How to Probate an Estate

Probate an Estate

California Sixth Edition

By Julia Nissley

Edited by Ralph Warner and Mary Randolph

Illustrations by Mari Stein

NOLO PRESS   BERKELEY, CALIFORNIA

YOUR RESPONSIBILITY WHEN USING A SELF-HELP LAW BOOK

We've done our best to give you useful and accurate information in this book. But laws and procedures change frequently and are subject to differing interpretations. If you want legal advice backed by a guarantee, see a lawyer. If you use this book, it's your responsibility to make sure that the facts and general advice contained in it are applicable to your situation.

KEEPING UP TO DATE

To keep its books up to date, Nolo Press issues new printings and new editions periodically. New printings reflect minor legal changes and technical corrections. New editions contain major legal changes, major text additions or major reorganizations. To find out if a later printing or edition of any Nolo book is available, call Nolo Press at (510) 549-1976 or check the catalog in the *Nolo News*, our quarterly newspaper.

To stay current, follow the "Update" service in the *Nolo News*. You can get the paper free by sending us the registration card in the back of the book. In another effort to help you use Nolo's latest materials, we offer a 25% discount off the purchase of any new Nolo book if you turn in any earlier printing or edition. (See the "Recycle Offer" in the back of the book.)

This book was last revised in: **October 1991.**

SIXTH EDITION	
First Printing	September 1991
Index	Sayre Van Young
Book Design	Keija Kimura
Printing	Delta Lithograph

Nissley, Julia P.
  How to probate an estate / by Julia Nissley ; edited by Ralph Warner and Mary
Randolph : illustrations by Mari Stein -- California 6th ed.
    p. cm.
  Includes index.
  ISBN 0-87337-169-0 : $34.95
  1. Probate law and practice--California--Popular works.
I. Warner, Ralph E. II. Randolph, Mary. III. Title.
KFC205.Z9N57 1991
346.79405's--dc20
[347.940652]   91-30702
                                                                  CIP

Acknowledgments

I would like to thank the many people whose energies are part of this book: Steve Elias, Mary Randolph, Jackie Clark, Stephanie Harolde, Keija Kimura, Glenn Voloshin, Carol Pladsen, and especially, Jake Warner, a splendid editor, for his invaluable assistance. I would also like to thank two practicing attorneys, Patricia S. Brady, a specialist in probate and estate planning in the West Los Angeles area and Warren Siegel, of Consumer Group Legal Services in Berkeley, both of whom reviewed the manuscript and made numerous suggestions for improvement. And finally, a special thank you to: My boss, Alan, for helping me learn so much about the subject; my children for their patience; and especially my husband, Ron, for always being there with encouragement and support.

RECYCLE YOUR OUT-OF-DATE BOOKS AND GET 25% OFF YOUR NEXT PURCHASE

OUT-OF-DATE = DANGEROUS

Using an old edition can be dangerous if information in it is wrong. Unfortunately, laws and legal procedures change often. Generally speaking, any book more than two years old is of questionable value. Books more than four or five years old are a menace.

To help you keep up-to-date, we extend this offer:

If you cut out and deliver to us the title portion of the cover of any old Nolo book, we'll give you a 25% discount off the retail price of any new Nolo book. For example, if you have a copy of *Tenant's Rights*, 4th edition, and want to trade it for the latest *California Marriage and Divorce Law*, send us the *Tenant's Rights* cover and a check for the current price of *California Marriage and Divorce*, less a 25% discount.

Information on current prices and editions is listed in the back of this book and in the catalog in the *Nolo News* (see offer at the back of this book).

This offer is to individuals only.

PAE 8/91

Table of Contents

CHAPTER 5

Preparing a Schedule of the Assets and Debts

CHAPTER 6

How to Identify the Best Transfer Procedure

CHAPTER 7

What About Taxes?

CHAPTER 15

Handling Property that Passes Outright to the Surviving Spouse

CHAPTER 16

If You Need Expert Help

Glossary

Appendix 1

Appendix 2

About the Author

Julia Nissley was Probate Administrator with the Los Angeles law firm of Silverberg, Rosen, Leon & Behr for many years. She is an honors graduate of the Attorney Assistant Training Program in Probate Administration at the University of California—Los Angeles School of Law and a member of the UCLA Attorney Assistant Alumni Association and the Los Angeles Paralegal Association. Julia is a native Californian and enjoys playing tennis and riding trains with her husband, Ron.

Julia now operates her own probate typing service for all California counties, handling all kinds of probate paperwork through the mail or in person. To contact her, write to:

P.O. Box 1832
Cathedral City, CA 92235-1832
or call
(619) 324-2573.

Introduction

HERE IS A BOOK about how to probate a simple estate in California. Our purpose is to provide a practical source of information for the person who wants the satisfaction and financial savings of settling a simple California estate through his own efforts, without having to hire an attorney. It contains all the up-to-date information on probate procedures you need to settle a routine or uncomplicated California estate. It is designed to be understood by non-lawyers. When the use of legal terms is absolutely necessary, translations into straightforward language are provided.

Probating an estate has gotten easier because California has enacted many "short cut" methods for transferring property on the death of the owner. A number of these can be accomplished in a matter of weeks. Even when a formal probate proceeding is required, much of the work has been eliminated. As long as the estate is relatively uncomplicated, court involvement is now minimal, and printed, fill-in-the-boxes court forms have now replaced the lengthy typewritten documents formerly required.

Tax reform has also played an important part in simplifying estate administration. Death taxes have now been substantially abolished for moderate-sized estates. For decedents who died in 1987 and after, no federal estate tax is due if the estate is worth less than $600,000. In addition, California's inheritance tax was repealed by the voters in 1982.

This book shows you how to:

- Identify the property the decedent owned, including assets you might have overlooked.

- Determine who has authority to wind up the decedent's affairs (executor or administrator).

- Determine who is legally entitled to inherit the estate, whether the decedent left a will or died without one.

- Transfer and clear title to property the decedent owned in joint tenancy with others.

- Handle a small estate competently and efficiently with a simple one-page affidavit.

- Transfer property to a surviving spouse in a matter of weeks with an abbreviated court proceeding.

- Transfer securities, real property, motor vehicles, money market fund accounts and most other property to the people who inherit it.

- Conduct a simple probate court proceeding entirely by mail without setting foot inside the courthouse; and

- File income tax and, if necessary, estate tax returns on behalf of the decedent.

This book also includes all the forms you'll need. A blank copy of each form is contained in the two Appendices. In most instances, you may simply tear them out, fill in the blanks according to our instructions, make extra copies using a photocopy machine and file them with the court, financial institution, transfer agent, etc.

But please be warned. Although this book can help you settle most California estates without an attorney, you may need legal help if you are dealing with a very large or complicated estate. In some instances, this will mean hiring a lawyer to advise you on one or more specific points. In others, it may require turning over the entire probate proceeding to an attorney. As we go along, we will discuss the factors which will help you determine whether or not you can use this book to settle your estate. However, if any of the following is true, be prepared to get help:

- The decedent was not a California resident.

- The decedent left real property (or tangible personal property) outside of California. It doesn't make any difference where intangible personal property such as securities and bank accounts is located as long as the decedent was a California resident.

- The decedent died before January 1, 1985.

- The decedent was involved in an ongoing business which needs to be wound up (unless it is an uncomplicated one and considerable pre-death planning was done).

- The decedent left a very large estate with a lot of assets and beneficiaries. There is no absolute rule here, but certainly if the decedent's assets are worth more than $1,000,000, you will want to get some help.

- Someone is planning to contest the decedent's estate plan.

Finally, just a word to those readers who, in the midst of grieving for a loved one, wonder if they can cope with the details, and, sometimes even, complexities, of settling that person's estate. The only advice we can offer is to give it a try. Many times the concentration needed to do bureaucratic work can be a positive form of therapy, especially when you realize that your efforts will help preserve the estate and/or distribute it as your deceased loved one intended. Good luck.

CHAPTER 1

An Overview

A. What Is Probate?

MANY PEOPLE AREN'T SURE what the term "probate" really means. They think of it only as some long, drawn-out and costly legal formality surrounding a deceased person's affairs. Technically, probate means "proving the will" through a probate court proceeding. A generation ago, virtually every estate had to be reviewed by a judge before it could pass to those who would inherit it. Today there are several ways to transfer property at death, some of which don't require formal court proceedings, so the term is now often used broadly to describe the entire process by which an estate is settled and distributed.

For example, a surviving spouse may now receive property outright from her deceased spouse without any probate proceedings at all. Joint tenancy property also escapes the need for formal probate, as does property left in a living (inter vivos) trust and property in a pay-on-death bank account (Totten trust). If an estate consists of property worth less than $60,000, it too can be transferred outside of formal probate. Fortunately, the paperwork necessary to actually transfer the property to its new owners in the foregoing situations is neither time-consuming nor difficult. We discuss all of these procedures, as well as how to do a formal probate court proceeding.

There is one thing you should understand at the outset: The person who settles an estate usually doesn't have much choice as to which property transfer method to use. That is, whether you are required to use a formal probate or a simpler method to transfer property at death depends on how much (or little) planning the decedent (deceased person) did before death to avoid probate. This is discussed in detail as we go along.

Both formal probate and some of the other non-probate procedures involve filing papers at a court clerk's office, usually in the county where the decedent resided at the time of death. In larger counties, going to the main courthouse and other government offices in person can be an ordeal. To avoid this, you may settle most simple estates entirely by mail, even if a formal probate court proceeding is required. In other words, most probate matters don't require that you appear in court before a judge. In fact, settling an estate by mail is now the norm in many law offices. We will show you how to do this as we go along.

B. What Is Involved in Settling an Estate?

GENERALLY, SETTLING AN ESTATE is a continuing process which:

- Determines what property is owned by the decedent;

- Pays the decedent's debts and taxes, if any; and

- Distributes all property that is left to the appropriate beneficiaries.

When a person dies, she may own several categories of assets. Among these might be household belongings, bank and money market accounts, vehicles, mutual funds, stocks, business interests and insurance policies, as well as real property. All property owned by the decedent at the time of her death, no matter what kind, is called her "estate."

To get this property out of the name of the decedent and into the names of the people who inherit it requires a legal bridge. As there are a number of types of property, there are several types of legal procedures or bridges to move it to its new owners. Some of these are the equivalent of large suspension bridges that will carry a lot of property while others are of much less use and might be more analogous to a foot bridge. We collectively refer to these procedures as "settling an estate."[1]

Most of the decedent's estate will be passed to the persons named in her will, or, if there is no will, to certain close relatives according to priorities established

---

[1]Lawyers often use the word "administrate" and call this process "administering an estate." But as this term tells us nothing new, we will stick with "settling."

by state law (called "intestate succession"). However, to repeat, no matter how property is held, it must cross an estate settlement bridge before those entitled to inherit may legally take possession. The formal probate process is but one of these bridges. Some of the other bridges involve community property transfers, clearing title to joint tenancy property, winding up living trusts, and settling very small estates which are exempt from probate. Again, we discuss all of these in detail.

C. How Long Does It Take to Settle an Estate?

IF A FORMAL PROBATE court procedure is required, it usually takes from seven to nine months to complete all the necessary steps, unless you are dealing with a very complicated estate. On the other hand, if the decedent planned his estate to avoid probate, or the estate is small, or everything goes to a surviving spouse, then the estate may be settled in a matter of weeks by using some easier non-probate procedures.

Warning: The procedures in this book are only for *California* estates. Real property and tangible personal property (see Chapter 4 for definitions) located outside of California are not part of a California estate and cannot be transferred following the instructions in this book. To transfer property located outside of California, you will either have to familiarize yourself with that state's rules (these will be similar, but by no means identical to those in effect in California) or hire a lawyer in the state where the property is located.

D. What This Book Covers

NOT ALL ESTATES CAN be settled entirely by using a self-help manual. Although most California estates can be settled easily with the procedures described in the following chapters, some will require at least some formal legal assistance. Therefore, it's important to know if the one you are dealing with is beyond the scope of this book.

First, an estate that can be settled using this book (a "simple estate," for lack of a better term) is one that consists of the common types of assets, such as houses, land, a mobile home, bank accounts, household goods, automobiles, collectibles, stocks, money market funds, promissory notes, etc. More complicated assets, such as complex investments, business or partnership interests, or royalties from copyrights or patents, are often not as easy to deal with because they involve additional factors, such as determining the extent of the decedent's interest in the property and how that interest is transferred to the new owner. However, it may be possible to include unusual assets in a simple estate if the person settling the estate is experienced in such matters or has help from an accountant or attorney along the way. When questions arise as to ownership of an asset, or when third parties (anyone not named in the will or by intestacy statutes) make disputed claims against the estate (as would be the case if someone threatened to sue over a disputed claim), you have a complicated situation that will require help beyond this book.

Second, for an estate to be "simple" there should be no disagreements among the beneficiaries, especially as to the distribution of the property. There is no question that dividing up a decedent's property can sometimes bring out the worst in human nature. If you face a situation where family members are angry and lawsuits are threatened, it is not a simple estate. To settle an estate without unnecessary delays or complications and without a lawyer, you need the cooperation of everyone involved. If you don't have it (for example, a disappointed beneficiary or family member plans to contest the will or otherwise engage in obstructionist behavior), you will have to try to arrange a compromise with that person by using formal mediation techniques or the help of a person respected by all disputants. If this fails, you will need professional help. (See Chapter 16.)

Third, and contrary to what you might think, a simple estate does not have to be small. A substantial estate may still be treated as a simple estate if the qualifications we have just outlined are present. The only additional concern with a large estate is federal estate taxes, which affect estates of $600,000 or over. Estate income tax returns may also be required. If you are dealing with an estate worth at least $600,000, you can hire an accountant who is familiar with estate taxes to prepare the necessary tax returns for you, leaving you free to handle the rest of the settlement procedures yourself. We provide an overview of estate taxation in Chapter 7.

Note on Selling Real Property: It is not difficult to transfer real property to the people who inherit it. It is not quite as easy to sell real property and distribute the proceeds, despite the existence of simplified procedures to accomplish this. It is not common to have to sell real property. However, if you must, you may conclude that you need the help of an expert.

E. Simple Estate Checklist

THE FOLLOWING CHECKLIST shows all the basic steps in settling a simple estate in California. Each step is thoroughly explained later in the book.

This list may appear a bit intimidating at first, but don't let it discourage you. Not all of these steps are required in every situation, and even then you won't find them difficult. As with so many other things in life, probating a simple estate is much like putting one foot in front of the other (or one finger in front of the other on your typewriter). If you take it step-by-step, paying close attention to the instructions, you should have little difficulty. Remember, if you get stuck, you can get expert help to solve a particular problem and then continue with the rest.

F. Important Terms Defined

AS YOU READ through this material, you will be introduced to a number of technical words and phrases used by lawyers and court personnel. We define these as we go along, with occasional reminders. If you become momentarily confused, refer to the Glossary which follows Chapter 16.

1. The Gross Estate and the Net Estate

You will encounter the terms "gross estate" and "net estate" while settling every estate. The distinction between the two is simple as well as important. The decedent's "gross estate" is the fair market value at date of death of all property that he owned. It includes everything in which the decedent had any financial interest—houses, insurance, personal effects, automobiles, bank accounts, unimproved land, etc.—regardless of any debts the decedent owed and regardless of how title to the property was held (for example, in a living trust, in joint tenancy or as community property). The "net estate," on the other hand, is the value of what is left after subtracting the total amount of any mortgages, liens or other debts owed by the decedent at the time of death from the gross estate.

Suppose Harry died, leaving a home, car, stocks and some cash in the bank. To arrive at his "gross estate" you would add the value of all his property without looking to see if Harry owed any money on any of it. Let's assume that Harry's gross estate was $500,000. Now, assume when we check to see if Harry owed money, we discover that he had a mortgage of $150,000 against the house. This means his "net estate" (the value of all of his property less what he owed on it) would be worth $350,000.

Checklist for Settling a Simple Estate

1. Locate the will, if any, and make copies.

2. Order certified copies of the death certificate.

3. Determine who will be the estate representative.

4. Determine the heirs and beneficiaries and get their names, ages and addresses.

5. Determine the decedent's legal residence.

6. Collect insurance proceeds, Social Security benefits and other death benefits.

7. Arrange for final income tax returns and estate fiduciary income tax returns, if required.

8. Assemble and list assets such as:

   - Bank accounts;

   - Cash and cash receivables, uncashed checks, money market funds;

   - Promissory notes and other debts owing to decedent;

   - Stocks and bonds (including mutual funds);

   - Business interests, copyrights, patents, etc.;

   - Real property;

   - Antiques and collectibles, motor vehicles, including motor homes;

   - Miscellaneous assets including household goods and clothing; and

   - Insurance.

9. Determine whether each item of property is community or separate property and how title is held (for example, in the decedent's name alone, in joint tenancy, etc.).

10. Estimate the value of each asset, and if the decedent was a co-owner, the value of her share.

11. List debts and obligations of decedent unpaid at date of death, including:

    - Funeral and last illness expenses;

    - Income taxes;

    - Real property taxes;

    - Encumbrances or liens on real or personal property;

    - Debts outstanding; and

    - Approximate expenses of administering the estate, such as court filing fees, certification fees, appraisal fees, etc. (These fees usually total less than $500, unless the estate is large.)

12. Determine priority of debts.

13. Pay debts having priority, as soon as estate funds are available.

14. Prepare and file U.S. estate tax return, if required.

15. Determine method of transferring assets:

    - Terminate joint tenancy title to property; transfer bank trust accounts to beneficiaries.

    - Transfer estates under $60,000 without formal probate administration.

    - Transfer property going outright to surviving spouse without formal probate.

    - If property is contained in a living trust, the trustee named in the trust document may transfer (or administer) the trust property in accordance with the trust's provisions.

    - Begin simple probate court proceedings if necessary to transfer other property. (A detailed checklist of the steps in the actual probate court process is in Chapter 13, Section B.)

How To Settle An Estate

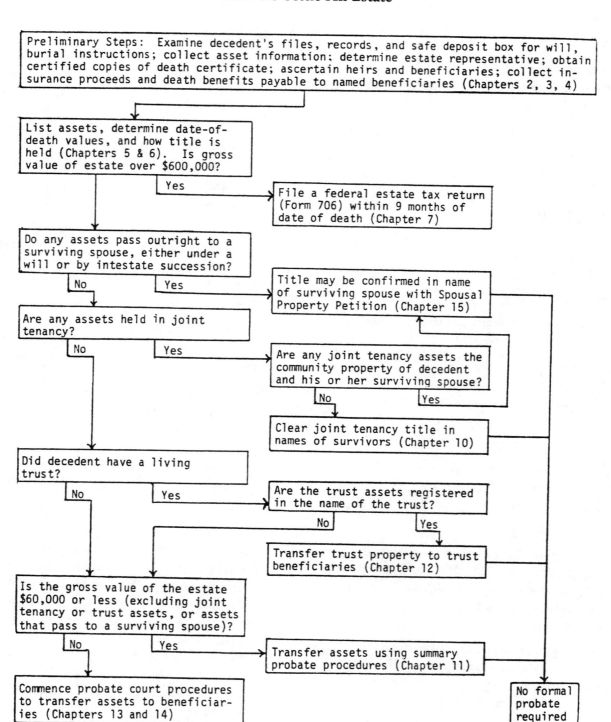

Preliminary Steps: Examine decedent's files, records, and safe deposit box for will, burial instructions; collect asset information; determine estate representative; obtain certified copies of death certificate; ascertain heirs and beneficiaries; collect insurance proceeds and death benefits payable to named beneficiaries (Chapters 2, 3, 4)

List assets, determine date-of-death values, and how title is held (Chapters 5 & 6). Is gross value of estate over $600,000?

Yes → File a federal estate tax return (Form 706) within 9 months of date of death (Chapter 7)

Do any assets pass outright to a surviving spouse, either under a will or by intestate succession?
No / Yes

Title may be confirmed in name of surviving spouse with Spousal Property Petition (Chapter 15)

Are any assets held in joint tenancy?
No / Yes

Are any joint tenancy assets the community property of decedent and his or her surviving spouse?
No / Yes

Clear joint tenancy title in names of survivors (Chapter 10)

Did decedent have a living trust?
No / Yes

Are the trust assets registered in the name of the trust?
No / Yes

Transfer trust property to trust beneficiaries (Chapter 12)

Is the gross value of the estate $60,000 or less (excluding joint tenancy or trust assets, or assets that pass to a surviving spouse)?
No / Yes

Transfer assets using summary probate procedures (Chapter 11)

Commence probate court procedures to transfer assets to beneficiaries (Chapters 13 and 14)

No formal probate required

If Bill and Lorie, husband and wife, together own as community property a house, car and savings account having a total gross value of $800,000, and owe $300,000 in debts, the net value of their community property would be $500,000. However, if Lorie died, only one-half of such property would be included in her estate because under California community property rules, discussed in detail in Chapter 4, the other half is Bill's. Thus, Lorie's gross estate would be $400,000 and her net estate $250,000.

2. The Probate Estate

The "probate estate," quite simply, is all of the decedent's property that must go through probate. This is very likely to be less than the total amount of property the decedent owned, because if an asset already has a named beneficiary, or if title is held in a way that avoids probate, then it isn't part of the probate estate. To return to the bridge analogy we discussed earlier, this means that property which is held in one of these ways can be transferred to the proper beneficiary using one of the alternate (non-probate) bridges. As a general rule, the following types of property need not be probated:

- Joint tenancy property;

- Life insurance with a named beneficiary other than the decedent's estate;

- Pension plan distributions;

- Property in living (inter vivos) trusts;

- Money in "savings bank trusts" which is to be "paid on death" to a named beneficiary (these are sometimes called "Totten trusts");

- Individual retirement accounts (IRAs) that have named beneficiaries;

- Community property or separate property that passes outright to a surviving spouse (this sometimes requires an "abbreviated" court procedure).

Thus, put another way, the "probate" estate (property that must cross the formal probate bridge) consists of all property except the property that falls into the above categories. Where there has been pre-death planning to avoid probate, little or no property will have to be transferred over the probate court bridge. Where little or no planning to avoid probate has been done, most, or all, of a decedent's property may have to be probated. To repeat, whether probate is needed is not in your hands. The decedent either planned to avoid probate, or she didn't—there is nothing you can do once death has occurred.[2]

I HOPE I AVOIDED PROBATE!

3. The Taxable Estate

Although this book is primarily about settling an estate, we include some mention of taxes because, as noted in Section D, above, estates over a certain value are required to file a federal estate tax return. Therefore, you should know how to compute the value of the decedent's estate for tax purposes, not surprisingly called the "taxable estate." Keep in mind that the property that must go through probate (probate estate) is not necessarily the same as the taxable estate. Not all assets are subject to probate, but they are all counted when determining whether estate taxes must be paid. In other words, the taxable

---

[2]There is a lot you can do to simplify the settlement of your own estate, however. The best resource covering this subject is *Plan Your Estate With a Living Trust*, by attorney Denis Clifford(Nolo Press).

estate includes all assets subject to formal probate, plus joint tenancy property, life insurance proceeds (if the decedent was the owner of the policy), death benefits, property in a "living trust," or property in any other probate avoidance device. However, if any of the assets are community property (discussed in Chapter 4), only the decedent's one-half interest is included in his taxable estate.

If the estate is large enough to require a federal estate tax return, any tax is computed on the net value of the decedent's property (net estate). That is, the tax is determined by the value of all property less any debts owed by the decedent and certain other allowable deductions.

G. Death Taxes

NOW THAT WE HAVE DEFINED the taxable estate, let's talk about death taxes themselves. The term "death tax" refers to the federal estate tax, since California inheritance taxes have been substantially abolished.[3] However, even the federal estate tax is not the major concern it used to be, except in large estates. A person who dies in 1987 or later may own up to $600,000 in property without having to pay any estate taxes. Estates having a gross value over these amounts must file a federal estate tax return. The tax is computed on the "net estate" after certain allowable deductions have been taken. If the deductions reduce the estate to a value below that which requires the filing of a federal estate tax return, a return must still be filed if the estate has a gross value over the relevant threshold amount, although no tax will be owed. For example, if a decedent dying in 1990 has a gross estate of $650,000 and debts of $60,000, a federal estate tax return must be filed, although no tax will be due because the net value of the estate is under the $600,000

exempt amount. We discuss this in more detail in Chapter 7.

The good news is that California's inheritance tax has been abolished. However, as a technical matter, if a federal estate tax return is filed. There will be a California estate tax to pay. This payment will equal the amount of state death tax credit allowed on the federal return. In other words, a small tax must still be paid to the state of California in some estates, but the entire amount of this state tax can be deducted from the federal return, which means no additional tax is actually paid.

Warning: Although most estates don't have to worry about federal estate taxes, if yours is a large estate for which federal estate taxes are due, the taxes should be paid before property is transferred to the people who inherit it. Many wills set aside money for the payment of taxes and therefore this isn't a problem. In other cases, the person who is settling the estate must take steps to make sure taxes are paid. Again, we discuss this in more detail in Chapter 7.

H. Do You Need An Attorney?

THE LAW DOES NOT REQUIRE you to hire an attorney to settle an estate. The average simple estate can be settled with the guidelines and background information in this book. Nevertheless, some complications that require special knowledge or handling may crop up even in an otherwise simple estate. Some examples are:

- Ambiguities in the will. For example: "I give $50,000 to the poor children in the County Hospital." This would raise several problems. Does "poor" mean low income or just unfortunate enough to be in the hospital? And what did the decedent intend when it came to dividing the money? Is it to be divided among all the children in the hospital on the date of decedent's death or did the decedent intend to set up a central fund to

[3]As we discuss in detail in Chapter 7, federal and state income tax returns for the decedent's last year and sometimes for the estate (if there is a formal probate) must also be filed, but these are not, properly speaking, death taxes.

be used to make life a little easier for all kids in the hospital?

- Contested claims against the estate (for example, a surviving spouse who claims a community property interest in property left by will to someone else);

- The decedent's unfinished contracts (for example, a sale of real property begun but not completed prior to death);

- Insolvent estates (more debts than assets);

- Claims against the estate by people who were left out or think they were given too little; or

- Substantial property given to a minor, unless legal provisions to handle this are made in the will.

It is beyond the scope of this book to tell you how to deal with each and every unusual situation that may arise. If you encounter a problem not adequately covered here, you will need the help of an expert. This doesn't mean, however, that you must turn the whole estate over to a lawyer. A sensible approach is to do the bulk of the work yourself and seek expert advice only when you need it. We discuss how to get expert help from an attorney or trained non-lawyer in Chapter 16.

Besides the satisfaction of doing the estate work yourself, another advantage is not having to pay attorneys' fees. In a probate court proceeding, attorneys' fees have been set by law and are based on a percentage of the gross estate (the gross value of the assets that are subjected to probate). (This may soon change, as discussed below.) Again, "gross value" refers to the total value of the property before subtracting any encumbrances or debts owed by the decedent. Computing attorney's fees based on the gross estate, of course, means lawyers do very well, since the gross value of the property is often higher than the value of what the decedent actually owned after the debts and encumbrances are subtracted. For instance, the gross value of your house may be $200,000, but after you subtract your mortgage, etc., you may actually only own a portion of this (say $50,000). Yet the attorney's fees are based on the $200,000 gross value figure.

The formula for computing attorneys' fees in a formal probate court proceeding is found in California's Probate Code §§ 901 and 910. An attorney may collect:

- 4% of the first $15,000 of the gross value of the probate estate;

- 3% of the next $85,000;

- 2% of the next $900,000;

- 1% of the next $9,000,000;

- 1/2% of the next $15,000,000; and

- a "reasonable amount" (determined by the court) for everything above $25,000,000.

Thus, in a probate estate with a gross value of $50,000 the attorney is allowed $1,650; in an estate with a gross value of $100,000 the attorney may collect $3,150, and so on. If, for example, a probate estate contains only one piece of real property, perhaps an apartment building worth $600,000, the attorney could collect $13,150 to transfer title in a probate proceeding, even if the building might have a substantial mortgage that reduces the decedent's equity to only $150,000. If an estate doesn't require formal probate because it can be settled in another way, such as a community property transfer to a surviving spouse or a joint tenancy termination, then an attorney is not entitled to receive a statutory fee. In these situations, an attorney will bill for his time at an hourly rate, which may vary from $50 to $300 an hour.[4]

---

[4]In a probate court proceeding (which we discuss in detail in Chapters 13 and 14) the court appoints a personal representative to handle the estate, called either an "executor" (if there is a will) or an "administrator" (if the decedent died without a will or without naming an executor in his will). This person is entitled to the very same fee, called the representative's "commission," as the attorney. In the above examples, the estate representative and the attorney could each receive the amount indicated. However, since the commission is subject to income tax and most probates are family situations where the executor or administrator is a close relative or friend who will inherit the same amount anyway, the executor's or administrator's fee is often waived.

Returning to Harry's estate for a moment (discussed in Section F, above), if a lawyer were hired to probate Harry's estate, her fee would be $11,150, computed on a gross estate of $500,000. Let's assume that Harry's will left all of his property to his daughter Millicent and son Michael, and one of them, acting as executor, probated Harry's estate without an attorney and waived the executor's fee. The entire job could be accomplished through the mail for a cost of approximately $650 (including filing, publication, certification and appraisal fees).

Happily, this fee system may be on its way out. The California Law Revision Commission has recommended that statutory fees be abolished, allowing clients and lawyers to agree on fees for probate work just as they do for all other matters. It's now up to the legislature to repeal the statutes setting attorneys' fees. Even if the statute isn't changed, you have the right to negotiate a fee with your lawyer.

Some people hire attorneys to settle even simple estates for much the same reason they order over-fancy funerals. When a friend or loved one dies, everyone close to the decedent is naturally upset. It often seems easier to hire an expert to take over, even one who charges high fees, than to deal with troublesome details during a time of bereavement. Obviously, there is nothing we can do to assuage your grief. We would like to suggest, however, that expending the time and effort necessary to keep fees to a minimum and preserve as much of the decedent's estate as possible for the objects of his affection is a worthy and honorable endeavor, and may even constitute a practical form of grief therapy.

Just because you do not wish to hire an attorney to probate an entire estate, however, does not mean you should never consult one as part of the estate settlement process. As we discuss in detail in Chapter 16, there are at least three times we believe a consultation with a lawyer is wise:

- *Complicated Estates:* As noted above, not all estates are relatively simple. If the estate you are dealing with is likely to be contested, or has complicated assets such as a going business owned by the decedent, or substantial income from royalties, copyrights, trusts, etc., see a lawyer.

- *Questions:* If after reading this book you are unsure of how to proceed in any area get some help. You should be able to consult an attorney at an hourly rate, clear up the problem area, and finish the estate settlement job on your own.

- *Checking Your Work:* If you face a fairly involved estate, you may want to do all the actual work yourself and then have it checked by a lawyer before distributing the estate. This will be much less expensive than paying the attorney to handle the whole job and, at the same time, it will make you feel more secure.

First Steps in Settling An Estate

WHEN SOMEONE DIES, everything stops in connection with the decedent's affairs, and someone must step in and take charge of things until the estate is settled and the property transferred to its new owners. This person is usually called the "estate representative," or sometimes the "decedent's personal representative."

You may already know that you are going to be the estate representative, either because you were named in the will as executor, because you are the closest living relative in a position to handle things, or because you inherit the bulk of the decedent's estate. If that's the case, you can safely skip or skim Section A of this chapter, which explains how the estate representative is normally chosen. Section B sets out your first responsibilities as representative.

A. Who Should Act as the Estate Representative?

WHO WILL SERVE as estate representative depends on a number of factors: whether or not the decedent left a will, whether the will named someone to be executor, whether that person is willing or able to serve, and so on. About the only definite legal requirement is that the estate representative, whether formally appointed or acting informally, must be over 18 years of age, of good moral character and competent.

1. If There Is a Will Which Appoints an Executor

If the decedent left a will naming an executor, normally this is who will be the estate representative unless the executor named in the will is unwilling or unable to serve. In that case the alternate executor named in the will is next in line to be the estate representative. If a formal probate court proceeding is necessary (discussed in Chapter 6), the executor named in the will is appointed by the court and issued a formal badge of office, called "letters testamentary." If no formal probate is necessary because you are dealing with a small estate (one that goes to a surviving spouse or one that for one of the reasons discussed in Chapter 6 qualifies as a small estate), then the executor named in the will (or the alternate if the first choice can't serve) normally serves as the informal estate representative.

2. If There Is No Will

If there is no will, an "administrator" is appointed as estate representative if a formal probate proceeding is necessary. If no formal probate is necessary because an estate is small, has been planned using probate avoidance devices such as joint tenancy, or because the estate goes mostly to the surviving spouse, then no administrator is formally appointed. In this situation, a close relative, often the person who inherits the bulk of the estate, serves as an informal estate representative.

Assuming probate is necessary, the administrator is appointed by the probate court according to a certain order of priority, with a surviving spouse or a child of the decedent usually handling the job. The administrator must be a United States resident. If a person having priority to be administrator does not want to serve , he may sign a document stating that although he is entitled to be administrator, he does not wish to assume the responsibility and wishes to nominate someone to act in his place. If the person making the nomination is a surviving spouse, child, grandchild, parent, brother, sister or grandparent of the decedent, this nominee has priority *after* those in the same class as the person making the request. For example, if a decedent's son does not wish to be the administrator and nominates someone to serve in his place, his nominee does not have priority over the decedent's daughter, but would have priority over more distant relatives.

The logic behind the priority system is simple. Relatives who are entitled to inherit part or all of the estate under intestate succession laws (we discuss these in

Chapter 3) are entitled to priority, because lawmakers feel that a person who is entitled to receive property from the estate is the person most likely to manage it to the best advantage of all the heirs. Here is the priority list for appointing an administrator which is contained in Section 8461 of the Probate Code.[1]

Reminder: If in your situation there is a will naming an executor, or if all property can be transferred outside of formal probate (for example, by joint tenancy, community property and other non-probate transfers), there is no need for you to read this section about naming an estate representative; you can skip to Section B. If you are in doubt as to whether or not probate will be required, read Chapter 6.

Andy died a resident of California, leaving no will. His surviving relatives are four children. He leaves no surviving spouse. Any or all of his children are entitled to priority as administrators of his estate; if none wishes to serve as administrator, any one of them may nominate someone else who need not necessarily be a relative of the decedent.

---

[1]For decedents who died before July 1, 1989, Section 422, which has a slightly different priority list, applies. You can look up Section 422 in a law library.

Priority List for Appointing an Administrator When Someone Dies Without a Will

- a. Surviving spouse[2]
- b. Children[3]
- c. Grandchildren
- d. Other issue (great-grandchildren, etc.)
- e. Parents
- f. Brothers and sisters
- g. Issue of brothers and sisters
- h. Grandparents
- i. Issue of grandparents (uncles, aunts, first cousins, etc.)
- j. Children of a predeceased spouse
- k. Other issue of a predeceased spouse
- l. Other next of kin
- m. Parents of a predeceased spouse
- n. Issue of parents of a predeceased spouse
- o. Conservator or guardian of the estate of the decedent acting in that capacity at the time of death
- p. Public administrator
- q. Creditors
- r. Any other person

---

[2]The surviving spouse of the decedent, a relative of the decedent or a relative of a predeceased spouse has priority only if one of the following conditions is satisfied: (a) the surviving spouse or relative is entitled to inherit all or part of the estate; (b) the surviving spouse or relative either takes under the will of, or is entitled to inherit all or part of the estate of, another deceased person who is entitled to inherit all or part of the estate of the decedent.

If the surviving spouse is a party to an action for separate maintenance, annulment or dissolution of marriage and was living apart from the decedent on the date of the decedent's death, the surviving spouse has priority after brothers and sisters and not the priority prescribed above.

[3]Normally, one child, selected informally within the family, will serve. However, two or more children may petition to be co-administrators.

3. If the Will Appoints No Executor or an Executor Who Can't or Won't Serve

Sometimes a will does not name an executor, or names a person who has since died, or names someone who for some reason does not want to act as the estate representative. If no co-executor or alternate executor is named, and formal probate is necessary, the court will appoint an "administrator with will annexed" (sometimes called an "administrator C.T.A.") to act as representative. An administrator with will annexed is appointed in the same order of priority as a regular administrator, except that any person who receives property under the will has priority over those who don't. (Probate Code § 8441.) Any person, regardless of her relationship to the decedent, who takes over 50% of the value of the estate under the will and is a resident of the United States has first priority to serve as administrator or to appoint any competent person to act as administrator with will annexed.

Sally died a resident of California, leaving a will giving all of her property to her boyfriend, Mort. Sally's will does not name an executor. Mort is entitled to priority as administrator with will annexed because he receives all property under Sally's will, even though Sally may have surviving relatives. If Mort does not wish to serve as administrator, he may appoint anyone of his choosing to be administrator with will annexed of Sally's estate, because he is entitled to inherit over 50% of the estate.

4. If Formal Probate Isn't Necessary

As you now know, many estates do not require a formal probate court proceeding. Avoiding probate is becoming more common, as many people now carefully plan their estates. Formal probate isn't necessary if most of the decedent's assets were held in joint tenancy or in a trust, or as community or separate property that passes outright to a surviving spouse, or in small estates containing property valued under $60,000. (See Chapter 11.)

If there is no necessity for a formal probate court proceeding, there is no court-appointed representative for the estate. This, of course, raises the question of who informally acts as the estate representative. Sometimes, where through extensive planning a decedent has left most property outside of the will, there will also be a will naming an executor. In this instance, the executor named in the will usually, informally, takes over and does whatever is necessary to help settle the estate and transfer the property. If there is no will naming an executor, a close relative or trusted friend is a logical choice—preferably one who will inherit most, or at least part, of the estate. Normally, families and friends decide this among themselves, and it is not uncommon for several people to share the responsibility. If there is a major dispute as to who this should be, you should see a lawyer.

B. Responsibilities of the Estate Representative

ACTING AS AN ESTATE representative can be a tedious job, but in most cases it doesn't require any special knowledge or training. Your main responsibilities are to be trustworthy and reasonably organized.

1. Organize Your Material

Organization is the best tool of anyone who wants to wind up the affairs of a deceased person efficiently and without frustrating delay. As you go along, the information and material you collect should be arranged in an orderly manner. A good way to do this is to have a separate legal-sized file folder (available at office supply stores) for each category of information. For instance, one folder may hold unpaid bills, another may hold copies of income tax returns, another could be for official documents like the will and death certificate, and still others may be reserved for information on specific assets, such as insurance, real property, stocks or bank accounts.

Then, when you get involved in one or another of the actual steps to transfer assets described in this book, you can set up an additional folder for each (for example, formal probate or community property transfers). The folders should be kept together in one expansion file or file drawer. If you have a lot of material to organize, you might find it helpful to arrange it in the same order as the checklist in Chapter 1, Section E.

2. The Estate Representative's Fiduciary Duty

The principal duty of the representative, whether court-appointed or acting informally, is to protect the estate and to see that it is transferred to the people who are entitled to it. In other words, the representative must manage the assets in the best interests of all persons involved in the estate (this includes creditors and taxing authorities) until the property is delivered to the beneficiaries. The law does not require the representative to be an expert or to display more than reasonable prudence and judgment, but it does require the highest degree of honesty, impartiality and diligence. This is called in law a "fiduciary duty."[4] As a fiduciary, the representative cannot speculate with estate assets and must keep all excess cash not needed to administer the estate in certain interest-producing investments approved by the court. (These include bank accounts or insured savings and loans accounts or obligations of the U.S. maturing in one year or less.)

If an estate representative breaches her fiduciary duty, she is personally liable for any damages. Specifically, if she commits a wrongful act that damages the estate, she is personally financially responsible; although, if she is without fault, she will be indemnified (paid back) by the estate. In addition, if an estate representative advances her own interests at the expense of the estate, the court can remove her as executor. Finally, if an estate

representative improperly uses estate money for her own needs, she will be cited to appear before the court and probably charged criminally.

In a formal probate court proceeding, the estate representative may have to post a bond (see Chapter 13, Section D) to guarantee she will carry out her fiduciary duties faithfully; however, the decedent's will or the beneficiaries acting together usually waive bond requirements, preferring to rely on the honesty of the representative. This makes sense, as normally the estate representative is a family member or close friend who stands to inherit a substantial part of the estate and who is highly unlikely to act improperly.

Note of Sanity: A few people may be reluctant to serve as a personal representative of an estate without a lawyer, fearing that even if they make an innocent mistake, they will be held personally liable. This is very unlikely in a simple estate where the assets and beneficiaries are clearly established. However, if you face an estate with a great many assets and a large number of beneficiaries, you may have a legitimate cause for concern. One way to feel secure that you have met your duty of care is to check all of your conclusions (and paperwork) with a lawyer before actually distributing assets. Since you will be doing all the actual work yourself, this needn't be expensive. We discuss how to hire and compensate a lawyer in Chapter 16.

C. Specific Duties of the Estate Representative

WHETHER ACTING formally or informally, your job as an estate representative is to take possession of the decedent's property, safeguard it until all obligations of the estate are met, and distribute the remaining assets to the proper persons. Here are some of your main responsibilities as representative.

---

[4]The duty to act with scrupulous good faith and candor.

1. Determine the Residence of the Decedent

In order for the estate to be settled under California law, the decedent must have been a resident of this state when she died. The principal factor which determines residence is the decedent's state of mind—whether at the time she died she considered California, and a particular place within this state, as her permanent residence. Sometimes it isn't absolutely clear what a decedent thought. Here are several factors important to making this determination:

- The length of time the decedent lived in the place;

- The location of the decedent's business assets and bank accounts; and

- The place where the decedent voted.

Note: If you are in doubt as to whether the decedent was a California resident because she only lived in California part of the year, or had moved here immediately prior to death, or for some other reason, see an attorney.

If she was a California resident, it is also necessary to determine the county of her residence, because this is where the court proceedings will be held, if any are required. Normally, where a person resides is clear enough, but occasionally, as would be the case if the decedent was ill or elderly and had moved to live with relatives or in a rest home, there may be a question as to whether she had changed her residence. In this situation, if the decedent was temporarily staying in a hospital or care facility at the time of death, while intending to return to her usual residence, her permanent home will ordinarily determine the county of her residence.

2. Locate the Will

Make a thorough search for the most recent will and any codicils that may exist. As we have mentioned, if there is no will, the decedent is said to have died "intestate" and the persons who will inherit his property are determined under state law. (See Chapter 3, Section F.)

Wills may be either "formal" or "holographic." A formal will is one that is fully typed and witnessed. A holographic will is one which is written and signed in the handwriting of the person making the will. (A commercially printed form will that is completed in the testator's own hand writing is valid as a holographic will. Probate Code § 6111 (c).) A holographic will need not be witnessed or dated. However, if it is undated and there is another will with inconsistent provisions, the holographic will is invalid to the extent of the inconsistency, unless the time it was signed can be established by other evidence. If you face this sort of highly unusual situation, see a lawyer.

A codicil is a later document which supplements or modifies a will. It may also be either formal or holographic. A formal, witnessed will can have a holographic codicil, although this is unusual. Normally, a codicil is used to make a relatively small addition, subtraction or change in a will, as would be the case if the decedent bought or sold a piece of property which would alter the will. Sometimes, however, codicils make major changes in a will that conflict with or are inconsistent with the language of the original will so that it's difficult to understand what the decedent intended. In this situation, you would be wise to have the will and codicil interpreted by a lawyer before continuing the probate process on your own. We discuss how to consult a lawyer to get particular questions answered in Chapter 16.

Most people either keep their will in a fairly obvious place, such as a desk, file cabinet (often at the office), a safe-deposit box, closet or shelf, or entrust it to their lawyer. Banks usually allow a member of the surviving family to open a safe-deposit box in the presence of a bank officer to search for a will or burial instructions. However, nothing else may be removed until the box is officially released. (See Section 5, below.)

When you find a will, make six photocopies, which will be needed at various stages of the estate work. Be sure each page of the photocopy is complete and that the signatures are legible. You are under no obligation to provide copies of the will to anyone. After a will is admitted to probate, it becomes public record.

Note: Probate Code § 8200 requires anyone in possession of a will to deliver it to the clerk of the superior court for safekeeping within 30 days after being informed of the death *and* mail a copy to the named executor. The usual procedure followed by attorneys, however, is to file the original will at the same time a Petition for Probate is filed, if such a proceeding will be commenced. This avoids the possibility of the original will being misplaced by the court, delaying the filing of the petition. In non-probate matters, where the original will is not required by the court, it is a good idea for the named executor to keep the will in a safe place with other valuable papers. If someone delivers a will to you, it is appropriate to give him a receipt if he requests one.

3. Obtain Certified Copies of the Death Certificate

When a person dies in California, an official death certificate is filed in the county health department or vital statistics office of the county where the decedent died.

Certified copies of the death certificate are needed to collect insurance proceeds and other death benefits, and to transfer joint tenancy property. The death certificate also provides important personal information about the decedent, such as her Social Security number, date of birth and occupation.

One easy way to obtain certified copies quickly is to ask the mortuary you deal with to obtain them for you and add the cost to its bill. If you prefer, you may order certified copies yourself by writing to the vital statistics office or county health department in the county where the decedent died. When writing, you must enclose a check to cover the nominal fee, and give the name of the decedent, date of death and city of death. You can get the address and fee by calling the county health department or vital statistics office. A month or so after the date of death you may also obtain copies from the County Recorder's office. A sample form letter is shown below.

Sample Request for Death Certificate

Bureau of Vital Statistics
[in proper county]
_____

_____
[Address]
_____
[City, State, Zip]

        Re: _____, deceased
        Date of Death: _____
        City/County of Death:_____

Will you please provide me with ___ certified copies of the death
certificate of the above-named decedent. A check in the amount of "not to
exceed $_____" and a stamped, self-addressed envelope are
enclosed.

Thank-you for your assistance.

                        Very truly yours,

                        _____
                        [Signature]
                        _____
                        [Address]
                        _____
                        [City, State, Zip]
                        _____
                        [Telephone]

4. Ascertain the Heirs and Beneficiaries

As we will discuss in more detail in Chapter 3, an "heir" is a person who inherits if there is no will or alternative estate plan, according to the laws of intestate succession. A "beneficiary," on the other hand, is a person who inherits under the terms of a will. If the decedent left a will, the names, ages and exact addresses of the beneficiaries named in the will should be determined. If any are deceased (or don't survive the decedent by any period of days specified in the will), the will should be read carefully to ascertain the names of alternative beneficiaries. We discuss how to do this in detail in Chapter 3. Occasionally, you will find that a beneficiary predeceases a decedent and no alternate beneficiary is named, or that there are other problems in determining who inherits. Again, we discuss this in detail in Chapter 3.

Even if an estate must go through formal probate (we discuss this in detail in Chapter 6), you must determine the names, ages and exact addresses of the decedent's heirs (the people who would inherit if there were no will). At first this may not make much sense; why do you need to figure out who would inherit in the absence of a will, if in fact there is one? The answer is simple. In a formal probate court proceeding (discussed in Chapter 14), the names of the heirs must be listed on a Petition for Probate so they can be notified, even if some or all of them actually inherit nothing under the terms of the will. The purpose is to let these people know that the decedent's affairs are being wound up so that they can object or otherwise participate if they wish. They rarely do.

In addition, if a decedent who died without a will was married and there will be a formal probate, you must list all heirs who might inherit something depending on whether the decedent's property is ultimately characterized as community or as separate property. Every person who could have an interest in the estate must be considered a possible heir. If there is no surviving spouse, there will be no community property and you need only list the heirs of the separate property.

You are not required by law to make impractical and extended searches, but you must make reasonably diligent efforts to locate all heirs and beneficiaries. Usually, questioning survivors is sufficient. Additional information may be obtained from telephone directories, U.S. Post Office forwarding procedures, advertising, or voting records.

5. Examine Safe-Deposit Boxes

Any safe-deposit boxes in the decedent's name should be examined for assets and important papers. Safe-deposit boxes are no longer "sealed" on the death of the box holder. In many instances, their contents can immediately be turned over to the person who inherits them. However, be sure to contact the bank before you visit, as each bank has its own procedures for opening and releasing boxes. A certified copy of the decedent's death certifi-

cate is usually required, and don't forget that you'll need the key. If it can't be found, an appointment will have to be made to have the box drilled, and the expense charged to the estate. If you suspect a box may exist at some bank, but have no proof, write the bank or inquire in person. Most banks will tell you whether or not there is a box if you present a certified copy of the death certificate.

The procedures followed by most banks depend on how the box was owned and who inherits its contents.

a. Joint Tenancy: A joint tenancy safe-deposit box is generally released to the surviving joint tenant without delay. If the survivor wishes to have title to the box re-registered in his name alone, the bank will require a certified copy of the decedent's death certificate.

b. Surviving Spouse Inherits Everything: When property (either community or separate) goes outright to a surviving spouse under the decedent's will or by the law of intestate succession, it may be collected by the surviving spouse without probate. (Probate Code § 13500.) This means a surviving spouse who, either by will or intestate succession, inherits all of the decedent's property can have the safe-deposit box released to her upon presenting to the bank a certified copy of the death certificate and a signed declaration in the form shown below, setting forth the facts that allow the box to be released to her. The bank will also probably wish to see a copy of the decedent's will, if there is one.

Restrictions: This declaration is for personal property only, not real property. And if any of the decedent's separate property or his one-half interest in any community property goes to someone other than the surviving spouse, or if the surviving spouse is given a qualified ownership in the property, the estate usually requires probate and this simple procedure can't be used. This is discussed in Chapter 15.

Declaration Regarding Property Passing to Decedent's Surviving Spouse Under Probate Code § 13500

The undersigned declares:

1. _____
died on _____, 19___, and on the date of death was a
resident of California.

2. On the date of death, decedent was married to
_____, who survives the decedent.

3. Among the decedent's assets was
_____ (insert description of
bank account, savings and loan account or safe-deposit box, by
account or box number, name and location of bank and balance of
account).

4. The decedent's interest in the described property passed to
decedent's surviving spouse upon decedent's death by the terms of
decedent's will and any codicils to it.

or

4. The decedent died intestate and the above described property is
the community property of the decedent and the decedent's surviving
spouse, having been acquired during the parties' marriage while
domiciled in California, and not having been acquired by gift or
inheritance, and passes to the decedent's surviving spouse by the
laws of inheritance governing passage of title from decedent in the
absence of a will.

5. Decedent's surviving spouse therefore is entitled to have the
described property delivered to that spouse without probate
administration, pursuant to California Probate Code § 13500.

The undersigned declares under penalty of perjury that the
foregoing is true and correct and that this declaration was executed
on _____, 19___, at _____, California.

_____
[Signature]

c. Safe-Deposit Box in Decedent's Name (Surviving Spouse Does Not Inherit Everything): Probate is commonly, but not always, required when the box is in the decedent's name alone, and a surviving spouse does not inherit all community and separate property. The exception to probate is when the decedent leaves a small estate which is broadly defined as having less than $60,000 of property, not counting property that passes outside probate. We discuss small estates and the procedures to deal with their assets without probate in Chapter 11. If probate is required, the bank requires a certified copy of the death certificate and a certified copy of the estate representative's letters issued by the probate court. We show you how to get these in Chapter 14.

d. Small Estates: When no probate is required, as is the case with small estates (generally those with assets of $60,000 or less), the bank will usually release the box to the heirs or beneficiaries of the estate when they present a certified copy of the decedent's death certificate and sign a form declaration provided by the bank. You should also present a copy of the decedent's will if there is one. This procedure, which can be used to bypass probate in a variety of small estate situations, is discussed in Chapter 11.

6. Collect the Decedent's Mail

If the decedent lived with relatives or friends, collecting her mail may not be a problem. If she lived alone, it is a good idea to notify the post office to have the mail forwarded to you so you may keep track of it. Assets, debts or other important information may come to light from this source. Usually, the mail will be forwarded if you submit a change-of-address card to the post office with a copy of the death certificate attached. A supply of these cards is kept in the lobby of the post office. Write the word DECEASED in large letters across the top of the card, put the decedent's name and old address in the upper section of the card, and in the lower section fill in your name and address where you want the mail forwarded. Then sign the card and mail it, with the death certificate attached, to the Postmaster in the zip code area where the decedent lived.

7. Cancel Credit Cards and Subscriptions

To prevent unauthorized use, all credit cards in the decedent's name should be either destroyed or cut in half and returned to the company promptly with a statement that the decedent died, giving the date of death. Because many credit card companies will cancel the balance due when a card holder is deceased if the amount owing is not substantial, it is worthwhile to inquire about this policy. Similar notices should be sent to businesses from which the decedent made purchases on credit. When the notices are sent, it is a good idea to enclose an extra copy of the letter and ask that receipt of the notice be acknowledged by signing and returning the copy. A sample letter is shown below.

Newspaper and magazine subscriptions should also be cancelled. Ask for reimbursement of the unused portion of the subscription price if the amount is enough to be worth the trouble.

Letter to Credit Card Issuer

[Name of credit card company]

[Address]

[City, State, Zip]

Re: _____, deceased

Date of Death: _____

    I am the representative of the estate of the above-named decedent.

Enclosed is the decedent's credit card, No._____, which has been cut in half and should be immediately cancelled. Please acknowledge receipt of the card and this notice by signing the duplicate copy of this letter and returning it to me in the enclosed stamped, self-addressed envelope.

                      Very truly yours,

                      [Signature]

                      [Address]

                      [City, State, Zip]

Receipt acknowledged by:

[Name]

[Title]

8. Notify Social Security Administration and/or the Director of Health Services

If the decedent was receiving monthly Social Security benefits, you should call the "800" number for Social Security listed in the telephone book and notify them that the decedent has died. In addition, the check for the month in which the decedent died must be returned (even if he died on the last day of the month), along with any checks received for later months. Checks issued at the beginning of a month (usually on the 3rd) are for the previous month. So if a recipient dies on April 28, the May 3rd check must be returned. Take the check in person or mail it to your local Social Security office and get a receipt. It is illegal for anyone to cash the checks or deposit them to the decedent's account. If they are cashed, the government will require reimbursement from the estate account or the beneficiary receiving the property. If the decedent's Social Security checks were being deposited directly into his bank account, notify the bank to return the funds to Social Security. It may take several weeks to stop the "direct deposit" of checks to an account, and such monies should be kept separate and not used by the estate. A sample letter that may be used to return the checks is shown below.

If a beneficiary or a person in possession of property of the decedent believes the decedent was receiving benefits under Medi-Cal, that person must notify the Director of Health Services of the death within 90 days. (See Chapter 14, Step 8.)

Letter to Social Security Administration

```
Department of Health, Education and Welfare
Social Security Administration
[Address of local office]
                      RE: _____ , deceased
                      Date of Death: _____

I am the representative of the estate of the above-named decedent.

Enclosed is the decedent's Social Security check for the month of
_____, which is being returned as required. Please
acknowledge receipt of the enclosed check by signing the duplicate
copy of this letter and returning it to me in the enclosed stamped,
self-addressed envelope. (Add, if applicable: Please stop the direct
deposit of the decedent's checks immediately.)


                         Very truly yours,

                         _____
                         [Signature]
                         _____
                         [Address]
                         _____
                         [City, State, Zip]

Receipt acknowledged by:

_____
[Name]
_____
[Title]
```

9. Obtain Basic Estate Information

You should learn as much about the decedent's business affairs as you can by examining all of her legal papers at the earliest possible time. If the decedent was not an organized person, it may take some detective work on your part to find out what her assets and liabilities are. Examine bankbooks, notes, deeds, stock certificates, insurance policies, recent tax returns and all other tangible evidence of property. Keep what you find in organized files with other important estate information. Again, a convenient way to do this is to have a separate file folder for each category of information. If original documents are valuable, you may want to keep them in a secure place and make copies for day-to-day reference.[5]

Studying the decedent's income tax returns is a good way of discovering assets. For instance, if it shows the decedent received stock dividends, you will know she owned stock. If the tax return reports interest earned, this is a clue there are savings accounts or promissory notes, or other kinds of interest-bearing assets. The decedent's accountant may also be able to provide important information.

10. Get Bank Accounts Released if Possible

Sometimes, immediate cash may be needed to pay some obligations of the decedent, or the decedent's family may need funds for living expenses. Many people think that as soon as a person dies, all his or her cash is immediately frozen for some indefinite period. This is not true.

---

[5]If you want to computerize your record-keeping, try *For the Record*, a Nolo software program. It is designed primarily as a way for people to organize their own affairs prior to death so that they will not leave a mess when they die, but it is also an excellent organizational tool for an estate representative. It provides a place to list the details concerning all major assets and investments.

As soon as a certified copy of the death certificate is available, obtaining the release of cash held in the name of the decedent in banks and savings and loan associations in California presents no substantial problems. The procedures for releasing bank accounts are similar to those required to release safe-deposit boxes:

a. If the decedent held an account in joint tenancy with someone else, the bank will release the funds immediately to the surviving joint tenant.

b. If the decedent held a bank account as trustee for another (called a Totten trust or a pay-on-death account), the bank will release the funds to the beneficiary if furnished with a certified copy of the decedent's death certificate.

c. If the account is in the decedent's name alone, and the value of the estate is under $60,000, the bank should release the funds without the necessity of probate upon being presented with a certified copy of the death certificate and a form affidavit (usually provided by the bank) signed by the heirs or beneficiaries entitled to the account. The requirements for this type of transfer are given in Chapter 11.

d. If the account is held in the names of the decedent and the surviving spouse, or the decedent alone, and the decedent's will provides for such property to go to the surviving spouse, or if the decedent didn't leave a will but the account is listed as community property (in which case it would go outright to the surviving spouse by the law of intestate succession—see Chapter 3), then the account may be released to the surviving spouse without probate under Probate Code § 13500. To accomplish this, the surviving spouse should submit a certified copy of the decedent's death certificate to the bank, along with a copy of the will (if there is one), and an affidavit or declaration signed by the surviving spouse setting forth the facts that allow her to receive the account without probate administration. A sample of such a declaration is shown above in Section C5 of this chapter, and a blank sample appears in Appendix 1. It is a good idea to attach a copy of Probate Code § 13500, a copy of which also appears in Appendix 1. Alternatively, the surviving spouse may obtain a Spousal Property Order from the probate court to obtain release of the account. The procedures for obtaining such an order are given in Chapter 15.

e. If the account is the separate property of the decedent and the decedent died without a will, or if the decedent willed his interest in community and/or separate property to someone other than a surviving spouse, probate proceedings will ordinarily be required. Before releasing the account (unless the estate is under $60,000 in value and the account may be released by the procedures outlined above), the bank will need a certified copy of the Letters (the formal authorization of the estate representative by the probate court) issued to an estate representative appointed in a formal probate court proceeding. The procedures for obtaining the Letters are detailed in Chapter 14. It usually takes about four or five weeks to obtain the Letters after the court proceeding has begun.

All funds released to an estate representative in a formal probate court proceeding should normally be placed in an estate account in the name of the representative as "Executor (or Administrator) of the Estate of _____." Obviously, if funds are released directly to a beneficiary under one of the procedures discussed just above, this isn't necessary.

11. Collect Life Insurance Proceeds

Life insurance claims are frequently handled directly by the beneficiary of the policy, and the proceeds are usually paid promptly. All that is usually required is a proof of death on the company's printed claim form signed by the beneficiary, a certified copy of the decedent's death certificate and the policy itself. If the policy can't be found, ask the company for its form regarding lost policies.

Always carefully examine the life insurance policy to make certain who the beneficiary is. Most policies name a primary beneficiary and a secondary beneficiary, meaning if the primary beneficiary predeceases the insured, the secondary beneficiary receives the proceeds. If the

beneficiary is a secondary beneficiary, a certified copy of the death certificate of the primary beneficiary is also required.

You must call or write the home or regional office of the life insurance company, inform it of the decedent's death and request a claim form to be sent to the beneficiary. The company will want the decedent's name, the date of death, the number of the life insurance policy and the name and address of the beneficiary.

Life insurance proceeds that are paid to a named beneficiary (other than the decedent's estate or personal representative) are not part of the decedent's probate estate and, thus, do not have to go before a probate court. The proceeds are payable under the life insurance contract, not by the terms of the decedent's will or the laws of intestate succession. However, the proceeds will be included in the decedent's "taxable" estate, if he was the owner of the policy. (We discuss ownership of life insurance in Chapter 7.) Many insurance policies do not indicate who the owner of the policy is, and you may have to ask the insurance company to verify this for you. It is a good idea to ask for this information when you return the claim form to the company. You should also ask the company for a copy of Life Insurance Statement, Form 712, which must be filed with the federal estate tax return, if one is required. A sample letter is shown below.

12. Collect Annuity Benefits

If the decedent had purchased annuities naming someone to receive the benefits on his death, the beneficiary may obtain the benefits by submitting a certified copy of the decedent's death certificate and a completed claim form to the insurance company issuing the annuity.

Letter to Insurance Company

[Name of Insurance Company]

[Address]

[City, State, Zip]

Attention: Death Claims Division

    Re: _____, deceased

    Date of Death: _____

    Policy No. _____

  Enclosed is your claim form executed by the named beneficiary under the above policy, along with a certified copy of the decedent's death certificate and the original policy.

  Please process this claim and forward the proceeds to the beneficiary at the address indicated on the claim form.

  Also, please provide an original and one copy of Life Insurance Statement, Form 712.

  Thank you for your cooperation.

      Very truly yours,

      _____
      [Signature]

      _____
      [Address]

      _____
      [City, State, Zip]

13. Collect Social Security Benefits

If the decedent was covered by Social Security, there will be a $255 lump sum death benefit. Mortuaries often assist with information on this. It is payable to one of the following people in the order of priority listed:

- The surviving spouse if he or she was living with the decedent at the time of death;

- The decedent's surviving spouse not living with the decedent but eligible on the decedent's earnings records; or

- Eligible surviving children (that is, a dependent child).

Minor children or children in college may also be entitled to survivor's benefits under the Social Security Act. A visit to the local Social Security office is the best way to find out what benefits are available. You will need a certified copy of the death certificate. The staff will assist in preparing the forms. Also, to get a better idea of the rights of all family members, we recommend *Social Security, Medicare and Pensions: A Sourcebook for Older Americans*, by Joseph Matthews (Nolo Press).

14. Collect Veteran's Benefits

Dependents of deceased veterans may be eligible for benefits. Information on veteran's benefits may be obtained by phoning the nearest Veterans Administration Office. Also, you will want to see the government publication "Federal Benefits for Veterans and Dependents," which can be obtained from the Government Printing Office, Washington, D.C. 20402; the GPO Bookstore, 450 Golden Gate Avenue, San Francisco, CA 94102; or the GPO Bookstore, Federal Building, 300 North Los Angeles Street, Los Angeles, CA 90012.

15. Collect Railroad Retirement Benefits

Death benefits and survivor's benefits may be available if the decedent was covered by the Railroad Retirement Act. If the decedent was employed by a railroad company, you should contact the nearest Railroad Retirement Board office for specific information and assistance.

16. Prepare Decedent's Final Income Tax Returns

You should also consider, at this time, preparation of the decedent's final state and federal individual income tax returns (Forms 1040—U.S. and 540—California) covering the period from the beginning of the decedent's tax year to the date of death. (We discuss this in detail in Chapter 7.) If the decedent is survived by a spouse, the final returns may be joint returns. An accountant can advise you in this regard.

17. Collect Miscellaneous Death Benefits

Survivors are often faced with a myriad of forms, questionnaires and regulations to claim certain disability and death benefits. These benefits are sometimes overlooked during mourning and then forgotten. Some examples are:

State Disability Income Payments: If the decedent was receiving state disability benefits at the time of death, make sure all benefits were paid through the date of death and notify the California Employment Development Department.

Worker's Compensation: If the decedent was receiving worker's compensation benefits at the time of death, notify the private insurance carrier who pays these benefits and make sure all benefits are paid.

Retirement or Disability Income from Federal Employment: If the decedent was a federal employee, the decedent's family or named beneficiaries may be entitled to benefits. Contact the agency the decedent worked for.

Benefits from Medical Insurance Through Decedent's Employment or an Association: Most employers and some unions provide group medical insurance which helps pay for medical expenses and, sometimes, funeral expenses. Claims should be made to cover any expenses of a last illness, and you should ask about any additional lump sum death benefits.

Group Life and Disability Income Benefits: Life insurance or disability benefits may be payable through a group policy provided by the decedent's employer, union or other organization. No one procedure to obtain the benefits will apply in all cases, and the administrator of the plan under which death benefits are payable (or the organization obligated to pay the benefits) should be contacted to ask about the procedure to follow. Usually a claim form must be signed and submitted with a certified copy of the decedent's death certificate. Death benefits are normally excluded from the decedent's probate estate if they are paid to a designated beneficiary (not the decedent's estate or personal representative), which means they can be collected without the approval of the probate court.

CHAPTER 3

Who Are the Heirs and Beneficiaries?

A. Introduction

STUDIES INDICATE that most people don't know who will inherit their property when they die. In one recent survey, 55% of the people interviewed had not made a will, but 70% of them believed they knew who would inherit their property if they died without one. Then, when each was asked to name his heirs and how much each would receive, only 40% were correct.

In this key chapter we give you, the estate representative, the information necessary to do an accurate job of determining what is in the decedent's estate and to figure out who is legally entitled to it. Obviously, this is one of the central tasks involved in settling any estate.

Mercifully, it is usually easy to figure out which beneficiaries or heirs receive which property if the decedent did one or more of the following:

- Left a simple will that effectively identified the beneficiaries (often a surviving spouse or children);

- Died without a will in a situation where it is clear which relatives will inherit under state law (the law of intestate succession); or

- Placed title to the bulk of her property in joint tenancy or a living trust.

Life is not always this easy, however. If a will is unclear, or the decedent died without a will and left no close relatives, or in some circumstances, if the will accidentally left a child or spouse out in the cold, it may be more difficult to decide who inherits the decedent's property.

If it is clear who inherits the property in the estate you are dealing with, skim the material in this chapter to be sure you haven't overlooked something, and then go on to the next. On the other hand, if you aren't sure who gets what property, study this chapter carefully. If it doesn't provide sufficient clarification, you will either need to do some additional research or see a lawyer.

Reminder: The information in this chapter is useful only if the decedent died after January 1, 1985, when a number of California laws having to do with inheritance rights changed.

B. Where to Start

Important Terms

There are two fundamental types of estates. The estate is "intestate" if there is no will and "testate" if there is.

Those who inherit when the state is intestate are called "heirs," whereas those who inherit under wills are termed "devisees" or "beneficiaries."

The identity of the heirs who stand to inherit from an intestate estate is determined by state laws, called the laws of "intestate succession." The identity of devisees or beneficiaries who stand to inherit from a testate estate is determined, as much as possible, according to the decedent's intent as reflected in the will.

When a person dies, her property (after debts and expenses are paid) is apportioned among the persons who are legally entitled to inherit it. The identity of these persons (beneficiaries or heirs) is normally decided by:

- The terms of the decedent's will; or

- State law (the law of intestate succession) if there is no will; or

- Estate planning devices such as life insurance, joint tenancy or living trusts, which the decedent established while still living; or, *more rarely*

- State law if a will provision turns out to be ineffective or if a few types of beneficiaries are accidentally left out of the will.

1. The Will

If you are dealing with an estate where there is a will, the chances are good that the beneficiaries will be clearly defined and the property they are to receive will also be accurately specified. An obvious example would be a will that simply states, "I leave all my property to my husband, Aldo Anderson," or "I leave my real property located at 112 Visalia St., Ukiah, CA to my husband, Aldo Anderson and all my personal property to my son, Alan

Anderson, and my daughter, Anne Anderson-McGee, in equal shares." If the will you are concerned with reads like this, you can skim or skip this chapter. Otherwise, read Section C.

2. The Laws of Intestate Succession

More people die without a will than with one. If this is the situation you face, you obviously don't have to interpret the decedent's will. This means that, with the exception of real property (and certain types of tangible personal property) located in another state, the decedent's property is divided according to California law.[1] The rules are normally fairly simple and are explained in Section F of this chapter.

3. Probate Avoidance Devices

Various types of assets pass to beneficiaries more or less "automatically" according to the terms of an estate plan devised by the decedent while still alive, with the idea of avoiding probate. Generally, property covered by a properly-drawn estate plan is not subject either to the terms of the decedent's will or to the laws of intestate succession. In such cases, the beneficiaries were selected by the decedent either in a contract or by some other probate avoidance arrangement. This category of probate avoidance devices includes:

---

[1]Real or tangible personal property located out of state and not covered by a probate avoidance device is divided according to the intestate succession laws of the state in which it is located. Succession laws in other states will be similar to, but not necessarily exactly the same as, those in force in California. To transfer this property, you must comply with the laws of the state where the property is located. This will require your figuring out the laws and procedures in this state and handling it yourself, or hiring an attorney located in the relevant state to help you.

- Life insurance policies with a named beneficiary;
- Property covered by a living (inter vivos) trust;
- Joint tenancy property;
- Property in a pay-on-death account (Totten trust); *and*
- Property placed in a life estate.

If the estate you are concerned with is entirely made up of these types of property, you can safely skip or skim this chapter because you already know who will take the property. In Chapter 6, you will find a summary of how these types of assets are transferred, with specific directions as to which of the "how to" chapters you should use to make the actual transfers.

Caution: We have tried to spot some common situations where you need not wrestle further with this chapter. If, however, you need to interpret unfamiliar language, resolve one or more ambiguities in a will, or are otherwise in doubt about an issue or problem, we urge you to carefully read the rest of this chapter so that your ultimate decision about who inherits the estate will be an informed one.

C. How to Read a Will

MOST WILLS ARE EASY to read and understand. However, at times what purports to be the "last will and testament" of the decedent may be filled with so much bewildering language that it is about as easy to decipher as the Rosetta Stone. How do you, as a non-lawyer personal representative, unravel this sort of will to discover the identity of the intended beneficiaries and what they inherit? We include here several suggestions that may help. But if, after applying the suggestions you read here, you are still not absolutely sure of what the will says, a consultation with a lawyer is definitely indicated. Put differently, if you aren't sure what the decedent intended, don't guess.

Some of the more common problems to watch out for are:

- Attempts to dispose of property not part of the decedent's estate (for example, a house or vehicles that were sold years ago or property held in joint tenancy);

- Attempts to leave property to people who have died before the decedent in a situation where no alternate has been named;

- Attempts to dispose of a surviving spouse's one-half of the community property; *and*

- Omissions of children or a spouse from the will.

1. Prepare a Chart of Beneficiaries

First, we suggest that you get a pencil and tear out the form entitled "Who Inherits Under a Will," contained in Appendix 1. (See sample on this page.) After you read this section carefully and study the will, insert in the left-hand column the names of the people, institutions and charities who might possibly inherit under it. These include named beneficiaries, unnamed beneficiaries, alternate beneficiaries (Section 5, below), and contingent beneficiaries (Section 6). There is a special category for assets left in trust. Most wills don't have trust provisions, but if the one you are dealing with does, list them here. We discuss trust property in Section c, below. Then list in the right-hand column the property the will says they inherit.

Note: In Chapter 5, you will be asked to prepare a schedule of all of the decedent's property. Because the property mentioned in the will might be different than the property actually existing when the decedent died (see Section D, below), you may wish to wait and fill in the right-hand side of the chart after you have finished the detailed schedule in Chapter 5.

The next section contains some sample will provisions and information to assist you in solving the many routine sorts of will interpretation problems you might encounter.

Who Inherits Under a Will?	
Beneficiaries Named in Will	Property Inherited

2. Common Clauses Used in Wills to Leave Property

Your first job is to read the will carefully. Most wills use several distinct types of clauses to pass property. Although the syntax and jargon in these clauses vary from will to will, they still accomplish basically the same things.

a. Clauses Which Designate Specific Property

One type of clause names beneficiaries of "specific" assets, such as a set amount of cash, certain defined securities, a particular parcel of real estate or a particular motor vehicle.[2] Here are some examples:

- "I give my house at 111 Apple St., Orange County, to my son Keith." (This is a specific devise of real property.)
- "I give my 1980 green Chevrolet Camaro automobile to my nephew Michael." (This is a specific bequest/devise of personal property.)

As noted above, once you determine the people, institutions and charities named to receive specific bequests or devises in the will, write their names on your list. Very simple, so far.

b. Residuary Clause

Wills also generally have what is termed a "residuary clause," which designates a beneficiary for the testator's residuary estate. This is all property not specifically disposed of by specific bequest or devise. The clause often refers to this remaining property as the "residue." Here are some examples:

---

[2]In wills prepared prior to 1985, personal property gifts are generally termed "bequests" and gifts of real estate are called "devises." Since 1985, all gifts, whether real or personal property, are called devises.

- "I give, devise and bequeath all other property, real, personal or mixed, not previously disposed of by this will to my son, Jasper Phillips."
- "I give all the rest, residue and remainder of my estate to the Sierra Club, San Francisco, California."

Here again, the people, institutions or charities named to receive the residue of an estate are usually clearly stated. Add them to your list. To determine exactly what they get, you will first have to go through the steps outlined in Chapter 5 to determine what the decedent owned at her death. Then, simply subtract the property left under the terms of the specific bequests and devises from the total estate. The residue is what's left.

The decedent, Tammy Rucker, died owning $50,000 cash, a 1984 Oldsmobile Cutlass automobile, a residence in San Jose, household furniture and furnishings, and personal effects. Tammy's will disposed of her property as follows: "I give the sum of $10,000 to my son Richard. I give my 1984 Oldsmobile Cutlass automobile to my nephew Reggie. I give all the rest, residue and remainder of my estate to my husband John." The residue of the estate going to John consists of the San Jose residence, the household furniture and furnishings, Tammy's personal effects and the remaining cash ($40,000), that is, all property that was not otherwise specifically disposed of.

---

c. Trust Provisions

Especially where minor children are involved, it is common for a will to leave property in a simple trust for one or more beneficiaries until they reach a certain age. You will know when this is happening because the magic word "trust" is always used. It is also common for an elderly person to leave his spouse some property in a simple trust. In this way, the surviving spouse can use the income during her life, with the principal going to the children (or other relatives or charities) when the surviving spouse dies. In larger estates, trusts are also used for a variety of tax planning purposes, many fairly complicated. If you are dealing with a large estate with a number of trust provisions, yours is not a simple estate and you will need to get professional help.

Any property placed in trust technically goes to the person named as "trustee" (the person to care for the property in the trust) to be held and used in trust for the designated beneficiaries, and turned over to them at the specified time. Here is an example:

- "I give 50 shares of IBM stock to my executor, as trustee, to be held for the benefit of my son Joseph until his twenty-first birthday. The trustee shall hold, administer and distribute the trust as follows." [Instructions would be spelled out here.]

If you discover one of these provisions in the will, you should list it under the trust section in the left-hand column of the Schedule of Assets (Chapter 5), and list the designated beneficiaries, as well as the trustee, in your beneficiary chart.

3. Terminology Used in Wills to Denote Groups of People

Once you find the main clauses described above, you may be uncertain about who is included in them. For instance, it is extremely common for wills to leave specific bequests and devises, and residuary bequests to groups of people designated as "my issue," "my children," or "my heirs."

Note: You may also run into the term "right of representation" (or "per stirpes"). This concept is dealt with in Section G of this chapter, and understanding it is important for both will interpretation and for figuring out who inherits if the decedent died intestate.

If you encounter these types of group terms, proceed very carefully. Here are some definitions. Please pay close attention to them, since even the apparently simple term "children" does not necessarily mean what you might think.

a. Issue

- "I give one-third of the residue of my estate to my sister Clara Peters. Should Clara predecease me, this gift shall go and be distributed by right of representation to her lawful issue."

A term generally meaning all natural children and their children down through the generations. Thus, a person's issue includes her children, grandchildren, great-grandchildren and so on. Adopted children are considered the issue of their adopting parents, and the children of the adopted children (and so on) are also considered issue. A term often used in place of issue is "lineal descendants."

b. Children

- "I give the sum of $1000 to each of the children of my two nephews, Edward Long and Charles Long, living at the date of my death."

Children include:

1. the biological offspring of the person making the will (the "testator") unless they have been legally adopted by another (but see below),

2. persons who were legally adopted by the testator,

3. children born out of wedlock if the testator is the mother,

4. children born out of wedlock if the testator is the father and has acknowledged the child as his under California law (this can be done in writing or by the conduct of the father—for more information see *The Living Together Kit*, Warner and Ihara), and

5. stepchildren and other children if the relationship began during the child's minority, continued throughout both parties' lifetimes, and if it is established by clear and convincing evidence that the decedent would have adopted the person but for a legal barrier.[3]

---

[3]One legal barrier to the adoption of a child is that the natural parent will not consent.

The relationship that must have existed during the child's minority and continued throughout the parties' lifetime is more than the mere stepchild-stepparent relationship that arises automatically upon the natural parent's remarriage. It must be a *family* relationship like that of a parent and child. Even in cases where a family relationship existed, there must still be clear and convincing evidence that the stepparent or foster parent would have adopted the stepchild or foster child but for a legal barrier.

Children who have been adopted are still considered, for purposes of inheritance, children of their natural parents if *both* the following requirements are met:

- the natural parent and the child lived together as parent and child, or the natural parent was married to or cohabiting with the other natural parent when the child was conceived but died before the child's birth; *and*

- the adoption was by the spouse of either natural parent or after the death of either natural parent. (Probate Code § 6408.5.)

c. *Heir*

- "I give $10,000 to my sister Julie Lee. Should Julie predecease me, this gift shall be divided among her heirs who survive me by 45 days."

An heir is any person who inherits in the absence of a will or who is entitled by law to inherit in the event an estate is not completely disposed of under a will.

4. Other Confusing Language

You are undoubtedly aware that the language used in wills can be extremely abstruse. Lawyers tend to repeat everything several times, and love to use "wherefores," "heretofores" and "parties of the third part." And even if the language in a will is relatively clear, you may encounter ambiguous statements. For instance, how

would you interpret this provision: "I give $15,000 to my three sons, Tom, Dick and Harry"? Does $15,000 or $5,000 go to each one?

To begin, if you read the will provision in question several times, it may become clear. Charting out the language can sometimes help. If you encounter strange words, or suspect that several words mean the same thing, you can consult the Glossary at the end of the book. Then see if the will provision makes sense. If it doesn't, which is very possible, consult an attorney. Unfortunately, we cannot anticipate the form or content of the muddled language that all too often creeps into wills.

5. Alternate Beneficiaries

Most wills specify who should get the property in the event a named beneficiary or one or more of the "class members" fail to survive the decedent.[4] These alternate beneficiaries should be listed in your chart. The language creating alternates is often quite straightforward:

- "If any of my children dies, then that child's share shall pass equally to my surviving children."

- "I give to my wife, Jane, all of my clothing, jewelry, furniture, books and all property of a personal nature. In the event she predeceases me,

---

[4]The term "class member" means a member of a group of beneficiaries who have been named in a will (for example, "children," "grandchildren," "uncles").

I leave all such personal property to my sister Ella."

- "I give to my son Richard my Porsche automobile, License No. _____, or, if I no longer own that automobile at my death, any automobile I own at the time of my death. Should he predecease me, my automobile shall be left as part of my residuary estate."

Again, only you can be the judge of whether the language is straightforward enough for you to understand it or if you need the opinion of a lawyer.

6. Conditional Bequests

Finally, and less commonly, you may find there are bequests or devises in the will that are left to people upon one or more conditions and which will go to other people in the event the conditions are not met. In this situation, you will need to identify for your beneficiary chart both the main or primary beneficiaries and the beneficiaries who contingently stand to inherit. For example, you might find a clause leaving a house to "my three sons so long as they live in it, but if they move out, then to my sister Hannah." In this case, who inherits if one son moves out but the others continue to live there?

There is no easy answer. Contingent and conditional gifts have long been responsible for many of the lawsuits that arise over the interpretation of wills. If you run into one of these clauses and are unsure of who is entitled to what, talk it over with the affected family members. If everyone is reasonable and a successful compromise is arrived at, you can probably continue to handle the estate settlement work yourself. However, if a dispute festers or threatens to do so, you have to face the fact that you're not dealing with a simple estate and need professional help.

7. Unenforceable Will Provisions

Wills are often filled with wishes, suggestions and, sometimes, unenforceable demands. As the executor or administrator of the estate, you have no duty to comply with these, although you may wish to carry out the decedent's intentions to the greatest degree possible. For instance, suppose you encounter a will which says something like this:

- "I give to my sister Bertha all my clothing, jewelry, furniture, furnishings, books and all other property of a personal nature, with the request that she give to my children as they come of age such articles as they might desire or need."

Because the clause suggests rather than mandates, it cannot be enforced and Bertha is legally entitled to keep all of the property.

8. Summary

We have briefly covered a lot of ground here. It may be helpful to review this section on will interpretation by studying the following chart. Normally, you will be able to identify both the beneficiaries of the will and the property they are to receive by:

- Locating the parts of the will that dispose of property;

- Interpreting the words that apply to groups of potential beneficiaries;

- Sorting out the syntax and learning the meaning of strange words;

- Identifying the alternate beneficiaries;

- Identifying contingent beneficiaries; and

- Rejecting language that suggests but doesn't command.

Interpreting Wills

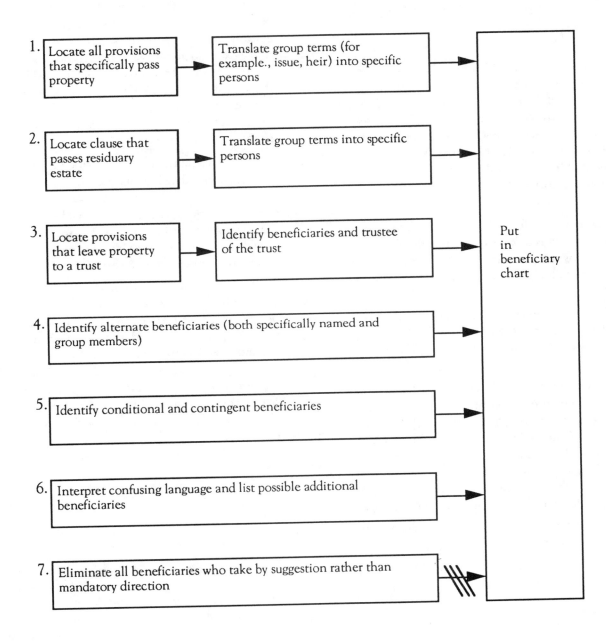

D. Compare Schedule of Assets (in Chapter 5) with Property Left in Will

NOW THAT YOU HAVE identified the beneficiaries of the will, your next job is to roughly compare the amount and character of the property the decedent actually left with the property she set out in the will. To say this another way, you must ask whether the property listed in the will was still owned by her when she died. We give you essential information about property in Chapter 4 and show you how to identify and list the decedent's property in Chapter 5.

As we noted briefly in the introduction to this chapter, sometimes this task is easy because the will doesn't give away any specific assets but instead leaves everything to a spouse or children in clearly defined portions. For example:

- "I give, devise and bequeath all of my estate, both real and personal, as follows: Two-thirds thereof to my wife, Mary, and one-third thereof to my son John."

However, if a decedent has left a long list of specific items to a long list of people, it can be a bit trickier. What happens, for example, if a decedent's will leaves his 1982 Dodge Omni to his son Herb, but the decedent sold the Omni and used the money for a vacation? Does Herb get anything? Or, suppose the decedent leaves his share of his house to Herb, but later places the property in joint tenancy with his wife. Here are some general rules that apply if a person does not keep his will up to date and dies without owning certain assets listed in it.

1. Specific Gifts

A gift of a particular thing, specified and distinguished from all others of the same kind belonging to the decedent, is a "specific" gift. If the specific asset is not, in fact, owned by the decedent when she dies (or if it has been put into joint tenancy or a trust in the meantime), the gift simply fails. (The legal word for this is "lapses.") The person named to receive the specific gift that no longer exists is not entitled to take another asset instead. Thus, in the example just above, if the decedent no longer has the 1982 Dodge Omni, no other property will do. But if the will said, "I give any automobile I may own at the time of my death to my son Herb," and decedent had sold the Omni and bought a jeep just prior to death, then Herb would take the jeep.

In some circumstances, if a specific item has "merely changed form," the original beneficiary may still have a claim—if, for example, a testator leaves a promissory note due her to a friend, and the note is paid before her death, leaving easily traceable proceeds.[5] In such a case, a court would look at the testator's intent to decide if the beneficiary should inherit from the estate.

If you face a situation where some assets have been replaced by others between the time a will was drafted and the decedent died, you should get professional help unless all people who stand to inherit agree in a sensible compromise. For instance, the decedent left Herb an Omni auto but sold the Omni and bought a jeep a few months before death. As everyone in the family agreed that the decedent wanted Herb to have the jeep but simply hadn't updated his will, you would be safe in honoring this intent.

---

[5]The concept of "tracing" is a complicated one. Normally it involves looking at what was done with the proceeds of the sale of an asset to see if they are still identifiable. Thus, if a car is sold and the money is placed in a new bank account, it's easy to trace. However, if the money is put in an existing bank account with other funds, and lots of money flows in and out, tracing is generally not possible. Lawyers and courts struggle with the tracing concept regularly, which is another way of saying that if you need to trace assets, you are not dealing with a simple estate.

2. General Legacies

Gifts of money are called "general legacies" or "bequests" because they are not tied to specific items but rather can be satisfied by the payment of cash. If there is enough cash in the estate to satisfy the terms of the will, fine and good. However, obvious problems can result if the will leaves a beneficiary money but insufficient cash is available when the testator dies. Suppose, for instance, that a decedent's will leaves $50,000 each to two different people (call them Herb and Cathy) and there is, in fact, only $60,000 in the decedent's estate. Here is what happens:

- If the decedent has other assets which form part of his residuary estate (that is, they have not been left to specific beneficiaries), Herb and Cathy as "named" beneficiaries of general legacies, first, split what money the decedent did leave, and then take assets of sufficient value from the residuary estate to make up the difference. Typically, this involves the sale of those assets and a corresponding decrease in the value of the assets received by the beneficiaries of the residuary estate;

- If the decedent dies leaving only $60,000 in cash and no other assets, Herb and Cathy would split the $60,000 in proportion to their original shares, assuming they were either both related or both unrelated to the decedent. In our example, Herb and Cathy were willed an equal amount so they would divide the $60,000 in half. However, if Cathy were related to the decedent and Herb were not, Cathy could receive her entire bequest ($50,000) while Herb would only receive the balance. This is because the law gives preference to a spouse or relative and would, thus, satisfy the relative or spouse's legacy first, unless the will stated a different intention. If you face this situation, consultation with a lawyer may be called for.

3. Property Left to Someone Who Fails to Survive Decedent

What happens if the decedent's will leaves property to someone and that person dies before the decedent? Obviously, the deceased beneficiary receives nothing. What happens to the gift? As discussed in Section C5, above, in the great majority of instances, wills provide for this by naming an alternate beneficiary. For example: "I leave $5,000 to Mary P. if she survives me. If she does not, I leave this money to Sally P."

If, however, the will does not specify an alternate beneficiary, the result will depend on the relationship of the original beneficiary and the decedent. The California laws that apply in these situations are discussed below.

a. Deceased Person Is Relative

If the gift was made to any relative of the decedent, or to a relative of a surviving, deceased or former spouse of the decedent, the property goes to the children, grandchildren or great-grandchildren (termed "issue") of the person named to receive it, by "right of representation." However, this doesn't apply if the beneficiary is required to survive for a specific period of time (30 days, for example). This law is called the "anti-lapse statute," and is set forth in Probate Code § 6147. The term "right of representation" refers to how shares are divided among the "issue" and is discussed in detail in Section G of this chapter.

b. Deceased Person Is Not Relative

If the beneficiary who does not survive the decedent was not a relative or a relative of a surviving or deceased spouse, and no alternate beneficiary was named, the gift simply lapses and is added to the residue of the estate. This means the relatives of the predeceased beneficiary inherit nothing, and the gift passes under the terms of the will's residuary clause. As you now know from our earlier discussion in Section C2, this is the clause which disposes of all property not covered by a specific devise or bequest.

A residuary clause usually states something like this: "I give any and all property, real, personal or mixed, not previously disposed of by this will, to my wife, Jane."

Assume Bill, who has never married, says in his will: "I give $1,000 to my housekeeper Jennie." Jennie dies before Bill, who never changed his will. Jennie receives nothing, because she's deceased. Similarly, her children or grandchildren receive nothing (unless Jennie was a relative of Bill), because under California law, the gift lapses. The money becomes part of the residuary estate.

Bill's will says "I give $5,000 to my sister Claudia," and makes no provision for an alternative beneficiary. If Claudia dies before Bill, Claudia's $5,000 will go to her issue (that is, children, grandchildren, etc.) because Claudia is related to the decedent.

If Claudia left a will when she died, it would have no bearing on the situation in Bill's estate or on how the $5,000 would be distributed—the money would still go to Claudia's children. On the other hand, if Bill's will says, "I give $5,000 to my sister Claudia, but if Claudia should fail to survive me, this gift shall go to Sally," then Claudia's issue receive nothing.

It may be easier to grasp how the anti-lapse laws work by studying the chart below.

E. Determining Identity of Beneficiaries and Heirs When Will Is Ineffective

AS WE INDICATED earlier in Section C4, wills sometimes don't have the effect that the testator may have intended. This primarily occurs in three situations:

- Spouses who are entitled to inherit are left out of the will;

- Children who are entitled to inherit are left out of the will; *and*

- The will was not updated after a divorce.

    Let's consider these areas one at a time.

1. Spouse Left Out of the Will

If a person marries after making her will and (a) doesn't provide for the new spouse in the will or in a codicil (or by any other means), and (b) doesn't indicate an intention in the will to exclude the spouse, and (c) dies first, then the surviving spouse will be entitled to all the community and quasi-community property (the decedent's half and the one-half already owned by the surviving spouse), plus up to one-half of the decedent's separate property. This is called the spouse's "statutory share" of the estate. (Probate Code §§ 6560 through 6562.)

    Looking at this rule from the opposite perspective, a person who married the decedent after she made a will and who is not provided for in the decedent's will may claim some of the estate unless:

- The decedent intentionally omitted such spouse (by language such as, "I intentionally omit any future husband"); *or*

Anti-Lapse Chart

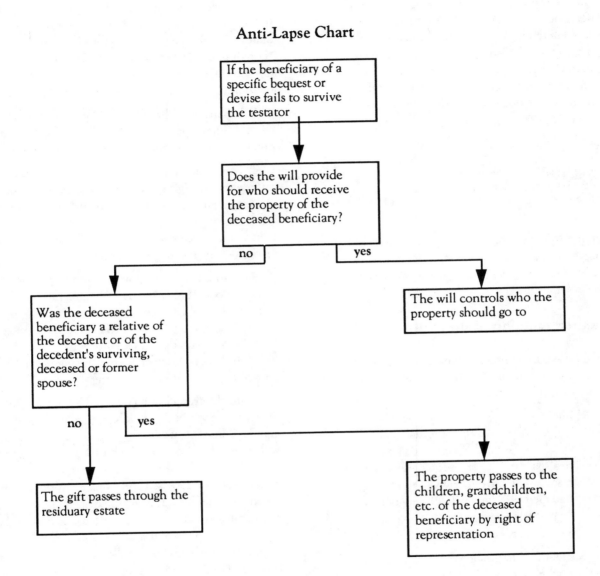

- The decedent provided for the spouse by property transfers outside the will instead (such as in a marriage contract, joint tenancy transfers or insurance proceeds), and it can be clearly shown by statements made by the decedent, by the amount of the transfer, or by other evidence that the decedent intended the transfer to be in lieu of a will provision; *or*

- The omitted spouse made a valid written agreement waiving the right to share in the decedent's estate.

The Pretermitted Spouse Chart, below, will further clarify these situations.

Warning: In the unusual event that you must deal with this situation, check your conclusions with a lawyer.

2. Children Left Out of the Will

Here are the rules that apply if the decedent failed to provide for one or more of his children in his will (see *Glossary* for definition of children):

- If at the time of writing a will the decedent was unaware of the birth of a child, or mistakenly believed the child was dead, the omitted child will receive a share in the estate equal in value to that which she would have received if the decedent had died without a will. Otherwise, the law assumes that the omission was intentional and the child inherits nothing;

- If the decedent fails to provide in his will for any of his children born or adopted after the execution of the will (and, thus, not foreseen at the time), the omitted child is entitled to receive a share in the estate equal in value to that which the child would have received had the decedent died without a will, unless one or more of the following conditions exists, in which case the omitted child does not receive a share of the estate:

a. It appears from the will that the omission was intentional, for example, the will says "I have intentionally omitted to provide in this will for my daughter Lynn," or "I don't like my daughter Lynn and leave her nothing." Or, the will could simply name Lynn as a child and leave her nothing;

b. When the will was signed, the decedent had one or more children and left substantially all the estate to the other parent of the omitted child;

c. The decedent provided for the child by transfer outside the will (gifts during the decedent's lifetime, life insurance, joint accounts) and the intention that the transfer be in lieu of a will provision is shown by statements of the decedent (oral or written), and/or from the amount of the transfer, or by other evidence.

Situations involving omitted children, covered by Probate Code §§ 6570 to 6573, can be intricate. If you face an estate where a child has not been mentioned in a will and has not otherwise been clearly and obviously provided for to that child's satisfaction, you have a problem. If it can't be resolved within the family, you should consult a lawyer before continuing.

Grandchildren Note: The law does not protect omitted grandchildren or more remote issue (great-grandchildren) of the decedent who are living when the will is signed. If a decedent's child is deceased at the time the will was signed and the decedent failed to provide for children of that deceased child (grandchildren of the decedent), that omission is treated as intentional and the grandchildren receive nothing. However, if a child who was living when the will was made is named as a beneficiary under the will and that child dies before the decedent, leaving a child or children surviving (grandchildren of the decedent), then the grandchildren will divide the deceased child's share absent other direction in the will. We discuss how this works in Section G, below.

Pretermitted Spouse Chart

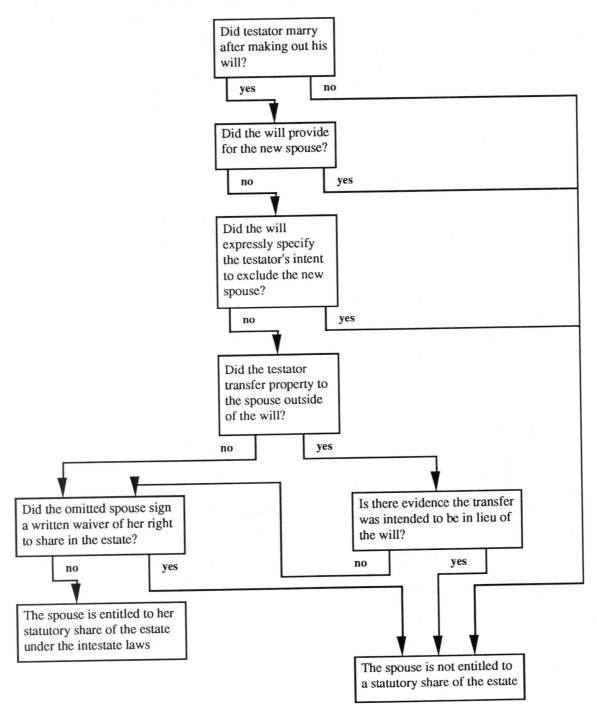

3. No Update After Divorce

If a decedent's will gives property to her spouse, but her marriage to that spouse was dissolved or annulled after the will was signed after January 1, 1985, any gift of property made to the former spouse by the will is cancelled unless the will specifically provides otherwise. The estate is then distributed as if the former spouse did not survive the decedent. However, if the divorce or annulment occurred prior to January 1, 1985, bequests to a former spouse stand, unless there is a provision made in the property settlement agreement that the parties waive their rights to inherit the estate of the other at the other's death.

Harold made a will while married to Sally that gave Sally $200,000 and the rest of his estate to his children in equal shares. The marriage was dissolved on July 1, 1986, but Harold never made a new will. Sally gets nothing on Harold's death. The $200,000 gift to her is added to the portion of the estate going to his children. However, if the divorce had occurred before January 1, 1985, Sally would get the $200,000.

F. Determining Heirs Under Intestate Succession Laws

WHEN A DECEDENT DIES without a will, you must determine the heirs of her estate under intestate succession laws. This should not be difficult if you refer to the Intestate Succession Chart, below. California's intestate succession laws are set out in Probate Code §§ 6400 to 6414.

Note that the portion of the decedent's estate going to each relative first depends on whether or not the decedent was married when she died and whether her estate contains both community property and separate property, only community property or only separate property. (We define and discuss community and separate property in Chapter 4.) Of course, if the decedent was not married, all of her property will be separate property.

By looking at the chart, you should get a good idea of what happens to property left by intestate succession. To summarize, if a person dies without a will:

• The surviving spouse inherits all community property;

• The surviving spouse inherits either one-third, one-half or all of the separate property, depending on whether the decedent is survived by one or more children or other close relatives;

• Separate property not inherited by the surviving spouse is divided into fractional shares and distributed to the children, parents, grandparents, or brothers and sisters.

Note: To inherit property from an intestate decedent who died after December 31, 1989, a person must survive the decedent for at least 120 hours. (Probate Code § 6403.)

If a decedent dies intestate with no alternative estate plan, and leaves only more distant relatives (no spouse, children, grandchildren, great-grandchildren, parents or their issue, or grandparents or their issue), then the property goes to the next of kin. Deciding who will inherit involves understanding a concept called "degrees of kindred." Each generation is called a "degree." The degrees are determined by counting up to a common ancestor and then down to a decedent.

Intestate Succession

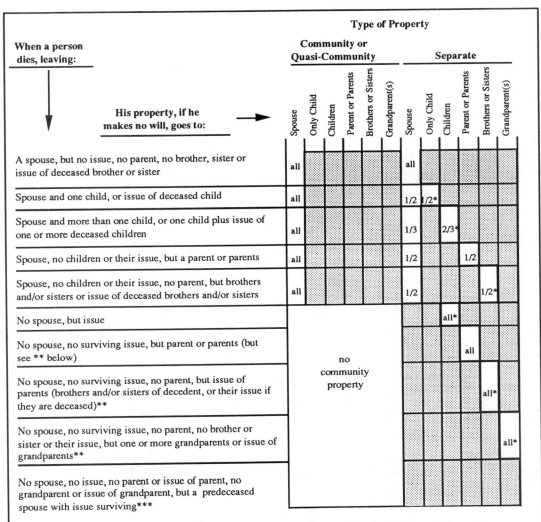

When a person dies, leaving: / His property, if he makes no will, goes to:	Community or Quasi-Community						Separate					
	Spouse	Only Child	Children	Parent or Parents	Brothers or Sisters	Grandparent(s)	Spouse	Only Child	Children	Parent or Parents	Brothers or Sisters	Grandparent(s)
A spouse, but no issue, no parent, no brother, sister or issue of deceased brother or sister	all						all					
Spouse and one child, or issue of deceased child	all						1/2	1/2*				
Spouse and more than one child, or one child plus issue of one or more deceased children	all						1/3		2/3*			
Spouse, no children or their issue, but a parent or parents	all						1/2			1/2		
Spouse, no children or their issue, no parent, but brothers and/or sisters or issue of deceased brothers and/or sisters	all						1/2				1/2*	
No spouse, but issue	no community property							all*				
No spouse, no surviving issue, but parent or parents (but see ** below)										all		
No spouse, no surviving issue, no parent, but issue of parents (brothers and/or sisters of decedent, or their issue if they are deceased)**											all*	
No spouse, no surviving issue, no parent, no brother or sister or their issue, but one or more grandparents or issue of grandparents**												all*
No spouse, no issue, no parent or issue of parent, no grandparent or issue of grandparent, but a predeceased spouse with issue surviving***												

* Issue take equally if they are all of the same degree of kinship to the decedent, but if of unequal degree, those o more remote degree take by right of representation (in the manner provided in Probate Code Sec. 2407).

** If decedent leaves no spouse or issue, but had a predeceased spouse who died within 15 years of the decedent, property in the decedent's estate attributable to the predeceased spouse goes to certain close relatives of the predeceased spouse (Probate Code sec. 6402.5).

*** Property goes to issue of predeceased spouse, issue taking equally if they are all of same degree of kinship to the predeceased spouse, but if of unequal degree, those of more remote degree take by right of representation. I decedent leaves no surviving spouse, issue, parents, grandparents, brothers or sisters or their issue, or issue of a predeceased spouse, all property goes to decedent's next of kin. If no next of kin, then all property goes to parents or issue of parents of predeceased spouse.

The Table of Consanguinity, below, shows the degree of different relatives. For instance, children are in the first degree, and nieces and nephews are in the third degree. Second cousins are in the sixth degree.

Table of Consanguinity

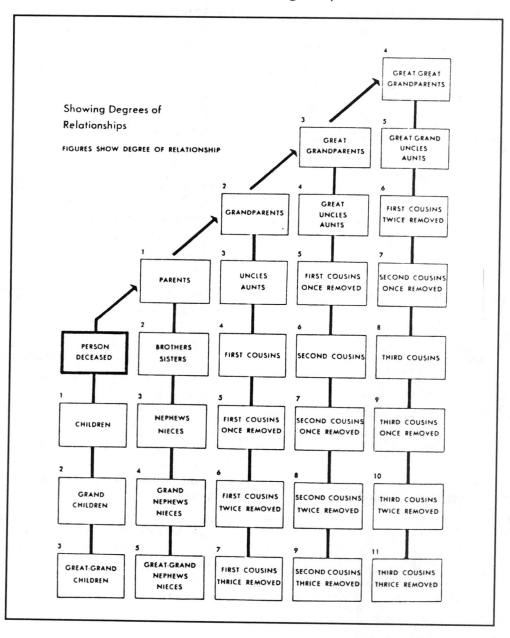

Note: In reading this chart and the ones that come later in this section you will see that legal terminology is often used to specifically differentiate between certain persons or classes of persons. Simple definitions of the most important terms are provided in the *Glossary*.

Although the definition of children discussed in Section C, above, applies when determining heirs under the intestate succession laws as well as identifying beneficiaries of a will, the statute contains some special rules for intestate succession situations. A child who has been adopted may still inherit from her natural parents:

- If the deceased parent was married to or cohabiting with the other natural parent at the time of the child's conception and died before the child was born; and if

- The adoption was by the spouse of either of the natural parents or took place after the death of either natural parent.

G. The Concept of Right of Representation

THE CONCEPT OF inheritance by "right of representation" (or "per stirpes") can be very important in determining whether particular people will inherit property under a will (and, sometimes, by intestate succession in the absence of a will) and if so, how much.

1. Right of Representation Defined

Let's start with a simple definition. "The right of representation" means that the descendants of a deceased beneficiary take the same share collectively that the deceased beneficiary would have taken if he had been living at the time of the decedent's death. For instance, assume John makes a bequest to his brother Tommy, and Tommy dies before John but leaves three children of his own. Unless the will provided otherwise, the children

would take the bequest by "right of representation"—that is, the children would equally divide Tommy's bequest.

While this concept may seem straightforward, it often is not. And to confuse matters further, a statutory change has left us with two different definitions of the "right of representation" concept—each of which applies in certain specific situations. In other words, there is just no way to make the concept of "right of representation" as simple as we would wish.

2. When You Need to Understand Right of Representation

Fortunately, most people will not have to deal with this material at all. However, if you face one of the four situations set out just below, it is essential that you understand the concept of right of representation; please read the following discussion carefully and see a lawyer to check your conclusions.

Situation 1: A will specifically leaves property to a group of beneficiaries using the words "by right of representation" or "per stirpes."

Daisy leaves her house "to my children Myra and Andrew, but if either of them should not survive me, then to that child's children by right of representation."

Situation 2: The will provides that issue of a predeceased beneficiary should inherit their ancestor's share, but doesn't specify the method by which to determine their shares.

Daisy leaves her house "to my children Myra and Andrew, but if either of them should predecease me, then to their issue."

Situation 3: A will leaves property to a relative of the decedent and:

- The relative died before the decedent, or failed to survive the decedent by the time specified in the will (often 45-180 days); and

- The will names no alternate beneficiary.

Albert left his sister Agnes $50,000 and made no pro-vision for what would happen if Agnes died before he did, which she did. Who will inherit the money depends on how the right of representation is applied. If, however, Albert had left the same amount to his faithful, but not related, nurse, Phil, who didn't survive Albert, the gift to Phil would be wiped out. The money would pass under the residuary clause of Albert's will. Because it wouldn't go to Phil's descendants, you wouldn't need to worry about right of representation.

Situation 4: There is no will, and the intestacy laws call for succession (inheritance) by right of representation.

Jane dies without a will. Two of her three children survive her, as does a child of her predeceased child. The relevant intestate succession statute (Probate Code § 6402) provides that Jane's issue (her children and grandchild) inherit her estate and that the grand-child takes by right of representation.

If you face one of these four situations, read on. If you don't, proceed to Chapter 4, where we discuss assessing different types of property.

3. The Two Meanings of Right of Representation

As mentioned, there are currently two methods or formu-las in use for determining who inherits in "right of repre-sentation" situations. It is essential that you understand which one applies to the estate you are dealing with:

- Formula 1 (set out in Probate Code § 240) is used when a will provides that issue of a deceased beneficiary take but doesn't specify by what method, or when a kindred beneficiary dies before the testator, and whenever the intestate succession laws call for division by right of representation (Situations 2, 3 and 4). It is discussed in Section a, below.

- Formula 2 (set out in Probate Code § 246) applies only when the will specifically calls for division by right of representation (Situation 1). It is discussed in Section b, below.

a. Formula 1

When Formula 1 applies, you must first identify the clos-est generation of issue that has living members. The clos-est possible generation is that of the children. If there are no children living, go on to the grandchildren's genera-tion, and so forth. The property is divided into as many shares as there are living members, and deceased members who left issue living, of that generation. Each living member of the generation gets a share, and the issue of a deceased member take their ancestor's share.

Assume John died without a will and all three of his children, Bob, Bill and Ben, survived him. The portion of his estate that would go to his children under the intestate laws would be divided equally among the children (the closest generation with a living member). It would look like this:

Right of Representation #1

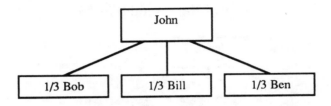

James makes a will in 1985 and leaves his house to his three children. Two of his children, Jill and Jack, are alive when James dies. One daughter, Joyce, has died before James, but after the will was signed, leaving two surviving children, Janice and Jake (James' grandchildren). James' house would be inherited as follows: each of his surviving children (Jill and Jack) would own a third and the two grandchildren (Janice and Jake), inheriting their deceased parent's share equally, would each own a one-sixth.[6]

Right of Representation #2

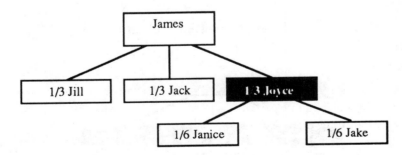

---

[6]However, if James' deceased daughter Joyce had died before he made his will, Joyce's children (James' grandchildren) would receive nothing, because they would be considered "intentionally omitted" under the law.

Jeffrey makes a will in 1985 and leaves all of his property to his three children, Phil, Paul and Peter. At Jeffrey's death, Phil survives, Paul is deceased, leaving two children of his own (Sarah and Sabrina), and Peter is deceased, leaving no children, but one surviving grandchild (Lew) of his own. Jeffrey's only surviving child, Phil, would receive one-third of the property. The two grandchildren, Sarah and Sabrina, would split their parent's share (one-sixth each), and the great-grandchild, Lew, would take his grandparent's share (one-third).

Right of Representation #3

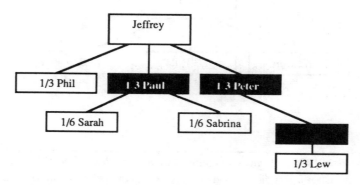

If all members in the closest degree of relationship are deceased, the property is equally divided at the next generation having a living member.

Suppose Angela leaves her property to her three children (Rosie, Marie and Josefa) and none of them survive. However, Josefa leaves four children of her own, Rosie leaves two children, and Marie leaves one child. Because there are no living members in the next closest generation to Angela (that is, her children), each of the grandchildren takes an equal share (that is, one-seventh of the property).

Right of Representation #4

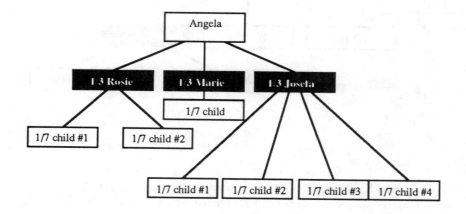

Suppose Rosie survived Angela. Then the other grandchildren would only take their parent's share. Thus the four grandchildren would have to split one-third of the property (one-twelfth each) while the single grandchild of the other deceased child would inherit one-third of the property.

Right of Representation #5

```
                        ┌──────────┐
                        │  Angela  │
                        └────┬─────┘
            ┌────────────────┼──────────────┐
      ┌───────────┐   ┌────────────┐  ┌────────────┐
      │ 1/3 Rosie │   │ 1/3 Marie  │  │ 1/3 Josela │
      └───────────┘   └─────┬──────┘  └────────────┘
                      ┌───────────┐
                      │ 1/3 child │
                      └───────────┘
```

| | 1/12 child #1 | 1/12 child #2 | 1/12 child #3 | 1/12 child #4 |

Here is a final example that demonstrates all these principles:

Grandpa dies without a will in 1985 and leaves a childless son (Harry) and three children of a deceased daughter (Rhoda). In this situation, the estate is first divided at his children's level into two shares: one for the decedent's surviving son Harry and the other for the deceased daughter Rhoda. Harry would get half and the three grandchildren would share the half that their mother would have had, or one-sixth each.

Right of Representation #6

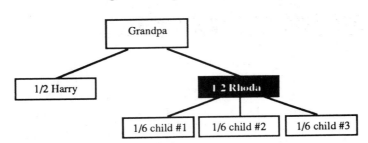

Suppose, however, the son also died before Grandpa and left a son. In this case, the four grandchildren would each get one-fourth. Why? Because Grandpa's property is divided first at the grandchildren's level (it being the generation closest the decedent with a living member) instead of the children's level. Because the grandchildren are all in the same generation and are all living, they share equally.

Right of Representation #7

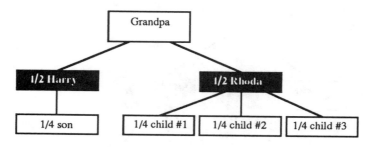

If one of the grandchildren had also died and left surviving children (great-grandchildren of the decedent), then the deceased grandchild's children would share the one-fourth their parent would have received.

Right of Representation #8

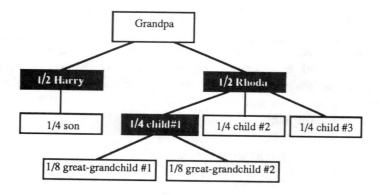

b. Formula 2

Formula 2 is used only if a will expressly directs that inheritance be by "right of representation" or "per stirpes." Under this system a generation that has no living members is not ignored; the estate is always divided first at the children's generation. This can make the distribution different than it would be under Formula 1.

For example, review the Right of Representation Chart #8, above. Under Formula 1, the estate is divided first at the closest generation with living members—here, the decedent's grandchildren. The three living grandchildren take one-fourth, and the fourth grandchild's share is split between his two children (the decedent's great-grandchildren.)

If, however, Grandpa had left a will leaving his estate to his children or their issue "by right of representation," the situation would be analyzed under Formula 2. The estate would be divided first at the children's level. Thus the estate would be divided in half, even though neither Harry nor Rhoda survived Grandpa. Harry's child would take his father's one-half share. Rhoda's two surviving children would take one-third of their mother's share (one-sixth each), and the great-grandchildren would split their parent's one-sixth share.

Right of Representation: Formula 2

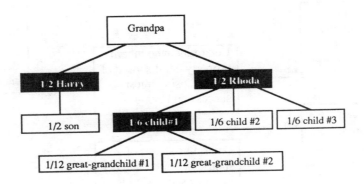

H. Summary Chart

WE STARTED OUT this chapter with the goal of identify-ing the beneficiaries or heirs and the property that they are supposed to inherit. Although it was necessary to take a number of side-trips into some dense legal forests, we hope to have always returned to the main path. Below is the Overview of Property Distribution chart that summarizes our analysis. By studying it, you should be able to gain a perspective of the entire chapter that may have been lost somewhere along the line.

Overview of Property Distribution

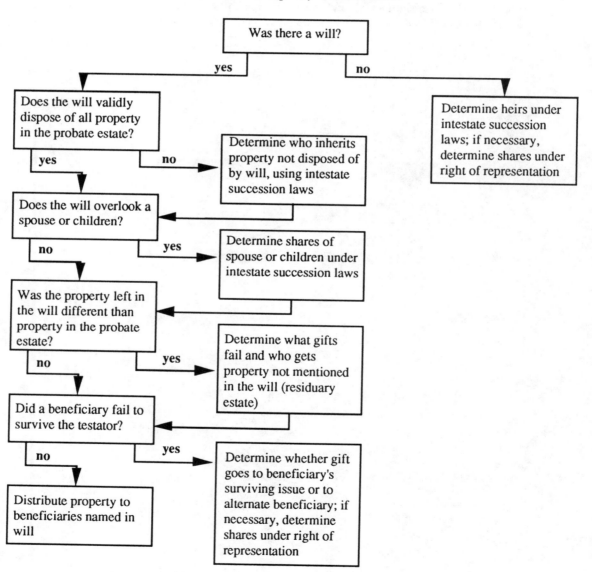

CHAPTER 4

What Is the Decedent's Estate?

TO SETTLE AN ESTATE, you must first be able to identify the decedent's property. Everything the decedent owned—from real estate, bank accounts, securities, insurance and antiques, to furniture, art, coin collections, copyrights, cars, campers, computers, collies and canoes—collectively makes up her estate. We specifically instruct you on how to prepare an inventory of whatever the decedent owned in the next chapter. Our goal in this chapter is to introduce you to the basic property law concepts you must know to make sense of this inventory.

Property can be viewed from two fundamental perspectives. First, property is whatever can be owned by humans. The air you breathe cannot be owned and is, therefore, not property. Oxygen captured in tanks, however, can be owned and, therefore, is property. When the Europeans approached the American Indians about selling their land, the Indians had no concept of the land as being property subject to sale. Europeans, on the other hand, had long viewed land as being the essence of property. Not surprisingly, the Europeans soon ended up with most of the property.

The second view of property has to do with the nature of ownership. This view of property focuses on the form in which it is owned (jointly, individually, contingently), and the quantitative nature of this ownership (total, partial, shared), and how much it is worth. Put differently, this view treats property only in relationship to how it is owned and how much it is worth.

We mention these two views of property because the law relating to the settlement of estates treats property differently depending on the form of the property itself and the type (and value) of the interest which the decedent possessed in the property. You will need to answer the following questions in respect to each item of the decedent's property:

- Is it real property or personal property?

- How was the property owned? In other words, did the decedent hold title to the property in his own name or jointly with someone else (for example, community property, joint tenancy, tenancy in common, etc.)?

Note: If personal property of the decedent is located outside of California at the time of his death, it is also important to understand if it is tangible or intangible. The reason for mastering this distinction, which we will develop in Section B, below, is that tangible personal property located outside of California must be transferred under the laws and procedures of the state in which it is located and can't be handled using the forms and instructions contained in this book. (More on this distinction below.)

The answers to these questions will not only help you define what property is included in the decedent's estate, but will also have a direct bearing on two other important points—who is entitled to the property, and what is the best method of transferring it to its new owner(s). While some very simple estates can be settled without mastering the information in this chapter, most require at least a passing knowledge of it. Start by reading this chapter carefully. We do our best to separate the simple property ownership situations from those that are more complex, and you may find that if your estate qualifies for the former category, you can safely leave this chapter and go on to Chapter 5 without digesting the whole thing.

Note: For now, don't worry about whether the decedent owed money on a particular piece of property. Once ownership rules are firmly established, it will be easy to subtract debts as part of valuing the property. (See Chapter 5.)

A. Real Property

ALL PROPERTY IS either real or personal (see Section B, below), and a number of the procedures used to settle the estate will depend on how each asset is classified. "Real property" is land and things permanently affixed to land, such as houses, trees and growing crops. If a mobile home or other structure is permanently attached to the land, it is treated as part of the real property, the same as a house. However, if it is registered with the Department of Motor Vehicles or the Department of Housing and Community Development and can be taken from place to place, it is personal property. Real property also includes condominiums,[1] leasehold interests in cooperatives and underground utility installations. A real estate lease with an unexpired term of ten years or longer, or a lease together with an option to purchase, or an oil or gas leasehold interest, is also treated as real property; any other leases are considered personal property. (Probate Code §§ 10203, 10204.)

Real property is transferred to its new owners following the laws and procedures of the state in which it is located. We only show you how to transfer real property located in California in this book. To transfer real property located outside of California, you will need to find self-help information or a lawyer in that state.[2] If the property was owned in joint tenancy with right of survivorship[3] or title had been transferred to a living trust, you can probably handle it yourself. If formal probate is required, you will probably need a lawyer.

Interest in real property is usually transferred from one person to another by a written document. When both parties are living, this is usually done with a deed. Various kinds of deeds are used for this purpose, some of which you may have discovered among the decedent's papers. Most deeds are clearly labeled, but just in case you aren't sure whether a particular document is a deed, here are the basic elements. A deed must contain the name of the grantee (purchaser or person receiving title to the property), name of the grantor (seller or person conveying title to the property), a legal description of the property, a granting clause which says, "I hereby grant to ..." (sometimes the words "transfer" or "convey" are used), and the

---

[1]Some life interests in condominiums and co-ops which do not survive the decedent are not considered real property.

[2]Even though real property located outside of California is not covered in this book, it is part of decedent's taxable estate as discussed in Chapter 7.

[3]In some states joint tenancy doesn't mean what it does in California. In Texas, for example, joint tenancy doesn't always carry with it a right of survivorship, while in Oregon the term "tenancy in common with right of survivorship" is used to mean what California calls "joint tenancy."

signature(s) of the grantor(s). Below are some of the more common deeds and what they are used for.

1. Grant Deed

This is the most commonly used deed in California. The grantor (seller) conveys the property and the grantee (buyer) receives it. The grantor in a grant deed makes certain implied warranties (guarantees) that he owns the property and has not previously conveyed (transferred), mortgaged or otherwise encumbered the property except as stated in the deed.

Grant Deed

RECORDING REQUESTED BY

Thomas B. Buyer and Helen A. Buyer

AND WHEN RECORDED MAIL THIS DEED AND, UNLESS OTHER-
WISE SHOWN BELOW, MAIL TAX STATEMENTS TO:

NAME Thomas B. Buyer and Helen
         A. Buyer
ADDRESS 35 Overview Lane
CITY &   San Francisco, Calif. 91378
STATE
ZIP

Title Order No. _____ Escrow No. _____

SPACE ABOVE THIS LINE FOR RECORDER'S USE

GRANT DEED

The undersigned declares that the documentary transfer tax is $ 70.65 _____ and is

☐ computed on the full value of the interest or property conveyed, or is

☒ computed on the full value less the value of liens or encumbrances remaining thereon at the time of sale. The land,
tenements or realty is located in

☐ unincorporated area   ☐ city of _____ and

FOR A VALUABLE CONSIDERATION, receipt of which is hereby acknowledged,

GEORGE S. SELLER and MARY M. SELLER, his wife

hereby GRANT(S) to   THOMAS B. BUYER and HELEN A. BUYER, his wife,

the following described real property in the City and
county of San Francisco   , state of California:

Lot 4 in Block 28, as designated on the map
entitled "Twin Peaks Tract, City and
County of San Francisco, State of California,"
filed in the Office of the Recorder of the
City and County of San Francisco, State of
California, on August 5, 1909, in Volume 3
of Maps, at page 8.

A.P.N. 1234 567 890

Dated June 26, 1986 _____   s/ GEORGE S. SELLER

                                    s/ MARY M. SELLER

STATE OF CALIFORNIA
COUNTY OF San Francisco   } SS.
On this the 26th day of June 19 86 before me the undersigned, a
Notary Public in and for said County and State, personally appeared George S. Seller and Mary M. Seller,

_____ personally known
to me or proved to me on the basis of satisfactory evidence to be the
person s_ whose name s they subscribed to the within instrument
and acknowledged that ✓ executed the same.

        s/ Nancy Notary
          Signature of Notary

FOR NOTARY SEAL OR STAMP

Assessor's Parcel No. _____

MAIL TAX STATEMENTS TO PARTY SHOWN ON FOLLOWING LINE; IF NO PARTY SO SHOWN, MAIL AS DIRECTED ABOVE.

Name   Street Address   City & State

CAL-1 (Rev. 8-82)

2. Quitclaim Deed

This type of deed is used when the grantor makes no warranties about title, saying in effect that whatever she has, she is conveying. Assuming the grantor owns the property, this type of deed is just as effective to transfer ownership as is a grant deed. It looks just like a grant deed except that it's labeled "Quitclaim Deed" and contains slightly different wording.

Quitclaim Deed

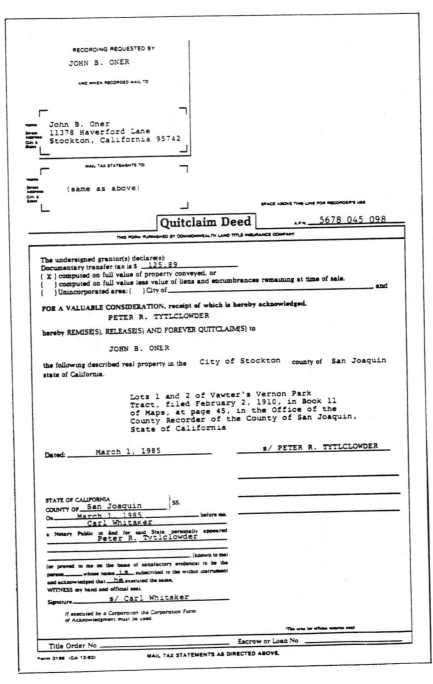

3. Joint Tenancy Deed

Joint tenancy is one way two or more people may own property. A "joint tenancy deed" is merely any deed that is used to convey property to two or more persons as joint tenants. Many printed deeds are titled "Joint Tenancy Deed," but this designation is unnecessary if the substance of the deed indicates that a joint tenancy has been created. In other words, any grant deed or quitclaim deed can be a joint tenancy deed if the language of the document identifies the grantees (persons who receive the property) as joint tenants as far as that particular property is concerned. Below is an example of the language used to express joint tenancy.

"FOR VALUABLE CONSIDERATION, receipt of which is hereby acknowledged, John Smith and Mary Smith hereby grant to Robert Doe and Mary Doe, as joint tenants, the following described real property in the City of Los Angeles, County of Los Angeles, State of California...."

Sometimes a person, let's call her Ellen, who owns real property will execute a joint tenancy deed transferring title to herself and another person (let's assume it's her son Bill) as joint tenants so that when Ellen dies, the property will be transferred to Bill with no need for probate. When this happens, the original owner, Ellen, has actually made a gift of one-half of the property to the other joint tenant, Bill, and she is responsible for federal gift taxes which are levied on the giver, not the recipient. A gift tax return may be required when the transfer is made, but not always.[4]

---

[4]If the receiver does not exercise his rights as owner of a half interest (such as selling his interest or borrowing against it), the taxation can be put off until the death of the giver (original owner who put up all the money) and any taxes will be assessed as part of the death taxes of the giver's estate.

Joint Tenancy Grant Deed

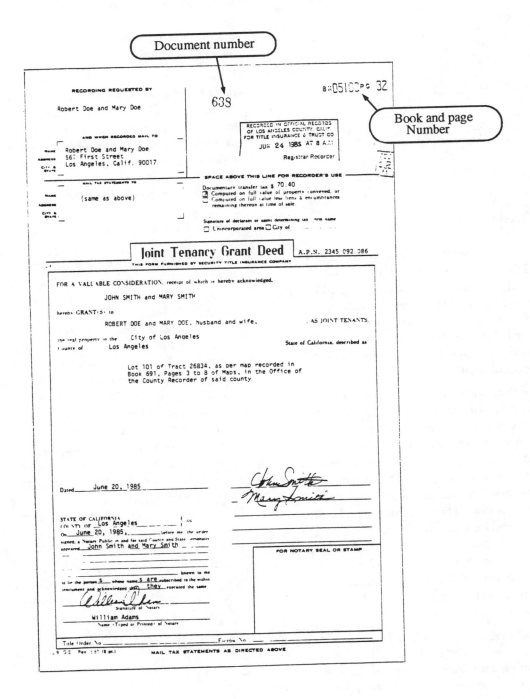

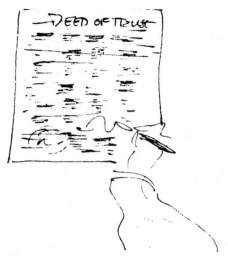

4. Trust Deed

This type of deed is commonly used when real property is purchased and the buyer borrows part of the purchase price from a third party such as a bank or savings and loan association. In some states this document is called a mortgage, but deed of trust is the term usually used in California. When a deed of trust is given, it is normally used with a grant deed, quitclaim deed or joint tenancy deed as part of a single transaction.

It works like this. A grant deed is executed by the seller to convey title to the purchaser who becomes the owner. If the purchaser needs additional money for the purchase price, she borrows it and executes a promissory note in favor of the lender. This involves the use of a second deed, in this case a trust deed. The trust deed, signed by the purchaser, is used to make the real estate security for money borrowed by the owner/purchaser from the bank, savings and loan, or other lender.[5] In signing a trust deed, the owner/purchaser, who is now officially called the trustor, does not actually transfer title of the property to anyone. Instead, the trust deed becomes an encumbrance on the real property. Trust deeds and

mortgages are recorded by their owner (usually, but not always, a financial institution) at the County Recorder's office where the property is located, so they will have priority over any liens on the real property that may be recorded afterwards.

When someone dies and leaves real property subject to a mortgage or encumbrance, as a rule the real property passes to the new owner along with the encumbrance, unless the decedent's will provides otherwise. The new owner of the property then becomes responsible for making the payment on the mortgage, taxes, etc. After the property is officially transferred, it is customary to notify the person or entity collecting the mortgage payments of the name and address of the new owner. No notice to the trustee is necessary.

Bruce and June want to purchase a house from Sol for $170,000, but only have $70,000 in cash for the down payment. Bruce and June find out they can borrow the balance of the purchase price from a savings and loan that will accept the property as security for payment of the loan. Sol executes a grant deed transferring title to the residence to Bruce and June. At the same time, Bruce and June execute a promissory note payable to the savings and loan and execute a deed of trust transferring the residence to a trustee to hold as security for the loan. Bruce and June then take the $100,000 they have borrowed, plus the $70,000 cash they already had, and give it to Sol, who receives all cash for the property. Bruce and June remain the owners of the property subject to the payment of the $100,000 loan owed to the savings and loan, which is an encumbrance against the property. In legal jargon, Bruce and June are known as trustors. The third party who holds the property subject to the deed of trust is the trustee, and the financial institution which lends the money is the beneficiary.

---

[5]The trust deed is actually transferred to a third party (neutral) trustee to hold "in trust" until the lender is paid off. The trustee is normally a title insurance company. When the buyer has paid in full, he asks the trustee to reconvey the title to him.

Short Form Deed of Trust and Assignment of Rents

RECORDING REQUESTED BY

AND WHEN RECORDED MAIL TO

Name

Street
Address

City &
State

SPACE ABOVE THIS LINE FOR RECORDER'S USE

SHORT FORM DEED OF TRUST AND ASSIGNMENT OF RENTS

TD 861 HC   181619

This Deed of Trust, made this _____ day of _____ , _____ , between
                                                                          (month)   (year)

(Names of signer(s))

, herein called TRUSTOR,

whose address is _____
                        (number and street)   (city)   (state)

(Name of title insurer) , a California corporation,   , herein
called TRUSTEE. and   *(Name(s) of beneficiary(ies))*

, herein called BENEFICIARY,

Witnesseth: That Trustor IRREVOCABLY GRANTS, TRANSFERS AND ASSIGNS to TRUSTEE IN TRUST, WITH POWER OF SALE,
that property in   *(City and County)*   County, California, described as:

(Description of property)

TOGETHER WITH the rents, issues and profits thereof, SUBJECT, HOWEVER, to the right, power and authority given to and conferred
upon Beneficiary by paragraph (10) of the provisions incorporated herein by reference to collect and apply such rents, issues and profits.
For the Purpose of Securing: 1. Performance of each agreement of Trustor incorporated by reference or contained herein. 2. Payment of the indebtedness evidenced by one promissory note of even date herewith, and any extension or renewal thereof, in the principal
sum of $ ___*(Amount)*___ executed by Trustor in favor of Beneficiary or order.
TO PROTECT THE SECURITY OF THIS DEED OF TRUST, TRUSTOR AGREES: By the execution and delivery of this Deed of
Trust and the note secured hereby, that provisions (1) to (14), inclusive, of the fictitious deed of trust recorded in Riverside County
June 24, 1968, and in all other Counties July 2, 1968, in the book and at the page of Official Records in the office of the County
Recorder of the County where said property is located, noted below opposite the name of such County, viz.:

COUNTY	BOOK	PAGE	COUNTY	BOOK	PAGE	COUNTY	BOOK	PAGE	COUNTY	BOOK	PAGE
			Kings	924	185	Placer	1204	632	Shasta	958	68
Alameda	2210	I.M.188	Lake	559	271	Plumas	182	83	Sierra	47	197
Alpine	10	483	Lassen	222	476	Riverside Account 59015		Year 1968	Siskiyou	560	897
Amador	175	234	Los Angeles	T5841	240	Sacramento	68-07-02	288	Solano	1514	628
Butte	1523	386	Madera	1013	455	San Benito	339	63	Sonoma	2338	981
Calaveras	259	342	Marin	222	399	San Bernardino	7053	298	Stanislaus	2227	171
Colusa	357	32	Mariposa	110	193	San Diego	Series 9	111626	Sutter	725	20
Contra Costa	5658	1	Mendocino	768	171		Book 1968		Tehama	514	275
Del Norte	135	256	Merced	1775	48	San Francisco	8254	261	Trinity	128	567
El Dorado	884	635	Modoc	204	156	San Joaquin	3221	96	Tulare	2790	157
Fresno	5586	264	Mono	95	17	San Luis Obispo	1481	591	Tuolumne	253	585
Glenn	509	75	Monterey	563	646	San Mateo	5496	67	Ventura	3328	548
Humboldt	966	322	Napa	789	862	Santa Barbara	2237	734	Yolo	585	163
Imperial	1264	201	Nevada	450	210	Santa Clara	8177	403	Yuba	469	398
Inyo	182	944	Orange	8648	347	Santa Cruz	1890	1			
Kern	4175	224									

(which provisions, identical in all counties, are printed on the reverse hereof) hereby are adopted and incorporated herein and made a part
hereof as fully as though set forth herein at length; that he will observe and perform said provisions; and that the references to property.
obligations, and parties in said provisions shall be construed to refer to the property, obligations, and parties set forth in this Deed of Trust.
    The undersigned Trustor requests that a copy of any Notice of Default and of any Notice of Sale hereunder be mailed to him at his address
hereinbefore set forth.

Signature of Trustor

State of California
County of _____
On this the _____ day of _____ 19___,
before me.
the undersigned Notary Public, personally appeared
    (names of signer(s))

☐ personally known to me
☐ proved to me on the basis of satisfactory evidence
to be the person(s) whose name(s) _____ subscribed to the
within instrument, and acknowledged that _____ executed it.
WITNESS my hand and official seal.

_____
Notary's Signature

(Signature)

(Typed name)

(Signature)

(Typed name)

Note Secured By Deed of Trust

NOTE SECURED BY DEED OF TRUST
(INSTALLMENT – INTEREST INCLUDED)

$ .... _(Place of execution)_ .... California.......... _(Date)_ ....

In installments as herein stated, for value received, I promise to pay to.......... _(Name(s) of payee(s))_ ....

at.......... _(Place of payment)_ .... or order.
the sum of..........
with interest from..........DOLLARS,
rate of.......... per cent per annum: principal and interest payable in installments of..........
or more on the.......... day of each..........Dollars,
on the.......... day of..........month, beginning

..........and continuing until said principal and interest have been paid.

Each payment shall be credited first on interest then due and the remainder on principal; and interest shall thereupon cease upon the principal so credited. Should default be made in payment of any installment when due the whole sum of principal and interest shall become immediately due at the option of the holder of this note. Principal and interest payable in lawful money of the United States. If action be instituted on this note I promise to pay such sum as the Court may fix as attorneys' fees. This note is secured by a Deed of Trust.

(Signature)

(Signature)

(Typed name)

(Typed name)

B. Personal Property

ALL PROPERTY that is not real property is "personal property." Personal property is divided into two broad categories, tangible and intangible, which are defined as follows.

1. Tangible Personal Property

Tangible personal property includes concrete items you can touch, such as books, automobiles, boats, animals, clothing, household furniture, farm equipment, jewelry, machinery, motor homes, firearms, tools, antiques and actual cash like coins or dollar bills. Like real property, tangible personal property is legally required to be transferred following the laws and procedures of the state in which it is located. However, in practice, many types of tangible personal property (for example, cars registered in California, jewelry, cash, etc.) are highly portable and of-ten find their way back to the state of a person's residence at death. If this occurs in a small or medium-sized estate, there is, in practice, normally no objection to transferring the property using the simplified procedures discussed in Chapter 11.

2. Intangible Personal Property

Intangible personal property is abstract. It is a right to be paid money or to legally exercise some type of power (for example, stopping others from using your patented invention). It is usually represented by a paper or document that states the nature of the rights associated with it. Some examples are promissory notes, bank passbooks, court judgments giving a right to receive money, mortgages, deeds of trust establishing an interest in property as security for a debt, stock or bond certificates giving an ownership interest in a corporation, mutual fund certificates, money market fund certificates, copyrights, patents and trademarks. Other examples of intangible personal property include contracts giving the right to future income, as would be the case with a publishing contract granting a royalty share of income derived from the sale of a book or a film contract providing a share of the gross receipts of a movie. Intangible personal property is transferred under the laws and procedures of the state in which its owner resides. In other words, if a California resident dies owning stocks and bonds located in a New York safe-deposit box, has $50,000 deposited in an Illinois bank and has placed $25,000 in a money market fund headquartered in Boston, then ownership of all this property (no matter where the decedent lived when it was purchased) can be transferred in California using the instructions contained in this book.

Note: We discuss intangible personal property acquired by California couples before they moved to California in Section I of this chapter.

C. What Establishes Ownership of Property?

TITLE IS A METHOD by which ownership of many, but by no means all, types of property is established. Most valuable assets have a written title document that shows who owns the property (establishes title). For instance, a bank issues a passbook showing the name in which a savings account is held. Stock certificates establish title to the ownership of shares in a corporation. "Pink slips" serve as title documents for motor vehicles, motor homes and boats. Some kinds of intangible personal property, like copyrights and patents, have documents issued by the federal government that to some extent act like certificates of title. If a decedent had executed a contract giving him a right to receive periodic payments in exchange for property or services, the contract itself takes the place of a title document showing proof of ownership of the future income. Title to real property, including condominiums and cooperatives, must always be in writing and is usually represented by a deed containing a legal description of the property.

Some kinds of personal property don't have formal title slips. Nevertheless, there is usually little doubt who owns them. For instance, you can normally assume things such as clothing, books, furniture and personal effects belonged to the decedent if he had possession of them when he died and if no one steps forward to claim them. Valuable objects, such as jewelry, furs or works of art don't come with a title document in the formal sense, but their purchase is normally accompanied by a receipt or bill of sale, which accomplishes a similar purpose. If not, questions of ownership surrounding these types of property can sometimes be resolved by reference to cancelled checks or by contacting the seller.

As a rule, you will find it relatively easy to figure out what property the decedent at least claimed to own by checking in all the obvious places (desk drawers, safe-deposit boxes, file cabinets, etc.). If as part of doing this you find an unfamiliar document and don't know what it means, it is best to consult an expert to be sure you're not overlooking any assets (or liabilities, for that matter).

D. How Was Decedent's Property Owned?

PROPERTY, BOTH REAL and personal, may be owned either separately (the decedent owned it all) or concurrently with other persons.

1. Separate Property Ownership

Separate ownership simply means ownership by one person. The sole owner alone enjoys the benefits of the property, but is also responsible for its burdens, such as mortgages or taxes. He may dispose of his separate property by will to anyone he chooses, and if he dies without a will the separate property goes to his heirs under intestate succession laws. All property owned by *unmarried* persons, whether or not they were previously married, is separate property, except for property owned in joint tenancy (discussed in Section 2, below).

A married person can also own separate property. This is because all property acquired prior to marriage and property received by an individual by gift or inheritance, whether before, during or after a marriage, remains separate property. In addition, if a married couple separates, the earnings and accumulations of each after the date of permanent separation are also separate property. Finally, even during marriage, the earnings of a husband or wife can be separate property if they sign a written contract providing for this result and, in fact, keep the property separate.

2. Concurrent Ownership

Concurrent ownership means ownership by two or more persons at the same time. Some estates, especially those of single individuals, contain no property owned concurrently with another person. If this is your situation, you can skip this entire section.

In California, concurrent ownership normally takes one of the following legal classifications:

- Tenancy in common

- Joint tenancy

- Community property

- Life tenancy (or life estate)

We discuss each of these forms of concurrent ownership just below. However, please note that the information on community property ownership applies only to decedents who were married at the time of death; therefore, if you are settling the estate of a single person, you can skip the discussion of community property. You also do not need to worry as much about whether or not property is community property if the decedent willed all of his property to his surviving spouse. Since the surviving spouse gets it all anyway, it's not necessary to understand technical rules as to who owned what portion. We discuss community property ownership last because it requires

more extended coverage, not because it is less important. It isn't.

a. Tenancy in Common

This occurs when two or more persons own an undivided interest in property, without an automatic right to inherit the property from each other if one owner dies. An undivided interest means a tenant in common does not own a particular portion of the property but rather a fractional share of the whole property. If you own a piece of land as a tenant in common with your sister, absent any agreement to divide it differently, you each own an undivided one-half interest in the whole property. However, co-tenants can own unequal shares in a property if a written contract so provides. Thus, one co-tenant may own one-tenth, another three-tenths, and a third may own the remaining six-tenths under the terms of a written agreement.

A tenancy in common is created when an ownership document states, for example, "Jill Evers and Finley Fox as Tenants in Common." In addition, whenever an ownership document does not specify that more than one owner acquire it in joint tenancy or as community property, it is presumed the owners hold the property as tenants in common. If any of the tenants in common dies, her interest is not acquired by the remaining tenants in common, but instead goes to the beneficiaries named in her will or to her heirs if she dies without a will.

b. Joint Tenancy

For property to be held in joint tenancy, it must be expressly stated in the deed or ownership document that the owners own it "as joint tenants" or "with right of survivorship," or the abbreviations "JTRS" or "WROS" must be used. In addition, registration of a motor vehicle in the names of two people joined by "or" is treated as joint tenancy, as are certain bank accounts held in this way. U.S. savings bonds held in co-ownership form also have the same legal effect as if the words "joint tenancy" were used.

Owning property in joint tenancy means if one of the joint tenants dies, her interest immediately becomes the property of the remaining joint tenant(s) by operation of law. A will has no effect on joint tenancy property, nor do the laws of intestate succession have any control over who gets the property. Persons who own property as joint tenants always own an undivided equal interest, and all have the same rights to the use of the whole property. Usually, only persons with a very close personal or family relationship to each other hold property this way, such as husband and wife, parent and child, unmarried couple or brothers and sisters. It isn't normally practical for others, such as business associates, to be joint tenants, because the families and relatives of a joint tenant would inherit nothing in such a situation. More than two persons may be joint tenants, but this is not common. If there are three or more joint tenants and one dies, the others acquire his interest and still remain joint tenants. Joint tenancy property need not go through a formal probate proceeding, but there are several formalities necessary to clear the joint tenancy title to the property so it appears in the name of the surviving tenant. We discuss how to do this in Chapter 10.

Warning: If a husband or wife puts a piece of community property into joint tenancy with someone other than his or her spouse, and the other spouse did not agree to it at the time, and after death the surviving spouse wishes to claim a one-half community property interest in the property, you have a problem and should see a lawyer.

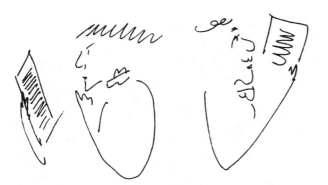

c. Life Tenancy (Life Estate)

A life tenancy (sometimes called "life estate") is a form of ownership used infrequently, but it deserves mention here. It is ownership of property for the period of a lifetime only. Life tenancies are sometimes created to allow an elderly person (often a spouse) to use property for the rest of her life and then to give the property to a person in the next generation without the necessity of probate proceedings. Or, a life estate can be used by a living person to avoid probate at his death.[6]

> *Wanda is an elderly widow who owns a home which she wishes to go to her son Steve upon her death. Wanda may deed the property to Steven during her lifetime, with the deed saying that "Grantor (Wanda) reserves to herself a life estate in said property." This will transfer the ownership to Steven, but subject to Wanda's life estate. It will accomplish Wanda's objective of avoiding probate of the home upon her death because she will die without ownership of the property. Her life estate will terminate at the moment of death and the home will be owned by Steven.*

d. Community Property

Married persons present another subclassification as far as the concurrent ownership of property is concerned. Several states, including California, have community property laws that apply to property acquired during marriage. Briefly, these laws give both husband and wife equal interest in property—including wages and other

---

[6]This sort of transfer can also save on federal estate taxes in larger estates if the person who gets the life estate (as opposed to getting the property outright) already has considerable property of his own. Since the life estate terminates at death, the property covered by it isn't included in that person's estate and therefore is not taxed as part of it. For more details on how this sort of estate planning (which must be done before death, of course) can save money, see *Plan Your Estate With a Living Trust*, by Denis Clifford (Nolo Press).

earned income and the property acquired with this income—they accumulate during their marriage. In other words, each spouse owns a one-half interest in the community property. Any property either spouse owned before marriage is not community property, but is the separate property of the owner spouse, who can deal with it as he or she wishes. The same is true if either spouse inherits or is given property during the marriage—such property remains the separate property of the spouse receiving it. Earnings from the separate property of either spouse are also separate property. Thus, if the wife owns an apartment house as separate property because she acquired it prior to marriage, or inherited it or received it as a gift after marriage, the rents from it are also her separate property.

Certain events during marriage, however, can alter the character of property owned by married persons. Thus, spouses can agree to change (transmute) community property into separate property, or vice versa. Or, spouses may combine their separate property and community property to such an extent that it all becomes community property. And commonly, an asset (such as a family business, house or pension) will be part community property and part separate property.

Accurately drawing the line between community property and non-community property can be both difficult and tedious. Accordingly, before you struggle through the rest of this rather intricate material, stop and think whether you really need to know if the decedent owned any community property. For instance, do any of the following situations apply to your estate?

- Was the decedent an unmarried person? If so, he did not own any community property. Only married persons can own property as community property.

- If the decedent was married, did he leave a will that gives his entire estate to his surviving spouse? In this case, it is not as important to know whether the property is community or separate, since it all goes to the surviving spouse anyway. The only reason you may want to clearly identify the community property in this situation is if the

estate might be large enough to require a federal estate tax return (although there will be no estate tax payments, as property transferred to a surviving spouse is tax exempt), or if you need a court order to transfer it to the surviving spouse. (See Chapter 15.)

The main reasons you will probably want to know if the decedent owned any community property are that:

- If a person dies without a will (intestate), all of the community property goes to the surviving spouse, including the decedent's one-half and the other half that is already owned by the surviving spouse.

- If a decedent uses a will or other estate planning device to try to transfer more than his one-half of the community property to someone other than his spouse, that spouse can object and claim her one-half.

E. How to Determine Whether Property Is Community or Separate

HERE IS A STEP-BY-STEP approach to determining whether any given property item is community property or separate property. Read it now for a general understanding of community property principles. Later on, when you are filling out your Schedule of Assets in Chapter 5, you will want to return and use this information. You will want to follow this analysis for each piece of property the decedent left, unless you can conclude that all property fits into the same basic category, in which case your task will be very easy.

Step 1: Is there an ownership document (deed, certificate of title, pink slip, bank account card) that says "John and Mary Doe, husband and wife," or "John and Mary Doe, husband and wife as community property," or "Mr. and Mrs. John Doe"? If so, the property is presumed to be community property. Go to Step 10. If not, go to Step 2.

Step 2: If the decedent and his wife were married for a long time and began their marriage with little or nothing, you can usually assume at the outset that all their property was community property. If so, go to Step 10. If not, go to Step 3.

Step 3: Was the property acquired during the marriage (after the wedding but prior to a permanent separation or divorce)? If so, go to Step 4. If not, go to Step 8.

Step 4: Does the property consist of earnings[7] of either spouse during the marriage, gifts or inheritances to the spouses jointly, or property purchased with such earnings, gifts or inheritances? If so, go to Step 10. If not, go to Step 5.

Step 5: Was the property acquired during the marriage through a gift[8] given to one of the spouses as an individual? If not, go to Step 6. If yes, go to Step 8.

Step 6: Was the property acquired during the marriage by an inheritance of one of the spouses as an individual? If not, go to Step 7. If yes, go to Step 8.

Step 7: Was the property acquired by one spouse as an award in a personal injury action? If not, go to Step 10. If yes, go to Step 8.

Step 8: Did the spouse who owned the property agree orally or in writing prior to January 1, 1985 to put it into community property form? See Section F, below. If so, go to Step 13. If not, go to Step 9.

Step 9: Did the spouse who owned the property agree in writing after January 1, 1985 to put it into community property form? See Section F, below. If so, go to Step 13. If not, go to Step 12.

Step 10: Did both spouses enter into an oral or written agreement prior to January 1, 1985 that the property be the separate property of one of the spouses? See Section F, below. If so, go to Step 12. If not, go to Step 11.

Step 11: Did both spouses agree in writing after January 1, 1985 that the property be the separate property of one of the spouses? See Section F, below. If so, go to Step 12. If not, go to Step 13.

Step 12: Was separate property mixed with community property (lawyers call this "commingling")[9] so that its separate nature can no longer be traced? If so, go to Step 14. If not, go to Step 15.

Step 13: Is the property a mix of community property and separate property such as a house, a contract for future payments, a family business or a pension that was only partially earned during the marriage? See Section G, below. If so, you might wish to obtain help from a lawyer or accountant in characterizing which portion of this asset is community property and which is separate property. If not, go to Step 14.

Step 14: The property should be treated as community property which means the decedent only owned one-half of it.

Step 15: The property should be treated as separate property, owned by whichever spouse acquired, inherited or was given the property as his or her separate property.

---

[7]Earnings include not only wages, but employment fringe benefits, such as insurance, pension plans, stock options, and so forth.

[8]Strictly speaking, a gift is a transfer of property without anything being paid by the person receiving the property (called "consideration" by lawyers). Commonly gifts made during marriage by one spouse to the other are considered the separate property of the receiving spouse unless the spouses agree differently. Sometimes these gifts can be quite valuable, such as furs, diamonds, etc.

---

[9]The most common example of commingling is when spouses deposit both separate and community property in a joint bank account and make withdrawals over the years that make it impossible to characterize the funds left in the account. See Section F, below.

F. Actions by Spouses That Change the Character of Property

IN THE ABOVE step-by-step analysis, we indicated that certain acts by the spouses could change the nature of property from community to separate and vice versa. Here we take a closer look at how this can occur.

The general rule is that the community or separate nature of property is determined by its source. However, you should clearly understand that no matter what its source, the community or separate nature of property can be changed by actions of the husband and wife. This is more likely to result in separate property becoming community property than the reverse, but both types of changes occur fairly frequently. Let's look at some common examples.

1. Commingling Assets

In general, property can change its physical form without changing its community or separate character. For instance, if money kept in a husband's checking account before marriage (separate property) is used during marriage to buy stocks and bonds, and if the stocks and bonds are later sold and the proceeds used to buy a house, then the house remains the husband's separate property.

Many married couples, however, change the separate or community nature of their property without realizing it. One common example of this phenomena is what lawyers call "commingling." The basic commingling rule, subject to a number of technical subtleties which are beyond the scope of this book, is that if separate property assets are mixed together (commingled) with community funds so that it is impossible to trace them to their source, the formerly separate property becomes community property.

A husband and wife open a savings account during the marriage in which they deposit money they have earned during their marriage. Assume the wife receives an inheritance of $3,000, which is separate property, and deposits it into the joint account. If no withdrawals are made from the account, she can trace her $3,000 to her inheritance. However, if a number of deposits and withdrawals are made by the parties over the years and the balance dips below $3,000, she will no longer be able to trace her money and it will be treated as having been given to the community.

Note: Rules as to how to trace property in commingling situations are so complicated, confusing and changing that they are the subject of endless litigation. If you find yourself dealing with a commingling problem, check your conclusion with a lawyer.

2. Agreement Between the Spouses

The separate property of either spouse may be "transmuted" (changed) into community property, and community property may be transmuted into separate property of either spouse merely by an agreement between them. Prior to 1985, this could be accomplished by an informal oral agreement whereby one spouse indicated to the other that he or she wished the property to be community rather than separate, or if both simply agreed that a community asset would become the separate property of one. Since January 1, 1985, a change in the nature of property must be made in writing, signed by the person whose property is adversely affected. This new law, however, does not apply to property whose character was changed by oral agreement prior to 1985.

The most important element of an agreement between spouses to change the status of property is the intention to do so. When there is no expressly stated intention, the courts will sometimes examine the actions and conduct of the parties. Up to 1985 the courts were quite liberal in implying such agreements from rather skimpy facts. For instance, in one case the court considered a statement by a husband that "I wanted to do something for my wife," as sufficient evidence of his intention to make his property community rather than separate.

Sometimes a husband and wife may also change the character of property owned by one of them by making a gift of it to the other. For example, when a single person who owns a house is then later married, the house is not automatically converted into community property by the fact of marriage. The house remains the separate property of the owner spouse. However, if the owner makes a deed after marriage which puts the house in the names of both spouses, thereby making a gift of it, it is converted into community property.

G. Property That Is a Mixture of Community and Separate Property

SOMETIMES WHEN PROPERTY is received over a period of time and a marriage or divorce takes place during that time, it can be difficult to determine how much of the property is community property and how much is separate. Let's look at some examples of this sort of situation.

1. Contract Rights

It is not uncommon for high-earning executives and entertainers to receive compensation payable over a period of several years. If the right to collect the money arises—that is, if the work is done before the marriage,

then any money received under such a contract is separate property, even though the payments are made during the marriage.[10] In other words, the test of whether the property is community normally depends on the time when the right to payment arises and not on the time when payment is actually made. In another situation, a writer could do substantial work on, or even complete, a book during marriage and if the marriage is later dissolved, the right to future royalties would be split equally between the husband and wife as community property, even though payment would be made after the divorce.

Warning: Sometimes it becomes extremely difficult to determine what is and isn't community property, so much so that thousands of court cases are litigated over this question every year. If you have difficulty determining which is which, see a lawyer.

2. Insurance Proceeds

The extent to which proceeds from life insurance on either husband or wife are treated as community property depends on what proportion of the premiums paid for such insurance came from community funds, not on who is named as the beneficiary. In other words, the surviving spouse's community property interest in the insurance proceeds must be recognized regardless of who is named as beneficiary of the policy. For example, if the husband purchases insurance on his life, naming his brother as beneficiary, and one-half of the premiums are paid from community funds, when the husband dies, his wife is entitled to one-fourth of the proceeds of the policy (that is, one-half of the community half), and the husband's brother is entitled to the rest. If all the premiums were

---

[10]However, if the work isn't done until after marriage, as might be the case when a sports figure or entertainer gets a large up-front payment for work to be done over several years, the money would be community property to the extent that the work needed to earn the money was performed after marriage.

paid with community property funds, the wife would be entitled to one-half of the insurance policy proceeds.

3. Improvements to Property

What happens when improvements are made to one type of property (community or separate) using funds that are a different type of property? For example, if one spouse has a separate property cabin or boat, and community property funds are used to fix it up, what happens when the property is left to a third person? Does the other spouse have a right to claim one-half of the value of the improvements? Similarly, if one spouse uses his separate property to improve the other spouse's separate property and feels unfairly treated by that spouse's will or alternative estate plan, what are his rights?

As you can probably gather, the law in this area can be complex. Put another way, you are dealing with an estate that isn't simple, and you need more information about the ins and outs of California marital property law than we can give you here. One good source of more information is *California Marriage and Divorce Law,* by Warner and Ihara (Nolo Press).

4. Pensions

A pension is regarded as compensation for services previously rendered, and a percentage of the pension right is deemed to have been earned during each year that the pensioner worked to qualify for the pension. Thus, if a pensioner worked for fifteen years, then married and worked for another five years before qualifying for a pension on the basis of twenty years' service, three-fourths of the pension payments (and anything accumulated with them) would be separate property and one-fourth would be community property. If the pensioner was married for the entire time he had the job, pension payments are community property.

5. Rents and Profits

The rents and profits received on community property (interest, dividends, royalties, rents, capital gains, etc.) are community property, and the rents and profits from separate property remain separate property.

6. Separate Property Businesses

It is often difficult to determine whether income from a separate property business in which a spouse works after marriage is community or separate property. The value of the business at the time of marriage is clearly separate property. Wages paid to the spouse who owns the business after marriage are clearly community property. But what about the increase in the value of the business itself? Is this just the natural growth of a separate property asset and, therefore, separate property, or is it the result of the continuing work of the spouse and, therefore, community property? Often the answer to this question is some combination of the two. For more information on this area, again, we recommend *California Marriage and Divorce Law* by Warner and Ihara (Nolo Press). However, it is an area of particular difficulty, and in some situations you will need professional help in deciding what is separate and what is community property.

H. Examples of Property Ownership

PERHAPS THE BEST WAY to review the material we have covered in this chapter is to examine several examples of community and separate property ownership.

Brad

Brad is a bachelor who moved to California from Nevada in 1978. While living in Nevada he inherited $50,000 from his father's estate in 1975 which he invested in a motel in Las Vegas. While living in California from 1978 until his death in 1986, he acquired 300 shares of Marvelous Corporation stock in which he took title as a joint tenant with his mother. He also purchased a 1980 Porsche automobile and a $10,000 life insurance policy naming his mother as beneficiary.

Since Brad was never married, all of his property is his separate property in which he has a 100% interest. His interest in the Las Vegas motel, being real property, will be transferred according to Nevada law and excluded from his California estate. The 300 shares of Marvelous Corporation stock, being held in joint tenancy, is not subject to probate because it automatically became his mother's property on his death by right of survivorship. However, title to this property must be cleared, a procedure we discuss in Chapter 10. The $10,000 life insurance proceeds are not subject to probate either, because Brad's mother is the named beneficiary under the policy and the proceeds will be paid under the insurance contract entered into between Brad and the insurance company. Brad's mother only needs to send a certified copy of the death certificate and a claim form to the insurance company to collect the proceeds. The remaining asset—his Porsche automobile—can probably be transferred using the simple affidavit procedure available for small estates which we discuss in Chapter 11. Who gets the Porsche will depend on whether Brad left a will or died without one (intestate).

Joe and Mabel

Joe and Mabel were married in 1975 and lived in California during the entire 10 years of their marriage. Prior to their marriage Mabel owned some valuable antiques and a $10,000 bank account. Joe owned a $20,000 promissory note secured by a deed of trust on real property located in San Diego, a boat which he kept at Marina del Rey (in Los Angeles County) and $5,000 in a California bank savings account. During their marriage, Mabel inherited 50 shares of AT&T stock from her aunt's estate. During their marriage they opened a bank account at Culver City Bank in California as tenants in common. They deposited their excess earnings into this account, plus the proceeds of the two bank accounts they each owned individually before marriage, periodically making withdrawals from and deposits into the account during their marriage. They also acquired with their combined earnings during marriage a condominium located in Culver City, California, and a 1984 BMW automobile. Joe died in 1986.

Joe's estate in California is determined as follows: The boat at Marina del Rey (tangible personal property) and the $20,000 trust deed note (intangible personal property) are Joe's separate property, having been acquired before his marriage to Mabel. The two bank accounts which Joe and Mabel owned prior to marriage have been commingled and are both community property, as is the Culver City Bank account which Joe and Mabel established after marriage. Therefore, Mabel owns a one-half interest in each of these. The AT&T stock is Mabel's separate property, since she acquired it by inheritance. The antiques which Mabel owned prior to marriage are also her separate property. The condominium and the 1984 BMW automobile acquired with the couple's earnings during marriage are California community property. Thus, Joe's estate in California consists of the following:

a. A 100% separate property interest in:

- $20,000 trust deed note;
- Marina del Rey boat.

b. A one-half community property interest (Mabel owns the other half) in:

- The Culver City condominium;
- 1984 BMW automobile;
- Culver City Bank account.

Beverly and Randolph

Beverly was a scriptwriter for a large motion picture studio in Los Angeles when she married Randolph, an aspiring actor, in 1970. At the time of their marriage, Beverly owned a home in Pacific Palisades, a 1969 Mercedes Benz automobile, and a $10,000 bank account. Also, at the time of their marriage, Beverly had completed 10 years of the necessary 25 years of service required to qualify for a $50,000 pension from the studio on her retirement. Beverly's daughter by a prior marriage was named contingent beneficiary of the pension. Randolph's property at the time of their marriage consisted of an interest in a motor home, worth about $15,000, and a $5,000 savings account. Randolph was also entitled to receive residual payments from several television commercials he completed prior to their marriage, which are still rolling in at an average rate of $500 per month. Shortly after their marriage, Randolph sold his interest in the motor home, and he and Beverly pooled their money and deposited all cash in joint bank accounts, paying their expenses from the accounts and also depositing their earnings during marriage into the accounts. In 1975, they improved the Pacific Palisades residence by building a lap pool and redwood deck, at a cost of about $20,000. Since the house was Beverly's separate property, Randolph generously agreed to treat the cost of the improvements as a gift to Beverly, and did not ask for reimbursement of his one-half interest in the community funds used for the improvements. Beverly died shortly after her retirement from the studio in 1985, after she and Randolph had been married 15 years. Their combined assets at the time of Beverly's death consisted of:

a. Pacific Palisades home;

b. 1969 Mercedes Benz automobile;

c. Cash in joint bank accounts of approximately $15,000;

d. Beverly's vested interest in her pension;

e. Randolph's rights to future residual payments from his TV commercials.

How do we know which of these assets are included in Beverly's estate? First, we know the Pacific Palisades house and Mercedes Benz automobile are Beverly's separate property, because she owned them prior to her marriage to Randolph. The improvements to the residence took on the same character as the house (because of Randolph's gift) and are, therefore, also her separate property, along with the house, even though they were made with community funds. Therefore, these two assets are indicated 100% as Beverly's separate property. Beverly's vested interest in her $50,000 pension was earned two-fifths prior to marriage and three-fifths during marriage (that is, she was married 15 of the 25 working years required to qualify for the pension, thus 15/25 = 3/5). This means two-fifths of the pension ($20,000) is separate property and three-fifths ($30,000) is community property, and Randolph owns a one-half interest in the community portion, or $15,000. Randolph would have to work out an arrangement with the pension plan administrators and Beverly's daughter to receive his share. If this can't be done, then Randolph would have to see an attorney.[11] Beverly's separate property portion ($20,000), plus her one-half interest in the community portion ($15,000) will go to her daughter, as the contingent beneficiary. Since the pension has named beneficiaries, it will not be subject to probate. Randolph's residual payments are his separate property, since the right to payment was earned prior to marriage, and they are not included in Beverly's estate. Beverly also has a one-half interest in the $15,000 in the couple's joint bank accounts. Her half interest is part of her gross estate but will not be subject to probate because the accounts were

---

[11]Of course, Randolph might not choose to claim his share and let it all go to Beverly's daughter, but he is entitled to $15,000 if he wants it.

held in joint tenancy. Therefore, Beverly's estate consists of the following assets:

a. Pacific Palisades home

b. 1969 Mercedes Benz automobile

c. $35,000 interest in pension

d. $7,500 interest in bank accounts

Unless Beverly has used an estate planning device, such as joint tenancy or a living trust, the home and automobile will be subject to probate in California. (See Chapter 14.)

I. Property Acquired by Couples Before They Moved to California

THIS SECTION APPLIES only if the decedent was a married Californian who acquired property during marriage prior to moving to California. To deal with this situation lawyers invented the term "quasi-community property." Quasi-community property includes all real property situated in California and all personal property, wherever located, which would have been community property if the owner had been a resident of California at the time he or she acquired it. The label is generally applied to property owned by married couples at the time they move to California from a non-community property state. The only exception is real property located outside of California which is not quasi-community property. Quasi-community property is treated the same way as community property in estates of persons who die while residents of California.

California also treats community property acquired by a married couple while living in another community property state as community property, even though such property would not be community property in California. For instance, some community property states classify income from separate property as community property when the income is received during marriage. Although such income would be treated as separate property in California, it is treated as community property when the

owner who acquired the property in such other community property state dies a resident of California.

If you have difficulty in establishing any of the decedent's out-of-state property as community or separate, you should seek the advice of an attorney.

Harry and Marsha

Harry and Marsha had only a small amount of cash between them and a few personal belongings when they were married in New York City in 1940. During their marriage, while living in New York City, they acquired with their earnings an apartment building and 200 shares of XYZ Corporation stock. They moved to California in 1960 where they lived as husband and wife until the time of Marsha's death in 1986. No property was acquired by either of them by gift or inheritance at any time. At the time of Marsha's death, the property owned by Harry and Marsha consisted of the following assets:

a. The apartment house in New York City, held in both their names;

b. 200 shares of XYZ Corporation stock, in Harry's name;

c. A residence in Van Nuys, California, in both names as community property;

d. Two automobiles, one in Marsha's name and one in Harry's name;

e. A joint tenancy bank account at Union Bank in Van Nuys.

What does Marsha's estate consist of for California purposes? First of all, it doesn't include the real property (apartment house) in New York City, which will have to be transferred independently under the laws of the state of New York. The XYZ Corporation stock is included in the California estate because it is intangible personal property. Since the stock was acquired with the combined earnings of Harry and Marsha during their marriage, it would be treated as community property in California even though the stock is in Harry's name alone and, therefore, is technically quasi-community property. The joint tenancy bank account (although obviously commu-nity property funds) is included in Marsha's estate, al-though it is not subject to probate and becomes Harry's property by operation of law immediately on Marsha's death. Thus, Marsha's estate in California consists of her one-half interest in the following assets:

a. 200 shares of XYZ Corporation stock

b. Van Nuys residence

c. Two automobiles

d. Union Bank account

CHAPTER 5

Preparing a Schedule of the
Assets and Debts

A. Introduction

BY NOW YOU SHOULD have examined the necessary papers and documents and gathered sufficient information to prepare a schedule of all property owned by the decedent at the time of her death. The schedule, once it is completed, will be used as a worksheet in conjunction with the remaining steps required to transfer the assets and settle the estate.

To help you with this project, we have included a blank Schedule of Assets in Appendix 1. Instructions for completing the schedule are contained in the following sections. Since this schedule will serve as your record of all property in which the decedent had any interest when she died—including assets that are subject to probate, as well as those that are not—you will refer to it often, and it should be as accurate as possible.

The assets should not only be listed but should be briefly and carefully described so you can easily identify each. A more detailed description of some items may be required on later documents, but a brief listing will do now. In addition, you should indicate for each asset, in the column provided for this purpose:

* The value of the asset;

* How the decedent owned it (for example, separate property - SP, community property - CP, joint tenancy property - JT, tenant in common - TC, or as trustee in a trust - T);

* The portion owned by the decedent and the value of the decedent's interest;

* Whether the asset is subject to formal probate or can be transferred in a simpler way.[1]

---

[1]We briefly review the information you need to know to make this determination in this chapter and discuss it more extensively in Chapter 6. If you are in doubt about whether a particular asset must be probated, leave this column blank until you read Chapter 6.

Note: The following four sections of this chapter (B, C, D and E) provide some information and tools to assist in the process of preparing your Schedule of Assets. After you finish with these sections, Section H shows you how to complete the schedule, item by item. Thus, your best approach is not to try to fill in the schedule until you have read this entire chapter. Please understand, however, that this book is not designed to provide you with extensive coverage of California property ownership rules, a large and sometimes complex area of the law. If, after reading the previous chapter and what follows, you are still unsure about how to characterize a particular asset, see a lawyer.

B. Describe Each Asset

IT IS HELPFUL TO GROUP assets such as cash items, bank accounts, real property, securities, etc., according to their general type as part of listing them on your schedule. Describe each asset briefly, including enough pertinent detail to identify it accurately. For example, a bank account might be described like this: "Personal checking account #57111; Bank of Occidental, Santa Rosa." At this point, don't worry about what percentage or type of ownership is involved, or how much the account is worth. Simply list every asset you are aware of that might be owned by the decedent. We provide more details on how to describe particular assets in Section H, below, so you may want to read this section as you make your list.

C. Value Each Asset (Column A)

AS WELL AS DESCRIBING each item of property, you must also determine the total date-of-death value of each asset as accurately as possible and put this amount in Column A. Here are some guidelines to help you do this. If you desire more detail on evaluation, consult the extended discussion in Section H for the type of asset in question, or see an accountant.

1. In placing a dollar value on an asset, the usual rule is to try to determine its "fair market value." The definition of fair market value is generally the price that a willing buyer would pay to a willing seller, both of them acting of their own free will and under no compulsion to buy or sell. Some assets have a definite record of value, such as stocks, bonds and bank accounts, while others are valued by special rules which we will discuss as we go along.

2. The *gross* value of each asset should be used in this column without regard to any liens or encumbrances against the property. In other words, for our purposes right now, do not subtract amounts owed on the property.

3. All assets and their values should be listed as of the *date of the decedent's death*, not as of the date you complete the schedule. This means that if a security is involved you need to do a little research. (See Section H, below.)

D. How to Determine Ownership of Property

NOW YOU MUST DETERMINE how each asset is owned. This information should be inserted in Column B. To do this, use the following abbreviations:

- Separate property (SP)
- Community property (CP)
- Joint tenancy (JT)
- Tenancy in common (TC)
- Life tenancy (LT)

For mixed property (items that are part one type of property and part another), put both designations indicating the percentage share of each (for example, one-third CP, two-thirds SP).

We include general California property ownership rules in Chapter 4. Also, consult the extended discussion in Section H for the type of item in question.

If you have any doubt about the ownership of any item in the decedent's estate, or you want to check your conclusions, take the following steps:

Step 1: Was the decedent married at time of death? If so, proceed to Step 2. If not, proceed to Step 3.

Step 2: Was the particular item community property or separate property? See Chapter 4, Section G, for how to answer this question. If the asset is a house, family business, pension, contract for future payment, or some other form of property that might be a mixture of community and separate property, also see Chapter 4, Section I. As stated above, if the property was community property, put CP in Column B and proceed to Step 6. If the property was a mixture of community property and separate property, put the respective portions in Column B (for example, one-fourth CP, three-fourths SP) and proceed to Step 6. If not, proceed to Step 3.

Step 3: Was the property held in joint tenancy (that is, jointly held with others with right of survivorship? See Chapter 4, Section D). If so, put JT in Column B and proceed to Step 6. If not, go to Step 4.

Step 4: Was the property held in tenancy in common (that is, jointly held with others with no right of survivorship)? See Chapter 4, Section D. If so, put TC in Column B, and proceed to Step 6. If not, go to Step 5.

Step 5: Was the item owned solely by the decedent as nearly as you can tell? If so, put SP in Column B. Otherwise, go to Step 6.

Step 6: Compute the share of the property owned by the decedent and put this fraction in Column C. For instance, if the decedent was married when she died, you may find that she owned a one-half interest in many assets as community property. Sometimes, you may find that the decedent and his spouse together owned (as community property or as joint tenants) a fractional interest in property with third parties. In this case, the decedent will have owned one-half of the fractional interest. For example, if the decedent and his surviving spouse owned a one-fourth community property interest in a commercial building with several other people, the decedent's interest would be one-eighth (that is, one-half of one-fourth).

Note: We discuss shared ownership situations in detail in Chapter 4. In most estates, determining what the decedent owned should not be a problem after you read this material. However, if a decedent was married and owned a number of pieces of property jointly with people other than her spouse, the portion of the property she owned may be in doubt or there may be a difference of opinion between the surviving spouse and the third party. If you face this situation, see an expert. (For information on finding and compensating lawyers, see Chapter 16.)

E. List the Value of the Decedent's Interest (Column D)

NOW THAT WE HAVE LISTED all the assets, evaluated them and determined the type of interest the decedent had in the property, it is time to insert the value of the decedent's interest in Column D. Fortunately this is normally easy. If the decedent owned the entire asset, the dollar figure you insert here is the same as listed in Column A. (Remember, the specifics of valuing assets are contained in Section H, below.)

If the decedent owned less than a full interest in any property, such as an undivided one-half interest as a tenant in common or a one-half interest as community property, include only the value of the decedent's fractional interest in Column D. For example, if the decedent owned a one-half community property interest in a residence valued at $170,000, the value of the decedent's interest in Column D is $85,000.

The total of Column D will give you the value of the decedent's gross estate to help determine if a federal estate tax return will be required. (See Chapter 7, Section E.)

Caution: If the decedent owned joint tenancy property with anyone other than his spouse, the IRS presumes

(for estate tax purposes) that he owned 100% of the property, so include 100% of the property's value in Column D. If the decedent in fact didn't contribute 100% of the purchase price of the property, you can rebut that presumption by showing that the surviving joint tenant contributed some of the purchase price.

F. Determine Whether Property Is Probate or Non-Probate Asset (Column E)

IN COLUMN E, indicate whether the asset must go through formal probate (P) or can be transferred outside of formal probate and is therefore a non-probate asset (N/P). As you will remember from our discussion in Chapter 1, probate assets are handled differently from non-probate assets in settling an estate, and even some assets which are theoretically subject to probate can be transferred with no need to go to court. These are primarily assets in small estates of $60,000 or less and property that passes to a surviving spouse.

Let's review the distinctions between the assets that do not have to go through probate.

• **Assets Not Subject to Probate:** Generally, non-probate assets are those for which the beneficiary has been predetermined by reason of a contract or by law, such as life insurance proceeds, death benefits, property held in trust (including living trusts and savings bank trusts), and joint tenancy property. The will doesn't affect disposition of the asset.

- **Assets Subject to "Summary" Probate:** Property that passes outright to a surviving spouse and property in small estates ($60,000 or under) can be transferred by simple "summary" probate procedures without a formal probate court proceeding. These procedures are so simple that we classify these assets N/P. After you have completed your schedule and add up the total gross value of the assets, you will be able to determine whether any assets which would otherwise be subject to probate in fact fall in this category.

- **Assets Subject to Formal Probate:** Everything not included in the above two categories requires formal probate court proceedings before the property can be transferred.

  Note: If any of this confuses you, leave this column blank until you read Chapter 6. Chapter 6 serves as a sort of road map to the rest of the book in that it directs you to the chapter containing instructions as to which property transfer procedure to follow.

G. List All Debts

WE HAVE ALSO INCLUDED a separate section at the end of the Schedule of Assets for listing debts and obligations owed by the decedent at the time of his death. This information is not necessary for the purposes of this chapter. However, it will serve as a valuable record of these items for your future use. Usually, the decedent's general debts as well as the expenses of administering the estate are paid from the general assets (residuary) of the estate, either during formal probate or a summary probate administration procedure. However, if specific assets carry with them their own obligations (such as property taxes, mortgage payments in the case of real property, or installment payments on "secured" items, such as motor vehicles, furniture, etc.), these obligations ordinarily are assumed by the beneficiaries receiving the particular item of property, unless the decedent's will provides otherwise. You can check this out by carefully reading the will provision that makes the specific devise. Information on debts of the decedent and other estate expenses is also needed in preparing the decedent's final income tax returns and, if necessary, estate income tax and federal estate tax returns.

H. Checklist of Property to List on Schedule of Assets

THIS SECTION CONTAINS an extended discussion of how to describe, evaluate and characterize the various kinds of assets commonly found in an estate. By this time, you should have a good start on your Schedule of Assets, and the material here is intended to fill in any gaps which might exist.

1. Cash Items

List all cash, checks, money orders, traveler's checks or other items that can be immediately converted to cash. The value of these items (Column A) is their face value, unless they are antique coins or something else of unusual value. These are normally community property assets if the decedent was married and separate property if he was single at the time of death. All items in this category are potentially subject to being transferred through a formal probate court proceeding unless they are (1) covered by a living trust or other probate avoidance device, (2) part of a small estate, or (3) to be transferred to a surviving spouse.

Examples:
Three American Express Traveler's Checks
Refund check, Watco Corporation
Miscellaneous cash on hand

2. Bank and Savings and Loan Accounts

Examine all bank books, statements or other evidence as to accounts or amounts on deposit with any financial institution, such as banks, trust companies, savings and loan associations or credit unions. Describe the type of account (checking account, savings account, savings certificate, money market account, or other), the number of the account or certificate, and the name and location of the institution where the account is held. You should always verify with the bank or institution as to how title to the account is held.

The amount to put in Column A is the balance on the date of death. Savings accounts and certificates should include accrued interest to the date of death, even if not credited to the account until the end of the quarter following the date of death. The accrued interest can be added as a separate item. The exact balances, including accrued interest, may be obtained directly from the bank or from a recent bank statement. Remember, you are going to insert the full value in Column A, even if it is a joint account or community property account. Then, if the decedent owned only a part interest, you will insert the amount of the fraction or portion he owned in Column C and the value of the fractional interest in Column D.

If the decedent was married and owned a certificate of deposit as community property, you would describe it like this:

	A	B	C	D	E
Certificate of Deposit, No. 10235, Lighthouse Savings & Loan Assn., Ventura, CA	20,000	CP	1/2	10,000	P*
accrued interest	150			75	

*As you will remember from our earlier discussion, if the decedent's estate is small ($60,000 or less) or it all goes to a surviving spouse, no formal court proceeding is required and you can put N/P here.

If the decedent wasn't married, or owned an account as his separate property, then you should list it like this:

	A	B	C	D	E
Interest-bearing checking account, No. 1001001, First National Bank, Malibu Branch, CA	5,000	SP	all	5,000	P*
accrued interest	15			15	

*See above footnote.

3. Pay-On-Death Accounts (Also Called Totten Trusts or Saving Bank Trusts)

Many people own what are called variously "Totten trust" accounts, "pay-on-death" accounts, or "savings bank trust" accounts. They all amount to the same thing. Title to this kind of bank account will be shown as "Mary Jones, Trustee for Harry Jones." This means the account is owned by Mary Jones, as trustee for the beneficiary, Harry Jones. On the death of the trustee (Mary Jones) the balance of the account automatically passes to the beneficiary, Harry Jones, and the funds are not subject to probate. If the decedent owned a Totten trust account, you should make a notation in Column B that it is owned in trust (T) and in Column E that it is a non-probate (N/P) asset. The balance on the date of death should be inserted in Column A. However, if community property was used to establish the trust, it is a community property asset, and only one-half of its value will be owned by the decedent because the other one-half belongs to the surviving spouse, no matter what it says on the trust document. Therefore, you would indicate in Column B that it is also community property (CP), and in Column C that the decedent owned one-half, and insert the value of the one-half interest in Column D.

	A	B	C	D	E
Trust savings account, No. 8903, Harbor Bank, San Pedro, in name of decedent as trustee for son, Jon	10,000	T/CP	1/2	5,000	N/P

4. Money Market Funds

A money market fund (as opposed to a bank money market account, which is simply another name for a bank account) is a mutual fund, much like a stock market mutual fund. Instead of investing in stocks or bonds, a money market fund lends money to various entities and the interest collected is paid out as "dividends" to the depositor, who is technically a "shareholder" in the fund. The fund's latest monthly statement will show the number of shares owned (normally, shares simply reflect the dollar amount invested; so 5,000 shares means a $5,000 investment) and the value of the decedent's interest in the fund, as well as the way she held title. If in doubt, call or write to the fund management at the address shown on the statement. Remember, even if the account is in the decedent's name alone it may very well be community property if the decedent was married. These accounts can also be held in joint tenancy, like other assets.

Assume that decedent left a separate property interest in a money market fund worth $3,175.

	A	B	C	D	E
3,175 shares, Executive Money Fund, Account No. 57632, E. F. Hutton, Beverly Hills	3,175	SP	all	3,175	P*

*If decedent's estate is small, these shares can be transferred outside of formal probate following the instructions in Chapter 11.

Now assume decedent was married and that the money market shares were community property.

	A	B	C	D	E
Cash Reserve Management Fund, Inc., Paine Weber, Toluca Lake	30,000	CP	1/2	15,000	P*

*See above footnote.

5. Real Estate

Carefully review all deeds to real property (real estate) to verify how title is held. If there is any doubt about how title is held, contact a title company and request a title search. The title company will then provide you with a Record Owner Guarantee, which is a report of all property owned by the decedent in any California county. The minimum fee is usually around $75 per name for each county that is searched, plus about $5 for each parcel over two reported. On the Schedule of Assets form list the common address of the property and the kind of property it is, such as "single family residence," "nine-unit apartment building" or "unimproved land." You do not need the legal description for our purposes here, although it may be required on later documents.

To determine the value of real property, consider the condition of the premises or property, the neighborhood and recent sales prices of comparable property in the area. Assessed values shown on real property tax bills generally do not reflect the true value and should not be used. A private appraisal by a licensed real estate appraiser is good evidence of the value of real property, and one may be obtained for approximately $150 or $200. Real estate brokers in the area will also provide written appraisals. If a formal probate proceeding is required, the real property will be appraised by a probate referee at a cost of one-tenth of one percent of the value of the property. If the decedent owned income property, you should obtain an appraisal from an expert in this field. The value of income property is based on such things as capitalization of income, the kind of financing, the quality of tenants and the effects rent control may have on such property, as well as a number of other factors, and is probably not something you should try to figure out on your own. The yellow pages of your phone book will list the names of private real estate appraisers in your area.

In addition to establishing the value of real property for your Schedule of Assets, consider getting a written appraisal. An appraisal is good evidence of the date-of-death value for establishing a new "stepped-up" federal income tax basis of the property in the hands of the new owners when computing capital gains tax, if and when the property is sold. (We discuss tax considerations, briefly, in Chapter 7.)

Let's assume the decedent had a separate property piece of land and owned a house with his spouse as community property. You would list the property like this:

	A	B	C	D	E
5 acres, unimproved grazing land, Alameda County	20,000	SP	all	20,000	P*

	A	B	C	D	E
Single family residence, 711 Hill St., Los Angeles, CA	300,000	CP	1/2	150,000	P*

*If this property was inherited by a surviving spouse, the simple community property transfer procedures set out in Chapter 15 can be used instead of formal probate.

Now assume the first piece of property was owned by decedent and his wife as joint tenants and the second piece was decedent's separate property, which was passed to his son by use of a living (inter vivos) trust. The Schedule of Assets should be filled in like this:

	A	B	C	D	E
5 acres, unimproved grazing land, Alameda County	20,000	JT	1/2	10,000	N/P

	A	B	C	D	E
Single family residence, 711 Hill St., Los Angeles, CA	300,000	SP	all	300,000	N/P

6. Stocks and Bonds

Information on the type of securities the decedent owned and the way she held title can be obtained from examining the stock or bond certificates. Stocks should be listed by the number and type of shares (that is, common or preferred) and the name of the company issuing the shares. For preferred stock, put down the dividend rate. For bonds, put down the total gross face amount (usually in multiples of $1,000), name of the issuer, interest rate and maturity date. For U.S. Treasury bills, list the total face amount and the maturity date. U.S. Treasury bills are issued either in a single name or in two names joined by "or." If issued in the decedent's name alone, they are included in the probate estate. If in co-ownership form, they pass to the surviving co-owner without probate; they are treated basically the same as joint tenancy assets and should be listed as such. For U.S. Series E savings bonds, list the issue date instead of the maturity date. The issue date is how the value is determined on Series E bonds.

Assume you have a decedent who owned some XYZ Telephone Company preferred stock and Series E savings bonds before his marriage as separate property. After marriage he acquired some Transpacific Corporation stock in joint tenancy with his brother, a $5,000 Antioch Drainage System bond as community property with his wife, and a $10,000 U.S. Treasury bill in co-ownership (joint tenancy) form with his wife. Since the assets acquired after marriage are presumed to be community property (although the records don't reflect this), one-half of the decedent's interest in the Transpacific Corporation stock acquired in joint tenancy with the decedent's brother belongs to the surviving spouse. Therefore, the decedent's interest in the Transpacific stock is actually one-fourth (one-half of one-half). The surviving spouse would probably have to file a Spousal Property Petition (see Chapter 15) to claim her community property interest in this asset. The remaining two assets ($10,000 Treasury bill and Antioch Drainage System bond) are community property and are owned one-half by the decedent. In this case, your descriptions will look like this:

	A	B	C	D	E
50 shares, Transpacific common stock	16,000	JT	1/4	4000	N/P
200 shares, XYZ Telephone Company 5% first preferred stock, par value $100	15,000	SP	all	15,000	P*
Three U.S. Series E savings bonds, face amount $100 each, issued July, 1967	300	SP	all	300	P*
$5,000 Antioch Drainage System, District of Contra Costa, 1980 Drainage bond Series B, 4-1/2% due June 1, 1990	5,000	CP	1/2	2,500	P*
$10,000 U.S. Treasury bill, due June 30, 1985	10,000	JT	1/2	5,000	N/P

*If decedent left a small estate or these assets were left to his surviving spouse, they can be transferred outside of probate following the instructions in Chapters 11 and 15.

Information on stock and bond values at the date of death can be obtained from newspaper financial sections; however, it takes a little arithmetic to compute the valuations. The value per unit or share is the mean (midpoint) between the highest and lowest quoted selling prices on the date of death. For example, if the high was fifteen-and-one-fourth and the low was fourteen-and-three-eighths, the mean would be determined by converting the fractions to decimals (15.25 and 14.375), adding these two figures together, for a total of 29.625, and dividing by two (2) for a mean value of 14.813. Then, by multiplying the unit (mean) value by the number of shares owned for each kind of stock, you will have the total value of the shares. To determine the value of bonds, divide the total gross face amount (par value) by $100 and then multiply that figure by the mean value.

Stock sold on date of death

Description of stock: 100 shares, General Motors, common

Highest selling price on date of death:	84	=	84.00
Lowest selling price on date of death:	81-7/8	=	81.875
			165.875

165.875 divided by 2 = 82.937 = mean selling price per share

82.937 multiplied by 100 (shares) = $8,293.70 = date-of-death value

If there were no sales on the date of death for the security you wish to value, but there were sales on the closest trading days before and after the date of death (for instance, if the decedent died on a Saturday or Sunday and the stock was traded on Friday and Monday), then take the average of the prices on the nearest trading dates before and after death.

No sales on date of death (decedent died on Sunday)

Description of stock: 20 shares, Natural Foods, common

Selling price on Friday (the nearest transaction date prior to death)

High:	12	
Low:	+ 10	
	22	(mean = 11)

Selling price on Monday (the nearest transaction date after death)

High:	14	
Low:	+ 12	
	26	(mean = 13)

The fair market value is obtained by averaging the Friday and Monday figures:

$$\frac{(11 + 13)}{2} = \$12.00$$

$12.00 multiplied by 20 (number of shares) = $240.00 = date-of-death value of the stock.

When the closest sales were made more than one trading day away from the date of death (that is, any day but a weekend or holiday), a slightly more complicated formula is used. The fair market value is determined by taking a weighted average of the mean price on the nearest date before the date of death and the mean price on the nearest date after the date of death. The average must be weighted inversely by the numbers of trading days between the selling dates and the valuation date, as in the following example.

Sales made two (2) trading days before date of death and three (3) trading days after date of death

Description of stock: 100 shares of AT & T, common

Selling price two (2) trading days before date of death:

High:	60
Low:	+ 58
	118 (mean = 59)

Selling price three (3) trading days after date of death:

High:	62
Low:	+ 60
	122 (mean = 61)

The fair market value is obtained by the following computation (note that the number of trading days before date of death (2) are multiplied by the mean value of the stock on the selling date after date of death, and vice versa):

$$\frac{(3 \times 59) + (2 \times 61)}{5} = \$59.80 \text{ (unit value per share)}$$

100 shares multiplied by $59.80 = $5,980 (value of shares)

Bond traded on date of death

Description of bond: $1,000 Sears Roebuck bond, 8-5/8%, due 1995

Highest selling price on date of death:	110-7/8	=	110.875
Lowest selling price on date of death:	110-1/2	=	110.50
			221.375

Mean selling price = 221.375 divided by 2 = 110.687

$1,000 (face value of bond) divided by 100 = 10

110.687 (mean) multiplied by 10 = $1,106.87 = value of bond at date of death

Sometimes stock dividends are declared before death but not paid until after death, and these should be included in valuing the stock. For example, if a stock pays a quarterly dividend of $216.00 per share for the quarter ending June 30 and the decedent died on July 3 of the same year, the $216.00 dividend should be added to the value of the stock, even though the dividend has not been received as of the date of death.

For bonds, any accrued interest due and unpaid on the date of death should be included in the valuation. To calculate accrued interest, you compute the daily rate of interest and multiply it by the number of days since the last payment to the date of the decedent's death.

The decedent owned a $10,000 bond that pays 6% interest annually on January 1 and July 1 each year.

$10,000   bond
x   .06
$600.00   (interest paid annually) ÷ 365 days = $1.64 daily interest

Date of death: July 15

Date of last interest payment: July 1

Days since last interest payment: 15

Accrued interest: 15 x $1.64 = $24.60

If you are perplexed by newspaper financial pages (as many people are) and have problems in determining the values of securities, or if the decedent owned a large number of securities, contact a brokerage firm to obtain the valuations. Many stock brokerage firms have an estate security valuation service for this purpose, and they will provide you with a report of all the information you need at a very modest cost based on the number of securities you wish evaluated. Again, remember to insert the full value of the securities in Column A, and, if they were in co-ownership form, compute the value of the decedent's fractional interest for Column D.

For mutual funds, list the number of shares in the fund, the name of the particular fund and the location of the fund management firm. Frequently, share certificates for mutual funds are actually held by the fund's custodian, not by the investor. Contact the fund management directly for information on the ownership and a description of the shares and the date-of-death value, or refer to the latest statement.

Assume a single person owned a major investment in a mutual fund as a joint tenant with her brother. You would list it like this:

	A	B	C	D	E
35,000 shares, Dreyfus Special Income fund, State Street Bank and Trust Co., New York	16,000	JT	1/2	8,000	N/P

7. U.S. Savings Bonds in Co-Ownership or Beneficiary Form

U.S. savings bonds in co-ownership form will be shown registered to "John Jones or Sally Jones," as owners. Bonds registered in beneficiary form appear as "John Jones payable on death [or abbreviated "P.O.D."] Sally Jones." John Jones is the registered owner in this case, and Sally Jones is the beneficiary. Bonds registered in co-ownership with someone, or in beneficiary form, pass to the surviving co-owner or beneficiary on the death of the co-owner or registered owner, much like a joint tenancy asset, and are not subject to probate. Most commercial banks have the forms for reissuing or redeeming U.S. savings bonds and will assist in these transactions. Only if the present decedent is the surviving co-owner, or survives the beneficiary in case of a beneficiary registration, will such bonds be subject to probate, because in such cases the present decedent is the only owner of the bonds (there being no co-owner or designated beneficiary living).

8. Insurance

List on the schedule only insurance policies that are owned by the decedent. The policy itself does not always indicate the owner, and often insurance policies on the decedent's life are owned by another person (for example, spouse or partner).[2] If you write to the insurance company, it will provide you with a written record of the name of the owner. And remember, any insurance policy on the life of the decedent or his surviving spouse may be community property if, and to the extent, the premiums were paid with community funds.

Conversely, the decedent may have owned an insurance policy on his surviving spouse (or someone else) when he died. Strange as it may seem, such a policy is considered an asset of the decedent's estate and the cash value of the policy on the date of the decedent's death is included in his probate estate. Usually, the cash value—as opposed to the face value—of the policy is only a few thousand dollars. If the decedent had such a policy (on the life of someone else), you should write the insurance company to verify ownership and to get a statement of the cash value of the policy on the date of the decedent's death. Upon request, the insurance company will send you a Life Insurance Statement (Form 712) setting forth a computation of what is paid in connection with policies on the decedent's life, as well as the cash value of any policies the decedent owned on the life of another.

In describing insurance owned by the decedent on the Schedule of Assets, list the name of the insurance company, the policy number and the name of the beneficiary. The value of an insurance policy on the decedent's life is the full amount of insurance proceeds paid, but the value of a policy the decedent owned on the life of another is the cash value provided by the insurance company.

Insurance proceeds on the decedent's life payable to named beneficiaries are non-probate assets. In rare cases, the decedent's estate is the beneficiary, and in this case the insurance proceeds are included in the probate estate.

---

[2]We discuss who owns insurance policies in more detail in Chapter 7, Section E.

Suppose a married decedent owned two life insurance policies as his separate property. One is a paid-up policy on the decedent's life purchased before his marriage to the surviving spouse and payable to his estate, and the other is on the life of his surviving spouse. Here's how to list them:

	A	B	C	D	E
Proceeds, Acme Insurance Policy No. 23456, on decedent's life, payable to estate as beneficiary	10,000	SP	all	10,000	P*
Decedent's interest as owner in Grand Insurance Co., Policy No. 654321, on life of decedent's spouse	1,500	SP	all	1,500	P*

*No formal probate will be necessary if decedent leaves a small estate or if this property is transferred to a surviving spouse.

What if the decedent purchased a policy on his life during his marriage, without assigning ownership to anyone else and naming his daughter by a previous marriage as beneficiary? Here's how to list it:

	A	B	C	D	E
Proceeds, Beneficial Life Policy No. 45609, on decedent's life, payable to decedent's daughter, Mary	20,000	CP	1/2	10,000	N/P

9. Retirement and Death Benefits Through Decedent's Employment

If the decedent was employed, his employer should be asked whether there are any unpaid salary, pension or survivor's benefits payable. If so, list the name of the company paying the benefit, the name of the beneficiary and the amount. Benefits payable to named beneficiaries are non-probate assets. The value of each benefit is the actual amount paid in a lump sum. If the decedent was married this is probably a community property asset.

	A	B	C	D	E
Death Benefit, Public Employees Retirement System, payable to decedent's spouse	50,000	CP	1/2	25,000	N/P

10. Amounts Due the Decedent

Any right the decedent had to receive money from another person or entity should be listed as an asset. List any personal loans, rents, dividends, unpaid fees, salary or commissions owed to the decedent, with the name of the payor, the amount due and a brief description of what it is for. The value of these items is the amount due, unless it is unlikely the debt will be collected, in which case it will have no value and should not be included. For instance, if the decedent made an unsecured loan to someone who refuses or is unable to pay it back, or the payments are extremely delinquent, or the person cannot be located, then this is not regarded as an estate asset. If any note is secured by a deed of trust on real property, a brief description of the property should be noted.

The value of the notes will be the principal balance still owing and unpaid as of the date of death, plus the amount of any accrued but unpaid interest to that date.

Assume Robert Morgan, the decedent, had loaned $50,000 to his son, J.P., to purchase a house and at the time of Robert's death J.P. had repaid $15,000. Robert was married to Ellen, and the loan is considered to be community property.

	A	B	C	D	E
$50,000 promissory note of J. P. Morgan, dated 3/1/69, interest at 8%, payable $350 on the first of each month, secured by deed of trust on real property located at 515 Sutter Street, San Jose; principal balance on date of death $35,000	35,000	CP	1/2	17,500	P*
accrued interest	150			75	

The accrued interest is computed by determining the daily amount of interest on the principal balance due (that is, .08 x $35,000 ÷ 365 = $7.66), and multiplying this figure by the number of days from the date of the last note payment to the date of death. For instance, if the last note payment was May 1, 1985, and the decedent died on May 5, 1985, there would be 5 days' accrued and unpaid interest due on the date of death, or $38.30 (5 x $7.66).

---

*Formal probate would not be necessary if this note was left to Ellen. See Chapter 15 for details on how to transfer property to a surviving spouse.

11. Tangible Personal Property

This category is for miscellaneous items of personal property. Personal effects that are not particularly valuable can be grouped together under the general heading of "furniture, furnishings and personal effects," and given a lump-sum value. Remember, you do not consider what these items cost, but what they are worth secondhand. This is generally a small fraction of their original purchase price. For example, the value of these items, except such things as valuable stereo equipment, pianos, home computers, etc., for a five-room house would probably be around $500 to $1000. For valuable jewelry, furs, coins, paintings, antiques, electronics equipment, musical instruments, etc., a private appraisal should be obtained from an expert in each field. The Yellow Pages of your telephone book will list appraisers who specialize in various types of assets. Any appraisal fees should be paid from estate assets as discussed in Chapters 13 and 14. All items in this category are usually probate items.

For an unmarried decedent, your descriptions will be in the following form:

	A	B	C	D	E
One Tiffany blue diamond ring, 2 carats	2,500	SP	all	2,500	P*
Antique coin collection in decedent's residence	3,000	SP	all	3,000	P*
Household furniture, furnishings and personal effects	750	SP	all	750	P*

*If you have a married decedent, the ring would probably be separate property, but the coin collection and personal effects would probably be community property and show a one-half interest.

12. Motor Vehicles

Examine the ownership certificate (pink slip) to see how title to each vehicle is registered. Any automobile held in the name of "Mary Smith *or* Andy Smith" is considered by the Motor Vehicles Department to be in joint tenancy ownership, and it may be transferred to the surviving owner without probate. (The procedures for transfer are given in Chapter 10.) Describe automobiles by the year, make and model. Automobiles are valued at the average between the wholesale and retail "blue book" price, unless the automobile is unusual (for example, antique, foreign, classic), in which case an appraisal should be obtained. You can find a blue book at any car dealer or public library.

	A	B	C	D	E
1978 Dodge Monaco, 4-door sedan, in name of John Doe and Mary Doe	1,000	CP	1/2	500	P*
1985 Cadillac Seville, 4-door sedan, in name of decedent	20,000	SP	all	20,000	P*

*If decedent left an estate of $60,000 or less (excluding joint tenancy property and property left to a surviving spouse), formal probate would not be necessary. See Chapter 11. Similarly, if he left an item of property to a surviving spouse, that item would not have to go through formal probate. See Chapter 15.

13. Business Interests

If the decedent had any interest in a business as a sole proprietor or partner or owned an interest in a closely held (private) corporation, you should list it here with the name of the business, partnership or corporation, and the decedent's percentage ownership and manner of holding title. You may need to contact the other parties involved to obtain this information. Assets like these are valued according to many technical rules and you will need to get an estimate of the value either from an accountant or a firm that is expert in business appraisals. Some CPA firms specialize in business appraisals; you can also ask a bank trust department to recommend an appraiser.

Assume the decedent owned an interest in a partnership as separate property which she left to her daughter by use of a living (inter vivos) trust, and a community property interest in a business. These would be described like this:

	A	B	C	D	E
Eureka Mining Co., a general partnership, 500 Unity Building, Banning, CA	15,000	SP	all	15,000	N/P
"The Rori Kennel," a sole proprietorship, 111 Bunratty Rd, Kelso, CA	70,000	CP	1/2	35,000	P*

*If the decedent left her community property interest to her spouse, formal probate would be unnecessary and this asset could be transferred following the instructions in Chapter 15.

14. Individual Retirement Accounts

If the decedent owned an individual retirement account (IRA), you should contact the institution where the investment was set up (bank, credit union, insurance company, stock brokerage) and ask for instructions on how to transfer the asset to the beneficiary. In most cases, a certified copy of the decedent's death certificate is all that is required. An IRA is not subject to probate unless it is payable to the decedent's estate. When the IRA is opened, the owner designates a beneficiary to receive the investment on the death of the owner. Usually, if the beneficiary is the surviving spouse, the IRA may be continued with the spouse as the new owner. If a beneficiary has not been designated, or the named beneficiary dies before the owner, payment is usually made in the following order of priority: (1) the surviving spouse, (2) the decedent's surviving child, or (3) the decedent's estate.

	A	B	C	D	E
IRA Account No. 13876-2, at Superior Savings and Loan, Kelso, California, payable to decedent's spouse	$2,500	CP	1/2	$1,125	N/P

15. Other Assets

List here any other assets not included in the above categories. Here again, you will probably need an expert appraiser to determine the value of such things as copyrights or royalty interests, patents or future residuals if the amount involved is large.

	A	B	C	D	E
Copyright on book *How to Play Tennis*, published 1982 by Harvest Pub. Co., Los Angeles, annual royalties approx. $5,000 with three-year life expectancy. (Approx.)	15,000	CP	1/2	7,500	P*
Estimated future residuals due decedent from Screen Actors Guild for services prior to death	500	SP	all	500	P*

*These assets would not be subject to formal probate if decedent's entire estate is worth $60,000 or less or were left to a surviving spouse. See Chapters 11 and 15.

I. Schedule of Assets for a Sample Estate

LET'S LOOK AT a sample estate, the *Estate of Sybil Sample, Deceased,* and see how its Schedule of Assets would take form.

Sybil Sample married Cyrus Sample in San Jose, California, in 1974. They lived in California continuously during their marriage until Sybil's death on February 16, 1986. Sybil left all of her community and separate property to Cyrus, except for her savings bonds, which she left to her cousin Alice.

At the time of marriage, Sybil owned an unimproved lot in San Bernardino County, three $500 U.S. Series E savings bonds, a savings account at Union Bank in Arcadia held in Sybil's name as trustee for her mother, Anne, and a $40,000 promissory note secured by a deed of trust on real property. Sybil also owned a $15,000 Sun Life insurance policy on her life, naming her mother as beneficiary, on which one-third of the premiums were paid with her earnings during her marriage to Cyrus.

Cyrus, a newspaper columnist, owned a home in San Jose at the time of his marriage to Sybil, which he sold in 1976 for $120,000, receiving cash of $100,000 and a $20,000 promissory note secured by the real property. Using the $100,000 as a down payment, Cyrus purchased a new home in which Sybil and Cyrus took title in both their names as husband and wife. Cyrus and Sybil, who was a school librarian, both continued to work after marriage, depositing all of their excess earnings into a joint savings account at Pacific States Bank. During their marriage, Cyrus purchased 200 shares of AT&T stock and a 1980 Oldsmobile Cutlass automobile with his earnings, taking title in his name alone. Sybil and Cyrus also invested money in Franklin Group Money Funds, a money market fund, and purchased a $10,000 Central High School District School bond, holding both of these assets as joint tenants. Cyrus also took out a $100,000 Aetna Life Insurance policy on his life during their marriage, and transferred complete ownership in the policy to Sybil. Sybil paid the premiums on the policy from her

separate funds. For their anniversary in 1982, Cyrus gave Sybil a three-quarter carat diamond ring.

At her death Sybil also had an uncashed refund check from a hardware store and $3.00 in cash. She and Cyrus were owed $2,000 by Joe Swinger, to whom they had made an unsecured non-interest loan. At Sybil's death a $5,000 pension plan death benefit became payable to Cyrus.

The Schedule of Assets for Sybil's estate is set out below. The information inserted on the schedule for each asset was determined by the following facts:

Item 1: Cash Items

The cash in Sybil's possession and the refund check are community property, having been acquired during her marriage. Thus, Sybil has a one-half vested interest in these items. These are technically part of her probate estate, but since Sybil left all of her community and separate property to Cyrus, they can be transferred without having to go through formal probate. See Chapter 15.

Item 2: Bank and Savings and Loan Accounts

The Pacific States Bank account, held in joint tenancy, passes to Cyrus outside of probate. Nevertheless, you should insert the full value of the account in Column A and the value of a one-half interest in Column D.

The savings account at Union Bank in Arcadia is a Totten trust account (sometimes called a pay-on-death account, or bank savings trust account), which passes to Sybil's mother as named beneficiary, without probate, on Sybil's death. The entire proceeds of the account are Sybil's separate property. She was the sole owner prior to death; she didn't transfer any percentage of ownership in the account to her mother when she made her a beneficiary, and didn't deposit any of her community property earnings in the account during marriage.

Item 3: Real Property

The residence is community property because title was acquired by Sybil and Cyrus during marriage as husband and wife, and one-half of the residence is included in Sybil's estate. The $100,000 which Cyrus received from the sale of his previous home was Cyrus' separate property, having been derived from a separate property asset he owned prior to his marriage. However, by using the $100,000 as a down payment on their new home during marriage and taking title as husband and wife, he made a $50,000 gift to Sybil from his separate property by converting it into community property. The $20,000 promissory note Cyrus received from the sale of his previous home (plus the income from the note) remains his separate property and no part of the note is included in Sybil's estate.

In the case of the residence, a formal probate court proceeding won't be necessary as it passes to Cyrus under Sybil's will. The simplified procedure to transfer property to a surviving spouse (Chapter 15) can be used.

The unimproved lot in San Bernardino is Sybil's separate property, since she owned it prior to marriage, and it is included 100% in her estate.

Item 4: Securities

Sybil owned the three U.S. Series E savings bonds prior to marriage, so they are her separate property and included 100% in her estate. They will be subject to probate because they were left to cousin Alice. The Franklin Group Money Fund shares and the $10,000 Central High School District School bond are held in joint tenancy and, therefore, are not subject to probate. Although it is held in Cyrus' name alone, the AT&T stock is community property, having been purchased during marriage with community property funds, and one-half of the stock is included in Sybil's estate. Because this property goes to Cyrus, no formal probate will be required. (See Chapter 15.)

Item 5: Insurance

The $15,000 Sun Life Policy which was owned by Sybil prior to her marriage was her separate property when she married Cyrus. However, because she paid one-third of the premiums during marriage with community property funds, she converted one-third of the policy proceeds into community property. Therefore, even though her mother is the named beneficiary, Cyrus owns a one-half vested interest in the community property portion of the proceeds, or one-sixth (one-half of one-third) of $15,000, which is $2,500. The policy proceeds are not subject to probate because there is a named beneficiary; however, since the premiums were paid from both separate and community property, the total value of the policy is apportioned between separate and community property, based on the portion of the total premiums paid from each. Thus, the amount included in Sybil's gross estate is $12,500 ($15,000 less Cyrus' one-half community interest of $2,500). In this case you put the total value of the proceeds ($15,000) in Column A, and the part owned by Sybil ($12,500) in Column D.

The $100,000 Aetna Life Policy on Cyrus' life is Sybil's separate property and the total cash value of the policy on her date of death is included in her estate. It would be subject to formal probate except that Sybil left all of her property to Cyrus and, therefore, it qualifies for the simplified spousal transfer provisions discussed in Chapter 15. Sometimes ownership of an insurance policy may be transferred simply by furnishing the carrier with a copy of the will.

Item 6: Retirement and Death Benefits

The $5,000 Pension Plan death benefit, payable to Cyrus, is not subject to probate, but one-half is included in Sybil's estate as community property because it is payable by reason of her employment.

Item 7: Amounts Due the Decedent

The $2,000 loan due from Joe Swinger is community property and one-half is included in Sybil's estate. It would be subject to formal probate except that it qualifies for the simplified spousal transfer provisions discussed in Chapter 15.

Item 8: Promissory Notes

The $40,000 trust deed note owned by Sybil prior to marriage is her separate property and included 100% in her estate. It would be subject to formal probate if it had been left to anyone but Cyrus.

Item 9: Tangible Personal Property

The household furniture and personal effects are included in Sybil's estate to the extent of her one-half community property interest. The gold diamond ring is Sybil's separate property, having been acquired as a gift, and is included 100% in her estate. Both of these would be subject to formal probate if they had not been left to a spouse.

Item 10: Automobiles

A one-half interest in the Oldsmobile Cutlass is included in Sybil's estate as community property, even though Cyrus took title in his name alone. Since Cyrus inherits this vehicle anyway, nothing need be done to transfer ownership to him.

An example of the Schedule of Assets for Sybil's estate is shown below. After you review it, go on to the next chapter to see how to actually transfer the assets in Sybil's estate.

Estate of _____SYBIL SAMPLE_____ , Deceased

Schedule of Assets

Description of Asset	A Total Value of Asset on Date/Death	B How is Asset Owned?	C Portion Owned by Decedent	D Value of Decedent's Interest	E Probate or Non-Probate
1. Cash Items:					
Cash in decedent's possession:	3.00	CP	½	1.50	P
Uncashed checks payable to decedent:					
Refund from Abco Hardware	5.60	CP	½	2.80	P
2. Bank and Savings and Loan Accounts: (Name and location of bank, type of account, account number, account balance)					
a. Sav. Acct. #1234, Pacific States	20,000	JT	½	10,000	NP
Bank, San Jose (acc. int.)	150	JT	½	75	NP
b. Sav. Acct. #0832, Union Bank,	6,000	T (SP)	all	6,000	NP
Arcadia (in trust for Anne) (acc. int.)	70	T (SP)	all	70	NP
3. Real Property: (common address, brief description)					
a. Single-family residence,					
930 Hill Street, San Jose	500,000	CP	½	250,000	P
b. Unimproved lot, San Bernadino					
County	15,000	SP	all	15,000	P
4. Securities: Stock: (Name of company, type and number of shares)					
200 shares AT&T common (in name	10,000	CP	½	5,000	P
of Cyrus Sample)					
Bonds: (Type of bond, face amount)					
$10,000 Central High School Dist. Bond,	9,800	JT	½	4,900	NP
Series C, 4%, 12-31-85 (acc. int.)	196	JT	½	98	NP
U.S. Savings Bonds/Treasury Bills: (Series, amount, date of issue)					
Three $500 U.S. Series E Savings	1,500	SP	all	1,500	P
Bonds, issued July 1957					

Mutual funds:
(Name of fund, number of shares)

50,000 shares Franklin Group Money Funds	50,000	JT	½	25,000	NP

5. Insurance:
(Name of company, policy number, name
of beneficiary, name of owner)
Policies on decedent's life:

$15,000 Sun Life Ins. Policy, No. 83792 (beneficiary: decedent's mother)	15,000	⅓ CP, ⅔ SP	⅙ as CP ⅔ as SP	12,500	NP

Policies owned by decedent on another:

$100,000 Aetna Life Policy No. 24487 on life of Cyrus Sample	4,000	SP	all	4,000	P

6. **Retirement and Death Benefits:**
(Description, beneficiary, amount)
Employee Benefits:

$5000 School Employee's Pension Plan (beneficiary: Cyrus Sample)	5,000	CP	½	2,500	NP

Pension, profit-sharing, savings plans:

Social Security/Railroad Retirement:

7. **Amounts Due the Decedent:**
(Name of payor, amount)

$2000 unsecured non-interest-bearing loan due from Joe Swinger	2,000	CP	½	1,000	P

8. **Promissory Notes:**
(Name of payor, date amount, balance)

$40,000 promissory note of Mynus Cash, 5% int., dated 7-1-59, secured by trust deed on real property at 123	35,000	SP	all	35,000	P
Main St., Los Angeles (acc. int.)	123.50	SP	all	123.50	P

9. **Tangible Personal Property:**
(Household furniture, furnishings,
personal effects, books, jewelry, artwork,
valuable collections, antiques, etc.)

a. Household furnishings and personal effects	1,000	CP	½	500	P
b. Lady's gold ring, ¾ carat diamond	1,500	SP	all	1,500	P

10. **Automobiles:**
(Year, make, model)

1980 Oldsmobile Cutlass, 2-door   4,000   CP   ½   2,000   P

11. **Business Interests:**
(Partnerships, sole proprietorships,
family corporations, brief description)

12. **Other Assets:**
(Copyrights, royalty interests, patents,
any other property not listed above)

Total Value of Decedent's Gross Estate . . . . $ 376,770.80

Deductions (for Federal Estate Tax Purposes):

a. Debts owed by decedent at date of death:

     Amount

Clark's Department Store : $1,180 (CP) $ 590.

b. Expenses of estate administration:

Appraisals, transfer fees, recording fees, court costs   800

c. Last illness expenses:

Richard Roe, M.D., medical services   150

Mary Smith, nursing care   60

d. Funeral expenses:

Chapel Mortuary   2,589

e. Sales contracts (automobiles, furniture, television):

C & D Financial (auto loan) : $1150 (CP)   575

f. Mortgages/promissory notes due:

Beneficial Sav. & Loan (house loan): $98,000 (CP)   49,000

Total: $ 53,814

CHAPTER 6

How to Identify the Best Transfer Procedure

AFTER YOU'VE FIGURED out what the decedent owned and who should get it, the next step is to determine the best method of actually transferring the property. This chapter does not actually deal with the "how to's" of making transfers, but serves as a road map to the detailed transfer instructions contained in the chapters that follow. In other words, after reading this chapter carefully, you should be able to identify the most direct route to your property transfer goal.

On your Schedule of Assets (Chapter 5), you labeled each asset (in Column B) as separate property, community property, joint tenancy property, trust property, etc. Let's briefly review the transfer rules for each.

A. Non-Probate Assets

ASSETS CONTAINED in estates where planning to avoid probate has been done avoid probate automatically. It's important to realize, however, that the following list of non-probate items does not include every kind of property that passes without formal probate proceedings. Because of several simplifications in California law in the last decade, some assets that used to have to be submitted to a probate court are now exempt from formal probate. Because a particular type of asset is not listed here does not mean that formal probate is required. It very well may not be. In Section B of this chapter we review all assets that are potentially subject to probate and help you to see if in fact you will have to file a formal probate proceeding or if you can use one of the simpler methods to transfer the property.

1. Joint Tenancy Assets

Joint tenancy assets are not subject to probate, and the decedent's interest in property held in this manner passes to the surviving joint tenant(s) by operation of law. Chapter 10 explains how to transfer title to the surviving joint tenant(s).

Surviving Spouse Note: In most situations, property held in joint tenancy by spouses is community property. You may transfer it either as a joint tenancy asset, or you may use a Spousal Property Order (discussed in Chapter 15) to officially establish the joint tenancy property as community property and obtain the favorable tax treatment that community property receives. We discuss these tax rules in Chapter 7. If after reading this discussion you are still confused, see an accountant.

2. Trustee Bank Accounts (Totten Trust Accounts or Pay-on-Death Accounts)

These accounts may be transferred outside of probate in the same manner as joint tenancy bank accounts by using the procedures explained in Chapter 10, Section E.

3. Living Trusts

Many people put their property in living (inter vivos) trusts to avoid probate. Any property held in a living trust created by the decedent is not subject to probate administration if the property was actually transferred to the trust, in which case title will be held in the name of the trust. Occasionally, a decedent may have signed a trust document describing the assets to be held in the trust but for some reason failed to sign documents actually transferring title into his or another's name as trustee. To check this, carefully examine all title documents such as real property deeds, stock certificates and motor vehicle pink slips. If the asset was transferred to the trust, the ownership document will show title held something like this: "The I.M. Smart Trust."

Miscellaneous items of personal property that don't have title documents can be included in a living trust without being formally transferred to the trust.

When the person who established a living trust dies, property held in the trust is transferred to the beneficiary (named in the trust document) by a successor trustee named in the trust. The procedure used to transfer property subject to a living trust is set out in Chapter 12.

4. U.S. Savings Bonds in Co-Ownership or Beneficiary Form

Bonds registered in this manner also avoid probate, and your local bank will assist in having these bonds redeemed or re-registered in the name of the new owner. The Federal Reserve Bank and many commercial banks have the required forms and will assist in preparing them. The original bond certificates and a certified copy of the decedent's death certificate are required to make the transfer.

5. Life Insurance and Death Benefits Payable to Named Beneficiaries

If life insurance and other death benefits payable to named beneficiaries have not already been collected, these benefits may be claimed by contacting the company or organization responsible for making payment. The company provides the necessary forms and will notify you of the other documents it requires (usually a certified copy of the decedent's death certificate and the policy). Instructions are in Chapter 2, Section C.

Insurance proceeds payable to the decedent's estate, as well as the cash value of any insurance policies the decedent owned on the life of another person, require probate unless the entire estate qualifies to avoid probate based on its small size (see Chapter 11) or unless the property is transferred to a surviving spouse. (See Chapter 15.)

6. Life Estates

A life estate is created when a person transfers real property to someone else but keeps the right to use the property for the rest of her life. We define life estates in detail in Chapter 4, Section D, and discuss transfers of property held in life estate in Chapter 12.

B. Assets That May Be Subject to Formal Probate

THE REMAINING ASSETS on your schedule may have to go through formal probate. They will fall into one of the following three groups: (1) property held "as community property," (2) property held in the decedent's name alone, and (3) property held in co-tenancy form, usually expressed in a deed or title slip "as tenants in common." Broadly speaking, determining the size of the estate and who the property is left to will tell you if formal probate is required.

1. Community Property or Separate Property That Passes Outright to the Decedent's Surviving Spouse[1]

Any property—community property or separate property—that goes outright (not subject to a life estate or in a trust) to the decedent's surviving spouse under the terms of the decedent's will or by intestate succession in the absence of a will does not require formal probate. (Probate Code § 13500.) Nevertheless, often a court order, called a "Spousal Property Order," is required to transfer title to certain types of assets, including real property or stocks and bonds. Chapter 15 describes the simple, informal court procedure for obtaining this court

---

[1] If the decedent wasn't married at death, you can skip this and go on to Section 2, below.

order. Procedures to transfer property to a surviving spouse can usually be commenced immediately after one spouse dies, unless there is a survival period required in the will.

To find out if any of a married decedent's assets fall into this category, examine the will carefully (if there is one) to see if property is given to the surviving spouse. Then, verify that such property passes to the surviving spouse without any limitations as to ownership. If the surviving spouse is given a qualified ownership in the property, such as in a trust, it is not eligible to be transferred in this way.

If there is no will, then all community property plus at least a part (and sometimes all) of the decedent's separate property, if any, will go outright to the surviving spouse under intestate succession laws. As you will know if you read Chapter 3, the amount of the separate property that a surviving spouse is entitled to under intestate succession depends on whether the decedent left any surviving children or other close relatives entitled to receive a portion of the separate property. Refer to Chapter 3, Section F, to see how a decedent's separate property is divided in the absence of a will. Again, if a court order is necessary to transfer this property, as it probably is in the case of real property or securities, see Chapter 15.

Note: If the decedent willed his interest in community property or separate property to someone other than the surviving spouse, then the procedures described in Sections 2 or 3, below, should be used to transfer it.

2. Property in Estates Under $60,000

California Probate Code §§ 13000 to 13209 provide a simple way to transfer property in estates that don't exceed a total gross value of $60,000. This means that for many Californians of modest means, no formal probate is required. All of the personal property may be transferred with a one-page affidavit. An affidavit procedure may also be used to transfer real property worth $10,000 or less,

and title to real property up to $60,000 in value may be passed by a simple court procedure. There is a waiting period, usually 40 days, before the transfers may be requested.

These summary procedures may, in many instances, be used for estates over $60,000, because several kinds of assets aren't counted in computing the $60,000 limitation. For example, all joint tenancy property (both real and personal) is excluded, as well as all property that goes outright to a surviving spouse (community or separate), and certain other property. Chapter 11 explains this simple method of transferring assets in more detail. Even if the estate you are dealing with contains somewhat more than $60,000 of personal property (and real property held in joint tenancy), you will want to read Chapter 11, Section B, to see if the various exclusions allowed by law permit the estate to qualify anyway.

3. Remaining Assets

All remaining assets that do not fall into one of the above categories require a formal probate court proceeding before title may be transferred. Generally, this includes remaining assets that are:

- Not held in trust;
- Not held in joint tenancy;
- Not community or separate property going outright to the surviving spouse;
- Not part of estates that are under $60,000 in value.

Fortunately, even if you find that an asset is subject to probate, you can still normally handle the necessary paperwork yourself. Probate court proceedings are not as cumbersome as they once were, and today a simple estate may normally be settled through court proceedings within nine months without the need to hire a lawyer. We tell you how to conduct a probate court proceeding in detail in Chapters 13 and 14.

C. Examples of How Assets Are Transferred in Typical Estates

LET'S RETURN NOW to the estate of Sybil Sample, which we introduced in the preceding chapter. Our idea here is to illustrate the process by which the assets of a typical estate are transferred. You may want to refresh your memory by reviewing the property in Sybil's estate before going on. If you analyze Sybil's Schedule of Assets in Chapter 5, you will find that the assets fall into the categories described above.

1. Joint Tenancy Assets

Sybil held three assets in joint tenancy with her husband, Cyrus: the savings account at Pacific States Bank, the $10,000 Central High School District School Bond, and the 50,000 shares of Franklin Group Money Fund. These all go to Cyrus without the need for probate. Chapter 10 shows how to transfer joint tenancy assets.

2. Trustee Bank Account

The proceeds in the Totten trust account at Union Bank in Arcadia (Item 2-b) should be transferred to Sybil's mother, Anne, as beneficiary using the procedures outlined in Chapter 10, Section E. (This is the same as for a joint tenancy account.) Since Sybil established this account prior to her marriage, Cyrus has no community property interest in it.

3. Insurance Payable to Named Beneficiary

The proceeds of the Sun Life Insurance Policy may be paid directly to the beneficiaries by contacting the company for the necessary claim forms and submitting a certified copy of the decedent's death certificate. Since Sybil's mother, Anne, is the named beneficiary of the policy, the insurance company will pay the proceeds to Anne unless it is advised otherwise. If Cyrus wants to collect his vested one-half community interest in the proceeds, he must contact the insurance company and work out an arrangement with the company and Sybil's mother. If it cannot be done on this basis, Cyrus would have to see an attorney. Alternatively, Cyrus could obtain a Spousal Property Order (see Chapter 15) confirming that $2,250 of the proceeds belongs to him as his one-half community property interest. Of course, as Cyrus gets most of the rest of the property, he might well conclude that for personal or family reasons he does not want to challenge Sybil's intent in naming Anne as beneficiary.

4. Pension Plan Death Benefit Payable to Named Beneficiary

The $5,000 School Employee's Pension Plan death benefit, payable to Cyrus as named beneficiary, may be collected by submitting a certified copy of the death certificate to the pension plan office and asking for the necessary claim forms.

5. All Other Assets

The other assets on the schedule make up the part of Sybil's estate that is potentially subject to probate, unless they fall within one of the exceptions to probate discussed in Section A of this chapter. The persons to whom these assets will pass and the method used to transfer such property depend on whether or not Sybil left a will naming who is to receive the property, or whether she died intestate.

D. Sample Estates

IN CHAPTER 5 we assumed that Sybil left a will, but here let's look at both possibilities and see what happens to the assets in each case. To make this easier, let's first divide Sybil's remaining assets into separate property and community property. Again, if you are not sure how to do this, please re-read Chapter 4.

Community Property (Sybil's 1/2 interest)	
Cash	$3.00
Abco Hardware Refund	5.60
San Jose Residence	250,000.00
AT&T Stock	5,000.00
Loan Due from Joe Swinger	1,000.00
Household Furnishings, etc.	500.00
Oldsmobile Cutlass	2,000.00
	$258,508.60

Separate Property (Sybil's 100% interest)	
San Bernardino Lot	$15,000.00
Series E Bonds	1,500.00
Aetna Life Insurance Policy	4,000.00
Mynus Cash T.D. Note	35,123.00
Diamond Ring	1,500.00
	$57,123.00

1. Sybil Dies With a Will

Assume Sybil left a will leaving Cyrus all property except her savings bonds, which she left to her cousin Alice. All of the property (both community property and separate property) left to Cyrus may be transferred to him without formal probate administration, with a Spousal Property Order, obtained by using the procedures outlined in Chapter 15. (See Section B above.)

A court order is not needed to transfer ownership of every asset to Cyrus. For instance, the AT&T stock and Oldsmobile Cutlass are already in his name, and since most of the other assets have no title documents, they will pass to Cyrus automatically under Probate Code § 13500. Therefore, the only assets for which an official transfer document (the Spousal Property Order) will be required are the San Jose residence, the San Bernardino lot and the Mynus Cash Trust Deed Note.

But as Sybil's will left some property to someone other than Cyrus (Cousin Alice), our next step is to see what the property consists of. If it is valued under $60,000, it may be transferred to the person(s) named in the will by using the affidavit procedure discussed in Chapter 11.

However, if Sybil willed property having a gross total value exceeding $60,000 to someone other than her surviving spouse, formal probate court proceedings are required before it can be transferred. Those proceedings are discussed in Chapter 14.

2. Sybil Dies Without a Will

If we assume Sybil died without a will, leaving Cyrus and her mother as her only heirs (there are no children), then intestate succession laws dictate that all of her community property would go outright to Cyrus and her separate property would be given one-half to Cyrus and one-half to her mother. (Remember, we show you how to figure out who inherits property in the absence of a will in Chapter 3).

In this case, the community property and Cyrus' one-half interest in the separate property may be transferred to Cyrus without formal probate by use of a Spousal Property Order, as discussed in Chapter 15. The other one-half interest in the separate property must go through probate or, if it is valued at less than $60,000, may be transferred by the simplified procedures in Chapter 11. At the close of the probate proceeding, the court will make an order distributing a one-half interest in the separate property to Sybil's mother. If Cyrus and Sybil's mother do not wish to own a one-half interest in each separate property asset (which might not be practical in the case of the diamond ring or the Aetna Life Insurance Policy), they may make an agreement for distribution after they obtain court orders.

3. Estate of Cyrus Sample, Deceased

Now for further illustration, let's see what happens to Cyrus' estate when he dies approximately two years later. Assume that Cyrus did not remarry after Sybil's death and was still a resident of San Jose, California, when he died on May 18, 1988. He had two children by a previous marriage, a daughter, Sally, and a son, Michael, who survived him. Prior to his death, Cyrus disposed of some of the assets he had received from Sybil's estate, and acquired others. To avoid probate of the bulk of his estate, Cyrus executed an inter vivos revocable "living trust" in 1986, and transferred the family residence and a limited partnership interest into the trust. The trust named his brother Sam as successor trustee and Cyrus' children Sally and Michael as beneficiaries.

At the time of his death, Cyrus' estate consisted of the following property:

- Savings Account No. 1234, Pacific States Bank, San Jose, California, having a principal balance of $20,000;
- 200 shares, AT&T common stock, worth $10,000;

- 10% interest in Westland Shopping Center, a limited partnership, in name of Cyrus Sample, as Trustee of the Cyrus Sample Revocable Trust, dated June 1, 1986, valued at $200,000;
- Family residence, 930 Hill Street, San Jose, in the name of Cyrus Sample, as Trustee of the Cyrus Sample Revocable Trust, dated June 1, 1986, having a value of $600,000;
- $100,000 Aetna Life Insurance Policy, on the life of Cyrus Sample, naming Sally and Michael as beneficiaries;
- 1987 BMW, Model 320i, 2-door sedan, having a value of $22,000.

Since Cyrus wasn't married when he died, all of his property is his separate property. His will (executed at the same time as his inter vivos trust) leaves his entire estate to his two children. As we examine the transfer procedures available for the assets in Cyrus' estate, we will see that no formal probate proceedings are required to transfer the property.

First of all, the successor trustee of the Cyrus Sample Revocable Trust (Sam) can transfer the family residence and the partnership interest immediately without probate to Cyrus' two children as the beneficiaries. The real property will require the preparation of a deed, signed by Sam as successor trustee, transferring the residence to Sally and Michael. The limited partnership interest will require an assignment executed by Sam, as successor trustee, assigning Cyrus' interest to his children. As noted in Chapter 1, transfers of significant business interests should normally be handled through an attorney.

The proceeds of the Aetna Life Policy will be paid to Sally and Michael, the named beneficiaries, without probate. The remaining personal property, consisting of the BMW automobile, AT&T stock, and the savings account at Pacific States Bank, all have a total gross value of $52,000. Thus, Sally and Michael, as the beneficiaries of Cyrus' will, may have each of these assets transferred to them without formal probate by using the affidavit procedure outlined in Chapter 11.

CHAPTER 7

What About Taxes?

ONE OF THE FIRST THINGS people want to know when they learn they will inherit property is whether or not taxes must be paid on the property. Fortunately, the burden of "death taxes" has been reduced substantially over the past few years. Today only relatively large estates have a tax imposed on the transfer of property to the beneficiaries. Most estates have some income tax matters to take care of, but normally these are not onerous.

This chapter will briefly review the various tax returns that may have to be filed in settling a decedent's estate. Tax laws pertaining to decedents' estates and to beneficiaries receiving property from a decedent can be complex, especially if the estate is large. For this reason a detailed discussion of how to prepare a federal estate tax return would require another book. If the estate you are settling has substantial assets or income to report, your best bet (absent a good self-help source) is probably to contact an accountant (or attorney) experienced in the area of estate taxes. Many technicalities are involved, and she may advise you on how to minimize the impact of all taxes on the beneficiaries and the estate. If an accountant (or attorney) prepares the returns, the fee is ordinarily paid from the general assets of the estate or shared by the beneficiaries in proportion to their interests in the estate. Accounting fees are a deduction to the estate either on the estate's income tax returns or on the federal estate tax return, if one is required.

Caution: Tax laws and regulations are bound to change in the years ahead, which means you should not rely on any of the dollar figures or detailed rules discussed here without checking recent IRS publications.

A. Decedent's Final Income Tax

IF THE DECEDENT receives more than a small amount of income in the taxable year in which the death occurred, final income tax returns may have to be filed for that year. The income levels at which returns must be filed may change from year to year. For 1990, for decedents who were not married at the time of death, a final federal income tax return is required if gross income exceeded

$5,300 ($6,100 if the decedent was 65 or older) for the taxable year up to the date of death. Gross income includes all income received in the form of money from property (for example, interest, dividends or rents) as well as income from employment, pension and other public and private benefit programs unless they are exempt from tax. If a married decedent was living in the same household with her spouse at the time of death and was eligible to file a joint return, a final federal income tax return must be filed if the combined gross income of the decedent and her spouse was $9,550 or more for the entire taxable year. The cut-off is $10,200 if one spouse was 65 or older and $10,850 if both spouses were 65 or older. A California income tax return must be filed (regardless of age) if an unmarried decedent had a gross income of $8,000 or over ($16,000 for a married couple).

Martha, an unmarried 68-year-old retired school teacher, earned gross income of $4,000 in the year of her death. Because Martha is a single taxpayer over 65, final income tax returns (both federal and California) do not have to be filed for Martha.

Jack and his wife, Jill, together earned a combined gross income of $20,000 in the year of Jack's death. Jack and Jill were entitled to file joint income tax returns. Final income tax returns, both California and federal, must be filed for Jack because Jack and Jill's combined gross income for the entire taxable year exceeds the $9,550 limit for federal purposes, and the $16,000 limit for California purposes.

If income tax has been withheld from the decedent's wages or she has paid any estimated tax, a final return should be filed even if it is not required. The purpose of such a return is to obtain a refund of the taxes paid or withheld. If a refund is due, you must file Form 1310 (Statement of Person Claiming Refund Due a Deceased Taxpayer) with the return to claim the refund. However, if a surviving spouse files a joint return with the decedent, Form 1310 isn't required.

The final income tax returns (federal Form 1040 and California Form 540) are due on the same day the decedent would have had to file them if he were living—the 15th day of the fourth month following the close of the decedent's regular tax year. This due date is usually April 15 of the year following death, unless the decedent had an accounting year different than a calendar year, which is rarely the case.

If the decedent died in the beginning of the year, before filing a return for the prior year, two returns may have to be filed. For example, if the decedent died on March 1, 1990, before filing his return for 1989, a return must be filed for 1989 on or before April 15, 1990, and the decedent's final return (if required), for the period from January 1, 1990, to March 1, 1990 (the date of death), would be due on April 15, 1991. If for some reason the tax returns cannot be filed on their due date, an extension may be applied for.

Ordinarily, it is the responsibility of the executor or administrator of the estate, assuming one has been formally appointed by the probate court, to file the final returns and any other returns still due for the decedent. Since the income tax returns are for the decedent, and not the estate, they are prepared and signed by the estate representative on behalf of the decedent. In this instance, the representative signs the return on the line indicated for the taxpayer. For example, "Joan Jones, Administrator of the Estate of Anne Rose, Deceased," or "Joan Jones, Executor of the Will of Anne Rose, Deceased."

If there is no court-appointed representative (as where the estate is not probated), the income tax returns should normally be filed by a surviving spouse. The spouse should sign the return and then write in the signature area "filing as surviving spouse." If the final income tax return is a joint return and a legal representative has been appointed (this will be the case only if a probate proceeding is required), both the legal representative and the surviving spouse must sign the return.

If there is no surviving spouse, administrator or executor, it is extremely important that an accountant or the IRS be consulted before property is distributed. In this situation the income tax return should be filed by a family member (usually one who stands to inherit) or a friend who assumes the responsibility of winding up the decedent's affairs. If this is not done, those who inherit the property, or have control of it, must jointly assume responsibility for filing or appoint one of their number to take charge of the estate for this purpose; if they do not, they may be subject to penalties for willful neglect or tax evasion. In cases where there is no court-appointed representative or surviving spouse, the income tax return should be signed by the heirs or beneficiaries jointly (or by one of them acting on behalf of all), followed by the words "Personal Representative(s) of the Estate of Joe Brown, Deceased."

In filling out the income tax return, the decedent's name should be put on the "name" line at the top of the return, followed by the word "deceased" and the date of death. If it is a joint return, both spouses' names should be included with "deceased" after the decedent's name, such as John Smith and Mary Smith, deceased." Also write "Deceased" across the top of the form.

An excellent source of information on this subject is IRS Publication 559, "Tax Information for Survivors, Executors and Administrators," available from the IRS Forms Distribution Center, P.O. Box 12626, Fresno, CA 93778.

B. Fiduciary Income Tax Returns

INCOME RECEIVED on assets in the decedent's estate after he has died is taxable like the income of an individual, and income tax returns must be filed for such income if the estate has more than $600 in gross income in a taxable year for federal purposes, or gross income of $7,000 in one year for California purposes. The tax returns used to report this income are called "fiduciary income tax returns." These should be prepared on federal Form 1041 and California Form 541.

Fiduciary returns are normally required only if a formal probate court proceeding is opened and an estate representative is appointed by the court. The reason for this is that a probate proceeding usually takes from six to nine months to complete, and in many cases even longer; thus, the legal representative of the estate must have a way to report the income received on the decedent's assets during the administration of the estate until the property is distributed to the new owners.

If the probate proceeding takes less than a year, fiduciary returns are required for just the short time the estate is open, assuming the estate receives sufficient income during that period. In this case, the returns are treated as "final" returns and the beneficiaries (not the estate) pay the taxes due, if any, because all income and deductions are passed through to the beneficiaries on a "K-1" form. However, if the estate is open more than a year (or through the Christmas holidays into a new tax year, if a calendar year is being used), the first returns are called the "initial" returns, and subsequent returns must be filed for each year the estate is open. The same forms (federal Form 1041 and California Form 541) are used for all fiduciary returns, and the taxes due, other than on the final returns, are paid from the estate assets.

When a formal probate court proceeding is not required, fiduciary returns are not normally necessary. This is because property is usually transferred promptly, and the income it generates is taxed to and reported on the personal returns of the persons receiving it.

For example, income received on joint tenancy property would be reported by the surviving joint tenant(s), since they became the owner(s) of the property immediately on the death of the decedent. Income received on community or separate property passing to a surviving spouse would, of course, be reported on the surviving spouse's income tax return. Similarly, others who receive property without probate under the simple affidavit procedure used for estates of $60,000 or less (see Chapter 11) would report income from such property on their personal income tax returns.

How to Apply for a Taxpayer Identification Number

If a probate proceeding is opened and fiduciary returns are to be filed, you will need a federal identification number for the estate. Federal Form SS-4 (Application for Employer Identification Number), which may be obtained from the Internal Revenue Service, is used for this purpose (even though the estate has no employees). The number should be requested as early as possible and all institutions reporting income paid on estate assets (banks, brokerage firms, etc.) should be notified immediately to use the new number instead of the decedent's Social Security number. It usually takes two to four weeks to obtain a tax identification number through the mail. If you need the number sooner, call the Fresno Service Center (7:30 a.m. to 2:30 p.m.) at (209) 456-5900, or the Ogden Service Center (6:30 a.m. to 6:00 p.m.) at (801) 625-7645. Whether you call Fresno or Ogden depends on the county where the decedent lived. If you get the number over the phone, you must complete the form before you call and then send in Form SS-4 with the assigned number inserted on the form.

Fiduciary returns are due no later than the 15th day of the fourth month after the end of the estate's taxable year. The taxable year may be a fiscal year chosen by the accountant or estate representative, or a calendar year. Depending on the length of time it takes to close the estate, the first tax year may be less than 12 months. If an asset is sold during probate administration, there may be a capital gain to report on this return.

C. Other Income Tax Returns

IF THE DECEDENT was engaged in a business, it is likely that there will be other returns required, such as business tax returns, employment tax returns, and sales and use tax returns. Also, if the decedent was a shareholder in a closely-held (private) corporation or a partner in a partnership, tax returns will be due. Usually, in these situations, it is appropriate to employ an accountant—often, the accountant who prepared such returns during the decedent's lifetime.

D. "Stepped-Up" Income Tax Basis Rules for Inherited Property

LET'S SLOW DOWN for a moment to understand the tax status of property which is inherited. For example, what are the tax obligations of a person who inherits property and immediately turns around and sells it?

When property, either real or personal (such as stocks), is sold for a price that differs from its tax basis (the market value of property at the time of its purchase or acquisition), the normal rule is that the seller must report the gain on his individual income tax return. Rules change, however, when a death occurs. For both federal and California income tax purposes, when property is acquired by inheritance, it gets a new "stepped-up" basis in the hands of the new owners equal to the fair market value of the property at the date of the decedent's death (or six months later, if the estate representative chooses to use this "alternate valuation date" for federal estate tax purposes). In other words, the new owners do not have to pay tax on the difference between the original purchase price and the current value of the property.

Heidi buys a home in 1967 for $75,000. Heidi dies in 1986 and the property passes under Heidi's will to her daughter, Dessa. The fair market value of the property at the time of Heidi's death is $250,000. Therefore, Dessa's basis for the property for reporting gain or loss when it is sold is $250,000.

In the case of community property, there is a substantial added tax benefit as a result of these stepped-up basis rules. This is because for state and federal income tax purposes the surviving spouse's one-half share of the community property is treated in the same manner as property the surviving spouse acquires from the deceased spouse. Thus, all community property (the decedent's and surviving spouse's shares) and all separate property included in the decedent's estate receives a new stepped-up basis equal to its fair market value as of the deceased spouse's death (or six months later, if the alternate valuation date is used on the federal estate tax return).

In 1960, Paul and Margaret purchase $50,000 worth of stock with community property funds. Paul dies in 1985, and his one-half community interest in the stock passes to Margaret. The fair market value of the stock at the time of Paul's death is $75,000. Therefore, Margaret's one-half interest, as well as Paul's one-half interest, receives a stepped-up basis for California and federal income tax purposes, meaning it will have a total tax basis of $75,000 if Margaret later sells the stock.

Many married couples hold title to their property as joint tenants to avoid probate. Unfortunately, this stepped-up tax basis does not apply to joint tenancy property owned by spouses unless it can be clearly established that the property is in fact community property. Only the decedent's interest in joint tenancy property gets a stepped-up basis for both federal and California income tax purposes. However, if joint tenancy property can be established as true community property held in joint tenancy for convenience, both the decedent's half and the surviving spouse's half will qualify for the stepped-up basis. One way to do this is to transfer the joint tenancy property to the surviving spouse as community property using a Spousal Property Petition, as described in Chapter 15, Section E.

E. Federal Estate Tax Return

A FEDERAL ESTATE tax return (Form 706) is due nine months from the date of death of a United States citizen or resident whose *gross estate* on the date of death exceeds $600,000.

This tax return must be filed if the gross estate is larger than this amount, even if no tax will be due. All assets transferred to the surviving spouse (and interspousal transfers which occur at death) are exempt from federal estate taxes. Thus, if a person dies leaving a million dollars to a surviving spouse, the gross value of the deceased spouse's estate requires the filing of a return, but no tax will be due.

To repeat, it is extremely important to note that for federal estate tax purposes the *gross* value of an estate is used to determine whether or not a federal estate tax return is required, even though the actual tax is computed on the *net* value of all property owned by the decedent at her death. As you will remember from our discussion of the "gross estate" and "net estate" in Chapter 1, the net value is arrived at by taking the total (gross) value of all of the decedent's property and subtracting such things as funeral expenses, expenses of settling the estate and any debts owed by the decedent. If you are hazy on the difference between the gross and net estate, please reread Chapter 1.

Because the value of the gross estate is often much larger than the net estate, many estates may be large enough to require the filing of a federal estate tax return (based on the gross estate), although no tax will be due based on the net estate.

Abel, who dies in 1990, has a gross estate valued at $625,000. A federal estate tax return must be filed because the estate is over the exemption amount of $600,000. However, if Abel had deductions in the way of debts (for example, a mortgage, car payments or money owed to a family member), taxes due, last illness and funeral expenses, and administration expenses (for example, attorneys' fees, accountant's fees, court costs, certification and publication fees) in excess of $25,000, this would bring the value of the net estate below $600,000 and no tax would be due even though a return is required.

Another important thing to remember is that the "net estate" for federal estate tax purposes is usually not the same as the estate that goes through probate, called the "probate estate." Again, as we discuss in Chapter 1, the difference is that the federal estate tax return must report *all* property in which the decedent had any interest when she died, including property that passes outside of probate such as joint tenancy property, pay-on-death accounts (also called Totten trusts), life insurance owned by the decedent, property held in living trusts, pensions, annuities, and profit-sharing and death benefits (regardless of whether payable to named beneficiaries or the decedent's estate). The probate estate, on the other hand, is only the property that must go through formal probate administration.

Ruth dies in 1989, leaving the bulk of her estate to her brother using a living trust and joint tenancy to transfer the property outside of probate. Only securities valued at $120,000 and miscellaneous personal property of little value are subject to probate. Ruth's estate has a gross value of $900,000. When a mortgage on the real property and various expenses associated with her death and the winding up of her affairs are subtracted, the net estate is valued at $680,000 for estate tax purposes. Because $600,000 is exempt from taxation, estate taxes are due on $80,000.

Insurance Note: The decedent's "taxable" estate will include the proceeds of life insurance on the decedent's life if:

- The proceeds are receivable by the estate; or

- The proceeds are receivable by another for the benefit of the estate; or

- The proceeds are not receivable by or for the benefit of the estate but the decedent possessed "incidents of ownership" in the policy.

Often a person who takes out an insurance policy will transfer ownership of the policy to someone else so the policy proceeds will not be included in his taxable estate when he dies. The most common example of this is in the case of a husband and wife. For instance, a husband may purchase an insurance policy on his life, naming his wife as beneficiary, and transfer ownership (including all "incidents of ownership") of the policy to his wife to avoid having to pay taxes on the proceeds upon his death.

In order for the policy proceeds not to be included in the husband's taxable estate, he must have given away complete control over the policy—in other words, he must no longer be able to do anything with it at all. Put another way, "incidents of ownership" includes not only the ownership of the policy in a technical, legal sense, but also the right of the insured or the insured's estate to the economic benefits of the policy. Thus, if the decedent had the power to change beneficiaries, to revoke an assignment, to obtain a loan against the cash value, to pledge the policy for a loan, or to surrender or cancel the policy, then he possessed "incidents of ownership" and the policy proceeds will be included in his taxable estate on his death even if he thought he had transferred policy ownership to another. If you are confused about this, check with the insurance company (see Chapter 2, Section C11), or an accountant or attorney experienced in estate tax matters.

To determine whether a federal estate tax return is required, you must compute the amount of the gross estate. This will be the total of Column D in the Schedule of Assets you prepared in Chapter 5. To arrive at the "taxable estate," subtract the total amount of all deductions listed on the last page of the Schedule of Assets.

Thereafter, many steps are needed to compute the actual amount of tax due, the details of which are beyond the scope of this book. The IRS has published a 20-page set of instructions for completing the federal estate tax return, which is very helpful, called "Instructions for Form 706." The instructions are usually provided with the Form 706 itself. Another IRS publication, called "Federal Estate and Gift Taxes" (Publication 448), is also helpful.

Briefly, to compute the amount of tax due, you must add to the "taxable estate" any taxable gifts[1] made after December 31, 1976, that are not included in the gross estate. Then, a "tentative tax" is arrived at by using the Unified Tax Rate Schedule from Table A in the instructions. (See Federal Estate Tax Return Chart.) If any gift taxes were paid by the decedent on gifts made after 1976, they are subtracted from the tentative tax. The actual tax payable is then determined by subtracting the credit allowed against federal estate taxes for the year of the decedent's death. (See Federal Estate Tax Return Chart.) Then, a credit for state death taxes is determined from Table C of the chart, and the amount of this credit is subtracted from the subtotal to produce a net tax payable.

---

[1]A taxable gift is a gratuitous transfer of property to another person. Gifts of less than $10,000 made to one person in one year are excluded from tax.

Molly Bright dies in 1990 with a gross estate of $769,000 and total allowable deductions of $39,000. She gave gifts to her grandchildren amounting to $12,000 in 1979, for which a gift tax of $300 was assessed. The death taxes in her estate would be computed as follows:

Gross estate	*$769,000*
Subtract allowable deductions	*(39,000)*
Taxable estate	*$730,000*
Add lifetime gifts made after December 31, 1976	*12,000*
	$742,000
Tentative tax on $742,000 (from Table A of instructions) ($155,800 + 37% of $242,000)	*$245,340*
Subtract unified credit for year of death (Table B of instructions)	*(192,800)*
Subtract credit for state death taxes (Table C of instructions) ($18,000 + 4.8% of $30,000)	*(19,440)*
Net tax due the federal government	*$ 33,100*

Note: A California estate tax return must also be filed for Molly's estate (see Section F, below), and a tax of $19,440 will be due to the state of California. The federal government allows a deduction for what goes to the state (in this case, $19,440), so the federal estate tax due is $33,100 instead of $52,540.

The federal estate tax, if any is due, must be paid in full when the return is filed unless an extension has been granted. The estate usually pays an estimated amount of tax when applying for the extension. When an extension to file and pay is granted, the estate will still be charged interest on any unpaid tax from the due date until it is paid. If the return is not filed on the due date (or on the extension date), there is a penalty of 5% of the amount of the tax for each month or part of a month between the date on which it should have been filed and the date on which it finally is filed, up to a maximum of 25%. The penalty is in addition to interest charged.

Most wills have a provision saying all taxes are to be paid from the residue of the estate. If there is no will, or the will makes no such provision and there are two or more beneficiaries, then the taxes are charged to each of the beneficiaries who receive a share of the estate, according to their percentage interests. Your accountant should be able to compute the amount chargeable to each beneficiary. Should there be insufficient cash to pay the taxes, then estate property must be sold or money borrowed to raise the necessary funds. For good cause (for example, hardship to the estate), an extension of time to pay will sometimes be granted on request.

The federal estate tax return (Form 706) may be obtained from an Internal Revenue Service office that furnishes tax information and forms generally (don't forget to ask for the instructions). It is a long and detailed tax return (16 pages), which includes many schedules. The schedules are used as worksheets to figure the amounts to be entered on the appropriate lines of pages 1 through 3. If you are dealing with a very simple estate and are used to preparing your own tax returns, you may wish to consider preparing Form 706 yourself, if one is required.

F. California Estate Tax Return

IN JUNE 1982, California's inheritance tax was repealed by the voters, and there is no inheritance tax due the state for decedents who die after that time. Nevertheless, when a federal estate tax return is filed, you may still have to pay a tax to the state of California. The amount due to California will be the same amount which is allowed as a state tax credit on the federal estate tax return. In other words, some of the tax that would go to the federal government goes to the state instead, so the estate actually pays no more. If a federal estate tax return isn't filed, there is no California estate tax.

Federal Estate Tax Return
(Table A of Instructions)

Unified Federal Estate Tax Rate Schedule			
Column A	Column B	Column C	Column D
net taxable estate over	net taxable estate not over	Tax on amount in column A	Rate of tax on excess over amount in column A
			(Percent)
0	$10,000	0	18
$10,000	20,000	$1,800	20
20,000	40,000	3,800	22
40,000	60,000	8,200	24
60,000	80,000	13,000	26
80,000	100,000	18,200	28
100,000	150,000	23,800	30
150,000	250,000	38,800	32
250,000	500,000	70,800	34
500,000	750,000	155,800	37
750,000	1,000,000	248,300	39
1,000,000	1,250,000	345,800	41
1,250,000	1,500,000	448,300	43
1,500,000	2,000,000	555,800	45
2,000,000	2,500,000	780,800	49
2,500,000	3,000,000	1,025,800	53
3,000,000	infinity		55 *

*This will be reduced to 50% after 1992.

Federal Estate Tax Return
(Table B of Instructions)

Decedents dying in	Credit against federal estate tax	Equivalent estate tax exemption
1981	$ 47,000	$175,625
1982	62,800	225,000
1983	79,300	275,000
1984	96,300	325,000
1985	121,800	400,000
1986	155,800	500,000
1987 and thereafter	192,800	600,000

Federal Estate Tax Return
(Table C of Instructions)

Maximum Credit for State Death Taxes (Based on federal adjusted taxable estate which is the federal taxable estate reduced by $60,000)			
Adjusted taxable estate equal to or more than— (1)	Adjusted taxable estate less than— (2)	Credit on amount in column (1) (3)	Rates of credit on excess over amount in column (1) (4)
0	$40,000	0	Percent None
$40,000	90,000	0	0.8
90,000	140,000	$400	1.6
140,000	240,000	1,200	2.4
240,000	440,000	3,600	3.2
440,000	640,000	10,000	4.0
640,000	840,000	18,000	4.8
840,000	1,040,000	27,600	5.6
1,040,000	1,540,000	38,800	6.4
1,540,000	2,040,000	70,800	7.2
2,040,000	2,540,000	106,800	8.0
2,540,000	3,040,000	146,800	8.8
3,040,000	3,540,000	190,800	9.6
3,540,000	4,040,000	238,800	10.4
4,040,000	5,040,000	290,800	11.2
5,040,000	6,040,000	402,800	12.0
6,040,000	7,040,000	522,800	12.8
7,040,000	8,040,000	650,800	13.6
8,040,000	9,040,000	786,800	14.4
9,040,000	10,040,000	930,800	15.2
10,040,000	....	1,082,800	16.0

The California estate tax return is a yellow, one-page form that may be obtained by calling the State Controller's office in your district. The return is due on the same date as the federal estate tax return (nine months from the date of the decedent's death). As in the case of the federal estate tax return, interest and penalties are assessed if it is not filed and the tax paid on time.

G. Tax Liability of Typical Decedents and Their Estates

LET'S LOOK AT some typical estates and see what tax returns must be filed for each.

Example 1: Estate of Abigail Apple, Deceased

Abigail died on October 11, 1986, at the age of 66. Her gross estate of $300,000 consisted of her one-half interest in community property owned by Abigail and her husband, Alfred, who is 68. Her estate did not require probate because all property passed outright to Alfred under Abigail's will. Abigail and Alfred received interest and dividend income of $20,000 during the period of January 1, 1986 to October 11, 1986 (the date of Abigail's death), one half of which ($10,000) was attributable to Abigail. Alfred is responsible for seeing that final income tax returns, both California and federal, are filed for Abigail for the period January 1, 1986 to October 11, 1986. They are due April 15, 1987. The returns for Abigail may or may not be joint returns with her husband, depending on which is the most advantageous way to file. No federal estate tax return or California estate tax return is required, because Abigail's estate is not large enough to require the filing of these returns. Fiduciary income tax returns are also not required, because Abigail's estate did not require probate and no legal representative was appointed. Alfred will report any future income he

receives from assets in Abigail's estate on his own personal income tax returns.

Example 2: Estate of Joe Brown, Deceased

Joe, a bachelor, died on March 12, 1990, owning a gross estate of $800,000. The estate consisted of a condominium worth $500,000, stock valued at $200,000, life insurance of $50,000, a 1980 Mercedes Benz automobile worth $20,000 and two bank accounts having a total balance of $30,000. Deductions from the estate amounted to $40,000, consisting of debts outstanding of $15,000, income taxes due of $15,000 and last illness and funeral expenses of $10,000, leaving Joe with a taxable estate of $760,000. Probate court proceedings were required for Joe's estate, and his brother, Jack, was appointed executor of the will by the probate court. Joe received a total of $30,000 from his employment, along with dividends and interest, for the period January 1, 1990 to March 12, 1990 (the date of death). Joe's income tax returns for 1989 had not yet been filed at the time he died. The tax returns that Joe's brother, Jack, must file as legal representative of Joe's estate are:

a. Joe's 1989 personal income tax returns, both California and federal, due April 15, 1990;

b. Joe's final income tax returns, both California and federal, for the period January 1, 1990 to March 12, 1990 (the date of Joe's death), due April 15, 1991;

c. Fiduciary income tax returns (Form 1041), reporting income received during the period of probate administration on the estate assets from March 13, 1990 (the beginning of the estate's income tax year), until the estate is closed and the assets distributed to the beneficiaries;

d. Federal estate tax return (Form 706), due on or before December 12, 1990 (nine months from the date of death); Joe's estate will owe $38,520 for federal estate tax;

e. California estate tax return (Form ET-1), also due December 12, 1990; Joe's estate will owe $20,880 in California estate tax.

Example 3: Estate of Ralph Rambler, Deceased

Reba and Ralph Rambler were married 25 years when Ralph died on April 20, 1986. His estate consisted of his one-half community property interest in a home in Pacific Palisades with a fair market value of $800,000, a six-unit apartment building in Santa Monica valued at $500,000, stocks valued at $200,000, a Cadillac automobile worth $20,000, and $200,000 in a money market fund. Ralph's will named Reba as executor and distributed his one-half interest in the house, automobile and money market account to Reba, and the apartment building and stocks in trust to his three children. Therefore, his estate required probate. Reba and Ralph received income of $125,000 during the period January 1, 1986 to April 20, 1986 (date of death), one-half of which was attributable to Ralph. Reba is responsible for seeing that the following tax returns are filed:

a. Ralph's final personal income tax returns for 1986, both California and federal, due April 15, 1987, covering the period January 1, 1986 to April 20, 1986, which may be joint returns with Reba;

b. Fiduciary income tax returns for Ralph's estate for the period beginning April 21, 1986, until the estate is closed;

c. Federal estate tax return (Form 706) due on or before January 20, 1987. Ralph's gross estate is $860,000 (one-half the value of the community property). For federal estate tax purposes, his estate will receive a deduction of $610,000 for his one-half interest in the property going outright to Reba (house, automobile and money market fund), leaving a taxable estate of approximately $250,000, which is below the amount for which a tax will be due. Thus, although a Form 706 must be filed, no federal estate tax is due.

d. California estate tax return, also due on or before January 20, 1987. No California estate tax will be due since the credit for state death taxes on the Form 706 was zero.

CHAPTER 8

Transferring Title to Real Property

IN THIS CHAPTER we, principally, discuss how to transfer real property owned by the decedent to its new owners. This basic nuts and bolts information is relevant no matter whether the real property is left in a will, passes by intestate succession or passes outside the will via one or another of the probate avoidance devices.

A. How to Transfer Property Ownership After Death

TO TRANSFER REAL PROPERTY belonging to a decedent, you will need to use a deed, affidavit or court order, depending on the way the decedent held title to the property and to whom it is left.

After you've obtained the appropriate document, it must be recorded in the office of the County Recorder where the real property is located. Section C explains how.

1. Transfers of Real Property to a Surviving Spouse

If the real property (whether community or separate) goes outright to the surviving spouse (either under the decedent's will or by intestate succession), you will need a Spousal Property Order, as explained in Chapter 15, unless the decedent's deed specifically shows title held "as community property" with the surviving spouse. In this latter case you may be able to clear title in the surviving spouse's name with a simple affidavit, which is also explained in Chapter 15.

2. Transfers of Real Property to a Surviving Joint Tenant

If title was held in joint tenancy, then an Affidavit—Death of Joint Tenant, which is explained in Chapter 10, may be used to remove the decedent's name from the title. However, for tax reasons discussed in Chapter 7, Section D, if spouses held community property in joint tenancy, the surviving spouse may instead want to use the Spousal Property Order procedure explained in Chapter 15.

3. Transfers of Real Property Left in a Living Trust

If title to the property is held in a living trust, a new deed must be prepared, usually by the successor trustee, transferring title to the beneficiaries named in the trust document. We show you how to accomplish this in Chapter 12.

4. Transfers of Real Property Subject to Formal Probate

If the decedent's interest in the real property goes to her heirs or the beneficiaries in her will (other than a surviving spouse), you must obtain an Order for Final Distribution through a formal probate court proceeding. The Order transfers ownership to the heirs or beneficiaries. A sample of the first page of an Order is shown below; note that it has recording information in the upper left corner. Instructions for preparing an Order are in Chapter 14, Step 19. However, see Chapter 11 for short-cut methods of transferring real property worth less than $60,000.

B. Basic Information on Recording Documents

ANY DOCUMENT AFFECTING title to real property (deed, court order, affidavit or deed of trust) should be recorded in the office of the County Recorder for the county in which the real property is located. This doesn't mean that an unrecorded document is null or void. Recording a deed isn't what conveys the title—delivery of the deed itself accomplishes this.

Of what significance, then, is recording? Recording a deed gives public notice of a person's rights in property, called "constructive notice" by lawyers. It informs the world of the ownership of the property and who has a mortgage on it. Once a deed is recorded, everyone (for example, banks, potential buyers and title companies) is said to have notice of this information. For example, if you buy a lot without a title search and do not check the public records yourself, you are considered to have knowledge of whatever the records would have shown. If there is a judgment lien against the property, you are responsible for paying it even though no one ever told you about it. In other words, you had "constructive notice" of all information the Recorder's office would have disclosed had you checked. This is why when you buy a house or other real property, the title company always checks the records at the Recorder's office to make sure the seller owns clear title to the property. Recording, then, is an orderly system of establishing ownership rights in and lien rights against property.

If a deed isn't recorded, the Recorder's office will not have current property ownership information, and if someone relies on the out-of-date information in good faith, she will be protected. For example, if you have some ownership right in property and do not record it, it can be cut off by a competing right acquired by another person without knowledge of yours.

The recording of a document takes effect the moment it is received in the Recorder's office. A deed, mortgage or court order is stamped as received for recording at the hour and minute received and given a document or instrument number (sometimes a book and page number are used). A photocopy is then made for the Recorder's records and bound with other similar documents in books of "Official Records" in the Recorder's office, which are there for the public to inspect. Using an alphabetical grantor-grantee index, one may find the proper page of these records to consult for a particular document. After a document is recorded, the original is returned to the person named on the deed to receive it—usually the one who requested the recording.

C. Change in Ownership Statements

USUALLY, A TRANSFER of an interest in real property or a mobile home triggers a reassessment for local property tax purposes. For this reason, certain forms must be filed with local officials whenever there is a change in ownership of real property.

1. Preliminary Change in Ownership Report

Whenever a deed, court order or other document affecting title to real property is recorded, it must be accompanied by a Preliminary Change in Ownership Report. A sample is shown below. You can get a copy by calling the county assessor's office. The form must be filed by the new owner at the time the transfer document is recorded. If the document is not recorded, the form must be filed within 45 days of the date of the change in ownership. (Rev. & Taxation Code § 480(a).)

Preliminary Change in Ownership Report

JOHN J LYNCH
COUNTY ASSESSOR
COUNTY OF LOS ANGELES
500 West Temple Street
Los Angeles California 90012-2770

THIS SPACE FOR RECORDERS USE

PRELIMINARY CHANGE OF OWNERSHIP REPORT
THIS REPORT IS NOT A PUBLIC DOCUMENT

(To be completed by transferee (buyer) prior to transfer of the subject property in accordance with Section 480.3 of the Revenue and Taxation Code.)

FOR ASSESSOR'S USE ONLY

Cluster:	
OC1	OC2
DT	INT
RC	SP $
DTT $	# PCL

SELLER/TRANSFEROR __Charity Taylor, deceased__

BUYER/TRANSFEREE __Jon Taylor__

ASSESSORS IDENTIFICATION NUMBER(S) __123 - 456 - 7890__

PROPERTY ADDRESS OR LOCATION __3311 - 22nd St.,__
__Santa Monica, California 90405__

A Preliminary Change in Ownership Report must be filed with each conveyance in the County Recorder's office for the particular where the property is located that particular form may be used in all 58 counties of California.

MAIL TAX INFORMATION TO

NAME __Jon Taylor__

ADDRESS __3311 - 22nd Street, Santa Monica, California 90405__

The property which you acquired may be subject to a supplemental assessment in an amount to be determined by the Los Angeles County Assessor. For further information on your supplemental roll obligation, please call the Los Angeles County Assessor at (213) 974-3211

PART I: TRANSFER INFORMATION   Please answer all questions

YES NO
- A. Is this transfer solely between husband and wife? (Addition of a spouse, death of a spouse, divorce settlement, etc.)
- B. Is this transaction only a correction of the name(s) of the person(s) holding title to the property? (For example, a name change upon marriage)
- C. Is this document recorded to create, terminate, or reconvey a lender's interest in the property?
- D. Is this transaction recorded only to create, terminate, or reconvey a security interest (e.g. cosigner)?
- E. Is this document recorded to substitute a trustee under a deed of trust, mortgage or other similar document?
- F. Did this transfer result in the creation of a joint tenancy in which the seller (transferor) remains as one of the joint tenants?
- G. Does this transfer return property to the person who created the joint tenancy (original transferor)?
- H. Is this transfer of property
  - 1. to a trust for the benefit of the grantor, or grantor's spouse?
  - 2. to a trust revocable by the transferor?
  - 3. to a trust from which the property reverts to the grantor within 12 years?
- I. If this property is subject to a lease, is the remaining lease term 35 years or more including written options?
- J. Is this a transfer from parents to children or from children to parents?
- K. Is this transaction to replace a principal residence located in _____ County by a person 55 years of age or older?

If you checked yes to J or K, an applicable claim form must be filed with the County Assessor.
Please provide any other information that would help the Assessor to understand the nature of the transfer

IF YOU HAVE ANSWERED "YES" TO ANY OF THE ABOVE QUESTIONS EXCEPT K, PLEASE SIGN AND DATE, OTHERWISE COMPLETE BALANCE OF THE FORM.

PART II: OTHER TRANSFER INFORMATION   (Not applicable)

A. Date of transfer if other than recording date
B. Type of Transfer. Please check appropriate box.
  - ☐ Purchase ☐ Foreclosure ☐ Gift ☐ Trade or Exchange
  - ☐ Contract of Sale – Date of Contract
  - ☐ Inheritance – Date of Death _____ ☐ Other: Please explain
  - ☐ Creation of lease. ☐ Assignment of a lease. ☐ Termination of a lease
  - Date lease began _____
  - Original term in years (including written options)
  - Remaining term in years (including written options)
C. Was only a partial interest in the property transferred? ☐ Yes ☐ No
  If yes, indicate the percentage transferred _____

PRELIMINARY CHANGE OF OWNERSHIP REPORT

Please answer, to the best of your knowledge, all applicable questions, sign and date. If a question does not apply, indicate with "N/A".

PART III: PURCHASE PRICE & TERMS OF SALE   (Not applicable)

A. CASH DOWN PAYMENT OR Value of Trade or Exchange (excluding closing cost)   Amount $

B. FIRST DEED OF TRUST @ _____ % interest for _____ years Pymts./Mo. = $ _____ (Prin. & Int. only) Amount $
  - ☐ FHA _____ (Prin. & Int. only) Amount $
  - ☐ Conventional   ☐ Fixed Rate   ☐ New Loan
  - ☐ VA   ☐ Variable Rate   ☐ Assumed Existing Loan Balance
  - ☐ Cal-Vet   ☐ All Inclusive D.T. $ _____ (Wrapped)   ☐ Bank or Savings & Loan
  - ☐ Balloon Payment ☐ Yes ☐ No   ☐ Loan Carried by Seller   ☐ Finance Company
  - Due Date _____   Amount $

C. SECOND DEED OF TRUST @ _____ % interest for _____ years Pymts./Mo = $ _____ (Prin. & Int. only) Amount $
  - ☐ Bank or Savings & Loan   ☐ Fixed Rate   ☐ New Loan
  - ☐ Loan Carried by Seller   ☐ Variable Rate   ☐ Assumed Existing Loan Balance
  - ☐ Balloon Payment ☐ Yes ☐ No   Due Date _____   Amount $

D. OTHER FINANCING Is other financing involved not covered in (b) or (c) above? ☐ Yes ☐ No
  Type _____ @ _____ % interest for _____ years Pymts./Mo = $ _____ (Prin. & Int. only) Amount $
  - ☐ Bank or Savings & Loan   ☐ Fixed Rate   ☐ New Loan
  - ☐ Loan Carried by Seller   ☐ Variable Rate   ☐ Assumed Existing Loan Balance
  - ☐ Balloon Payment ☐ Yes ☐ No   Due Date _____   Amount $

E. IMPROVEMENT BOND ☐ Yes ☐ No   Outstanding Balance   Amount $

F. TOTAL PURCHASE PRICE (or acquisition price, if traded or exchanged include real estate commission if paid.)   Total Items A through E $

G. WAS A BROKER INVOLVED IN THIS SALE? ☐ Yes ☐ No
  Please explain any special terms of financing and any other information that would help the Assessor understand the purchase price and terms of sale

PART IV: PROPERTY INFORMATION   (Not applicable)

A. IS PERSONAL PROPERTY INCLUDED IN THE PURCHASE PRICE? ☐ Yes ☐ No   (Attach itemized list of personal property)
  (other than a mobilehome subject to local property tax)?
  If yes, enter the value of the personal property included in the purchase price $

B. IS THIS PROPERTY INTENDED AS YOUR PRINCIPAL RESIDENCE? ☐ Yes ☐ No
  If yes, enter date of occupancy _____ Month _____ / _____ Day _____ 19 _____ or intended occupancy 19 _____

C. TYPE OF PROPERTY TRANSFERRED:
  - ☐ Single-Family residence   ☐ Agricultural   ☐ Timeshare
  - ☐ Multiple-Family residence (no. of units _____)   ☐ Co-op/Own-your-own   ☐ Mobilehome
  - ☐ Commercial/Industrial   ☐ Condominium   ☐ Unimproved lot
  - ☐ Other (Description _____)

D. DOES THE PROPERTY PRODUCE INCOME? ☐ Yes ☐ No
E. IF THE ANSWER TO QUESTION D IS YES, IS THE INCOME FROM:
  - ☐ Lease/Rent   ☐ Contract   ☐ Mineral rights   ☐ Other-explain
F. WHAT WAS THE CONDITION OF THE PROPERTY AT THE TIME OF SALE?
  - ☐ Good   ☐ Average   ☐ Fair   ☐ Poor

Enter here or on an attached sheet, any other information that would assist the Assessor in determining value of the property such as the physical condition of the property, restrictions, etc.

I certify that the foregoing is true, correct and complete to the best of my knowledge and belief.

Signed _____   Date __April 1, 1989__
New Owner/Legal Representative/Corporate Officer

Please Print Name of New Owner/Legal Representative/Corporate Officer __Jon Taylor__
Phone No. where you are available from 8:00 a.m. – 5:00 p.m. (213) 369-5670
(NOTE: The Assessor may contact you for further information)

If a document evidencing a change of ownership is presented to the recorder for recordation without the concurrent filing of a PRELIMINARY CHANGE OF OWNERSHIP REPORT, the recorder may charge an additional recording fee of twenty dollars ($20). The additional fee shall not be charged if the document is accompanied by an affidavit that the transferee is not a resident of California.

AFFIDAVIT OF NONRESIDENT TRANSFEREE

The Transferee (buyer) named above is a resident of _____ and not a resident of the State of California.

Signed _____   Date _____
New Owner/Legal Representative/Corporate Officer

2. Change in Ownership Statement

In a formal probate court proceeding, if the estate contains real property, the executor or administrator must also file a Change in Ownership Statement with the county *assessor's* office when the inventory and appraisement is filed with the court. (Rev. & Taxation Code § 480(b).) (This statement is in addition to the Preliminary Change in Ownership Report, discussed above, which is filed when the actual transfer is made.) Each county has prepared its own form for this purpose, which is similar to the one-page form used in Los Angeles County, shown in Chapter 14. This form must be filed in each county where the decedent owned real property at the time of death, accompanied by a copy of the death certificate.

The assessor's office treats the date of death as the date of the change in ownership, regardless of when title is actually transferred to the new owner.

3. Claim for Reassessment Exclusion

Transfers to a surviving spouse or to a revocable trust are excluded from reassessment. In addition, transfers of a personal residence (and certain other property) between parents and their children (including transfers into and out of trusts) may be excluded. (Rev. & Taxation Code Sec. 63.1.) "Children" includes sons- and daughters-in-law, stepchildren and children adopted prior to age 18. Even though these transfers are excluded from reassessment, a Preliminary Change in Ownership Report is still required. To claim the parent-child exclusion, you must file a "Claim for Reassessment Exclusion for Transfer Between Parent and Child," sometimes called "Proposition 58 Claim Form," with the county assessor's office. To obtain the form, call the assessor's office.

D. How to Record Your Document Transferring Title

RECORDING A TRANSFER document is not difficult; you can even do it by mail. Just follow these steps:

1. Select and prepare the appropriate document from the ones discussed in Section C.

2. Type or print the assessor's parcel number on the document. (You can find this number on the property tax bill.) Some printed forms of grant deeds and affidavits have a place to insert the number; if not (as in the case of a court order), the number should be typed or printed vertically in the margin on the side of the document preceded by the letters "A.P.N."

3. Type the name and address of the person to whom the document should be returned, and where the property tax bills are to be sent, on the document, usually in the upper left-hand corner. This person is usually the new owner. Printed documents have a place for this as a rule, but in the case of a court order the name and address of either the surviving spouse or the estate representative will already be typed in the upper left-hand corner of the document. Often these individuals are also the ones requesting the recording of the court order. If this is the case, you may type above the name and address the words: "Recording requested by, and after recording mail to:" If the person is also the new owner of the real property, you may type below his or her name and address, "Mail tax statements same as above." However, if the person who requests the recording of the court order is not the new owner of the property, you should type at the bottom of either the first or last page of the court order the words, "Mail tax statements to: (name and address of new owner)," or the tax statements will continue to go to the old address. There is not a lot of room on court documents, but you can usually squeeze all the information in. (If the new owner is a minor, the property must be held in the name of a court-appointed guardian for the minor. If one has not been appointed, an attorney should be consulted.)

Sample Order of Final Distribution
on Waiver of Account
(First Page)

RECORDING REQUESTED BY AND,
WHEN RECORDED, MAIL TO:

1

JON TAYLOR
3311-22nd Street
2   Santa Monica, California 90405
Telephone: (213) 209-4490
3   (Mail tax statements same
        as above)
4

5

6   SUPERIOR COURT OF CALIFORNIA

7   COUNTY OF LOS ANGELES

8   Estate of   )   No. p 555 666
9   )
            CHARITY TAYLOR,   )   ORDER OF FINAL DISTRIBUTION
10   )
                    Deceased,   )   ON WAIVER OF ACCOUNT
11   )
)
12   )

13   JON TAYLOR, as Executor of the Will of the above-named decedent,

14   having filed a petition for final distribution without rendering account,

15   and the report and petition coming on this day, September 27, 1985,

16   regularly for hearing in Department No. 11 of the above-entitled Court, the

17   Honorable Andrew Specht, Judge presiding, the Court, after examining

18   the petition and hearing the evidence, finds that due notice of hearing of

19   the petition has

20   been regularly given as prescribed by law; that all of the allegations of

21   the petition are true; that no federal estate taxes were due from the

22   estate; that all personal property taxes due

23   and payable by said estate have been paid, and that said report and account

24   should be approved and distribution ordered as prayed for;

25   IT IS THEREFORE ORDERED, ADJUDGED AND DECREED by the Court   that

26   notice to creditors has be duly given as required by law, and that

27

28   (This is a court-ordered conveyance or decree that is not pursuant

            to a sale (R & T 11911) and is exempt from tax)

4. The document that you plan to record must normally be the original document, and the signatures of the persons signing the document must be acknowledged by a notary public, except for joint tenancy transfers, which only require a declaration under penalty of perjury. (See Chapter 10.) However, if you record a court order, it must be a copy certified by the court clerk.

5. A recording fee must accompany the document. This is usually around $5 for the first page, and $2 for each additional page. (Call the Recorder's office for the exact amount.) An additional $10 "monument" fee is collected on some property if it has a longer "metes and bounds" legal description.

6. Sometimes a documentary transfer tax is collected by the Recorder's office on the recording of certain documents. Usually, this applies only when real property is sold. Probate court orders are not subject to this tax.

However, Recorders in some counties require that the following statement appear on the face of the probate order: "This is a court-ordered conveyance or decree that is not pursuant to sale (Rev. & Tax Code § 11911) and is exempt from tax." An Affidavit—Death of Joint Tenant is also exempt from tax when it is recorded, but no statement to this effect is needed when the affidavit is recorded.

7. Record the document along with a Preliminary Change in Ownership Report at the County Recorder's office in which the property is located. If the real property is subject to a mortgage, the new owner should notify the person or company collecting the payments on the mortgage of the name and address of the new owner. Below is a sample letter that may be adapted for use when sending in documents for recording.

```
County Recorder
227 North Broadway
Los Angeles, CA 90012


RE: Estate of John Doe, Deceased

Enclosed is a certified copy of the Court Order for Final
Distribution made in the estate of the above-named decedent. Also
enclosed is a Preliminary Change in Ownership Report.

Will you please record the Order, and after it is recorded return
it to the name and address of the person indicated in the upper
left-hand corner of the first page. A check in the amount of
$15.00 is enclosed to cover your recording fee.

Thank-you for your assistance.

     Very truly yours,



     _____
     (your signature)
```

E. Mortgages

WHEN SOMEONE DIES and leaves real property subject to a mortgage or encumbrance, as a rule the real property passes to the new owner along with the encumbrance, unless the decedent's will provides otherwise. The new owner of the property then becomes responsible for making the payment on the mortgage, taxes, etc. After the property is officially transferred, it is customary to notify the person or entity collecting the mortgage payments of the name and address of the new owner.

CHAPTER 9

How to Transfer Securities

SECURITIES, INCLUDING stocks, bonds, debentures or mutual fund shares owned by a decedent, must be re-registered in the name(s) of the new owners at some point during settlement of the decedent's estate. The actual transfers, except in the case of mutual fund shares, are made by a "transfer agent," whose name and address normally appear on the face of the stock or bond certificate. However, because transfer agents change frequently, it is a good idea to write or call in advance (or check with a stock brokerage firm) to verify the name and address of the current transfer agent before mailing any of the transfer documents. A sample form letter is shown below.

Sample

```
     (Address of stock transfer agent)

               Re:_____ ,deceased

               Date of death:

     Dear People:

       This is to notify you that the above-named decedent died on the date
     indicated.

       The decedent's records indicate that at the time of death he was the
     owner of the following described securities registered in the name(s) of:

     Name of                    Par Value or
     Certificate    Number      Number of Shares    Type of Security    Company




       Please indicate on the enclosed copy of this letter whether or not this
     agrees with your records. If so, please advise the documentation you will
     require to transfer title to the new owner(s). If you do not currently act
     as transfer agent for the company, please advise the name and address of
     the current transfer agent.

       Thank-you for your assistance.

               Very truly yours,
```

Shares in mutual funds are transferred by the company that manages the fund, and it should be contacted to find out its requirements for selling, redeeming or changing record ownership of the shares. You may get the name, address and telephone number of whom to contact from the last monthly statement. Usually, the same documentation discussed in this chapter for other types of securities is required to transfer mutual funds.

A. Documents Required to Transfer Securities

SEVERAL DOCUMENTS are required to transfer securities after a death, depending on how the securities were originally owned (and sometimes depending on who they are transferred to).

1. Transferring Securities in a Probate Court Proceeding

You will normally need a probate court order to transfer securities if the estate exceeds $60,000 in value and the securities were either in the decedent's name alone or with another person as tenants in common.[1] Ownership as tenants in common normally occurs when an asset is owned by two or more people, unless title is specifically held as community property or in joint tenancy.

Note: If the securities pass outright to a surviving spouse, whether community property or separate property, go to Item 3, below. If the estate is under $60,000, see Item 4, below.

---

[1]The procedure for obtaining the court order is explained in Chapter 15.

When a decedent owned securities as a tenant in common with a surviving person, the decedent's interest is subject to probate and the surviving person's is not. Although two new certificates must be issued, one in the name of the new owner of the decedent's interest, and one in the name of the surviving tenant in common, a probate court order is required only for the transfer of the decedent's shares.

Marsha died owning 300 shares of stock as a tenant in common with her sister Clara. A new certificate for 150 shares must be issued in the name(s) of the person(s) who receive Marsha's one-half interest, and another certificate issued in the name of Clara as sole owner of the other 150 shares.

Documents to be submitted to the transfer agent:

a. Original stock certificate, bond or debenture;

b. Certified copy of letters testamentary or letters of administration (Letters), certified within 60 days before they are sent to the transfer agent (we tell you how to get these in Chapter 13);

Note: Although the court issues an order at the end of probate naming the persons that the securities are to be transferred to, the transfer agent only requires a certified copy of the Letters.

c. A stock power signed by the personal representative, with the signature guaranteed (see Section B of this chapter);

d. Affidavit of Domicile, signed by you as personal representative, with signature notarized (see Section C of this chapter); and

e. Transmittal letter requesting the transfer, and giving the name(s), Social Security number(s), and address(es) of the new owner(s) (see Section D of this chapter).

2. Transfer of Securities to a Surviving Joint Tenant

Securities registered in joint tenancy form will usually appear as "John Brown and/or Ruth Brown, as joint tenants" or, instead of "as joint tenants," it might say "JTRS" (Joint Tenants with Right of Survivorship) or "WROS" (With Right of Survivorship). All of these terms and abbreviations mean the same thing.

It is relatively easy to transfer securities held in joint tenancy, as no probate is required. This means transfer of joint tenancy property can be done almost immediately after death.

If there are no surviving joint tenants, the stocks belong to the last joint tenant to die and will be subject to probate in her estate. If it has not already been done, title must still be formally transferred to the last surviving joint tenant before it is then again transferred as part of her estate. To accomplish this, the transfer agent will need a certified copy of the death certificate of the first joint tenant to die, along with the other documents listed below.

Assume that Jerome and Alvah own a house as joint tenants. Alvah dies, which means that Jerome is the sole owner of the house. If Jerome does not have the deed changed over to his name and, subsequently, dies with it still showing the joint tenancy, the joint tenancy deed must first be transferred to Jerome before it can again be transferred to whomever inherits the house under his estate.

Documents required:

a. Original stock certificate, bond, debenture or other security;

b. Stock power signed by surviving joint tenant(s) with signature guaranteed (see Section B of this chapter);

c. Certified copy of death certificate (see Chapter 2);

d. Affidavit of Domicile signed by surviving joint tenant(s), with signature(s) notarized (see Section C of this chapter); and

e. Transmittal letter signed by surviving joint tenant(s) (see Section D of this chapter).

3. Transfer of Securities to a Surviving Spouse

If the decedent was married at the time of death she may very likely have owned securities as community property with her spouse. She may also have owned other securities which were her separate property. Remember, however, that securities can be held in the name of either spouse alone and still be community property. If the securities are already held in the name of the surviving spouse, no transfer is required. See Chapter 4 for a detailed discussion of community property and separate property.

If the securities have been left to a surviving spouse outright by a will, or pass to a surviving spouse by intestate succession, you may make the actual transfer easily with the following documents.

Documents required:

a. Original certificate, bond or debenture;

b. Stock power, signed by surviving spouse, with signature guaranteed (see Section B of this chapter);

c. Certified copy of Spousal Property Order (we discuss how to get this in Chapter 15);

d. Affidavit of Domicile, signed by surviving spouse, with signature notarized (see Section C of this chapter);

e. Transmittal letter signed by the surviving spouse (see Section D of this chapter).

4. Transfer of Securities in Small Estates

When the total value of the decedent's property in California is under $60,000, not counting certain property going to a surviving spouse or property owned in trust or in joint tenancy (real or personal), the securities may be transferred by means of an affidavit signed by the person(s) entitled to receive the securities. This procedure, which is explained in detail in Chapter 11, usually applies when the securities are registered in the decedent's name alone or as a tenant in common with another. It can also be used as a simple way of transferring community property securities to a surviving spouse, if the estate is small and meets the requirements to use this procedure.

Documents required:

a. Affidavit given pursuant to California Probate Code § 13100, signed by person(s) entitled to receive the securities, with the signatures notarized (see Chapter 11);

b. Original stock certificate, bond, debenture or mutual fund certificate;

c. Certified copy of the decedent's death certificate (see Chapter 2);

d. Affidavit of Domicile signed by person(s) entitled to the securities, with signature(s) notarized (see Section C of this chapter);

e. Transmittal letter signed by person(s) entitled to the securities (see Section D of this chapter); and

f. Stock or bond power, signed by persons entitled to receive securities (see Section B of this chapter).

5. Transfer of Securities Left in a Living Trust

To transfer securities held by the decedent (or someone else as trustee) in a living (inter vivos) trust, the best procedure is to write to the transfer agent for each security to make specific arrangements for the transfer. Usually, in this instance, the securities are held in the name of the decedent (or someone else) as trustee, and the living trust document names a successor trustee to take over on the death of the original trustee. The transfer agent will itemize the documents needed to make the transfer. Usually, a certified copy of the decedent's death certificate, a stock or bond power and Affidavit of Domicile executed by the trustee or successor trustee are required. Sometimes a copy of the living trust document is requested, although the transfer agent should already have a copy, as it is normally needed to transfer the securities into the trust initially.

Note: If a living trust was established but the securities in question were never formally transferred to it, you probably will not be able to use this procedure, as the trust was never properly established in the first place. In this instance, you will probably need to transfer the securities under the terms of a formal probate unless they are part of a small estate (see Chapter 11) or pass to the surviving spouse.

B. The Stock or Bond Power

THE "STOCK OR BOND POWER" authorizes the actual transfer of the securities. It must be executed by a person having the authority to sign on behalf of the decedent. In each of the foregoing transfer situations, we have indicated who should sign the stock or bond power. Most stock, bond and mutual fund certificates have the stock or bond power printed on the back. However, a separate but very similar form is normally used, called "Stock or Bond Assignment Separate from Certificate," or "Irrevocable Stock or Bond Power," which may be obtained from a bank, stockbroker or stationery store. As you will notice in the sample just below, the form has a space to fill in the name of the person acting as attorney in fact. This person is normally an employee of the transfer agent who actually transfers the stock on the books of the corporation; leave this space blank.

Because transfer agents have no means of identifying the signature of the person who signs the stock power, they usually insist that the signature be "guaranteed." This may be done by a bank officer at the bank of the person executing the stock or bond power or by a broker handling the securities transfer. In either case, the bank or brokerage office stamps the stock or bond power "Signature Guaranteed," followed by the name of the bank, trust company or brokerage firm. The person guaranteeing the signature signs just below the stamp.

Irrevocable Stock or Bond Power

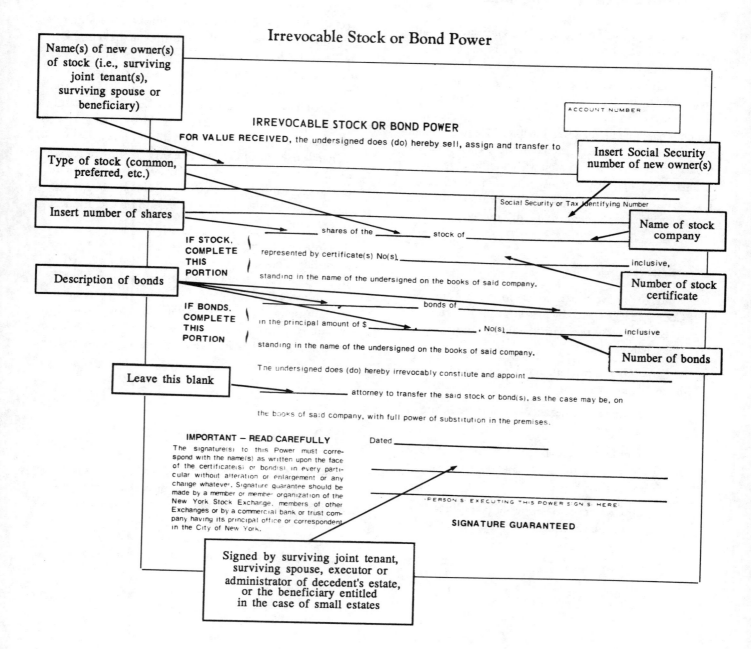

C.   The Affidavit of Domicile

THE AFFIDAVIT OF DOMICILE (sometimes called "Affidavit of Residence") is required as proof that the decedent was a resident of California and not of the state in which the corporation is organized, in which case transfer taxes might be due. Many transfer agents require this affidavit as a matter of routine, so it is best to prepare it and send it along with the other documents to avoid delays. Banks and stockbrokers usually have these forms on hand or you may type your own form by following the sample here. The signature on the affidavit must be acknowledged by a notary public.

Affidavit of Domicile

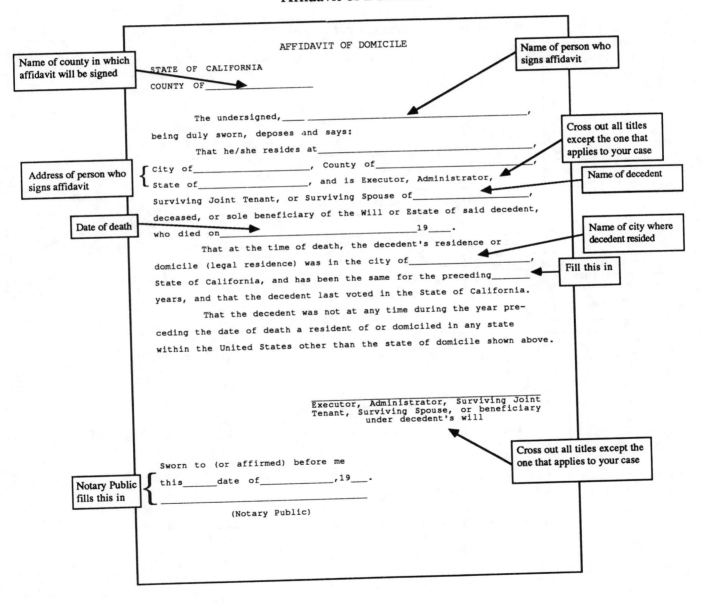

D.   The Transmittal Letter

A TRANSMITTAL LETTER must accompany the original stock and bond certificates and other documents when they are sent to the transfer agent. A sample letter that may be adapted to various situations appears below. Note that the name or names of the new owners of the securities, along with their addresses and Social Security numbers, must be provided. If the securities are to be apportioned between two or more persons, be sure to indicate the number of shares going to each. Original certificates should be sent by registered mail, return receipt requested, and should be insured. Many attorneys also recommend that the original certificates be sent separately (but at the same time) from the transfer documents to guarantee that if the certificates are misdelivered no one will have the power to make a fraudulent transfer.

Transmittal Letter

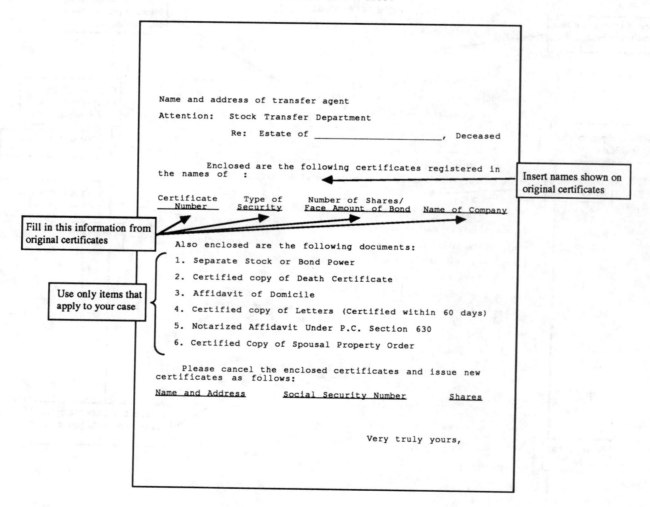

Name and address of transfer agent

Attention: Stock Transfer Department

Re: Estate of _____, Deceased

Enclosed are the following certificates registered in the names of :

Insert names shown on original certificates

Certificate Number	Type of Security	Number of Shares/ Face Amount of Bond	Name of Company

Fill in this information from original certificates

Also enclosed are the following documents:

1. Separate Stock or Bond Power
2. Certified copy of Death Certificate
3. Affidavit of Domicile
4. Certified copy of Letters (Certified within 60 days)
5. Notarized Affidavit Under P.C. Section 630
6. Certified Copy of Spousal Property Order

Use only items that apply to your case

Please cancel the enclosed certificates and issue new certificates as follows:

Name and Address	Social Security Number	Shares

Very truly yours,

Note: If the decedent owned securities held for him by a stockbroker or a bank as a custodian (meaning they were not registered in the decedent's name), you should contact the broker or custodian and arrange to have them put in the name(s) of the new owner(s).

E. How to Sell Securities

SOMETIMES BENEFICIARIES may prefer to have securities sold or liquidated, rather than have them re-registered in their names as the new owners. When securities are sold, the transaction is handled by a stockbroker. The same documentation is required to sell securities as to have securities transferred, and the broker will help you with the forms.

F. The Stock Transfer Tax

IF THE TRANSFER AGENT is located in New York state, as is common, there will be a stock transfer tax to pay. The tax is presently 2.5 cents per share, and you must send a check payable to the transfer agent for the amount of the tax along with the transfer documents. It is a good idea to write or call the transfer agent in advance to verify the exact amount of tax. New York and Florida are the only states with a stock transfer tax. Because of this you should select a transfer agent located in another state, if you have the option.

As you can see, transferring title to securities involves a fair amount of detail work. Rather than tackle this project yourself, you might want to consider having a bank or stock brokerage firm handle the transfers for you. They are experienced in this area and will help with the documentation and process the transfers for a nominal charge.

CHAPTER 10

Joint Tenancy Property

IT'S NOT UNUSUAL to find many of a decedent's assets held in joint tenancy. Real estate brokers, bank officers and stockbrokers often recommend joint tenancy ownership for married couples, and sometimes for other joint owners. Other people, aware that joint tenancy property avoids probate, use it for this reason. Sometimes elderly or ill persons place their bank accounts in joint tenancy with a younger relative or trusted friend so the relative or friend can conveniently cash checks, make deposits and carry on business for the elderly or ill person.[1]

A. About Joint Tenancy

FOR OUR PURPOSES, the important characteristic of joint tenancy ownership is that it is one way to avoid probate. The moment one of the co-owners dies, her interest in the property shifts to the surviving joint tenants, leaving no estate to be administered. Property held in joint tenancy doesn't pass under the provisions of the decedent's will, nor does it go to the decedent's heirs if the decedent died without a will (unless, of course, the heirs or beneficiaries happen to be the surviving joint tenants). However, even though probate is avoided, a few simple formalities must be completed to remove the decedent's name from the title, deed, certificate or other record of ownership, if the survivors wish to hold clear title to the property.[2]

When the last joint tenant dies, the property will be transferred as part of that person's estate and will be subject to formal probate unless it passes to a surviving spouse (see Chapter 15) or as part of a small estate, as discussed in Chapter 11. We explain how to do this here.

The first step is to verify that you are dealing with joint tenancy property. Examine deeds to real property and other ownership documents to make sure title is actually held in joint tenancy, and not in sole ownership, tenancy in common or as community property. (It is also a good idea to check with a title company because the decedent may have broken the joint tenancy prior to death without telling the other joint tenants.) Unless the title document (for example, deed, bank book or stock certificate) says "as joint tenants" or "with right of survivorship" (sometimes this is abbreviated as "JTRS" or "WROS"), it is probably not joint tenancy. An exception to this is an automobile or other motor vehicle registered in the names of two people with the word "or" between their names, which is considered joint tenancy ownership as far as the Department of Motor Vehicles is concerned. Bank accounts, stocks, bonds, promissory notes, as well as real property, may be held in joint tenancy. A bank account held in the names of two persons connected by "or" without saying "as joint tenants" is treated as joint tenancy ownership by most banks, and the account will pass to the survivor when one of the owners dies.

Note on Joint Tenancy and Death Taxes: As discussed in Chapter 7, joint tenancy property does not avoid estate taxes, although many people mistakenly think it does. Even though property held in joint tenancy is excluded from probate, it is included in the decedent's taxable estate. For instance, when a decedent has added someone as a joint tenant to his bank account for convenience or conveyed his interest in real property to someone as a joint tenant to make it easier to transfer the property on his death, the decedent's original interest in the property is included in his taxable estate, unless a gift tax return was filed at the time of the transfer. Therefore, if the gross value of the decedent's estate is sufficient to require a federal estate tax return (see Chapter 7), you should discuss the handling of joint tenancy property with an accountant or other person experienced in estate tax matters.

---

[1] A better way to provide for the management of your property should you become incapacitated is by use of a Durable Power of Attorney. See *The Power of Attorney Book*, by Denis Clifford (Nolo Press).

[2] If there are two or more surviving joint tenants, the survivors remain joint tenants as far as that particular property is concerned.

B. How to Clear Title to Real Property in Joint Tenancy

REAL PROPERTY, as we discussed in Chapter 4, is land or things permanently affixed to land, such as houses, trees and fences. It includes condominiums, cooperatives (although some cooperatives in which the decedent's interest is a very limited one are treated as personal property), and may also include mobile homes permanently attached to land if the person who owns the mobile home also owns the land.

Step 1. Prepare an Affidavit—Death of Joint Tenant

This is the easiest way to clear joint tenancy title to real property, and the method most commonly used. All you need is a form called "Affidavit—Death of Joint Tenant." You will find a blank form in Appendix 1. The affidavit, which is self-explanatory, states that the decedent named on the death certificate (which must be attached to the affidavit) is the same person named on the original deed to the property (quoting the decedent's name as it appears on the deed) as a joint tenant. Sometimes the names on the deed and on the death certificate may be different—initials might be used on one and a given name on the other. This isn't a problem unless the names are significantly different, in which case you will have to offer proof that the decedent and the joint tenant were the same person. A sample of the affidavit with instructions on how to prepare it is shown here. Much of the information needed to complete the affidavit is obtained from the original joint tenancy deed. The affidavit may either be signed by the surviving joint tenant in the presence of a notary public or it may be signed using a declaration under penalty of perjury.

As mentioned above, if you are dealing with the estate of the last joint tenant to die, but the interests of predeceased joint tenants were never formally ended, you must first terminate the interest of the first joint tenant(s) so

that the record will show title held solely in the name of the last surviving joint tenant. The Affidavit—Death of Joint Tenant for the first joint tenant to die should be signed by the personal representative (executor or administrator) of the estate of the last surviving joint tenant, and recorded as discussed below.

Step 2. Obtain a Certified Copy of the Decedent's Death Certificate

A certified copy of the decedent's death certificate must be stapled to the affidavit. If you don't have one, see Chapter 2, Section C(3) for instructions on how to obtain one.

Step 3. Fill Out Preliminary Change of Ownership Report (If Necessary)

All documents, including Death of Joint Tenant Affidavits, that transfer real property must be accompanied by a Preliminary Change of Ownership Report when they are recorded. You may also need to fill out a supplement to this form, if the property is being transferred from parent to child. (See Chapter 8, Section C.)

Affidavit—Death of Joint Tenant

(Page One)

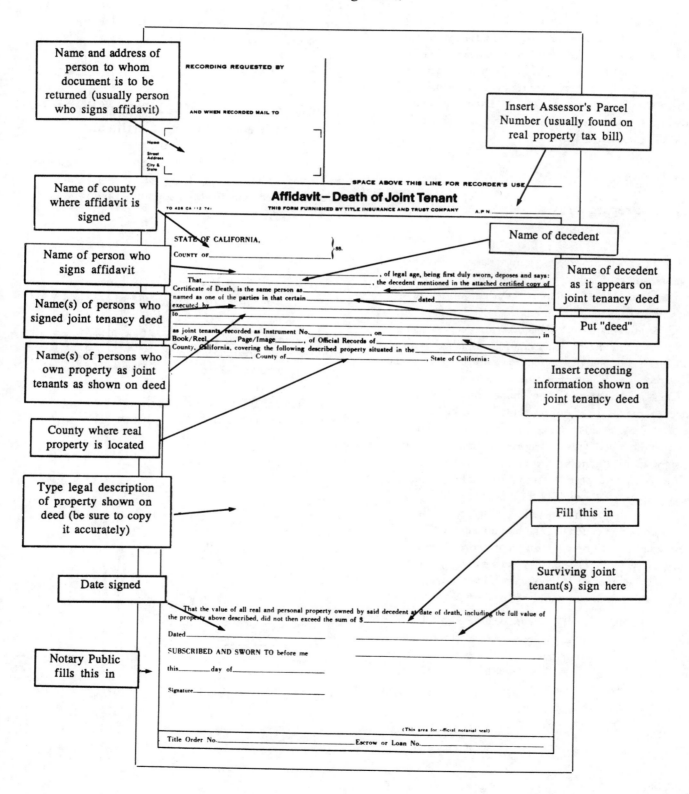

Affidavit—Death of Joint Tenant

(Page Two)

RECORDING REQUESTED BY

Mary Doe

AND WHEN RECORDED MAIL TO

Name Mary Doe
Street
Address 567 First Street
City &
State Los Angeles, Calif. 90017

___ SPACE ABOVE THIS LINE FOR RECORDER'S USE ___

Affidavit—Death of Joint Tenant

THIS FORM FURNISHED BY TITLE INSURANCE AND TRUST COMPANY   APN 2345 092 086

TO 426 CA   74

STATE OF CALIFORNIA.   }ss.
COUNTY OF Los Angeles

Mary Doe _____ of legal age, being first duly sworn, deposes and says:
That Robert Doe , the decedent mentioned in the attached certified copy of
Certificate of Death, is the same person as Robert Doe
named as one of the parties in that certain deed dated June 20, 1985
executed by John Smith and Mary Smith
to Robert Doe and Mary Doe, husband and wife

as joint tenants, recorded as Instrument No. 85-58892 on June 24, 1985 , in
Book/Reel D5100 Page/Image 32 of Official Records of Los Angeles
County. California. covering the following described property situated in the City of Los Angeles
, County of Los Angeles , State of California:

Lot 101 of Tract 26834, as per map
recorded in Book 691, Pages 3 to 8
of Maps, in the Office of the County
Recorder of said county

That the value of all real and personal property owned by said decedent at date of death, including the full value of
the property above described. did not then exceed the sum of $. I declare under penalty
of perjury under the laws of the State of California that the foregoing is true and correct.
Dated

SUBSCRIBED AND SWORN TO before me   (signed) Mary Doe

this _____ day of _____

Signature

(This area for official notarial seal)

Title Order No   Escrow or Loan No.

Step 4:   Record the Affidavit with the County Recorder

The final step is to record the affidavit at the County Recorder's office in the county where the real property is located. This should be done as soon as possible after the death. Mail it to the County Recorder with a cover letter requesting that it be recorded and returned to the address indicated in the upper left-hand corner of the document. Call the Recorder's office to ascertain the amount of the modest fee. An affidavit with a death certificate attached is considered two pages for recording purposes.[3] It isn't necessary to record a new deed when you record the affidavit. The purpose of the affidavit is to remove the deceased person's name from the title so ownership appears solely in the name of the survivor(s).

Note on the Spousal Property Order Alternative: Another way to transfer real property held in joint tenancy is through a Spousal Property Order. (See Chapter 15, Section G.) This method may be preferable if (1) the property is going to the surviving spouse, and (2) the property is community property. As explained in Chapter 7, establishing (through the court order) that the joint tenancy property was in fact community property can have advantageous tax consequences when the property is later sold.

---

[3]Information on recording documents with the County Recorder is given in Chapter 8.

C. How to Clear Title to Securities Held in Joint Tenancy

DETAILED INFORMATION on how to transfer securities is given in Chapter 9.

D. How to Clear Title to Motor Vehicles and Small Boats Held in Joint Tenancy

IF THE PINK SLIP (ownership document) shows a vehicle or boat is registered in the names of two persons joined by "or" (for example, "Bob Smith or Sarah Lee"), this creates a joint tenancy under the Vehicle Code. If the pink slip names the decedent "and" another person (for example, "Bob Smith and Sarah Lee"), it is joint tenancy ownership only if it so states (for example, "Bob Smith and Sarah Lee, as joint tenants"). Automobile clubs will assist in transferring title to motor vehicles, or you may go in person to the Department of Motor Vehicles and submit the following items:

1. Copy of the deceased joint tenant's death certificate (not necessarily a certified copy) (see Chapter 2);

2. Vehicle or boat ownership certificate (pink slip) signed in the proper place on the back by the survivor;

3. Registration card for the vehicle;

4. Certificate of compliance with the smog pollution control law, unless the surviving joint tenant who is taking title is the spouse or child of the decedent.

Transfer of Ownership of Motor Vehicle

Held in Joint Tenancy

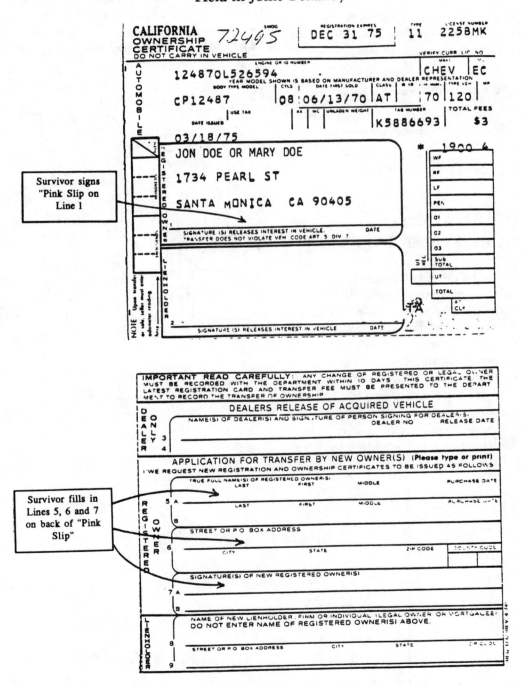

Survivor signs "Pink Slip on Line 1"

Survivor fills in Lines 5, 6 and 7 on back of "Pink Slip"

Survivor should take "Pink Slip and current registration card, with $7 transfer fee to nearest Department of Motor Vehicles office to have new "Pink Slip" issued in name of survivor.

E. How to Clear Title to Joint Tenancy Bank Accounts (and Totten Trust Accounts)

BANKS OR SAVINGS AND LOAN associations will transfer a joint account or Totten trust (pay-on-death) account to the survivor when presented with the following documents:

1. Certified copy of the decedent's death certificate (see Chapter 2);

2. Savings account passbook or a check drawn for the balance of the checking account.

F. How to Clear Title to Money Market Funds and Mutual Funds

MUTUAL FUNDS AND MONEY market funds are usually transferred by the fund management instead of a transfer agent, and, as a rule, the share certificates are held by the fund's custodian instead of by the owner of the shares. Consequently, transferring these types of assets is easier than with ordinary common stocks and bonds. The best procedure is to write or call the fund management directly and ask what they require to sell, redeem or change the record ownership of the shares when the funds are held in joint tenancy. In almost all cases, a certified copy of the death certificate will be required.

G. How to Clear Title to U.S. Savings Bonds in Co-Ownership

MOST LOCAL BANKS will help transfer jointly owned bonds to the surviving co-owner. If you take the bonds along with a certified copy of the death certificate to the bank, it will provide the forms and help you fill them out.

CHAPTER 11

Transferring Small Estates Under $60,000

A. Overview of the Simplified Transfer Procedure for Small Estates

SMALL ESTATES WITH ASSETS worth $60,000 or less may be settled without formal probate proceedings, using relatively simple transfer procedures. This summary form of probate is available regardless of whether the assets are real property or personal property, as long as:

- No administration proceedings are pending or have been conducted for the decedent's estate; and

- The gross value of all real and personal property owned by the decedent in California on the date of death is no more than $60,000. (This figure is the value of the property, not counting any money owed on the property.)

Actually, the $60,000 figure is a little misleading because, as we discuss in detail below, certain assets are not counted in computing whether or not the estate falls within the limitation. As a result, many apparently larger estates qualify to use these summary procedures to collect or transfer minor assets that would otherwise require a formal probate court proceeding. (See Section B, below.)

There are actually three separate procedures for small estates:

1. For personal property (Probate Code §§ 13100-13115);

2. For real property not exceeding $10,000 in value (Probate Code §§ 13200-13208); and

3. For real property not exceeding $60,000 in value (Probate Code §§ 13150-13157).

If the estate qualifies, anyone entitled to inherit property from the decedent, whether as a beneficiary under the will or as an heir under intestate succession laws, may obtain title or possession of the property with these abbreviated transfer procedures. (Probate Code § 13006.)

The trustee of an inter vivos (living) trust created by the decedent during his lifetime may use the procedures if the trust is entitled to receive property under the decedent's will. In addition, a guardian, custodian or conservator of the estate of a person who is entitled to receive property from the decedent may act on behalf of the person. (Probate Code § 13051.)

The waiting period required by these transfer procedures is to allow creditors and legitimate claimants a chance to protect their interests in the property. It also allows a reasonable period of time within which to determine whether the estate will require probate. Transferees who receive a decedent's property under these procedures are liable for the decedent's debts to the extent of the net value of the property received by the transferee.[1]

Note: Transferring personal property (household furniture, clothing, keepsakes), is often handled independently by the family. When an asset has no title document and isn't worth much to begin with, it's reasonably safe and certainly efficient to simply hand it over to whomever is entitled to it under the decedent's will or under the laws of intestate succession.

---

[1]In the case of decedents dying on or after January 1, 1991, actions against a transferee must be commenced within one year after the date of death. (Code of Civil Procedure § 353.)

Kind of Property	Procedure	Waiting Period
Personal property	Affidavit	40 days
Real property not exceeding $10,000 in value	Affidavit filed with probate court	6 months
Real property not exceeding $60,000 in value	Petition filed with probate court	40 days

B. How to Determine Whether You Can Use Summary Procedures

TO FIND OUT IF SOME or all of the decedent's assets may be transferred with these simplified procedures, you must first compute the gross value of all property the decedent owned when he died. We show you how to do this in Chapter 5. Summarized briefly, an estate's gross value is the fair market value on the date of death of all property owned by the decedent without subtracting any liens against the property, or debts or mortgages owed by the decedent.

Lily died owning stocks worth $20,000, a car with a blue book value of $8,000, a $5,000 savings account and an apartment full of furniture and antiques worth about $10,000. This comes to a total value of $43,000. Lily owes $6,000 on her car and $5,000 on her apartment furniture. The total gross value of Lily's estate is $43,000 because the money owed on her car and furniture is not considered in computing the gross value of her estate.

Fortunately, you can ignore several types of assets in computing whether the estate's gross value is under $60,000. (Probate Code § 13050.) The following property isn't counted:

- Real property outside California
- Joint tenancy property (real or personal)
- Property (community, quasi-community or separate) passing outright to a surviving spouse

- Life insurance, death benefits or other assets not subject to probate that pass to named beneficiaries
- Multiple party accounts and pay-on-death accounts
- Any manufactured home, mobile home, commercial coach, floating home or truck camper registered under the Health and Safety Code
- Any vessel numbered under the Vehicle Code
- Any motor vehicle, mobile home or commercial coach registered under the Vehicle Code
- Amounts due the decedent for services in the armed forces
- Salary or other compensation not exceeding $5,000 owed the decedent
- Property held in trust, including a living (inter vivos) trust, or in which the decedent had a life or other estate that terminated on the decedent's death.[2]

As you can see from the above list, if an estate has substantial joint tenancy assets or other assets that are excluded from probate, or consists largely of property that passes outright to a surviving spouse, it may well qualify for summary probate proceedings. You can use the simplified procedure to transfer many items of personal property that might otherwise require probate, such as stocks,

---

[2]Probate Code § 13050 does not specifically state that property held in a living trust is excluded; however, since trust property passes outside probate, it presumably is disregarded in calculating the dollar limitation.

bonds, bank accounts or property held in storage, or even real property up to $60,000 in value.

Before we look at how to transfer a small estate by summary administration, let's look at some examples of situations where it can be used.

Curt, a young bachelor, was a California resident when he died, leaving an estate consisting of a $30,000 mountain cabin in Flagstaff, Arizona (real property), a $10,000 savings account in a Santa Barbara bank, and stocks worth $30,000, all in Curt's name alone. Curt left no will, and his heirs under intestate succession laws are his parents. The mountain cabin in Arizona will not be included in computing the $60,000 limitation because it is real property located outside California. Therefore, his parents may use summary procedures to have the stocks and bank account transferred to them, because the total gross value of these two assets is under $60,000. The cabin would probably be subject to probate in Arizona, something not covered in this book.

Millie was a widow living in Pasadena when she died. Her will left all of her property to her three children, Marvin, Milton and Mary, equally. Her estate consisted of an unimproved lot in San Bernardino County having a market value of $9,950, furniture and furnishings valued around $1,000, a $15,000 bank account, and 3,000 shares in a mutual fund valued at $20,000, all in her name alone. Millie also had some old furniture stored in Bekins Van and Storage Co. worth around $1,500. Since the gross value of Millie's probate estate is under $60,000 ($47,000, to be exact, including the real property), Marvin, Milton and Mary can use the summary procedures to have all of these assets, including the real property, transferred to them as the new owners. To use this procedure, the children must all act together in signing the required affidavit, explained below.

Harry, a used-car salesman in Long Beach, owned the following property at the time of his death: a $250,000 home, held as community property with his wife, Rita; a $20,000 joint tenancy savings account; and two automobiles worth $10,000 each. His estate also contained a mountain cabin in Harry's name alone, having a gross value of $39,500, and a $5,000 personal note from his brother, both of which were acquired before his marriage to Rita. Harry's will leaves the mountain cabin and the $5,000 note to his sister, Pam, and everything else to Rita. Because the community property home passes outright to Rita under Harry's will (see Chapter 8 for transfer information), and the joint savings account passes to Rita as surviving joint tenant (see Chapter 10 for transfer information), they are not included in computing the value of the estate for summary procedure purposes. The two automobiles are also not included because of the vehicle exemption (although, in this case, they could also be excluded as property passing outright to the surviving spouse). Harry's sister Pam may use summary procedures to have the mountain cabin and the $5,000 personal note transferred to her.

C. How to Transfer the Property

AS MENTIONED, there are three different summary procedures for transferring or clearing title to property in small estates. The methods vary depending on whether you are dealing with:

1. Personal property;

2. Real property not exceeding $10,000 in value; or

3. Real property not exceeding $60,000 in value.

In all cases, the gross value of the decedent's assets (excluding the property described in Section B, above) must not exceed $60,000, and no probate proceedings may be conducted for the estate.

1. Personal Property

To receive property via this streamlined procedure, the person or persons entitled to the property (the "successor in interest") need only present an affidavit to the person, representative, corporation or institution having custody or control of the property, or acting as a registrar or transfer agent of the property, requesting that the property be delivered or transferred to them. We include a tear-out affidavit in Appendix 1.

When there are several assets to be transferred, they may all be included on one affidavit, or a separate affidavit may be used for each. A simple way to do this is to type one "master"copy of the affidavit of transfer, leaving out the description of the asset in Paragraph 5, and make as many photocopies as you will need. Then, simply insert the description of each asset to be transferred on one of the photocopies and have it signed by the person or persons entitled to receive the asset.

As a rule, if more than one person is entitled to inherit a particular asset, all beneficiaries must sign one affidavit.

Note: Minors cannot sign the affidavit. If the decedent's will nominates a custodian under the Uniform Transfers to Minors Act, the custodian may sign the affidavit on behalf of the minor. If not, and the minor has no court-appointed guardian of her estate, and the amount to be distributed is not large, it may be possible for the parent having custody of the minor to sign the affidavit and receive the property on behalf of the minor if the person or entity holding the property is agreeable. Otherwise, an attorney would have to be consulted to arrange for a guardian or custodian of the minor to be appointed. (See Chapter 14.)

The form in Appendix 1 provides a place for the signatures to be acknowledged by a notary public. Although the Probate Code says a declaration under penalty of perjury is sufficient when dealing with personal property, a notarized affidavit is required by many institutions, especially when securities are involved. Check with the institution before you send in your request; it may save you the trouble of finding a notary to witness your signature.

These rules apply when using this affidavit procedure to collect or transfer personal property:

- At least 40 days must have elapsed since the death of the decedent before the affidavit or declaration is presented to the holder of the property.

- No administration proceedings may be pending or have been conducted for the decedent's estate.

- A certified copy of the decedent's death certificate must be attached to the affidavit.

- Evidence that the decedent owned the property, such as a stock certificate, promissory note, bank passbook, storage receipt or bill of sale, must be presented with the affidavit. This requirement protects the holder or registrar of the property, who might be liable to another person who later makes a claim to the property. If there is no evidence of ownership, the holder of the property may require an indemnity bond or some other method of indemnification before he hands over the property.

- Reasonable proof of identity must be furnished by the persons signing the affidavit. This requirement is satisfied if (1) the signatures on the affidavit are acknowledged by a notary public, or (2) the person signing the affidavit is personally known to the holder of the property, or (3) the affidavit is signed in the presence of the holder of the property and the person who signs it presents a valid driver's license, passport or other suitable identification.

- An Inventory and Appraisement of all *real property* owned by the decedent in California (excluding property in joint tenancy or in trust, etc.) must be obtained and attached to the affidavit. The appraiser must be a probate referee who has been appointed by the State Controller to appraise property in the county where the property is located. The form and procedures for preparing the Inventory and Appraisement are generally the same as in a formal probate court proceeding. (See Chapter 14, Step 15.) However, in this case, you may choose the referee (appraiser) yourself, rather than using one selected by the court. Simply call the court clerk for a list of the names, addresses and telephone numbers of the referees who qualify.

If these requirements are satisfied, the holder of the property is discharged from liability on delivery of the property to the successor. However, the person receiving the property is made personally liable for any unsecured debts of the decedent. The liability is limited to the fair market value of the property received, less the amount of any liens and encumbrances on the property.

Mary receives a living room set worth $500 under the terms of Sally's will. Mary is liable for up to $500 of Sally's unsecured debts (debts that don't have collateral pledged to guarantee their payment).

Anyone who falsifies information or uses the affidavit fraudulently is liable to the rightful owner in an amount three times the value of the property. The rightful owner may sue anytime within three years after the affidavit or declaration was presented to the holder of the property.

A sample affidavit is shown below with instructions on how to complete it.

Item 1: Insert name of decedent, and date and place of death.

Item 2: Attach certified copy of death certificate.

Item 5: If estate contains real property, check the first box, have property appraised by a probate referee and attach the Inventory and Appraisement form to the affidavit. Otherwise, check the second box.

Item 6: Describe property with enough detail to be identifiable. If there is not enough space, put "See Attachment 6" and prepare a full-page attachment describing the property in detail.

Item 7: Insert name(s) of the person(s) entitled to the property.

Item 8: Check first box if the persons named in Item 7 will sign affidavit. Check second box if a guardian, conservator or custodian will sign affidavit on their behalf.

Here are instructions for collecting or transferring various types of personal property with an affidavit.

Affidavit for Collection of Personal Property
Under California Probate Code § 13100

The undersigned state(s) as follows:

1. _____CURT MORRIS_____ died on ____June 10_____, 19_89_, in the County of _____Santa Barbara_____, State of California.

2. At least 40 days have elapsed since the death of the decedent, as shown by the attached certified copy of the decedent's death certificate.

3. No proceeding is now being or has been conducted in California for administration of the decedent's estate.

4. The gross value of the decedent's real and personal property in California, excluding the property described in Section 13050 of the California Probate Code, does not exceed $60,000.

5. ☐ An inventory and appraisement of the real property included in the decedent's estate is attached; ☒ There is no real property in the decedent's estate.

6. The following property is to be paid, transferred, or delivered to the undersigned under the provisions of California Probate Code Section 13100:

   a. Savings Account No. 321-51, Santa Barbara Savings Bank, 100 State Street, Santa Barbara, California;
   b. 500 shares, PDQ Corporation, common stock

7. The successor(s) of the decedent, as defined in Probate Code Section 13006, is/are: _____Mary Morris and Michael A. Morris_____.

8. The undersigned ☒ is/are successor(s) of the decedent to the decedent's interest in the described property, or ☐ is/are authorized under California Probate Code Section 13051 to act on behalf of the successor(s) of the decedent with respect to the decedent's interest in the described property.

9. No other person has a right to the interest of the decedent in the described property.

10. The undersigned request(s) that the described property be paid, delivered or transferred to the undersigned.

I/we declare under penalty of perjury under the laws of the State of California that the foregoing is true and correct.

DATED: _____July 20_____, 19_89_

_____   _Mary Morris_____,
_____   _Michael A. Morris___
_____   _____

(See reverse side for Notarial Acknowledgments)

a. Securities (Stocks and Bonds)

A transfer agent of any security is required to change the registered ownership on the books of the corporation from the decedent to the successors upon being presented with the affidavit of transfer. (Probate Code § 13105.) Chapter 9 tells you in detail how to transfer securities. In this type of transfer you should send the following documents (you will find most in the Appendices) to the transfer agent:

- Affidavit (of transfer), signed by the persons entitled to receive the stock, with signatures notarized;

- Stock or bond power, signed by the persons entitled to receive the securities, with signatures guaranteed by a bank or stock brokerage firm (we discuss this in Chapter 9);

- Affidavit of Domicile, signed by the persons entitled to the securities, with signatures notarized (see Chapter 9);

- Certified copy of the decedent's death certificate (see Chapter 2);

- Original stock or bond certificates (see Chapter 9);

- Transmittal letter signed by the persons entitled to the securities (see Chapter 9).

Even though you send this information, some companies, especially if they are out-of-state, may ask for certified letters testamentary. Make it clear in your cover letter that no probate is being filed, and therefore no Letters can be obtained.

Chapter 9 tells you where and how to send these documents.

b. Bank Accounts and Safe-Deposit Boxes

California banks are familiar with the procedures for transferring bank accounts and safe-deposit boxes under summary administration procedures, and many of the larger banks and savings and loans have their own form of affidavit. Call to find out if they do. If so, save yourself the time and use theirs. They prefer using forms they are familiar with. In any event, the following documents will be required:

- Affidavit (or declaration);

- Certified copy of the decedent's death certificate;

- Bank passbook for savings accounts, bank money market accounts or certificates of deposit;

- Safe-deposit box key, if applicable.

c. Money Market Funds

Mutual funds and money market funds are usually transferred by the fund management instead of a transfer agent, and, as a rule, the share certificates are held by the fund's custodian instead of by the owner of the shares. Consequently, transferring these types of assets is easier than with ordinary common stocks and bonds. The best procedure is to write or call the fund management directly and ask what it requires to sell, redeem or change the record ownership of the shares. In almost all cases, a certified copy of the death certificate will be required, along with the affidavit or declaration.

d. Motor Vehicles, Small Boats, Mobile Homes, Etc.

Title to automobiles, trailers and other vehicles registered under the Vehicle Code may be transferred immediately by means of a special form available from the Department of Motor Vehicles verifying that the deceased owner "left no other property subject to probate." The value of the vehicle is immaterial, and there is no waiting period. To have title changed, the person entitled to the property should present the following items to the DMV:

- Certificate of ownership and registration card, if available; and

- Certificate for Transfer of Vehicle or Vessel Without Probate, (available from the DMV).

A similar procedure is used for manufactured homes, mobile homes, floating homes, and commercial coaches or truck campers registered under the Health and Safety Code, except there is a 40-day waiting period before these types of vehicles may be transferred. To transfer title to larger mobile homes (double- or triple-wide), contact the Department of Housing and Community Development at (800) 952-8356.

e. Miscellaneous Personal Property

The affidavit can be used to transfer other miscellaneous property, such as property held in storage under the decedent's name, promissory notes, or checks or money due the decedent for salary or retirement. All that is required is the affidavit describing the property and a certified copy of the decedent's death certificate. The documents should be presented to the persons holding the property and the property should be released to the persons entitled to it.

f. Trust Deed Notes

If the property transferred is an obligation secured by a lien on real property, such as a trust deed note, the affidavit must be recorded in the office of the County Recorder where the real property is located. (Probate Code § 13106.5.) Chapter 8 explains how to record documents. The description in the affidavit should include the recording reference of the deed of trust or other document creating the lien, or the legal description of the real property securing the debt, or both. After it has been recorded, a copy of the affidavit should be sent to the person or entity making payments on the obligation, with the request that future payments be sent to the new owner.

2. Real Property Not Exceeding $10,000 in Value

If the estate contains real property not exceeding $10,000 in value (such as an unimproved desert lot), the successors of the decedent may obtain title to the property by filing an Affidavit re Real Property of Small Value with the superior court and then recording a certified copy with the County Recorder. Some special requirements apply to this procedure:

- The affidavit may not be filed until six months after the decedent's death.

- No probate proceedings may be pending or have been conducted in California for the estate.

- A complete legal description of the real property must be included in the affidavit.

- The signature of the person or persons signing the affidavit must be notarized.

- Funeral expenses, last illness expenses and all unsecured debts of the decedent must have been paid before the affidavit is filed.

- A certified copy of the decedent's death certificate, and a copy of the will, if any, must be attached to the affidavit.

- An appraisal by a probate referee must be attached to the affidavit showing that the gross value of all real property (excluding real property held in joint tenancy or in a living trust, or that passes outright to a surviving spouse) the decedent owned in California does not exceed $10,000. See Section 1, above, for instructions on obtaining the Inventory and Appraisement.

When the affidavit and all attachments are complete, the original and one copy should be filed (in person or by mail) with the superior court of the county in which the decedent resided at the time of death, along with a filing fee of $35. If the decedent was not a California resident, the affidavit should be filed in the county in which the decedent owned real property. (See Chapter 13, Section C, on how to file court documents.) The court clerk will file the original affidavit and attachments and issue a certified copy without the attachments. To clear record title to the property in the name of the new owner, the certified copy should be recorded in the office of the County Recorder of the county where the real property is located. See Chapter 8 for instructions on how to record documents. A tear-out affidavit is included in the Appendix. A sample is shown below with instructions on how to fill it in.

Instructions for Preparing Affidavit re Real Property of Small Value

Heading

First box: Insert the name, address and telephone number (including area code) of the person who is entitled to the property and who will sign the affidavit. If there is more than one, list the one to whom the recorded affidavit will be mailed.

Second box: Insert the name of the county and address of the Superior Court where the affidavit will be filed.

Third box: Insert the name of the decedent exactly as it appears on the real property deed.

Items 1-4: Fill in the requested information.

Item 5-a: Insert the legal description of the real property, taken exactly from the deed. If there is not enough room, check the box under 5-a and copy the legal description on 8 1/2" x 11" paper as Attachment 5-a. Proofread the description carefully to make sure it is accurate.

Item 5-b: Indicate what percentage interest of the property the decedent owned and whether he owned it as community property or separate property. For example, you might put "an undivided 1/3 interest as decedent's separate property" or "an undivided 1/2 community property interest."

Items 6-a and 6-b: If the decedent left a will, check box 6-a and attach a copy of the will to the affidavit. All beneficiaries entitled to an interest in the property under the will must sign the affidavit. If there is no will, check box 6-b, and have each heir entitled to receive a portion of the property under intestate succession laws (Chapter 3, Section F) sign the affidavit.

Item 7: If the decedent had a guardian or conservator at the time of death, fill in the requested information. Otherwise, check "none."

When the affidavit has been completed and signed, and the signatures notarized, make sure the following documents are attached before you file it:

- Certified copy of the decedent's death certificate;
- Copy of the decedent's will, if any; and
- Inventory and Appraisement of all California real property owned by decedent.

Affidavit re Real Property of Small Value

ATTORNEY OR PARTY WITHOUT ATTORNEY (Name and Address): TELEPHONE NO.

MARVIN MURDOCH
301 Green Street   (213) 918-7270
Pasadena, California 91000

ATTORNEY FOR (Name):   In Pro Per

SUPERIOR COURT OF CALIFORNIA COUNTY OF LOS ANGELES
STREET ADDRESS: 300 East Walnut
MAILING ADDRESS: Pasadena, California 91101
BRANCH NAME: Northeast District

MATTER OF (NAME):
MILLIE MURDOCH,
                                    DECEDENT

CASE NUMBER:

AFFIDAVIT RE REAL PROPERTY OF SMALL VALUE
($10,000 or Less)

FOR RECORDER'S USE ONLY

1. Decedent (name): Millie Murdoch   died on (date): January 2, 1989
2. Decedent died at (city, state): Pasadena, California
3. At least six months have elapsed since the date of death of decedent as shown in the certified copy of decedent's death certificate attached to this affidavit. (Attach a certified copy of decedent's death certificate.)
4. a. [X] Decedent was domiciled in this county at the time of death
   b. [ ] Decedent was not domiciled in California at the time of death Decedent died owning real property in this county
5. The following is a legal description of decedent's real property claimed by the declarants (copy description from deed or other legal instrument).
   [ ] described in an attachment labeled "Attachment 5a."

Real property in the County of San Bernardino, State of California, legally described as:

Lot 5 of Tract 5721, as per Map recorded in Book 63, Page 31 of Maps in the office of the County Recorder of said county. (Assessor's Parcel No. 800-10-3000)

6. b. Decedent's interest in this real property is as follows (specify): 100% separate property
   b. Decedent's interest in this real property is as follows (specify):
   6. Each declarant is a successor of decedent (as defined in Probate Code section 13006) and a successor to decedent's interest in the real property described in item 5a, and no other person has a superior right, because each declarant is
      a. [X] (will) a beneficiary who succeeded to the property under decedent's will. (Attach a copy of the will.)
      b. [ ] (no will) a person who succeeded to the property under Probate Code sections 6401 and 6402
7. Names and addresses of each guardian or conservator of decedent's estate at date of death
   [X] none [ ] are as follows* (specify)
8. The gross value of all real property in decedent's estate located in California as shown by the inventory and appraisal, excluding the real property described in section 13050 of the Probate Code (joint tenancy property passing to decedent's spouse, etc.), does not exceed $10,000
9. An inventory and appraisal of decedent's real property in California is attached. The inventory and appraisal was made by a probate referee appointed for the county in which the property is located. (You may use Judicial Council form DE-160.)
10. No proceeding is now being or has been conducted in California for administration of decedent's estate

*You must personally serve or mail a copy of this affidavit with attachments to each person named in item 7
(Continued on reverse)

AFFIDAVIT RE REAL PROPERTY OF SMALL VALUE
(Probate)
Probate Code § 13200

MATTER OF (NAME):   MILLIE MURDOCH,
                                    DECEDENT

CASE NUMBER:

11. Funeral expenses, expenses of last illness, and all known unsecured debts of the decedent have been paid. (NOTE: You may be personally liable for decedent's unsecured debts up to the fair market value of the real property and any income you receive from it.)

I declare under penalty of perjury under the laws of the state of California that the foregoing is true and correct.

Date: July 5, 1989
Marvin Murdoch
(TYPE OR PRINT NAME)   (SIGNATURE OF DECLARANT)

Date: July 5, 1989
Milton Murdoch
(TYPE OR PRINT NAME)   (SIGNATURE OF DECLARANT)

Date: July 5, 1989
Mary Steele
(TYPE OR PRINT NAME)   (SIGNATURE OF DECLARANT)

NOTARY ACKNOWLEDGMENTS   (NOTE: No notary acknowledgment may be affixed as a rider (small strip) to this page. If additional notary acknowledgments are required, they must be attached as 8½- by 11-inch pages.)

STATE OF CALIFORNIA, COUNTY OF (specify): LOS ANGELES
(Name): Marvin Murdoch   whose name is subscribed to the foregoing affidavit,
on (date): July 5, 1989   personally appeared before me and acknowledged that he or she executed the affidavit, and
a. [X] is known to me to be that person, or
b. [ ] was proved to me to be that person by satisfactory evidence.
                                    (SIGNATURE OF NOTARY PUBLIC)   NOTARY SEAL

STATE OF CALIFORNIA, COUNTY OF (specify): LOS ANGELES
(Name): Milton Murdoch   whose name is subscribed to the foregoing affidavit,
on (date): July 5, 1989   personally appeared before me and acknowledged that he or she executed the affidavit, and
a. [X] is known to me to be that person, or
b. [ ] was proved to me to be that person by satisfactory evidence.
                                    (SIGNATURE OF NOTARY PUBLIC)   NOTARY SEAL

STATE OF CALIFORNIA, COUNTY OF (specify): LOS ANGELES
(Name): Mary Steele   whose name is subscribed to the foregoing affidavit,
on (date): July 5, 1989   personally appeared before me and acknowledged that he or she executed the affidavit, and
a. [X] is known to me to be that person, or
b. [ ] was proved to be that person by satisfactory evidence.
                                    (SIGNATURE OF NOTARY PUBLIC)

CLERK'S CERTIFICATE

I certify that the foregoing, including any attached notary acknowledgements and any attached legal description of the property (but excluding other attachments), is a true and correct copy of the original affidavit on file in my office. (Certified copies of this affidavit do not include the (1) death certificate, (2) will, or (3) inventory and appraisal. See Probate Code section 13202.)

Date: Clerk, by _____, Deputy

SEAL

AFFIDAVIT RE REAL PROPERTY OF SMALL VALUE
(Probate)

DE-305 (Rev. January 1, 1989)

Page two

(Photocopies need to look or on two sheets)

3. Real Property Not Exceeding $60,000 in Value

If the decedent owned real property in California not exceeding $60,000 in value, the heirs or beneficiaries (successors of the decedent) may file a printed form petition with the Superior Court asking for an order determining their right to take the property without probate administration. This abbreviated court procedure is very similar to the petition for determining that property passes to a surviving spouse, described in Chapter 15. The following limitations apply:

- The petition cannot be filed until 40 days after the decedent's death.

- The petition is only for real property.

- The procedure is available only when the gross value of the real and personal property in the estate does not exceed $60,000 (again, not counting property excluded by Probate Code § 13050, discussed in Section B, above). You must attach an Inventory and Appraisement by a Probate Referee of the real *and* personal property showing the gross value. Do not list on the Inventory any property that is excluded in determining the $60,000 limitation.

This abbreviated proceeding can be used to transfer title to real property under $10,000 more quickly than is allowed under the affidavit procedure described above (which has a six-month waiting period), or if the unsecured creditors have not been paid.

The petition is filed in the Superior Court of the county where the decedent resided, or if the decedent was not a California resident, in the county where the decedent owned property.

Here is a checklist that shows you how to obtain the court order:

1. Prepare and file with the court:

- Petition to Determine Succession to Real Property (obtain Inventory and Appraisement of all real and personal property and attach to petition)

- Notice of Hearing, if required (see Chapter 15, Step 3, for instructions)

- Certificate of Assignment, if required (see Chapter 14, Step 3)

- Filing fee (call court for amount)

2. Before the hearing date on the petition:

- Mail Notice of Hearing

- File original Notice of Hearing, showing date of mailing

- Prepare Order Determining Succession to Real Property (shown below)

- File Order, if required

- Check calendar notes at court (see Chapter 13, Section D)

3. After hearing:

- File Order Determining Succession to Real Property

- Record certified copy of Order in county where real property is located

- File Preliminary Change in Ownership Report with the Order (see Chapter 8)

- Samples of the Petition and Order are given below. For other instructions (for example, Notice of Hearing) see Chapter 15.

Petition to Determine Succession
to Real Property

ATTORNEY OR PARTY WITHOUT ATTORNEY *(Name and Address)*
PAM REESE
700 Harbor Way
Long Beach, California 91176

TELEPHONE NO: (213) 234-7794

Petitioner in Pro Per

SUPERIOR COURT OF CALIFORNIA, COUNTY OF LOS ANGELES
STREET ADDRESS: 825 Maple Avenue
CITY AND ZIP CODE: Torrance, California 90503
BRANCH NAME: Southwest District

MATTER OF (NAME): HARRY REESE, aka
HARRY C. REESE, DECEDENT

PETITION TO DETERMINE SUCCESSION TO REAL PROPERTY
(Estates $60,000 or Less)

FOR COURT USE ONLY

CASE NUMBER

HEARING DATE

DEPT   TIME

1 Petitioner *(name of each):* Pam Reese

requests a determination that the real property described in this petition is property passing to petitioner and that no administration of decedent's estate is necessary.

2 Decedent *(name):* Harry Reese
   a. Date of death: April 25, 1989
   b. Place of death *(city, state):* Long Beach, California

3 At least 40 days have elapsed since the date of decedent's death.

4 a. [X] Decedent was a resident of this county at the time of death.
   b. [X] Decedent died owning property in this county.

5 Decedent died
   [ ] intestate   [X] testate and a copy of the will and any codicil is affixed as attachment 5 or 12a.

6 No proceeding for the administration of decedent's estate is being conducted or has been conducted in California.

7 Proceedings for the administration of decedent's estate are necessary in another jurisdiction
   a. [X] have not been commenced.   and completed.
   b. [ ] have been commenced. *(Specify state, county, court, and case number):*

8 The gross value of all real and personal property in decedent's estate located in California as shown by the inventory and appraisal attached to this petition, excluding the property described in Probate Code section 13050 (joint tenancy, property passing to decedent's spouse, etc.), does not exceed $60,000. *(Attach an inventory and appraisal as attachment 8.)*

9 a. The decedent is survived by
   (1) [X] spouse   [ ] no spouse as follows: [ ] divorced or never married   [ ] spouse deceased
   (2) [X] child as follows: [ ] natural or adopted   [ ] natural adopted by a third party   [ ] step   [ ] foster
   (3) [X] no child
   b. Petitioner   [ ] issue of a predeceased child   [X] no issue of a predeceased child
      [X] has no actual knowledge of facts reasonably giving rise to a parent child relationship under Probate Code section 6408(b).

10 *(Complete if decedent was survived by (1) a spouse but no issue (only a or b apply); or (2) no spouse or issue. Check the first box that applies)*
   a. [ ] All surviving children and issue of predeceased children have been listed in item 14.
   b. [X] The decedent was survived by a parent or parents who are listed in item 14.
   c. [ ] The decedent was survived by a brother, sister, or issue of a deceased brother or sister, all of whom are listed in item 14.
   d. [ ] The decedent was survived by other heirs under Probate Code section 6400 et seq., all of whom are listed in item 14.

11 The legal description of decedent's real property passing to petitioner and decedent's interest in the property are stated in attachment 11. *(Attach the legal description of the real property and state decedent's interest.)*

(Continued on reverse)

Form Approved by the
Judicial Council of California
DE 310 (Rev. January 1, 1989)

PETITION TO DETERMINE SUCCESSION TO REAL PROPERTY
(Probate)

Probate Code 1-13151

MATTER OF (NAME):
ESTATE OF HARRY REESE,   DECEDENT

CASE NUMBER

12 Each petitioner is a successor of decedent (as defined in Probate Code section 13006) and a successor to decedent's interest in the real property described in item 11 because each petitioner is
   a. [X] [ ] will a beneficiary who succeeded to the property under decedent's will
      [ ] who succeeded to the property under Probate Code sections 6401 and 6402.
   b. [ ] (no will) a person who succeeded to the property described in item 11 [ ] is stated in attachment 13

13 The specific property interest claimed by each petitioner in the real property described in item 11 [X] is as follows *(specify):* 100% interest

14 The names, relationships, ages, and residence or mailing addresses of (a) all persons checked in items 9 or 10, (b) all other heirs of decedent, and (c) all devisees of decedent (persons designated in the will to receive any property), so far as known to petitioner, including stepchild and foster child heirs and devisees to whom notice is to be given
   [X] are listed below   [ ] are listed in attachment 14

NAME AND RELATIONSHIP	AGE	RESIDENCE OR MAILING ADDRESS
Rita Reese, wife	Adult	28 Surfside Avenue, Long Beach, California 91070
Pam Reese, sister	Adult	700 Harbor Way, Long Beach, California 91176

15 The names and addresses of all persons named as executors in decedent's will
   [X] are listed below   [ ] are listed in attachment 15   [ ] none named   [ ] no will.
   Rita Reese (see address above)

16 The petitioner is the trustee of a trust that is a devisee under decedent's will. The names and addresses of all persons interested in the trust, as determined in cases of future interests pursuant to paragraphs (1), (2), or (3) of subdivision (a) of Probate Code section 15804 [ ] are listed in attachment 16

17 Decedent's estate was under a [ ] guardianship [ ] conservatorship at decedent's death. The names and addresses of all persons serving as guardian or conservator [ ] are listed in attachment 17

18 [X] Number of pages attached: 4

I declare under penalty of perjury under the laws of the State of California that the foregoing is true and correct.

Date: June 15, 1989

Pam Reese
(TYPE OR PRINT NAME)   *(SIGNATURE OF PETITIONER)*

....
(TYPE OR PRINT NAME)   *(SIGNATURE OF PETITIONER)*

* See Probate Code section 13151(a) for the requirement that a copy of the will be attached in certain instances. If required, include as attachment 5 or 12a

DE 310 (Rev. January 1, 1989)   PETITION TO DETERMINE SUCCESSION TO REAL PROPERTY   Page two
(Probate)

```
Estate of Harry Reese, deceased

PETITION TO DETERMINE SUCCESSION TO REAL PROPERTY

Attachment 11--Legal Description of Real Property:

Decedent's 100% separate property interest in real property situated
in the County of San Bernardino, State of California, improved with a
single dwelling, commonly known as 85 Pine Street, Crestline, and
legally described as:

Lot 23, block 289, in Tract XYZ, per Map recorded in Book 70, Pages 91
and 92 of maps, in the office of the County Recorder of said county

Assessor's Parcel No. 234-56-7700
```

Instructions for Petition to Determine Succession to Real Property

Caption: Fill in the boxes at the top of the form just as you have filled them in on your other court forms. Leave the case number and hearing date boxes blank; when you file the petition, the clerk will give you this information.

Item 1: The petitioner (or his guardian or conservator) is the person who is entitled to succeed to the real property under the will or by intestate succession. If there is more than one such person, list all of them as petitioners. If there isn't enough room, type "See Attachment 1" and list them on a separate 8 1/2" x 11" paper and attach it to the petition.

Items 2-4: Fill in the requested information.

Item 5: If the decedent left a will, check "testate" and attach a copy of the will, labeled "Attachment 5." Otherwise, check "intestate."

Item 7: Indicate whether or not probate proceedings have been begun for the decedent in another state.

Item 8: Before filing the petition, you must obtain an Inventory and Appraisement of all property required to be considered in determining whether the estate is within the $60,000 limitation. The procedure for obtaining the Inventory and Appraisement is the same as that used in a formal probate proceeding (see Chapter 14, Step 15), but in this case you may choose the referee yourself. Attach the Inventory and Appraisement form to the petition.

Items 9 and 10: For instructions, see Items 5, 6 and 7 of Step 1, Chapter 14 on how to prepare the Petition for Probate.

Item 11: Put the legal description of the real property (from the deed to the property) on a plain 8 1/2" x 11" paper and label it as Attachment 11. Indicate what interest the decedent owned and whether it was community or separate property.

Item 12: If the decedent left a will, check box 12-a and attach a copy of the will. Each beneficiary entitled to receive an interest in the real property under the will must sign the petition. If there is no will, check box 12-b and have each heir of the decedent who is entitled to a portion of the property sign the petition.

Item 13: List the interest in the property claimed by each petitioner. For example, if there is only one petitioner, put "100% interest." If three successors are inheriting equally, put "John Doe, Jane Doe and Robert Doe, each as to an undivided 1/3 interest."

Item 13: List the interest in the property claimed by each petitioner. For example, if there is only one petitioner, put "100% interest." If three successors are inheriting equally, put "John Doe, Jane Doe and Robert Doe, each as to an undivided 1/3 interest."

Item 14: List persons potentially interested in the estate, to give them notice of the petition. If the decedent left a will, list the name, relationship, age, and residence or mailing address of everyone (whether living or deceased) mentioned in the will as a beneficiary. Also list this information for all persons listed in items 9 and 10 (the decedent's heirs). Before completing this item, read the instructions for Attachment 8 to the Petition for Probate (Chapter 14, Step 1).

Item 16: If the petitioner is also the trustee of a trust that is entitled to receive property under the will, check this box and list in an attachment the names and addresses of all living persons who are potential beneficiaries of the trust.

Item 17: Check the first box only if the decedent had a guardian or conservator at the time of death. If so, list the guardian or conservator's name and address on a separate piece of paper labeled Attachment 17, and attach it to the petition.

Item 18: Check the box and enter the number of attachments.

When the petition is filed with the court with the appropriate filing fee (approximately $100; the exact amount may be determined by calling the court clerk), the clerk will set a hearing date for three to four weeks later. You will not be required to appear at the hearing unless there is a problem. At least 15 days before the hearing, written notice of the hearing must be mailed or personally given to all persons listed in items 14, 15 and 16 of the petition (heirs, devisees or trustees named in the will, and trust beneficiaries). The procedures for giving the Notice of Hearing are the same as for the spousal property petition described in Chapter 15.

Before the hearing, you should also prepare the Order Determining Succession to Real Property for the judge to sign when she approves the petition. A sample is shown below. Some counties require the Order to be submitted to the Court several days *before* the hearing, so check your local court rules.

If the court approves the petition, the judge will sign the Order at the hearing or shortly thereafter. When the Order is signed, the successor of the decedent becomes personally liable for the unsecured debts of the decedent to the extent of the fair market value of the real property at the date of death, less liens and encumbrances. The new owner should record a certified copy of the Order with the County Recorder in the county where the real property is located. Chapter 8 gives instructions on how to record the Order.

Instructions for Order Determining Succession to Real Property

Caption: Fill in the boxes at the top of the form just as you filled them in on the petition, except that you can now fill in the case number.

Item 1: Fill in date, time and place of the hearing.

Item 3: Fill in the date of death and check the correct boxes.

Item 7: Check the correct box.

Item 9a: Fill in legal description of property. If there isn't enough room, check the box and put the description on a piece of paper labeled Attachment 9a.

Item 9b: Insert same information as in Item 13 of petition.

Item 10: Leave this box blank.

Item 11: Check the box and enter the number of pages attached, if any.

Box beneath judge's signature line: If you have attachments, check this box and at the end of the last attachment page, type a place for the date and a signature line for the judge.

Order Determining Succession
to Real Property

ATTORNEY OR PARTY WITHOUT ATTORNEY (Name and Address)

[X] Recording requested by and return to

PAM REESE
700 Harbor Way
Long Beach, California 91176
ATTORNEY FOR (Name) In Pro Per

TELEPHONE NO (213) 234-7561

FOR RECORDER'S USE ONLY

SUPERIOR COURT OF CALIFORNIA, COUNTY OF LOS ANGELES
STREET ADDRESS 825 Maple Avenue
MAILING ADDRESS
CITY AND ZIP CODE Torrance, California 90503
BRANCH NAME Southwest District

MATTER OF (NAME):

HARRY REESE, aka
HARRY C. REESE,   DECEDENT

ORDER DETERMINING SUCCESSION TO REAL PROPERTY
(Estates $60,000 or Less)

CASE NUMBER
SW 1234

FOR COURT USE ONLY

1. Date of hearing 7-15-89   Time 9:00 A.M. Dept 3   Rm

THE COURT FINDS

2. All notices required by law have been given.
3. Decedent died on (date) April 25, 1989
   a. [X] a resident of the California county named above.
   b. [ ] a nonresident of California and left an estate in the county named above.
   c. [ ] intestate [X] testate
4. At least 40 days have elapsed since the date of decedent's death.
5. No proceeding for the administration of decedent's estate is being conducted or has been conducted in California.
6. The gross value of decedent's real and personal property in California, excluding property described in Probate Code section 13050, does not exceed $60,000.
7. Each petitioner is a successor of decedent (as defined in Probate Code section 13006) and a successor to decedent's interest in the real property described in item 9a because each petitioner is
   a. [X] (will) a beneficiary who succeeded to the property under decedent's will.
   b. [ ] (no will) a person who succeeded to the property under Probate Code sections 6401 and 6402.

THE COURT FURTHER FINDS AND ORDERS

8. No administration of decedent's estate is necessary in California.
9. a. The following described real property is property of decedent passing to each petitioner (give legal description)
      [ ] described in attachment 9a.

   Real property situated in the County of San Bernardino, State of California, improved with a single dwelling, commonly known as 85 Pine Street, Crestline, and legally described as:

      Lot 23, Block 789, in Tract XYZ, per Map recorded in Book 70, Pages 91 and 92 of Maps, in the office of the county recorder of said county.

   Assessor's Parcel No. 234-56-7700

   b. Each petitioner's name and specific property interest [ ] is stated in attachment 9b [X] is as follows (specify):

      Pam Reese - 100% interest

10. [ ] Other (specify)

Date

11. [X] Number of pages attached 0

JUDGE OF THE SUPERIOR COURT
[ ] Signature follows last attachment

Form Approved by the
Judicial Council of California
DE 315 Rev January 1 1990
396 3

ORDER DETERMINING SUCCESSION TO REAL PROPERTY
(Probate)

Probate Code § 13154

CHAPTER 12

How to Transfer Trust Property and Property Subject to Life Estates

PEOPLE SEEKING TO AVOID the delay and expense inherent in the probate process often adopt estate planning devices such as gifts, joint tenancy transfers, trusts and, less often, life estates to transfer their assets without a will. Someone who sets up a living (or inter vivos) trust specifies in the trust document how, when and to whom the property in trust is to be distributed. For example, Mary P. might set up a living trust with herself as trustee and her daughter Sue as beneficiary. She would then formally transfer items of property to the trust by putting the name of the trustee on the relevant deeds, title slips, etc.[1] At Mary's death, whomever she designates as successor trustee on the living trust document simply transfers the proceeds of the trust to Sue, and no probate is required.

A life estate can be used to accomplish much the same thing. In this instance, a person ensures that real property will pass without probate, upon his death, by deeding it to the intended beneficiary but retaining a life estate—that is, the right to use the property for the rest of his life.

A. Trust Property

SOMETIMES YOU MAY FIND that the decedent signed a trust document designating certain assets to be held in trust but for some reason failed to actually transfer title into the name of the trust. As a general rule, assets not transferred to the living trust are still subject to probate. Therefore, you should carefully examine all title documents (for example, real property deeds, stock certificates and motor vehicle pink slips) to see if title was actually transferred to the trust. If the asset was transferred to the trust, the ownership document will show title held something like this: "The I.M. Smart Trust" or the "I.M. Smart, Trustee Under Declaration of Trust dated June 1, 1985." Property that doesn't have formal title documents,

however, such as miscellaneous items of personal property, can be included in a living trust without being formally transferred to the trust. They need only be listed in the trust document.

B. How to Transfer Property Held in Living Trusts

THE PROCEDURES USED to transfer property held in living trusts to the beneficiaries of the trust are similar to those used to transfer assets not held in trust.

1. Real Property

If real property is held in the trust, you will need to prepare some documents to show the transfer of title from the trustee to the beneficiaries of the trust. To do this, the trustee (or successor trustee, if the decedent was the original trustee) need only record a deed from himself, as trustee to the beneficiaries. A sample of such a deed is shown below. The transfer to the beneficiaries is exempt from the documentary transfer tax, and the statement shown on our sample should appear on the face of the deed. Instructions for recording the deed are given in Chapter 8. However, before a title company will insure title in the names of the beneficiaries, it will also require a certified copy of the death certificate of the trustee or creator of the trust and a copy of the trust document.

---

[1] If you are interested in using a living trust to plan your own estate, see Clifford, *Plan Your Estate With a Living Trust*, by Denis Clifford (Nolo Press).

Grant Deed

RECORDING REQUESTED BY

Betty Beneficiary

AND WHEN RECORDED MAIL THIS DEED AND. UNLESS OTHER-
WISE SHOWN BELOW. MAIL TAX STATEMENTS TO

NAME
ADDRESS
CITY &
STATE
ZIP

Betty Beneficiary
12345 Circle Terrace
San Bernardino, Calif. 90557

Title Order No.   Escrow No.

SPACE ABOVE THIS LINE FOR RECORDER'S USE

GRANT DEED

Note: This conveyance is a termination of the trust and transfers title
to the beneficiary of the trust.

The undersigned declares that the documentary transfer tax is $ ___ Ø ___ and is
☐ computed on the full value of the interest or property conveyed, or is
☐ computed on the full value less the value of liens or encumbrances remaining thereon at the time of sale. The land,
tenements or realty is located in
☐ unincorporated area   ☐ city of _____   and

FOR A VALUABLE CONSIDERATION, receipt of which is hereby acknowledged,

    Fred Fiduciary, Successor Trustee Under Declaration of Trust
    dated May 1, 1985, which acquired title as I. M. Smart, Trustee,

hereby GRANT(S) to   Betty Beneficiary

the following described real property in the   City of San Bernardino
county of   San Bernardino   , state of California:

    Lot 22, Block 19 of Tract 7730 as designated
    on the map entitled "Ramona Acres, City and
    County of San Bernardino, State of California,"
    filed in the Office of the County Recorder of
    said county on May 5, 1903, in Volume 4 of
    Maps, at page 9

Dated___October 31, 1985___   (signed) Fred Fiduciary
                                     Fred Fiduciary

STATE OF CALIFORNIA
COUNTY OF _San Bernardino_ } ss.
On this the ___31st___ day of ___October___ 19_85_, before me the undersigned, a
Notary Public in and for said County and State, personally appeared
___Fred Fiduciary___

_____, personally known
to me or proved to me on the basis of satisfactory evidence to be the
person ___ whose name _is_ subscribed to the within instrument
and acknowledged that _he_ executed the same.

(signed) Nora Notary
        Signature of Notary

FOR NOTARY SEAL OR STAMP

Assessor's Parcel No

MAIL TAX STATEMENTS TO PARTY SHOWN ON FOLLOWING LINE. IF NO PARTY SO SHOWN, MAIL AS DIRECTED ABOVE

Name   Street Address   City & State

CAL-1 (Rev 8-82)

2. Securities

For general information on how to transfer securities, see Chapter 9. The transfer agent for securities held in trust should be sent the following documents:

- Certified copy of the death certificate;

- Copy of the trust document (if the transfer agent did not receive one when the securities were transferred into the trust);

- The original certificates for the securities;

- A stock power signed by the trustee or successor trustee, with the signature guaranteed by an officer of a bank or brokerage firm;

- An Affidavit of Domicile; and

- A letter of instructions for the transfer from the trustee to the beneficiaries. The letter should include the name, address and Social Security number of each beneficiary receiving the securities.

3. Bank or Savings and Loan Accounts

Title to bank or savings and loan accounts can usually be transferred to the successor trustee and to a beneficiary on termination of the trust by submitting to the bank or savings and loan association a copy of the trust document and a certified copy of the death certificate.

4. Totten Trust Accounts

Totten trust accounts, sometimes called "pay-on-death accounts," are accounts in the name of someone as trustee for one or more beneficiaries. (See Chapter 5, Section H3.) The bank or savings institution will transfer funds in these kinds of accounts to the beneficiaries on the death of the trustee if it is presented with a certified copy of the trustee's death certificate.

Totten trust accounts are often set up for children or grandchildren. If the beneficiaries are minors, special requirements may apply to distribution of the funds. If the amount exceeds $5,000, either a guardianship, "blocked account," or a custodianship under the Uniform Transfers to Minors Act (Probate Code §§ 3900-3925) will probably have to be established to hold and account for the money. (Probate Code § 3413.) Amounts not exceeding $5,000, however, can be ordered paid to the minor's parents to be held for the benefit of the minor without a guardianship. (Probate Code § 3413(d).) If you are dealing with minor beneficiaries, you may need to see an attorney.

5. Miscellaneous Trust Assets

For other assets held in trust, contact the principal parties involved to find out what is needed to have the assets transferred to the beneficiaries. In most cases, a copy of the trust document and a certified copy of the death certificate will be required. In addition, an assignment form may be needed for assets such as a trust deed note or partnership interest. The payor on the trust deed note or the general partner of a limited partnership interest should be able to assist you. For automobiles and other motor vehicles held in trust, the successor trustee should contact the Department of Motor Vehicles, which will provide the forms and instructions to transfer the vehicle.

C. Life Tenancy (Life Estate)

A LIFE TENANCY (sometimes called a "life estate") is not a common form of ownership, but it deserves mention here. A life tenancy is ownership of property for the period of a lifetime only. Life tenancies, like trusts, are sometimes created to avoid the necessity of probate proceedings.

Wanda is an elderly widow who owns a home which she wishes to go to her son Steven upon her death. Wanda may deed the property to Steven during her lifetime, with the deed saying that "Grantor (Wanda) reserves to herself a life estate in said property." This will transfer the ownership to Steve, but subject to Wanda's life estate. It will accomplish Wanda's objective of avoiding probate of the home upon her death because she will die without ownership of the property. Her life estate will terminate at the moment of her death, and the home will be owned by Steven.

Life estates are handled in much the same way as joint tenancy property on the death of the life tenant. To clear title to real property in which there was a life estate, you simply use the "Affidavit—Death of Joint Tenant" discussed in Chapter 10, and cross out the word "Joint" and replace it with the word "Life." Then your affidavit will say "Affidavit—Death of Life Tenant." The affidavit is then recorded in the office of the County Recorder in which the real property is located (discussed in Chapter 10), along with a certified copy of the death certificate. If other assets are subject to life estates, such as securities, the same procedures for clearing joint tenancy property should generally be followed, which are discussed in Chapter 10.

CHAPTER 13

An Overview of the Probate Court Process

LET'S START IN THIS CHAPTER by providing you with an overview of what is involved in settling a simple estate through a superior (probate) court proceeding using the new streamlined procedures. Again, keep in mind we are dealing with simple estates. (This is discussed in more detail in Chapter 1.) Generally, this means there should be no complications such as large, disputed Creditor's Claims, disagreements among beneficiaries, questions of title to property, ambiguities in the will, or any other unusual or antagonistic situations—in short, nothing that requires special handling.

When you first read this material, probating an estate may seem difficult. Please don't be discouraged. Even though there are a number of steps involved, none is truly hard. If you carefully follow our instructions, you should have little difficulty in completing a court proceeding successfully. Before you start, we suggest you relax and read this chapter through one or two times to familiarize yourself with what is required. Then, read Chapter 14, which describes what you must do step-by-step. Whenyou feel comfortable that you know basically how to proceed, you can begin the paperwork.

A. Do You Really Need a Probate Court Proceeding?

BEFORE YOU BEGIN a probate court proceeding, you should study the decedent's assets to see if any, or even all, of them fall into categories that don't require probate. We discuss this in detail in Chapter 6 and do not repeat the details here.

B. Probate Checklist

THE CHECKLIST BELOW sets out all the steps in a simple probate court proceeding. Each step will be explained in detail in the same order in the next chapter. You will probably want to refer to this checklist frequently as you proceed.

Formal Probate Court Proceeding Checklist

	Basic Steps	Time Frame or Deadline
First Month: Open Estate	1. File Petition for Probate; obtain hearing date (Steps 1 and 5)	Any time after death (no deadline or time limit)
	2. File original will and codicils, if any (Step 2)	Filed with Petition for Probate as separate filing
	3. Publish "Notice of Petition to Administer Estate" (Step 4)	Three times before hearing date; first publication must be at least 15 days prior to hearing
	4. Mail "Notice of Petition to Administer Estate" (Step 4)	At least 15 days prior to hearing date
	5. File proof publication and proof of mailing "Notice of Petition to Administer Estate" (Step 4)	As early as possible before hearing date
	6. File proof of will, if required (Steps 6 and 7)	As early as possible before hearing date
	7. Check calendar notes (Step 10)	Two days or more before hearing
	8. File Order for Probate (and probate bond, if required) (Step 9)	Time requirements vary between counties; check with court

Letters Issued	9. File Letters and "Duties and Liabilities of Personal Representative" form (Steps 11 and 12)	At same time or after filing Order for Probate
Next 4 to 5 Months: Administer Estate	10. Apply for Employer Identification Number (Chapter 7, Section B)	As early as possible after Letters are issued
	11. Notify Director of Health Services of decedent's death (Step 8)	Within 90 days of death, if decedent received Medi-Cal
	12. Open estate bank account (Chapter 13, Section D)	After Letters are issued
	13. Arrange for preparation of income tax returns (Chapter 7)	As soon as possible after Letters are issued
	14. Prepare Inventory and Appraisement and send to Referee (Step 15)	As soon as possible after Letters are issued
	15. Mail "Notice of Administration" to creditors; pay debts without requiring formal claims (Step 16)	Within four months after Letters are issued or within 30 days after first discovering a creditor
	16. File Approval or Rejection of formal Creditor's Claims (Step 16)	Anytime before Petition for Final Distribution
	17. File Inventory and Appraisement with court (Step 15)	Within four months after Letters are issued
	18. File change in Ownership Statement with county assessor if Inventory lists real property (Step 15)	When Inventory and Appraisement is filed with court
	19. File federal estate tax return if gross estate is $600,000 or more (Chapter 7)	Within nine months of date of death
Last Month: Close Estate	20. File Petition for Final Distribution (Step 17)	From four months to one year after Letters are issued (within 18 months, if federal estate tax return is required)
	21. Mail Notice of Hearing to heirs and beneficiaries (Step 18)	Within 15 days of hearing date on petition
	22. File proof of mailing Notice of Hearing (Step 18)	As soon as possible before hearing date on petition
	23. File Order for Final Distribution (Step 19)	Procedures vary between counties; check with court
	24. Transfer assets and obtain receipts (Step 20)	Anytime after Order for Final Distribution s signed
	25. File Receipts and Affidavit for Final Discharge (Step 21)	After assets are distributed and all matters concluded

C. Dealing with the Probate Court

IF ALL THE ASSETS in the estate you are settling can't be transferred by the methods discussed in Chapter 6, probate will be necessary. Here are the basics of what's involved in a probate court proceeding.

1. What Court Do You Use?

As you probably know, different courts in our legal system handle different matters. All probate cases are handled by the superior court of the county in which the decedent resided at the time of her death, no matter where she died or left property.

When a superior court is dealing with a probate procedure, it is often called the "probate court." Some counties have branch courts whose locations can be determined by calling the main courthouse. If you live in one of the branch court districts, the probate proceeding may be commenced there.

If a decedent leaves real property in a state of which he isn't a resident, that property will be governed by the laws of that state, and proceedings to have title transferred must be commenced in the state where the property is located. When there are assets in more than one California county, the estate will be administered in the superior court of the county in which a petition to commence probate proceedings is first filed.

Although all superior (probate) courts follow the basic procedures outlined in the California Probate Code, they each have a few special procedural rules of their own. Most counties have these court rules set out in small printed pamphlets, often called "Probate Rules," or sometimes "Probate Policy Manual" or "Rules of Probate Practice." This booklet (or instruction sheet) tells you such things as when particular forms must be presented to the court, what must be included in court documents and where to call for information. Call the probate department of the court where you will be filing your papers and arrange to obtain a copy.

2. Who Will Represent the Estate?

The estate representative (executor or administrator) will represent the estate in the court proceeding. We discuss selection of the estate representative in detail in Chapter 2. To review very briefly:

- If there is a will which names an executor and that person can serve, that person is the estate representative.

- If there is no will (the decedent died intestate), the court will choose the estate representative, who is called an "administrator."

- If there is a will but no executor is named, or the person named is unable to serve, the court will choose the estate representative, who is called an "administrator with will annexed" (sometimes referred to as "administrator C.T.A.").

The responsibilities of each are basically the same. In all cases, the representative must be over 18 years old and competent. If two or more executors are named in the will and appointed by the court, when one or more is absent from the state, the remaining executors cannot act alone without a court order.

3. Preparing Court Documents

As we mentioned, most forms now used in superior (probate) court matters are preprinted and officially prescribed by the state of California. The facts of each situation are merely written in or checked off in boxes provided. Use of these printed forms is mandatory, and only in a few instances must a document be completely typed. Even though a copy of most required forms is included in Appendix 2 to this book, you may want additional copies. We discuss how to get them in Section G, below.

All court forms and documents should be completed with a typewriter using a black ribbon and standard size type. In the few cases where a printed form is not available, you must type the entire document (following instructions we provide later in this book), and the following format must be followed.

- Use 8 1/2" x 11" white bond paper with lines numbered consecutively on the side; stay within the margins on each side when you type.

- Documents must be double-spaced, using only one side of the paper, and each page must be numbered consecutively at the bottom.

- If attachments or exhibits are needed, they must be the same size (8 1/2" x 11").

- All papers must be fastened together at the top.

- The first page of all documents must be in the following form:

    a. Commencing with line 1 in the upper left-hand corner, type the name of the petitioner, office or residence address, and telephone number;

    b. Leave the space blank between lines 1 and 7 to the right of the center of the page for the use of the clerk;

    c. On or below line 8, type the title of the court;

    d. Starting on line 11, in the space left of the center, type the title of the case;

    e. To the right, opposite the title, put the case number;

    f. Immediately below the case number, put the nature of the document (for example, "Petition for...," "Supplement to...").

Most of the documents that must be typed are simple forms that are easy to copy from examples given in the next chapter. The only document of any length that must

be completely typed in a probate court proceeding is the final petition requesting distribution of the estate. A sample of this petition is shown in detail in Chapter 14, Step 17, and the format should be easy to duplicate.

4. Petitions and Orders

A petition is a document that requests something from the court and includes information to help the court determine if the petition should be granted. In a simple probate proceeding you are required to file two petitions. The first requests that the court admit the will to probate (if there is a will) and that a representative (executor) be appointed. If there is no will, it only requests the appointment of the representative (administrator). The second petition requests an order closing the estate and distributing the assets to the beneficiaries.

The person who prepares and files a petition is called the "petitioner." A petitioner who acts without an attorney is identified as "Petitioner In Pro Per." (This is an abbreviation for "In Propria Persona," a Latin phrase meaning you're representing yourself without a lawyer.)

If the court approves a petition, it will issue an order to that effect. Court orders are usually prepared by the petitioner and presented to the court for the judge's signature before or at the time of the hearing on the petition. Some courts allow the order to be submitted after the hearing date, so local rules should always be checked.

5. Verifications

All statements in petitions should be verified at the end of the document by the petitioner. The verification paragraph is usually as follows:

"I declare under penalty of perjury under the laws of the State of California that the foregoing, including any attachments, is true and correct. Executed this _____ day of _____ , 19__, at _____, California."

The verification has the same effect as a sworn statement or an affidavit witnessed by a notary so that a personal appearance in court is not necessary. All printed court forms have the declaration (verification) printed on them, if one is required. If you have to type a document that needs to be verified, be sure to include the verification. For instance, a supplement to a petition must be verified in the same manner as the petition. Always be sure to insert the date when the verification is signed—it's easy to overlook this.

6. Filing Court Documents

Court documents are filed by either mailing them or presenting them in person to the county clerk's office at the courthouse. As a general rule, it is a good idea to include two copies of all documents in addition to the original because some courts require them. The original document is always retained by the court, and any copies not needed will be returned to you. When you file your papers by mail, always keep a copy of each for your records in case the others get lost, and always include a stamped, self-addressed envelope so the court will return your conformed (stamped "filed" by the clerk) copies.

When the first petition is filed, the court clerk stamps it with a case number, which should be used on every court document you prepare thereafter. In addition, each petition is given a hearing date. This is the time and date the court will decide whether or not it will approve the petition.

The court will collect a filing fee when you file the first petition, but except for a few instances, no fee is collected for any documents filed after that. The filing fee is different in each county, but is usually around $100.

In some counties, blue document backers, with the title of the document typed at the bottom, must be attached to original court documents (other than printed court forms) when they are filed. Other courts do not use these covers and may return documents if they are attached, so check local practice. You can get "blue-

backs" at most office supply stores. The blue back is attached by folding the top edge (about 3/4") over your document and stapling it at the top in the center and at each side. Some courts also require that all documents have two holes punched at the top with a standard two-hole punch. The holes should be centered.

7. Certified Copies

A certified copy of a court document is one that has been certified by the clerk as a true and correct copy of the original document on file with the court. Certified copies of court documents may be needed at various times during the administration of the estate and may be ordered from the court for a nominal fee. Call the court for the exact amount or ask for a copy of the fee schedule.

D. Beginning the Probate Process

A PROBATE PROCEEDING may begin at any time after someone dies. There is no time limit or deadline. In most cases, however, the process is initiated as soon as possible.

1. Filing the Probate Petition

The probate proceeding is started by filing a petition with the clerk of the superior court in the county where the decedent resided at the time of his death, no matter where he died or where he left property. (We show you how to do this in Chapter 14.) If there is a will, the original is filed separately, at the same time, and a copy is attached to the petition. The petition asks the court to admit the will (if any) to probate and appoint someone to act as estate representative. The petition also gives the court certain information, such as the names of the decedent's heirs, the beneficiaries in the will, where the decedent lived, what kind of property he owned, and where and when he died. The court clerk gives the petition a hearing date, which will be not less than 15 nor more than 30 days after it is filed. In most situations there is no opposition to the petition and it is automatically approved and the representative appointed without anyone having to appear in court.

It is probably a good idea to file your first papers in person, especially when there is an original will that must be presented to the court at the same time as the first petition. You may then pick up forms from that court for filing future documents and also obtain a copy of their probate court rules at the same time.

The person requesting to be appointed the estate representative (either the executor, administrator or administrator with will annexed) files the probate petition. He is called the petitioner, and from now on in this chapter we will assume you are the petitioner and will be the estate representative.

2. The Independent Administration of Estates Act

The probate petition will request that the court grant the estate representative permission to handle the estate under the Independent Administration of Estates Act. (Probate Code §§ 10400-10600.)[1] This Act is designed especially for simple estates (regardless of size) where there are no disputes among the beneficiaries. It allows the representative to do many things without having to obtain prior permission from the court. This is referred to as administering an estate "without court supervision." If all of the heirs and beneficiaries have a cooperative attitude toward the representative, authority to settle the estate under the Act should always be requested, because it saves a lot of time and paperwork. For instance, an

estate representative who has been granted this authority may without court approval:

- Allow, pay, reject or contest any claim against the estate;

- Make repairs or improvements to estate property; *and*

- Pay taxes and expenses of administration.

Generally, however, a personal representative must obtain approval from the court to buy estate property, exchange estate property for property of the personal representative, or pay or compromise claims by the personal representative against the estate, unless the personal representative is also the sole beneficiary, or all known beneficiaries have consented to the transaction. (Probate Code § 10501.)

Many other powers are granted to a personal representative who has authority to administer the estate without court supervision. (Probate Code §§ 10550-10564.) However, those actions we have described above are the ones most often used for a simple estate.

Other actions may be taken without court supervision by giving prior notice, called "Notice of Proposed Action," to beneficiaries whose interests will be affected. The purpose of the Notice is to give the beneficiaries a chance to object if they don't wish the action to be taken. Actions that require such notice are listed in Probate Code §§ 10510-10538. Those that may be useful in simple estates are:

- Selling or exchanging real property (a bond may be required by the court when real property is sold for cash under this procedure, unless the will waives bond);

- Selling or exchanging nonperishable personal property;

- Leasing real property for a term in excess of one year;

- Investing funds of the estate (other than in banks and savings and loan accounts, or direct obligations of the United States maturing in five years

---

[1]The estate representative cannot use the simplified procedures allowed by the Act if the decedent's will prohibits its use—something which almost never happens.

or less), or in direct obligations of the state of California maturing in one year or less);

- Completing a contract entered into by the decedent to convey real or personal property; *and*

- Borrowing money, executing a mortgage or deed of trust or giving other security.[2]

A sample of the "Notice of Proposed Action" form is shown in Chapter 14. It includes a space for the recipient to object or consent to the proposed action. A copy of the Notice form must be mailed or personally served to all heirs and beneficiaries whose interest will be affected at least 15 days before the proposed action will be taken. Although the Probate Code doesn't require it, some courts require that proof of the mailing be presented to the court. Therefore, it is a good idea to have the Notice form mailed or personally served (by someone who is over 18 years old and not interested in the estate) and then file an affidavit with the court stating when and how she served the Notice.

If the proposed action involves selling or granting an option to buy real property, the Notice must include the material terms of the sale and any payment that is to be made to a broker or agent.

Persons entitled to receive Notice forms may waive, in writing, their right to notice. They must use a printed form, called "Waiver of Notice of Proposed Action," which is available at the probate court. The Waiver can apply to all actions taken by the personal representative, or only certain actions specified on the form. Persons who should have received notice may also consent to an action that has already been taken. A person who fails to object to a proposed action gives up his right to have a court review the action later.

What happens if the will prohibits the use of the Independent Administration of Estates Act? You can still do your own probate and use the procedures outlined in the next chapter for simple probate court proceedings.

---

[2]Only a personal representative who has "full authority" under the Act may borrow money with the loan secured by an encumbrance on real property. (Probate Code § 10514.)

The only difference is that you will not be able to do the things listed in Probate Code §§ 10510-10564 without prior court approval; however, most simple estates can be settled without these transactions anyway. The only two that might affect you are paying Creditors' Claims or selling estate property without prior court approval. Obtaining court approval to pay formal Creditor's Claims is simple and merely means mailing the original claim and a copy to the court asking that it be approved for payment and that a conformed copy be returned to you. However, selling real property without the authority of the Independent Administration of Estates Act is more involved and requires special documents and procedures not covered in this book. See Section E4[d] below.

3. The "Notice of Petition to Administer Estate"

When you file the probate petition, the court clerk assigns a hearing date. Notice of the time, date and place of the hearing must then be given to all heirs, beneficiaries, creditors and persons who may be interested in the estate. This is done by publishing a "Notice of Petition to Administer Estate" in a newspaper in the city where the decedent lived at the time he died (or where he left property, if he is not a California resident). The notice of the hearing date must also be mailed to all heirs and beneficiaries within 15 days of the hearing date. This gives them an opportunity to appear at the hearing and assert their rights, if they wish to do so. Procedures vary in different court districts as to who arranges for the preparation, publication and mailing of the notice. In some counties the petitioner does all the work, while in others the court clerk and the newspaper do everything. However, seeing that the notice is properly given is the responsibility of the petitioner, even though the job is delegated to a newspaper in some counties. We will discuss this in more detail in Chapter 14.

Note: The Notice of Petition to Administer Estate also advises interested persons that they may serve the personal representative with a written "Request for

Special Notice" of the filing of certain documents. It is rare to receive these requests in a simple, uncontested estate; however, if one is filed you must notify the interested person in writing when the inventory and appraisement and petition for final distribution are filed, as well as when a Notice of Proposed Action is given. We explain how to do this in the next chapter.

4. Proving the Will

If there is a will, it must be "proven" in a probate court hearing (unless it is a "self-proving" will—see Subsection 5, below). To prove a will, it must be shown either that (1) the decedent signed it in front of witnesses, declaring that it was his will, or (2) the witnesses understood it was his will. You do this by finding the witnesses and having them sign a declaration to this effect. The declaration is a simple printed court form with a photocopy of the will attached showing the signature of the witnesses and the filing stamp of the court clerk. We provide a sample in Step 6 of the next chapter. If the decedent left a

holographic will (one in which the signature and material provisions are in the decedent's handwriting), you need a declaration from someone who knows the decedent's handwriting and who will verify that the will was written by the decedent.[3] Any person having knowledge of the decedent's handwriting may sign the declaration, even if that person stands to inherit all or a part of the estate. This declaration is also a simple printed court form, and is shown in Step 7 of the next chapter.

5. Self-Proving Wills and Codicils

Many formal wills and codicils are "self-proving," meaning they were executed in such a way as not to require a declaration from one of the witnesses. A self-proving will or codicil is one signed by the witnesses under penalty of perjury declaring the document was executed according to law. (Probate Code § 8220.) If the paragraph preceding the signature of the witnesses is in the following basic form, it is usually sufficient to prove the will, or codicil, if no one appears to contest the probate

---

[3]A printed form will is a valid holographic will and a statement of testamentary intent may be in the testator's own handwriting or part of a commercially printed form will. (Probate Code § 6111 (c).)

Sample of "Self-Proving" Clause of Will

On the date written below, [name of decedent] declared to us, the undersigned, that this instrument, consisting of three (3) pages including the page signed by us as witnesses, was his will and requested us to act as witnesses to it. He thereupon signed his will in our presence (or acknowledged to us that he had signed it as his will), all of us being present at the same time, and we understand it to be his will. We now, at his request, in his presence, and in the presence of each other, subscribe our names as witnesses. We declare that at the time of signing this will the said testator appeared to be of sound and disposing mind and memory and not acting under duress, menace, fraud or the undue influence of any person whomsoever.

Executed at _____, on _____, 19__. We declare under penalty of perjury under the laws of the State of California that the foregoing is true and correct.

_____ residing at _____

_____ residing at _____

If, however, the validity of the will is questioned during the probate proceeding, the court may require evidence beyond this clause. Some courts always require a written declaration by at least one witness, regardless of whether or not the original will is self-proving, so local practice should be checked. Technically, therefore, wills in California are never completely "self-proving."

6. Probate Calendar Notes

In most of the larger counties, after a petition is filed, checkers, probate attorneys or commissioners examine the petition before the hearing. They look to see if it conforms to certain requirements, such as whether notice of the probate proceeding has been given to the proper people (Chapter 14, Step 10), whether the petition is properly signed and verified, and whether all necessary information has been given. Each court keeps a calendar sheet of cases scheduled for hearing. Calendar notes are notations made by the probate examiner on the calendar sheets after the petition has been reviewed. If all is well, the probate examiner stamps on the calendar the letters "RFA," which means "Recommended for Approval." This means no one need show up (appear) in court and the petition will be approved routinely. If, however, a problem exists, or more information is needed, the probate examiner notes on the calendar sheet what is required before approval can be granted. In some counties, including Los Angeles, if you attach a self-addressed, stamped envelope to the petition when it is filed, the probate examiner will mail the calendar notes to you before the hearing so you will know in advance if it will be approved. In other counties, the clerk will call you and explain the problems.[4]

---

[4]Some courts (for example, the Los Angeles Central District) will FAX the notes to you if you request it when you file the petition and pay a small fee.

Not all counties have a staff of probate examiners, however. If the court does not mail calendar notes, you may call the court's probate department two or three days before the hearing is scheduled and inquire if the petition has been approved. Some courts post calendar notes at the courthouse; others have a telephone number you call for a recording of all petitions that were approved. If your petition isn't granted, you should talk to one of the "clearing attorneys," preferably in person, and find out what the problem is. Don't worry. Most problems, once they are explained, are easy to correct, and the worst thing that will happen is that your hearing will be postponed about three or four weeks to allow you time to correct the problem. Probate departments in larger counties are extremely busy, and the probate examiners do not have time to discuss the notes in detail nor advise what should be done. However, courts in smaller districts are usually very helpful.

Here are some abbreviations used on calendar notes:

Aff	"affidavit" (when used alone means affidavit of mailing by the county clerk—applies to Notice of Hearing)
Appr	"appraisement" or "appraisals" (refers to an appraisal of the assets by the probate referee—see discussion in Section E).
Benef	"beneficiary"
Bond w	"bond waived" (see discussion in Section D)
Bond req	"bond required" (see discussion in Section D)
C/P	"community property"
D/D	"date of death"
Inc	"no certificate from franchise tax board" (applies to estates over $400,000—see discussion in Section E)
JTD	"judge to determine" (usually means an appearance in court is required for approval of an item)
N/D	"Notice of Death" (refers to the published and mailed notice required to be given to the heirs and beneficiaries where the petition for probate is filed)
Off-Cal	"off calendar" (means the petition has been removed from the court's calendar and new notice will have to be given when a new hearing date is obtained)
O/W	"otherwise"
PPM	"probate policy memoranda" (refers to the court's pamphlet setting forth the rules of the court)
Pub	"publication" (refers to published notice to persons interested in the estate of the filing of the petition for probate—see discussion in Section D)
RFA	"recommended for approval without a court appearance"
S/P	"separate property"
Supp	"supplement" or "supplemental"
Verif	"verification" (statement that the end of a petition whereby the petitioner swears under penalty of perjury that the statements in the petition are true—see Section C)

7. Supplements to the Petition

If the calendar notes indicate additional information is required, or corrections should be made, you may prepare a supplement to the petition providing the necessary information and file it before the hearing date. (See instructions in Chapter 14, Step 10.)

Correcting information on a petition that is already filed with the court is a lot of extra work. It is far better to examine the petition carefully before it is filed to make sure every detail has been taken care of. If you can't get the petition approved in time for the hearing, the court will continue it to a new date (usually about three or four weeks later) to give you time to do whatever is necessary to have it approved. Some courts have a rule that a matter may be continued only once, and others will take the petition "off calendar" if it is continued three times. If a petition is marked "off calendar," rather than given a new date, this means the court has removed the petition from its calendar of cases and it has lost jurisdiction to act on the petition. However, this is not as bad as it sounds. All you need to do is request a new hearing date when you are ready and start over by giving notices of the hearing when the petition is re-set.

8. Probate Bonds

Before being appointed by the court, the executor or administrator must ordinarily post a bond (a sum of money or insurance policy) as insurance that he will faithfully perform his duties as representative, unless bond is waived in the decedent's will. Most wills include this waiver provision. To find out if a bond is required or waived, simply read the will.

If the will doesn't waive the bond, all beneficiaries under the will, or heirs if there is no will, may waive the bond as long as they are all adults and competent. The waivers must be in writing and attached to the petition for probate when it is filed with the court. The waivers can usually be obtained easily in a simple estate where the beneficiaries are all friendly. A waiver form is shown in Chapter 14, as Attachment 3d to the petition for probate.

The court will usually not require a bond if it is waived in the will; however, the court may still impose a bond if it sees a need. Some courts require at least a minimum bond (around $6,000), even if written waivers are obtained. Following are some situations where a bond may be required:

a. One of the beneficiaries is a minor, and therefore not qualified to sign a waiver of bond;

b. The will names two or more persons to serve as executors and all do not serve, and the will does not waive bond for fewer than the number specified;

c. The executor or administrator resides outside of California, notwithstanding that the will waives bond;

d. The executor named in a will that waives bond does not qualify, and an administrator with the will annexed (see Section C, above) is appointed in his place.

When the estate is represented by an attorney, probate bonds are most often obtained from authorized surety companies. The amount of the bond is fixed at the value of all the personal property plus the probable value of the annual rents, issues and profits from all property (including real property) in the estate. However, most surety companies will not provide a bond for personal representatives who are acting in pro per without an attorney.

If you cannot get a bond from a corporate surety, individuals may act as sureties instead, subject to the following limitations:

a. At least two individual sureties must be used;

b. The amount of the bond must be not less than twice the value of the personal property and twice the value of the probable annual income from the real and personal property;

c. The principal (estate representative) may not be one of the sureties;

d. The individuals must be California residents and either "householders" or owners of real property in California;

e. Each individual's net worth must be at least the amount of the bond in real or personal property, or both, in California.

In lieu of bond, alternate security can be provided by putting estate assets beyond the immediate control of the representative to be released only on court order. (Probate Code § 8483.) For instance, you may:

- Deposit estate money in an insured account in a financial institution in California (Probate Code § 9700);

- Deposit estate securities (stocks and bonds) or other estate assets (for example, jewelry, fine art, precious metals) with a trust company (Probate Code § 9701). Most banks are authorized trust companies, but not always.

Arrangements for the deposits may be made before or after the Petition for Probate is filed. The request that the blocked account be allowed is made by checking the appropriate box on the Petition for Probate (Item 2d). The money, securities or other assets deposited are then excluded from the computation of the amount of bond required. This task is easier if the securities or money are already on deposit with an authorized bank; otherwise it might be difficult to obtain possession of the assets before the representative is appointed by the court. Alternatively, you may allege in the petition that the money and/or other property will be deposited with an authorized institution promptly after appointment of the representative, subject to withdrawal only upon court order. In any event, a written receipt from the depository, including the statement that withdrawals will not be allowed except on court order, must be obtained and filed with the court.

To sum up, if bond is not waived in the will or if there is no will, you should obtain written waivers of bond from all adult heirs or beneficiaries and attach them to the petition for probate. In addition, we recommend you request authorization in the petition to deposit some or all of the estate's personal property and funds not needed for estate expenses in blocked accounts with an authorized bank or trust company. If the court still imposes a bond, it should be minimal and individual sureties easily obtained. As an alternative, check with the court to see if it will accept a blocked account of your personal funds in twice the amount of the bond requirement in lieu of the bond.

9. Order for Probate and Letters

As discussed in detail in Chapter 14, when the court approves the petition, you must prepare and send in an Order for Probate for the judge's signature. This is a simple printed form. The Order appoints the estate representative, admits the will to probate and usually appoints a probate referee to appraise the estate assets. At the same time the Order is signed, the court will issue "Letters" to you. This document is your "badge of office" as estate representative. The original of the Letters stays in the court file, and certified copies are supplied to you when you need evidence that you are authorized to act on behalf of the estate. "Letters testamentary" are issued to the executor, "letters of administration" are issued to the administrator, and "letters of administration with will annexed" (or "letters of administration C.T.A.") are issued to the administrator with will annexed. They all amount to the same thing.

10. Probate Register

Every court keeps a journal page for each probate case, which carries information on everything that happens in the court proceeding, such as when a petition or order has been filed, the hearing date on a petition, whether the petition is approved, if bond is required and when the estate inventory is filed. In most courts you may call the probate department at the courthouse, give them the probate case number and obtain the information over the phone.

If you are interested, you may go to the courthouse and examine the probate register as well as some probate files. These records are open to the public and you may find the information helpful.

E. Taking Care of the Estate During Probate

ONE OF THE ESTATE representative's primary duties is to take good care of estate property while the probate process chugs along. This section discusses some of the tasks you'll run into.

1. Probate Referee/Inventory and Appraisement

When the Order for Probate is signed, a "probate referee" is appointed by the court.[5] The referee's job is to appraise certain assets in the estate as of the date of the decedent's death. The referee is paid a fee of one-tenth of one percent of the total value of the assets appraised (minimum of $75), not to exceed $10,000. The referee is also reimbursed for necessary expenses, such as mileage if he must inspect real property.

You are responsible for preparing the inventory of the assets subject to probate, for the referee to appraise. This is done on an "Inventory and Appraisement" form, with attachments describing the assets owned by the decedent at his death, including all property except joint tenancy property, property held in trust, and insurance proceeds or death benefits payable to a named beneficiary. Property passing outright to a surviving spouse that will be the subject of a Spousal Property Petition (see Chapter 15) should also not be included in probate inventory, as a

rule. Preparation of the inventory should be started as early as possible so the administration of the estate is not unnecessarily prolonged. When the form is complete, send it to the probate referee, who appraises the assets listed on the attachments (with the exception of certain cash items which are first appraised by the representative). The referee will place the values on the inventory schedule and return it to you to file with the probate court.

Under Probate Code § 8903, you may request that the court waive the appointment of a referee, either when the petition for probate is filed or by a separate petition setting forth the facts that justify the waiver. The petition will be given a hearing date and all heirs and beneficiaries must be notified. You also have the option of using an independent expert to appraise unique assets. More on this in Chapter 14.

2. Handling Debts and Creditor's Claims

Anyone who winds up a deceased person's affairs must see that all legitimate debts are paid. Claims are received in two ways. At the formal level, the Notice of Petition to Administer Estate published in the newspaper (see Section D, above) gives legal notice to all creditors to file their claims within four months after issuance of your letters. The claims must be filed with the court and a copy sent to the personal representative. A Creditor's Claim form is available for this purpose. In uncomplicated estates, few formal claims are submitted.

---

[5]In some counties, the probate referee is appointed on the day the probate petition is filed. If this is done, the referee's name and address will be stamped on your copy of the Petition for Probate or later on the Order for Probate.

In addition, you must give written notice within four months after the Letters are issued to all known creditors and must continue to give notice as you become aware of new creditors. The written notice advises the creditors that administration of the estate has been commenced and that claims must be filed with the court. (Probate Code § 9050 et seq.)[6]

The second level at which claims are made is the informal one, where you find that the decedent's bills keep coming to the decedent's last address. The usual ordinary expenses can be taken care of with a minimum of paperwork under two code sections. Probate Code § 10552 allows you to pay debts at your discretion without court approval or without requiring a formal claim if you have independent administration authority. In addition, when there has been a written demand for payment, Probate Code § 9154 allows you to pay debts incurred by the decedent before death within 30 days after the claim period ends without requiring a formal claim, unless for some reason you dispute the amount or legitimacy of the debt. As a rule, all of the decedent's debts should be paid from the estate assets. If the decedent was heavily in debt or there are complicated or large disputed claims against the estate, you should probably seek help from an attorney.

3. How To Handle Assets During Administration

After Letters are issued (see Section D, above) there is a four-month waiting period before the estate may be closed and distributed, during which the creditors are allowed to file their claims. During this period questions sometimes arise on how to deal with certain assets until they can be distributed. Here are some suggestions on how to treat various types of assets.

---

[6]If you first acquire knowledge of the claim during the last 30 days of the period or after the four-month period has run, the Notice must be mailed within 30 days after acquiring knowledge. This is explained in more detail in the next chapter.

a. Bank Accounts

All accounts in the decedent's name (including out-of-state bank accounts) should be transferred to estate accounts in your name as the estate representative. Contrary to what many people believe, bank accounts in the name of a deceased person are not frozen for long periods of time, and banks will release the funds to you if you present a certified copy of your letters. All money received during the administration of the estate (such as stock dividends) should be deposited into the estate account, and the decedent's debts and expenses of administration (such as court costs and publication fees) should be paid from the estate account. Keep an accurate record of each disbursement, indicating the reason for the payment and the date. For each deposit, keep a record of the source of the funds and the date received. This detailed information on receipts and disbursements will be needed to prepare the estate's income tax returns, if they are required.

Excess cash must be held in insured interest-bearing accounts (Probate Code § 9652) or invested in government obligations maturing in five years or less, or in direct obligations of the state of California maturing in one year or less. (Probate Code § 9730.) Be sure not to mix any of your personal funds with the estate's funds. With the exception of the initial court filing fee, it is best not to pay estate expenses with your personal funds and later reimburse yourself, as this may raise questions as to why you took money from the estate.

Note: The estate is a separate taxpayer, and before opening the estate account most banks will require you to obtain a taxpayer identification number. Application for the number is made on Form SS-4 (Application for Employer Identification Number), available from the Internal Revenue Service. The same number is used for state income tax purposes. See Chapter 7, Section B, for instructions on how to obtain the number.

b. Rent

If the decedent rented rather than owned her residence, you have some decisions to make:

- Whether to pay additional rent on the decedent's apartment in order to safeguard the furniture and furnishings;

- Whether to store the items at the estate's expense; or

- Whether to permit the beneficiaries to take possession of the items to which they are presumptively entitled.

In most instances the last alternative is preferable and usually not objectionable as long as the items are not of unusual value, no problems are anticipated, and you obtain a receipt. Keep in mind, however, that it is the duty of the estate representative to protect estate property, so reasonable prudence should be exercised. If rented premises are to be vacated, you should immediately contact the landlord and give the required notice—usually 30 days—and arrange for a refund of any security deposit. If a long-term lease is involved, you should give prompt written notice and move out. The landlord has the duty to mitigate his damages, which means he must try to re-rent the property. Assuming he accomplishes this at the same or a higher rent, or reasonably could have done so if he had tried, the estate is off the hook for additional rent from the day of the new rental. If you have more questions about mitigation of damages, see *Tenants' Rights*, by Moskovitz and Warner (Nolo Press).

c. Motor Vehicles

If the decedent owned a motor vehicle (auto, motor home, motorcycle, etc.) in his name alone, the identity of the person entitled to it is not in doubt (either under the will or by intestate succession), and it is clear there will be no objections, then the vehicle may be transferred to the new owner prior to the closing of the estate. (Vehicle Code Section 5910.) However, you or the new owner should make sure there is adequate insurance coverage to eliminate any chance that a claim could be made against the estate based on a subsequent accident. Although the Vehicle Code does not specifically permit it, a transfer on the signature of the representative is normally honored by the Department of Motor Vehicles if submitted with a certified copy of your letters. If the vehicle is owned in joint tenancy with someone else, it may be transferred by the procedures outlined in Chapter 10. If money is owed on the vehicle, this obligation is normally assumed by the new owner, unless the decedent's will says otherwise. [7]

d. Stocks and Bonds

The easiest way to handle stocks and bonds is to leave them in the decedent's name and transfer them to the beneficiaries on final distribution of the estate. Dividend checks and checks for interest on bonds or debentures will, of course, be made payable to the decedent, but you can endorse the checks and deposit them to the estate bank account. Usually, there is no problem with the checks being honored.

4. Sales of Estate Property

Sometimes it may be necessary or desirable to sell some estate assets before the estate is closed to raise cash to pay debts or to avoid the expense of caring for the property during probate. Selling property may also facilitate distribution of an asset, as when beneficiaries do not wish to own fractional interests in an asset (such as a one-third interest in a computer or a one-half interest in a stamp collection). Property may be sold during probate administration and distribution made in cash, if the beneficiaries agree. If you have authority to administer the estate under the Independent Administration of Estates Act, you may sell estate property (real or personal) for cash or

---

[7] If none of the beneficiaries wants the vehicle, it is probably wise for the estate representative to sell it at an early date as a depreciating asset (see Section 4-a) to avoid the expense of caring for it during administration of the estate.

on credit, and for the price you determine, subject to the following rules:

a. Depreciating Personal Property

Personal property that will depreciate in value, or that will cause loss or expense to the estate if retained, may be sold without prior court approval and without prior notice to any person interested in the estate. Automobiles and furniture are frequently sold under this provision. In addition, if the cost of collecting, maintaining and safeguarding tangible personal property would exceed its fair market value (for example, junk cars and garage sale leftovers), you may abandon or otherwise dispose of the property after giving written notice to the heirs. The minimum notice period is ten days by mail or five days by personal delivery. If an heir objects in writing within that period, you can demand that the objecting heir take the property into his possession at the heir's own expense. (Probate Code § 9788.)

b. Securities, Stocks and Bonds

Securities listed on a stock or bond exchange may be sold for cash at the best price on the stock exchange without notifying the beneficiaries in advance or obtaining prior court approval.

c. Other Personal Property

You may sell other personal property without prior court approval as well, but (except for property noted in paragraphs a and b) you must first give a Notice of Proposed Action to the beneficiaries whose interest will be affected by the sale. See Section D, above, regarding the Notice of Proposed Action procedure.

d. Real Property

An estate representative who has **full** authority under the Act may also sell real property without court supervision by giving an Notice of Proposed Action to the beneficia-

ries whose interest in the property will be affected. The usual requirements that apply to sales of real property during probate administration, such as publication of notice of sale, court approval of the sale price and of agent's and broker's commissions, do not apply to sales under the Act. You may sell the property at a price and on terms you find acceptable. The Notice of Proposed Action must, however, include the material terms of the transaction, including the sales price and commission paid an agent or broker. We recommend that the title company be notified in advance that the sale will be made without court supervision. Usually, the title company will want assurance that the Notice has been given properly and will require a certified copy of the Letters, as well as an "Executor's Deed" in the form shown in the next chapter.

5. Income Taxes

You should contact an accountant early in the proceedings to arrange for preparation of the decedent's final state and federal income tax returns. Of course, you can do the paperwork yourself, but the moderate fee you will pay to have an experienced person do the work is probably worth the trouble you save. In addition, if the estate remains open long enough, it may receive enough income to require the filing of income tax returns for the estate. These are called "fiduciary" income tax returns. An accountant may advise you in this regard. Income taxes are discussed in more detail in Chapter 7.

6. Federal Estate Tax Return

If the value of all the decedent's property (this includes probate assets, joint tenancy property, insurance proceeds when the decedent owned the policy at death, death benefits and property in trust) is high enough, a federal estate tax return will have to be prepared and filed within nine months of the date of death. See Chapter 7.

7. Personal Property Taxes

Probate Code § 1024, which required that all personal property taxes must be paid before final distribution of the estate, has been repealed.

8. California Income Tax Clearance

A California Income Tax Clearance must be obtained before the estate may be closed if the estate has a gross value exceeding $400,000, and assets of $100,000 or more will be distributed to one or more beneficiaries who are not residents of California. This clearance takes the form of a California Franchise Tax Board certificate which says, in effect, that all income taxes of the estate or the decedent have been paid or adequately secured.

F. Closing the Estate

WHEN YOU'VE TAKEN CARE of all the claims made on the estate and filed all the right papers, you're ready to ask the court to wind up the probate and "close" the estate.

1. Petition for Final Distribution

The estate may be closed anytime after the expiration of the creditor's claim period (four months from the date Letters are issued to you) if:

- All claims have been paid or sufficiently secured; and

- There are no problems that prevent the closing of the estate.

If all of the steps to this point have been taken with diligence, you should be ready to close the estate within five to seven months (nine months, if a federal estate tax return is required) from the time you filed the petition to open the estate.

To close the estate you must file a "Petition for Final Distribution" with the court, showing that the estate is in a condition to be closed and requesting that distribution be made to the beneficiaries. This final petition is not a printed form; it must be typed on numbered court paper according to special rules. (See Chapter 14, Step 17.) We recommend that you obtain a supply of this numbered paper in advance, either from a stationery store or other source, so you will have it on hand when you need it. A sample of the petition, which may be adapted to your circumstances, is shown in Chapter 14 with instructions on how to prepare it. After the petition is filed and approved, the court will sign an Order for Final Distribution. In Los Angeles County, the Order is prepared by the court, but in most other counties, it must be prepared by the petitioner.

2. Representative's Commissions

The law provides that the estate representative is entitled to compensation for her services to the estate, referred to as "commissions," which are paid out of the estate assets. You may request or waive the commissions in the Petition for Final Distribution. The amount of the commissions is based on a percentage of the gross value of the probate estate (probate assets only, not joint tenancy or trust property or life insurance proceeds). The following shows you how it is computed:

4% of the first	$15,000
3% of the next	$85,000
2% of the next	$900,000
1% of the next	$9,000,000
1/2% of the next	$15,000,000
"reasonable amount" for everything above	$25,000,000

If you are the sole beneficiary, it is probably unimportant whether you claim the commissions or not, since you will receive all the estate anyway. However, if there are several beneficiaries and you have done all the work, you may want to have a discussion to decide whether you will claim or waive the commissions to which you are entitled. You may also request less than the statutory amount. If the commissions are paid to you, they are treated as taxable income and must be reported on your personal income tax return.

3. Waiver of Accounting

Ordinarily, when a Petition for Final Distribution is filed, the court requires a detailed accounting of all monies or other items received, and all monies paid out, during administration. However, the accounting may be waived when all persons entitled to receive property from the estate have executed a written waiver of accounting. Probate Code § 10954 describes the conditions for obtaining the waivers. This simplifies the closing of the estate. When all beneficiaries are friendly, there is usually no problem in obtaining the waiver. The waivers may be signed by the following persons:

a. Any beneficiary who is an adult and competent;

b. If the distributee is a minor, by a person authorized to receive money or property belonging to the minor—parent, guardian (attach a certified copy of Letters of Guardianship), or custodian named in the will (see Chapter 14, Step 17);

c. If the distributee is a conservatee, by the conservator (attach a certified copy of Letters of Conservatorship);

d. If the distributee is a trust, by the trustee, but only after the trustee has first filed a written Consent to Act as Trustee;

e. If the distributee is an estate, by the personal representative (attach a certified copy of Letters);

f. By an attorney-in-fact for the distributee.

We show you how to get the accounting waived in the next chapter in the instructions for paragraph 13 of the Petition for Final Distribution.

4. Distributions to Minors

If there is a minor beneficiary who is entitled to receive non-cash estate assets worth more than $10,000 and the minor does not have a court-appointed property guardian, or a custodian was not named in the decedent's will to receive the property of the estate of the minor, you should contact an attorney. A court order may have to be obtained to have a guardian appointed for the minor's estate in a separate court proceeding.

5. Transferring the Assets

After the court signs the Order for Final Distribution (Chapter 14, Step 19), the property may be transferred to the beneficiaries. This is relatively easy with most assets. All beneficiaries must sign a receipt for the assets they receive, which you will file with the court along with another form requesting that you be discharged from your duties as estate representative, and this concludes the court proceeding. See Chapter 14, Steps 20 and 21.

G. Necessary Court Forms

VIRTUALLY ALL DOCUMENTS used in a simple probate court proceeding are official printed forms, with the exception of the last petition and order. Below is a list of the main forms you will need, although some counties may require a few additional local forms. You will find one copy of each in Appendix 2. To obtain additional copies, you can either photocopy the forms given in the Appendices (be sure you get clear copies), or purchase additional ones from the court. Photocopies may also be used as worksheets.

Probate forms may be ordered from the court by mail if you indicate the ones you want and enclose a check payable to the "County Clerk" to cover the cost, plus tax and postage. The cost for forms varies from county to county, so your best bet is to write a check for "Not to exceed $5.00." (Type or write these words just *under* the line where you normally write in the amount of the check.) In your cover letter, ask the clerk to also send you any additional local forms required, along with an explanation of what they are for.

Standard Probate Forms

Petition for Probate

Certificate of Assignment (for filing in branch courts)

Notice of Petition to Administer Estate

Proof of Subscribing Witness
(used only when there is a will)

Proof of Holographic Instrument
(used only for handwritten wills)

Order for Probate

Letters

Duties and Liabilities of Estate Representatives

Notice of Administration (Notice to Creditors)

Application and Order Appointing Probate Referee

Inventory and Appraisement

Inventory and Appraisement (attachment)

Allowance or Rejection of Creditor's Claim

Notice of Hearing (Probate)

Affidavit of Final Discharge and Order

Here is a sample letter:

```
(date)

Clerk of the Superior Court
111 North Hill Street
Los Angeles, CA 90012


Will you please provide me with two copies
of each of the following probate forms:

Petition for Probate
Notice of Petition to Administer Estate
Proof of Subscribing Witness
Order for Probate
Letters
Duties and Liabilities of Estate
  Representative
Application and Order Appointing Probate
  Referee
Inventory and Appraisement
Inventory and Appraisement (attachment)
Allowance or Rejection of Creditor's Claim
Notice of Hearing (Probate)
Affidavit of Final Discharge and Order

Will you also please send me two copies of
any additional local forms you require,
along with an explanation of what they are
used for. A check for "Not to Exceed $5.00"
is enclosed to cover your fee.

Thank-you for your assistance.


          Very truly yours,
```

CHAPTER 14

Conducting a Simple Probate
Court Proceeding

NOW THAT YOU HAVE a general idea from Chapter 13 of what a probate court proceeding involves, this chapter will tell you exactly how to do it. It provides samples of all forms, with detailed explanations of how they should be prepared. You will find a complete set of tear-out printed court forms in Appendix 2. Extra copies can be made on a good photocopying machine or ordered from the court. (See Chapter 13.) Remember, when you file documents with the court, always submit at least one extra copy and keep a copy for your files.

Step 1: Prepare the Petition for Probate

THIS IS THE DOCUMENT that initiates the probate proceeding. It requests that the will (if there is one) be admitted to probate and that a representative be appointed to administer the estate. The same form is used whether you file a "Petition for Probate" (when there is a will) or a "Petition for Letters" (when there is no will). The distinction is made by checking the appropriate box. Be sure all attachments are full-sized sheets (8 1/2" x 11").

Box 1 (Attorney or Party Without Attorney): Your name and address (as the petitioner and proposed personal representative of the estate) should be inserted in the upper left-hand corner box. You will find this general format on all printed court forms. After the words "Attorney For," type "Petitioner in Pro Per," as in the sample form. This means you are acting as your own attorney.

Box 2 (Name and Address of Court): Type in the name of the county and the street address of the court. The county will be the one in which the decedent resided at the time he died. (See Chapter 13, Section C, for more on how to determine the correct county.)

Box 3 (Estate of): Simply type the name of the decedent, including all name variations under which he held property. All of these names should be carried forward to all probate documents filed with the court. If the decedent used more than one name, put the name he used most often for legal purposes followed by "aka" ("also known as") and then the other names he used for business purposes. For example, if John Doe held most of his property in that name but had several bank accounts and a car registration under Jack Doe and John L. Doe, you would insert "John Doe, aka Jack Doe, aka John L. Doe." If you are dealing with a female decedent who had prior marriages, you may find different last names, such as "Jane Storm, aka Jane Merryweather."

Box 4 (Petition for): Two boxes should be checked after the words "Petition for":

a. If there is a will and you are the executor named in the will, check the box which says "Probate of Will and for Letters Testamentary."

If there is a will but no executor is named, or the named executor is unable or unwilling to act and no co-executor or successor is named, you will be petitioning to serve as "administrator C.T.A." (see Chapter 13, Section C). Check the box which says "Probate of Will and for Letters of Administration with Will Annexed."

If there is no will, check the box which says "Letters of Administration."

The box saying "Letters of Special Administration" should be left blank.

b. The second box to be checked is the next to last one, which says "Authorization to Administer Under the Independent Administration of Estates Act." Make sure the will doesn't prohibit this. (See Chapter 13, Section D.) Even if it does, you can probably still use the procedures outlined in this chapter, but you shouldn't check the box requesting authorization to use independent administration procedures.

Special Form for San Francisco

If you file for probate in San Francisco, your Petition for Probate must be accompanied by a new local form called a "Declaration of Real Property." You can get the form from the court—it's very easy to fill out.

Petition for Probate
(front)

ATTORNEY OR PARTY WITHOUT ATTORNEY *(Name and Address):*

BILLY M. KIDD
1109 Sky Blue Mountain Trail
Billings, Montana 48906

TELEPHONE NO. (715) 392-6408

ATTORNEY FOR *(Name):* Petitioner in Pro Per

FOR COURT USE ONLY

SUPERIOR COURT OF CALIFORNIA, COUNTY OF LOS ANGELES
STREET ADDRESS: 1725 Main Street
MAILING ADDRESS:
CITY AND ZIP CODE: Santa Monica, California 90401
BRANCH NAME: West District

ESTATE OF (NAME): ANABELLE KIDD, aka
ANABELLE O. KIDD, DECEDENT

CASE NUMBER:

HEARING DATE:

DEPT.: TIME:

PETITION FOR

(For deaths after December 31, 1984)

- [X] Probate of Will and for Letters Testamentary
- [ ] Probate of Will and for Letters of Administration with Will Annexed
- [ ] Letters of Administration
- [ ] Letters of Special Administration
- [X] Authorization to Administer Under the Independent Administration of Estates Act [ ] with limited authority

1. Publication will be in *(specify name of newspaper):* Evening Outlook
   a. [ ] Publication requested.
   b. [X] Publication to be arranged.

(Signature of attorney or party without attorney)

2. Petitioner *(name of each):* BILLY M. KIDD
   requests
   a. [X] decedent's will and codicils, if any, be admitted to probate.
   b. [X] *(name):* BILLY M. KIDD
      be appointed (1) [X] executor (3) [ ] administrator
      (2) [ ] administrator with will annexed (4) [ ] special administrator
      and Letters issue upon qualification.
   c. [X] that [X] full [ ] limited authority be granted to administer under the Independent Administration of Estates Act.
   d. [X] bond not be required for the reasons stated in item 3d.
      [ ] $_____ bond be fixed. It will be furnished by an admitted surety insurer or as otherwise provided by law. *(Specify reasons in Attachment 2d if the amount is different from the maximum required by Probate Code, § 8482.)*
      [ ] $_____ in deposits in a blocked account be allowed. Receipts will be filed. *(Specify institution and location):*

3. a. Decedent died on *(date):* June 18, 1989 at *(place):* Santa Monica, California
      [X] a resident of the county named above.
      [ ] a nonresident of California and left an estate in the county named above located at *(specify location permitting publication in the newspaper named in item 1):*
   b. Street address, city, and county of decedent's residence at time of death: 9560 Euclid Street,
      Santa Monica, Los Angeles County, California
   c. Character and estimated value of the property of the estate
      (1) Personal property .... $ 48,500
      (2) Annual gross income from
          (i) [X] real property .... $ None
          (ii) [X] personal property ...... $ 3,400
          Total ...... $ 51,900
      (3) Real property: $ 305,000 *(If full authority under the Independent Administration of Estates Act is requested, state the fair market value of the real property less encumbrances.)*
   d. [X] Will waives bond. [ ] Special administrator is the named executor and the will waives bond.
      [ ] All beneficiaries are adults and have waived bond, and the will does not require a bond. *(Affix waiver as Attachment 3d.)*
      [ ] All heirs at law are adults and have waived bond. *(Affix waiver as Attachment 3d.)*
      [ ] Sole personal representative is a corporate fiduciary.

(Continued on reverse)

Form Approved by the
Judicial Council of California
DE-111 [Rev. July 1, 1989]

PETITION FOR PROBATE

Probate Code, §§ 8002, 10450

Petition for Probate
(back)

ESTATE OF (NAME): ANABELLE KIDD, DECEDENT	CASE NUMBER:

3. a. ☐ Decedent died intestate.
   ☒ Copy of decedent's will dated: July 1, 1980 ☐ codicils dated: are affixed as Attachment 3e.
   ☒ The will and all codicils are self-proving (Probate Code, § 8220).

   Attach a typed copy of a holographic will and a transla-tion of a foreign language will.

   f. Appointment of personal representative (check all applicable boxes)
   (1) Appointment of executor or administrator with will annexed
   ☒ Proposed executor is named as executor in the will and consents to act.
   ☐ No executor is named in the will.
   ☐ Proposed personal representative is a nominee of a person entitled to Letters. (Affix nomination as Attachment 3f(1).)
   ☐ Other named executors will not act because of ☐ death ☐ declination ☐ other reasons (specify in Attachment 3f(1)).
   (2) Appointment of administrator
   ☐ Petitioner is a person entitled to Letters. (If necessary, explain priority in Attachment 3f(2).)
   ☐ Petitioner is a nominee of a person entitled to Letters. (Affix nomination as Attachment 3f(2).)
   ☐ Petitioner is related to the decedent as (specify):
   (3) ☐ Appointment of special administrator requested. (Specify grounds and requested powers in Attachment 3f(3).)
   g. Proposed personal representative is a ☐ resident of California ☒ nonresident of California (affix statement of permanent address as Attachment 3g) ☒ resident of the United States ☐ nonresident of the United States.

4. ☒ Decedent's will does not preclude administration of this estate under the Independent Administration of Estates Act.

5. a. The decedent is survived by
   (1) ☐ spouse ☒ no spouse as follows: ☐ divorced or never married ☒ spouse deceased
   (2) ☒ child as follows: ☒ natural or adopted ☐ natural adopted by a third party ☐ step ☐ foster
       ☐ no child
   (3) ☒ issue of a predeceased child ☐ no issue of a predeceased child
   b. Petitioner ☒ has no actual knowledge of facts ☐ has actual knowledge of facts reasonably giving rise to a parent-child relationship under Probate Code section 6408(b).
   c. ☒ All surviving children and issue of predeceased children have been listed in item 8.

6. (Complete if decedent was survived by (1) a spouse but no issue (only a or b apply); or (2) no spouse or issue. Check the first box that applies):
   a. ☐ The decedent is survived by a parent or parents who are listed in item 8.
   b. ☐ The decedent is survived by issue of deceased parents, all of whom are listed in item 8.
   c. ☐ The decedent is survived by a grandparent or grandparents who are listed in item 8.
   d. ☐ The decedent is survived by issue of grandparents, all of whom are listed in item 8.
   e. ☐ The decedent is survived by issue of a predeceased spouse, all of whom are listed in item 8.
   f. ☐ The decedent is survived by next of kin, all of whom are listed in item 8.
   g. ☐ The decedent is survived by parents of a predeceased spouse or issue of those parents, if both are predeceased, all of whom are listed in item 8.

7. (Complete only if no spouse or issue survived the decedent) Decedent ☐ had no predeceased spouse ☐ had a predeceased spouse who (1) ☐ died not more than 15 years before decedent owning an interest in real property that passed to decedent,
   (2) ☐ died not more than five years before decedent owning personal property valued at $10,000 or more that passed to decedent,
   (3) ☐ neither (1) nor (2) apply. (If you checked (1) or (2), check only the first box that applies):
   a. ☐ The decedent is survived by issue of a predeceased spouse, all of whom are listed in item 8.
   b. ☐ The decedent is survived by a parent or parents of the predeceased spouse who are listed in item 8.
   c. ☐ The decedent is survived by issue of a parent of the predeceased spouse, all of whom are listed in item 8.
   d. ☐ The decedent is survived by next of kin of the decedent, all of whom are listed in item 8.
   e. ☐ The decedent is survived by next of kin of the predeceased spouse, all of whom are listed in item 8.

8. Listed in Attachment 8 are the names, relationships, ages, and addresses of all persons named in decedent's will and codicils, whether living or deceased, and all persons checked in items 5, 6, and 7, so far as known to or reasonably ascertainable by peti-tioner, including stepchild and foster child heirs and devisees to whom notice is to be given under Probate Code section 1207.

9. ☒ Number of pages attached: 4

Date: July 5, 1989

▶ _____   ▶ *[signature]*
   (SIGNATURE OF PETITIONER*)   (SIGNATURE OF PETITIONER*)

I declare under penalty of perjury under the laws of the State of California that the foregoing is true and correct.
Date: July 5, 1989
.... BILLY. M. .KIDD. ....   ▶ *[signature]*
       (TYPE OR PRINT NAME)   (SIGNATURE OF PETITIONER*)

* All petitioners must sign the petition. Only one need sign the declaration.

DE-111 [Rev. July 1, 1989]   **PETITION FOR PROBATE**   Page two

Important: If the estate contains real property, the court will require the representative to post a bond for the value of the cash that would be received on the sale of the real property, unless bond is waived in the decedent's will. Some courts require such a bond even if the heirs and beneficiaries have all filed written waivers. Therefore, unless the will waives bond, or unless real property of the estate will be sold during probate, we recommend you also check the last box, before the words "with limited authority," which means you are requesting all of the powers granted by the Independent Administration of Estates Act except the power to sell, or otherwise deal with, real property. If you do need to sell real property during probate, see Step 14.

Item 1: This item pertains to publication of the Notice of Petition to Administer Estate, which is discussed in Step 4, below. Selection of the proper newspaper is very important. The best way to handle this is to ask the clerk for newspapers, if any, in the city where the decedent lived at the time of death and go in person to make arrangements for publication of the Notice. Most newspapers are familiar with the requirements. However, you should ask if they will prepare and file the required affidavit giving proof of the publication with the court, or whether you will have to do it yourself. (See Step 4.) As a rule, you must pay the newspaper publication fee in advance, which is around $150. After you have determined the newspaper you will use, type in its name in Item 1, and check box 1-b indicating that publication is being arranged for.

Item 2: Type in your name, as petitioner, on this line. If there are two petitioners, type both names.

Item 2-a: If there is a will, check this box.

Item 2-b: Check the first box and on the same line type in your name. Check box (1), (2) or (3), whichever applies to your situation. (See Chapter 13, Section C, if you are in doubt.) Leave box (4) blank.

Item 2-c: Check the first box (unless the will prohibits the use of the Independent Administration of Estates Act). If the estate contains real property and the will does not waive bond (or if there is no will), we recommend you request limited authority. If the estate does not contain real property (or if it contains real property that will be sold during probate), then check the box requesting full authority under the Act.

Item 2-d: Remember, the representative usually does not have to post a bond when all beneficiaries or all heirs waive the bond, or if the will waives the requirement of a bond, unless the court orders otherwise. (See Chapter 13, Section D, paragraph 8.) Assuming you will be able to get waivers (if bond isn't waived by the will), check the first box that says "bond not be required." In addition, if estate assets will be placed in blocked accounts, check the last box and fill in the name and address of the institution. A receipt for the deposit in the form shown below must be obtained from the depository and filed with the court, preferably before the hearing date on the petition.

Item 3-a: Type in the date and city and state of the decedent's death and check the appropriate box under Item 3-a. The petition must be filed in the county of the decedent's residence, no matter where she died. (Chapter 13, Section D.) If she was a non-resident of California, the petition must be filed in the county where she left property. If the decedent was a resident of the county in which you are filing your petition, check the first box. If she was a non-resident of California but left real or tangible personal property here, check the second box and type in the address of the property.

Item 3-b: Type in the street address, city and county where the decedent lived at the time of death.

Item 3-c: Type in, where indicated, the estimated value of all the real property (less encumbrances) and all the personal property (taken from inventory of assets—see Chapter 5), plus the annual estimated income from any items of property that produce income. Include only property that is being probated and, if any of the assets are community property, include only the decedent's one-half interest. (See Chapter 4.) This information is used to determine the amount of bond, when one is required, and as a basis for appointing the probate referee.

Receipt and Agreement by Depository

```
 1   Name:
 2   Address:
 3
 4   Telephone No.:
 5   Petitioner in Pro Per
 6
 7
 8                     SUPERIOR COURT OF CALIFORNIA
 9                     COUNTY OF _____
10
11   Estate of                )      NO. _____
                              )
12     (name of decedent)     )      RECEIPT AND AGREEMENT BY
                              )
13            deceased.       )      DEPOSITORY (Probate Code
                              )
14   _____)   Section 541.1)
15        The undersigned acknowledges receipt from _____
16   _____, personal representative of the estate of the
17   above-named decedent, of the following items of personal property:
18        a.  200 shares of Miracle Corporation, common stock;
19        b.  Cash in the sum of $12,000
20        The undersigned agrees that the foregoing cash and
21   securities will be held by the undersigned for the personal
22   representative, and will permit withdrawals only upon express
23   order of the above-entitled Court.
24        DATED: _____, 19___
25                          WESTERN STATES BANK
26                          By_____
27                               (authorized officer)
28
```

Item 3-d: If the will waives the requirement of a bond, check the first box. If it doesn't waive bond, but does not specifically state that bond is required, check the box just below the first one and attach a Waiver of Bond as Attachment 3-d (as shown below) signed by all beneficiaries named in the will. If there is no will, check the third box under Item 3-d and attach a Waiver of Bond signed by all the heirs as Attachment 3-d. Leave the fourth box blank.

Item 3-e: If the decedent did not leave a will, check the first box. If he died with a will, check the second box, type in the date of the will, and attach a copy of the will to your petition labeled Attachment 3-e. If there are any codicils, the same information is needed plus a copy of the codicil. If the will is holographic (written in the decedent's handwriting), prepare an accurate typed copy and attach it along with a photocopy of the handwritten will as Attachment 3-e. If the typed and witnessed will and all codicils are "self-proving" (language in the will makes further verification by the witnesses unnecessary), check the box under Item 3-e that indicates this. See Chapter 13, Section D(5) for an explanation of self-proving wills and codicils. Be sure to check if your county accepts self-proving wills. Otherwise, you must file a Proof of Subscribing Witness form (discussed in Step 6) before the hearing date on your petition.

Waiver of Bond
Attachment 3-d

```
 1      Estate of _____, Deceased
 2
 3                         WAIVER OF BOND
 4
 5          The undersigned, as (an heir/a beneficiary under the will) of the
 6      above-named decedent, hereby waives the requirement of a bond by
 7      _____, while serving as estate representative.
 8          DATED: _____, 19___.
 9
10
11
12                        _____
13
14
15
16
```

Item 3-f(1): The boxes under Section (1) of Item 3-f apply only if the decedent left a will. If there is no will, skip Section (1) and go to Section (2) under Item 3-f.

Complete Item 3-f(1) as follows:

- If the proposed executor (you) is named as executor in the will, check the first box.

- If the will does not name an executor, check the second box.

- If the executor named in the will is unable or unwilling to act (he is dead, has disappeared, is too ill or has declined to act), check the fourth box (indicating the reason by checking one of the additional boxes that follow) and prepare either a Declination to Act signed by the person who declines to serve (as shown below) or your statement as to why the named executor cannot act, and attach it to the petition as Attachment 3-f(1). (See Chapter 2, Section A(3) for the rules governing how an administrator with will annexed is chosen under these circumstances.) If you are petitioning as the co-executor or successor executor named in the will, you should check the first box in addition to the fourth box.

- If you are being nominated to be the personal representative, check the third box and attach a nomination as Attachment 3-f(1). The wording of the nomination should be the same as in the sample nomination (Attachment 3-f(2), for intestate situations) shown below.

Item 3-f(2): Section (2) under Item 3-f is for intestate estates (where the decedent died without a will). Review the discussion in Chapter 13, Section C(2) before completing Section (2). If you are entitled to priority to be administrator, check the first box. If you are being nominated to be administrator by someone who would otherwise have priority to be administrator, check the second box and attach a nomination as Attachment 3-f(2), as shown in the sample below. If you, as the proposed administrator, are related to the decedent, check the third box and indicate the relationship.

Item 3-g: A person does not have to be a resident of California to be an administrator, but must be a resident of the United States. An executor named in the will may reside anywhere. However, if any proposed personal representative (whether an executor, administrator or administrator with will annexed) is a non-resident of California, he must attach to the petition a signed statement, Attachment 3-g, setting forth his permanent address. A sample statement is shown below.[1]

Item 4: Before checking this box, read the will to make sure it does not prohibit you from using the procedures of the Independent Administration of Estates Act. It is extremely rare for a will to prohibit this, but even if it does, many of the procedures outlined in this chapter may still be used. See the comments in Chapter 13, Section D(2) regarding this situation.

Note on Items 5, 6 and 7: These items request information necessary to determine the decedent's heirs (those persons who inherit the estate in the absence of a will). Before completing these sections, *carefully review Chapter 3*, which gives detailed information on how the heirs of a decedent are determined. Chapter 3 also explains the meaning of certain common legal terminology, such as "issue," "predeceased spouse" and "child."

---

[1]Some courts (for example, Riverside County) require the non-resident's signature to be notarized.

Sample Statement
Attachment 3-f(1)

```
 1    Estate of _____, Deceased
 2    Attachment to Petition for Probate of Will
 3
 4
 5         The Executor named in the decedent's will is unable to manage his
 6    own personal affairs and is currently under a conservatorship.  Therefore,
 7    he is unable to serve as Executor of the decedent's estate.
 8
 9
10
11
12
13                              _____
14                                   Conservator
15
16
17
18
19
20
21
22
23
24
25
26
27
28
```

Attachment 3f(1)

Declination to Act
Attachment 3-f(1)

```
 1    Estate of _____, Deceased
 2
 3         RENUNCIATION OF RIGHT TO LETTERS TESTAMENTARY AND NOMINATION
 4
 5         The undersigned is a resident of the United States and entitled to
 6    receive more than 50% of the value of the decedent's estate.  I am named
 7    in the decedent's will as executor, but hereby decline to act and request
 8    that _____ be appointed to administer
 9    the decedent's estate.
10         DATED: _____, 19__.
11
12
13                              _____
14
15
16
17
18
19
20
21
22
23
24
25
26
27
28
```

Attachment 3f(1)

Statement of Permanent Address
Attachment 3-g

Estate of ANABELLE KIDD, Deceased

Petition for Probate of Will and Letters Testamentary

STATEMENT OF PERMANENT ADDRESS

Petitioner, a nonresident of California, states that his permanent

address is:

Billy M. Kidd

1109 Sky Blue Mountain Trail

Billings, Montana 48906

Telephone: (715) 392-6408

Billy M. Kidd
Billy M. Kidd

Attachment 3-g

Nomination of Administrator
Attachment 3-f(2)

Estate of _____, Deceased

Petition for Letters of Administration

NOMINATION OF ADMINISTRATOR

The undersigned, a resident of the United States, is the

of the above-named decedent and entitled to

succeed to a portion of his estate. I am unable to assume the

administration of the estate and hereby nominate

to be administrator of the estate.

DATED: _____, 19___.

Attachment 3f(2)

Item 5-a: For (1) under this item, check the box that indicates whether or not the decedent left a surviving spouse. If no spouse, check one of the next boxes indicating whether divorced, never married or spouse deceased. For (2), if the decedent left surviving children you should check the first box and then indicate (by checking one or more of the additional boxes on the same line) whether the child is natural or adopted, natural adopted by a third party, a stepchild, or a foster child. (See Chapter 3, Section C for a definition of "child" as it pertains to each of these situations.) If there are predeceased children, or no children, check the last box under (2). For box (3), if the decedent had a child who died before the decedent (a predeceased child), and the predeceased child left issue (child, grandchild, great-grandchild, etc.) who are now living, check the first box under (3). If there are no issue of a predeceased child now living, check the second box under (3).

Item 5-b: Check the second box only if you know of a parent-child relationship (as defined in Chapter 3, Section C, paragraph 3-b) between a foster parent and foster child, or stepparent and stepchild, that might allow someone to inherit through the decedent's will or by intestate succession. You are required to give such persons notice of the probate proceeding. Otherwise, check the first box.[2]

Item 5-c: Check this box, and be sure to list all children in Attachment 8 (discussed below), as well as any surviving children or grandchildren, etc., of a dead child of the decedent.

Item 6: If deceased is survived by any issue (children, grandchildren, etc.), skip Item 6. Only one box should be checked under Item 6. To determine which one to check, follow these two steps:

1. If the decedent is survived by a spouse, then check only box a or b, depending on the situation:

Box 6-a: If the decedent is survived by a spouse and a parent or parents, check this box.

Box 6-b: If there is a surviving spouse, no surviving parents, but surviving brothers or sisters or issue of deceased brothers or sisters, check this box.

Note: If there is a surviving spouse, but no parent, brother, sister, or issue of deceased brothers or sisters, don't check any box under Item 6. In this situation, the surviving spouse is the only heir under intestate succession and you should make a notation in Attachment 8 (discussed below) that "The decedent is survived by a spouse, but no issue, no parent, no brother or sister, or issue of deceased brother or sister." This will alert the court that you did not inadvertently omit checking any of the boxes under Item 6.

2. If the decedent left no spouse and no children or issue of deceased children (grandchildren, etc.), then check the first box under Item 6 that applies:

Box 6-a: If there is a parent (or parents) surviving, check box a and no other.

Box 6-b: If no parents are living, but there are children of deceased parents living (brothers or sisters of the decedent), or if there are issue of deceased brothers or sisters living (nieces or nephews of the decedent), then check box b only.

Box 6-c: If the decedent is survived by a grandparent or grandparents, but none of the people listed for boxes a and b, check this box.

Box 6-d: If there are issue of the decedent's grandparents surviving (uncles, aunts or cousins of the decedent), but none of the people listed in boxes a through c, check box d.

Box 6-e: This box applies if the decedent had a predeceased spouse (a spouse who died before the decedent while married to the decedent), whose issue (children, grandchildren, etc.) are living. In this case (if boxes a, b, c or d do not apply), check box e and list the issue of the predeceased spouse in Attachment 8, below.

---

[2]Many attorneys recommend that notice be served on all known stepchildren or foster children in any event, regardless of whether or not you reasonably believe they might have had a parent-child relationship with the decedent, as described in Probate Code § 6408(b).

Box 6-f: If boxes a through e do not apply, check box f and then determine the next of kin by studying the charts shown in Chapter 3. List them in Attachment 8.

Box 6-g: This box applies if a parent or parents of a predeceased spouse or their issue are living.

Item 7: Complete Item 7 only if the decedent left no surviving spouse or issue. If the predeceased spouse died not more than five years before the decedent and owned personal property totaling $10,000 or more, and the property is still part of the present decedent's estate, Probate Code § 6402.5 provides that the property will pass by intestate succession (if there isn't a valid will) to the issue or next of kin of the predeceased spouse. The issue in this case would be from a prior marriage of the predeceased spouse, because the decedent left no issue. If this is your situation, check the applicable numbered boxes plus the first box (a, b, etc.), that applies and list the relatives of the predeceased spouse under Attachment 8, below. Generally, "property owned by the predeceased spouse" is property which was formerly the predeceased spouse's separate property or a one-half interest in community property.

Joe and Ruth owned a home together as community property when they were married. Ruth died, leaving her half interest in the house to Joe. Joe never had children; Ruth had a child from a previous marriage. When Joe dies 14 years after Ruth without a will, leaving no spouse or issue, the one-half interest in the house that Ruth owned when she died goes to Ruth's child. (Note: Even if Joe left a will, you would be required to list Ruth's child in the petition as a possible intestate heir along with the beneficiaries in the will. If Joe's will is later admitted to probate as his valid will and the will gives the property to someone else, Ruth's child does not inherit anything.)

Item 8: Prepare an "Attachment 8" on a separate sheet of paper (make sure it is 8 1/2" x 11") listing the name, relationship, age, and residence or mailing address of everyone mentioned in the decedent's will and codicils (if any) as a beneficiary, whether living or deceased, *plus* all persons checked in Items 5, 6 and 7, above. You are

not required to make impractical and extended searches, but you must make reasonably diligent efforts to ascertain all heirs and beneficiaries of the decedent (Probate Code § 8002(a)(3).) You should also list alternate and second alternate executors named in the will, if any. Everyone listed in Attachment 8 will be mailed a notice of the hearing on the petition. A sample of what Attachment 8 should look like is shown below. Persons not related to the decedent by blood are designated as "strangers." The ages may be shown as either "under eighteen" or "over eighteen." This alerts the court to the possible need of a guardian if assets will be distributed to a minor.

When listing persons named in the decedent's will and codicils, here are some things you should watch for to make sure you list everyone the court will require:

1. If any of the beneficiaries named in the will or codicil died before the decedent, you must list the deceased beneficiary's name, relationship to the decedent, and approximate date of death, if known. If the deceased beneficiary was related to the decedent (kindred), then list the deceased beneficiary's issue, if any (that is, children, grandchildren, etc.), specifically identifying them as "daughter of...." The reason for this is that the issue of a deceased beneficiary who was kindred of the decedent will inherit the deceased beneficiary's share of the estate. (See Chapter 3.) If the deceased beneficiary had no issue, you should so state. For example, "Robert Jones (deceased 12-5-81; no surviving issue)."

2. If the decedent's will or codicil makes a gift to someone who is not related to the decedent and who has died before the decedent, then the gift lapses. (See Chapter 3.) It is not necessary to list the deceased beneficiary's issue as they will not inherit part of the estate. However, be sure to list any alternate beneficiaries named in the will. For instance: "I give my stamp collection to my friend Sam. In the event Sam predeceases me, I give my stamp collection to my friend John." In this case, Sam should be listed as a deceased beneficiary (if he died before the decedent) and John should be listed as the alternate beneficiary.

ESTATE OF ANABELLE KIDD, DECEASED

Petition for Probate of Will and for Letters Testamentary

Attachment 8 - Heirs, Beneficiaries, Persons Named in the Will

Name and Address	Relationship	Age
Mary Kidd Clark 789 Main Street Venice, California 90410	Daughter	Over 18
Billy M. Kidd 1109 Sky Blue Mountain Trail Billings, Montana 48906	Son	Over 18
Jon Kidd (deceased 4-5-82)	Son	--
Carson Kidd 711 Valley Road Owens, California 98455	Grandson (Son of Jon Kidd)	Over 18
Calvin Kidd (deceased 11-3-86)	Spouse	--
Pat Garret 25 So. Corral Street Santa Fe, New Mexico 57256	Alternate Executor	Over 18
Albertine Terreaux 17 Rue Madeleine Paris, France	Stranger	Over 18
Consulate of France 8350 Wilshire Blvd. Los Angeles, California 99035		

Attachment 8

3. If the will requires any beneficiary to survive the decedent for a certain period of time, list by name the persons who would receive any property if the beneficiary does not survive for the required period. For example: "I give all my jewelry to my sister Mary if she survives me for a period of six months. In the event my sister Mary does not survive me for a period of six months, I give all of my jewelry to my niece, Ellen." In this case, you should list Ellen as a contingent beneficiary who will inherit the jewelry in the event Mary does not survive for six months following the decedent's death. It isn't necessary to label Ellen as a "contingent beneficiary"; her name and address will merely be included with the other beneficiaries.

4. List any person named as a beneficiary in the will but subsequently deleted in a codicil. For example, if paragraph four of the will says, "I give $5,000 to my brother, Robert," and a later codicil says, "I delete paragraph four of my will in its entirety," then Robert should be listed in Attachment 8. The reason for this is that if the codicil is proven to be invalid, Robert would inherit the $5,000. Again, you don't have to explain why Robert is listed (that is, that he is a "contingent beneficiary"); the probate examiners will pick up his name from the codicil and recognize the reason he has been included.

5. You should list any executor named in the will who is not joining in the petition. For example, if the will names two persons to act as executors and only one signs the petition requesting to be appointed, then you should list the non-petitioning executor in Attachment 8 as a person interested in the estate. If the will lists alternate executors, they should be listed as well. Again, there is no need to identify them as "non-petitioning co-executor" or "alternate executor."

6. If the will refers to people only by category, such as "my children" or "my issue" or "my brother's children," you should list the names of all people in this category in Attachment 8 and specify their relationship. For instance, if the will gives property to "my brother's children," then you would list them by name and specify their relationship as "son of decedent's brother Alfred," or "daughter of decedent's brother Alfred." See Chapter 3 for definitions of the more commonly used group terms,

especially if your situation involves adopted children, stepchildren or foster children.

7. If it appears that property may pass to a citizen of a foreign nation, the consul of that nation must be listed in Attachment 8 and given notice of the filing of the petition. For example, if the will leaves property to Francoise Terreaux, a French citizen, you would list Francoise as the beneficiary, giving her address, and you would also list the French Consul and its local address. The local addresses of the consulate offices are listed in major metropolitan telephone books, usually under the heading "Consulate Generals." If an heir or beneficiary is a United States citizen merely residing in a foreign country, you do not have to list the foreign consul. In this latter case, you should indicate that the beneficiary is a United States citizen.

Item 9: Fill in the number of pages of attachments.

Signature and Verification: As you will notice from our sample form, the petitioner must sign the petition on the back of the first page in the two places indicated near the bottom. The second signature block is the verification (under penalty of perjury) declaring that all statements in the petition are true and correct. Be sure to fill in the dates in the spaces provided.

Step 2: File the Original Will

THE ORIGINAL WILL, if any, should be filed with the court at the same time the petition is filed (Step 5, below). Don't forget to file any original codicils as well. If the will or codicil is holographic (written in the decedent's handwriting), type a transcript of it. (See Chapter 13, Section D.)

Step 3: Prepare the Certificate of Assignment

THIS FORM IS REQUIRED in some counties if you file your papers in a branch court. Branch courts are usually found in larger counties. They are smaller courts in out-lying districts that serve the same function as the main court. The form requests the court to assign the probate matter to a particular branch court because the representative lives in that court district. You may still file at the main courthouse in the county seat, however, even if you live in a branch area. A completed sample of the form required in Los Angeles County is shown below. The clerk will stamp in the case number. Call the court for the name of the district to insert in the first paragraph. If you don't file in a branch court, you may skip this step. If you do file in a branch court in another county, ask if there is a local form.

Step 4: Prepare the Notice of Petition to Administer Estate

AS STATED PREVIOUSLY, when you file the Petition for Probate the court clerk gives it a hearing date. Notice of the time and date of the hearing must then be given to certain persons. If the Notice is not properly given, the petition will not be approved, so you should give careful attention to these procedures. The Notice is a printed form called "Notice of Petition to Administer Estate," which is given in two ways.

A. Published Notice

The Notice must be published in a newspaper of general circulation in the city where the decedent resided at the time of death (or, if the decedent was a non-resident of California, where he left property). If there is no such newspaper or if the decedent did not reside in a city, the notice must be published in a newspaper of general circulation in the county that is circulated in the area of the county in which the decedent lived. (Probate Code § 8121.) The published Notice gives a general notice to creditors and any other persons who may be interested in the estate. (Step 16 explains how to give individual written notice to certain known creditors.) To find the right newspaper, ask the court clerk if there are any newspapers published in the city where the decedent lived. If there are no newspapers published in that city or if the decedent didn't live in a city, then find out about newspapers published in the same county. If you have a choice, call to find out price and publication schedule. You may be surprised at the difference in cost among newspapers. Daily papers are usually the most expensive. As long as the newspaper has been approved by the county, you may pick the least expensive and still meet the legal requirement.

In some counties, including Los Angeles, the court clerk will deliver the Notice to the newspaper for publication. If he does not, you will have to see that the newspaper gets a copy.

The Notice must be published three times before the date of the court hearing, and the absolute deadline for the first publication is 15 days before the date of the hearing. Three publications in a newspaper published once a week or more often, with five days between the first and last publication dates, not counting those dates, is sufficient. Most newspapers are familiar with the publication rules. After the Notice is published, a proof of publication must be filed with the court before the hearing date on the petition. Most newspapers have their own form. It must contain a copy of the Notice and show the date of its first publication.

Find out if the newspaper will file the proof of publication directly with the court; otherwise, you will have to file it. Be sure to check the published Notice for accuracy as to the case number, title of the Notice, dates of publication and wording. For example, a Notice is defective and void if it does not show the name of the court. Also, be sure the Notice states that the petition requests authority to administer the estate under the Independent Administration of Estates Act (unless, of course, you have not requested the authority).

Certificate of Assignment

SUPERIOR COURT OF CALIFORNIA, COUNTY OF LOS ANGELES

Estate of ANABELLE KIDD, aka ANABELLE O. KIDD, Deceased	CASE NUMBER **CERTIFICATE OF ASSIGNMENT**

File this certificate with all tort cases and all other civil actions or proceedings presented for filing in districts other than Central.

[X] The undersigned declares that the above entitled matter is filed for proceedings in the District of the Los Angeles Superior Court under Section 392 et seq., Code of Civil Procedure and Rule 300 Sections 3 and 4 of this court for the reasons checked below.

The address of the accident, performance, party, detention, place of business, or other factor which qualifies this case for filing in the above designated district is:

Anabelle Kidd, the decedent   9560 Euclid Street
(NAME — INDICATE TITLE OR OTHER QUALIFYING FACTOR)   (ADDRESS)

Santa Monica,   California   90405
(CITY)   (STATE)   (ZIP CODE)

	NATURE OF ACTION	GROUND
☐ 1	Abandonment	Petitioner resides within the district
☐ 2	Adoption	Petitioner resides within the district
☐ 3	Adoption	Consent to out-of-state adoption, consentor resides within the district
☐ 4	Appeal from Labor Commission Decision	Labor hearing was held within the district
☐ 5	Conservator	Petitioner or conservatee resides within the district
☐ 6	Contract	Performance in the district is expressly provided for
☐ 7	Equity	The cause of action arose within the district
☐ 8	Eminent Domain	The property is located within the district
☐ 9	Family Law	One or more of the party litigants resides within the district
☐ 10	Forcible Entry	The property is located within the district
☐ 11	Guardianship	Petitioner or ward resides within the district
☐ 12	Habeas Corpus	No action pending, the person is held within the district
☐ 13	Mandate*	The defendant functions wholly within the district
☐ 14	Name Change	The petitioner resides within the district
☐ 15	Personal Property	The property is located within the district
☒ 16	Probate	Decedent resided or petitioner resides within the district
☐ 17	Prohibition*	The defendant functions wholly within the district
☐ 18	Review*	The defendant functions wholly within the district
☐ 19	Small Claims Appeal	The lower court is located within the district
☐ 20	Title to Real Property	The property is located within the district
☐ 21	Tort	The cause of action arose within the district
☐ 22	Tort	One or more defendant(s) reside within the district
☐ 23	Transferred Action	The lower court is located within the district
☐ 24	Unlawful Detainer	The property is located within the district
☐ 25	_____	Rule 300 allows filing in Central (non-torts only).

I declare under penalty of perjury under the laws of the State of California that the foregoing is true and correct and this declaration was executed on ___July 5, 1989,___ at ___Santa Monica___ , California.

THE COURT MAY IMPOSE SANCTIONS OR OTHER PENALTIES FOR FAILURE TO FILE IN THE PROPER DISTRICT	(SIGNATURE OF ATTORNEY) Petitioner in pro per

* Prerogative writs concerning a court of inferior jurisdiction shall be filed in Central District.

4 76C134
RC 013/R8-89   CERTIFICATE OF ASSIGNMENT   RULE 300 LASCR

Checklist for Publication of Notice of Petition to Administer Estate

- The Notice must be published in a newspaper of general circulation in the city where the decedent resided at the time of death (or where he left property, if non-resident). If there is no such newspaper or if the decedent didn't reside in a city or if the property isn't in a city, publication may be made in a newspaper of general circulation in the county that is circulated in the area of the county in which the decedent lived.

- Notice must be published three times before the date of the court hearing, and first publication must be at least 15 days before the hearing date.

- There must be three publications in a newspaper published once a week or more often, with five days between the first and last publication dates, not counting those dates.

- Proof of the publication (by way of an affidavit from the newspaper) must be filed with the court before the hearing date on the petition.

- If the petition requests authority to administer the estate under the Independent Administration of Estates Act, the Notice must specify this.

B. Mailed Notice

The Notice must be mailed by first class mail to all heirs and beneficiaries and other persons named in Item 8 of the petition (see Step 1, Item 8, above) at least 15 days before the hearing date. The Notice doesn't have to be mailed to the petitioner or anyone joining in the petition. You also don't have to mail this Notice to known creditors—they are given mailed Notice on a different form, discussed in Step 16. The person doing the mailing (who cannot be yourself or any other person interested in the estate) must sign a declaration under penalty of perjury on the form, giving proof of the mailing which is filed with the court prior to the hearing.

Procedures vary in the different court districts as to who prepares the Notice of Petition to Administer Estate and who attends to the mailing and publication of the Notice. In Los Angeles County this is all done for you—the clerk prepares the Notice, mails it, prepares and files proof of mailing, and delivers the Notice to the newspaper named in the petition, which also prepares and files the proof of publication directly with the court. In other counties, the petitioner must do everything.

Call the court clerk and ask how it is handled in your county. To be safe, you may prepare the Notice according to the instructions below, leaving the date of hearing blank, and submit the original and as many copies as you will need for mailing (plus an extra one to be stamped by the court and returned to you for your records) to the court clerk when you file your petition. She will either insert the date of hearing on the Notices and return them to you, or notify you of the hearing date by stamping or writing it on your copy of the petition. In some counties the petitioner is required to fill in the date of hearing according to certain days of the week when such matters are heard in that court. If this is the case, the clerk will advise you. If you pick a date be sure you give yourself enough time to mail the Notice 15 days prior to the hearing.

It is your responsibility to see that the Notice is published and mailed and that proof of the publication and mailing is filed with the court, no matter what procedure is followed.

Notice of Petition to Administer Estate
(front)

<table>
<tr><td>ATTORNEY OR PARTY WITHOUT ATTORNEY (Name and Address):
  BILLY M. KIDD
  1109 Sky Blue Mountain Trail
  Billings, Montana 48906

ATTORNEY FOR (Name): Petitioner in Pro Per</td><td>TELEPHONE NO:
(715) 392-6408</td><td>FOR COURT USE ONLY</td></tr>
</table>

SUPERIOR COURT OF CALIFORNIA, COUNTY OF LOS ANGELES

STREET ADDRESS: 1725 Main Street

MAILING ADDRESS:

CITY AND ZIP CODE: Santa Monica, California 90401

BRANCH NAME West District

ESTATE OF (NAME):
  ANABELLE KIDD, aka
  ANABELLE O. KIDD,
                       DECEDENT

NOTICE OF PETITION TO ADMINISTER ESTATE
OF (name): ANABELLE KIDD, aka ANABELLE O. KIDD

CASE NUMBER:
WEP 14813

1. To all heirs, beneficiaries, creditors, contingent creditors, and persons who may otherwise be interested in the will or estate, or both, of (specify all names by which decedent was known):
    ANABELLE KIDD, aka ANABELLE O. KIDD

2. A PETITION has been filed by (name of petitioner): BILLY M. KIDD
in the Superior Court of California, County of (specify): Los Angeles

3. THE PETITION requests that (name): BILLY M. KIDD
be appointed as personal representative to administer the estate of the decedent.

4. [X] THE PETITION requests the decedent's WILL and codicils, if any, be admitted to probate. The will and any codicils are available for examination in the file kept by the court.

5. [X] THE PETITION requests authority to administer the estate under the Independent Administration of Estates Act. (This authority will allow the personal representative to take many actions without obtaining court approval. Before taking certain very important actions, however, the personal representative will be required to give notice to interested persons unless they have waived notice or consented to the proposed action.) The independent administration authority will be granted unless an interested person files an objection to the petition and shows good cause why the court should not grant the authority.

6. [ ] A PETITION for determination of or confirmation of property passing to or belonging to a surviving spouse under California Probate Code section 13650 IS JOINED with the petition to administer the estate.

7. A HEARING on the petition will be held

   on (date): July 25, 1989   at (time): 9:30 A.M.   in Dept.: A   Room:

located at (address of court): 1725 Main Street, Santa Monica, California 90401

8. IF YOU OBJECT to the granting of the petition, you should appear at the hearing and state your objections or file written objections with the court before the hearing. Your appearance may be in person or by your attorney.

9. IF YOU ARE A CREDITOR or a contingent creditor of the deceased, you must file your claim with the court and mail a copy to the personal representative appointed by the court within four months from the date of first issuance of letters as provided in section 9100 of the California Probate Code. The time for filing claims will not expire before four months from the hearing date noticed above.

10. YOU MAY EXAMINE the file kept by the court. If you are a person interested in the estate, you may file with the court a formal Request for Special Notice of the filing of an inventory and appraisal of estate assets or of any petition or account as provided in section 1250 of the California Probate Code. A Request for Special Notice form is available from the court clerk.

11. [X] Petitioner [ ] Attorney for petitioner (name): BILLY M. KIDD

   (address): 1109 Sky Blue Mountain Trail, Billings, Montana 48906

                                  ▶ _Billy M. Kidd_
                                  (SIGNATURE OF [X] PETITIONER [ ] ATTORNEY FOR PETITIONER)

12. This notice was mailed on (date): July 8, 1989   at (place): Santa Monica,   , California.
                                (Continued on reverse)

NOTE: If this notice is published, print the caption, beginning with the words NOTICE OF PETITION, and do not print the information from the form above the caption. The caption and decedent's name must be printed in at least 8-point type and the text in at least 7-point type. Print the case number as part of the caption. Print items preceded by a box only if the box is checked. Do not print the italicized instructions in parentheses, the paragraph numbers, the mailing information, or the material on the reverse.

Form Approved by the
Judicial Council of California
DE-121 (Rev. July 1, 1989)

NOTICE OF PETITION TO ADMINISTER ESTATE
(Probate)

Probate Code, § 8100

Notice of Petition to Administer Estate
(back)

ESTATE OF (NAME):		CASE NUMBER
ANABELLE KIDD, DECEDENT		WEP 14813

PROOF OF SERVICE BY MAIL

1. I am over the age of 18 and not a party to this cause. I am a resident of or employed in the county where the mailing occurred.

2. My residence or business address is (specify):

   2328 - 20th Street, Santa Monica, California

3. I served the foregoing **Notice of Petition to Administer Estate** on each person named below by enclosing a copy in an envelope addressed as shown below AND

   a. [X] depositing the sealed envelope with the United States Postal Service with the postage fully prepaid.

   b. [ ] placing the envelope for collection and mailing on the date and at the place shown in item 4 following our ordinary business practices. I am readily familiar with this business' practice for collecting and processing correspondence for mailing. On the same day that correspondence is placed for collection and mailing, it is deposited in the ordinary course of business with the United States Postal Service in a sealed envelope with postage fully prepaid.

4. a. Date of deposit: July 8, 1989   b. Place of deposit (city and state): Santa Monica, California

5. [ ] I served with the Notice of Petition to Administer Estate a copy of the petition and other documents referred to in the notice.

I declare under penalty of perjury under the laws of the State of California that the foregoing is true and correct.

Date: July 8, 1989

...............Hilton Waller.....................   ► _Hilton Waller_ _____
(TYPE OR PRINT NAME)   (SIGNATURE OF DECLARANT)

NAME AND ADDRESS OF EACH PERSON TO WHOM NOTICE WAS MAILED

Mary Kidd Clark
789 Main Street
Venice, California 90410

Carson Kidd
711 Valley Road
Owens, California 98455

Pat Garret
25 So. Corral Street
Santa Fe, New Mexico 57256

Albertine Terreux
17 Rue Madeleine
Paris, France

Consulate of France
8350 Wilshire Boulevard
Los Angeles, California 90035

DE-121 [Rev. July 1, 1989]   **NOTICE OF PETITION TO ADMINISTER ESTATE**   Page two
                                                (Probate)

Instructions for Preparing Notice of Petition to Administer Estate

Heading: Fill in same information as on Petition for Probate. In the last box of the heading (opposite the case number), be sure to type in all names by which decedent was known.

Item 1: Fill in decedent's name and all variations.

Items 2 and 3: Your name goes here. Insert the name of the county in Item 2.

Item 4: Check this box if there is a will. If not, leave it blank.

Item 5: Check this box if you are requesting independent administration authority.

Item 6: This item refers to estates in which the surviving spouse may file a Spousal Property Petition to have property confirmed to her without formal probate proceedings, as discussed in Chapter 15. If a Spousal Property Petition is filed along with the Petition for Probate, check this box to indicate that the hearing is on the Spousal Property Petition as well as the Petition for Probate. As a rule, both petitions are set for hearing by the court on the same date.

Item 7: Leave this blank until the court clerk gives you this information.

Item 11: Check the first box and type in your name and address where indicated. Sign the Notice on the signature line and check the box for "petitioner."

Item 12: Fill in the date and place (name of city) where the Notice was mailed.

Back of Form

Fill in the decedent's name and the case number at the top. Complete the Proof of Service by Mail as follows:

Item 2: Fill in the address of the person who mails the Notice.

Item 3: Check box "a" if the Notice was mailed directly by the individual. Box "b" pertains to businesses (usually law firms) where the Notice has been placed for mailing along with other business correspondence on the date and place shown.

Item 4: Fill in date of mailing, and the city and state where mailed.

Item 5: You don't have to check this box unless you prefer to mail a copy of the Petition for Probate along with the Notice.

Type in the name of the person who mails the Notice, and the date, where indicated. The person who mails the Notice should sign the original after the copies of the Notice have been mailed. In the space at the bottom of the form, type in the names and addresses of all persons to whom a copy of the Notice was mailed. This will be everyone listed in Attachment 8 of the petition.

Step 5: File Your Petition for Probate

AFTER YOU'VE TYPED and signed the petition, you're ready to get it and some other documents ready for your first trip to the courthouse.

A. Check Petition for Probate for Accuracy

Review the petition carefully to make sure the appropriate schedules are attached and all the proper boxes are checked. If there is a will, file the original and be sure a photocopy of it and any codicils are attached to the petition as "Attachment 3-E." Make sure all other attachments are properly numbered. All petitions will have at least one attachment (Attachment #8). It is also important that the signatures on the photocopies be clear and legible.

B. Make Copies of Petition for Probate

Make three photocopies of the petition. Send the original and two copies to the court; one copy will be stamped "filed" by the clerk and returned to you, and the other will be given to the legal newspaper to pick up addresses for mailing Notices to the heirs and beneficiaries if the newspaper mails the Notices. Keep one photocopy for your files. Staple a self-addressed, stamped envelope to the petition so the court may mail you the calendar notes (if your court mails calendar notes—see Chapter 13, Section D). You can check with the court to see if it will FAX the notes to you for a small fee, which is usually added to the filing fee.

C. Make Copies of Notice of Petition to Administer Estate

Make enough copies of the Notice of Petition to Administer Estate to mail to all persons listed in Attachment 8 of the petition, plus an extra copy for your file. (If the newspaper mails the Notice, you don't have to do this.)

D. Make Copies of Will and Codicils

Make about four photocopies of the will and each codicil, if any (and a transcript if either is handwritten), for the court clerk to stamp with the probate case number and filing date and return to you for future use. Make sure the signatures on the copies are clear and legible.

E. File the Petition and the Original Will and Codicils

The original will and codicils, if any, are filed with the court at the same time you file the petition. These documents are presented separately to the court clerk, in their original form, and do not require any preparation for fil-ing. You can file these documents in person or through the mail. If you mail them to the court, include a cover letter such as the one shown below. Send the original of the will by certified mail. Be sure to include a self-addressed, stamped envelope for the court to return your conformed copies in, and be sure to keep a file copy of everything you send to the court for your records. You'll need to include a check for the filing fee (see Step 6), so call the court clerk to find out the amount.

Note: When you file the petition, you may request that the court waive the appointment of a probate referee if there is good cause. (See Step 15-C, below.)

F. Pay Filing Fee

You must pay a filing fee when you file the Petition for Probate, but no additional filing fee is collected for any other documents filed during the court proceeding. The fee, which will be in the neighborhood of $100, varies with the county, so call to check. Make your check payable to the "County Clerk." The filing fee should come out of the estate assets as an expense of administration. If it is necessary for you (or someone else) to advance the fee from personal funds, reimbursement should be made from the estate's assets as soon as an estate bank account is opened. (See Chapter 13, Section D.)

Step 6: Complete the Proof of Subscribing Witness Form

IF THE WILL IS A HOLOGRAPHIC one—that is, in the decedent's handwriting—go on to Step 7. This form is required only if the decedent left a formal typed and witnessed will or codicil that does not have what is known as a "self-proving" clause. A self-proving will contains language that makes verification by witnesses unnecessary. (See Chapter 13, Section D.) The Proof of Subscribing Witness form is a declaration by one of the witnesses to the will (or codicil) that it was signed and witnessed according to the requirements of the law. Only one proof is required to prove a will or codicil if no one contests the validity of the documents. If there are any codicils, you must prepare a separate proof form for each. A photographic copy of the will (or codicil) showing the court clerk's filing stamp must be attached to the Proof of Subscribing Witness form. (You should have this as a result of filing the will in Step 5, above.) The signature on the copies of the will should be clear and legible.

When you have completed the Proof form, mail it (with the photocopy of the will or codicil attached) to the witness and ask that it be signed and returned to you. Enclose a self-addressed, stamped envelope for the convenience of the witness. After one Proof of Subscribing Witness form is signed (it should always have a photocopy of the will or codicil stapled to it), file it with the court. These documents should be on file as far in advance of the hearing date as possible. If you get more than one Proof of Subscribing Witness form, keep the extras as a reserve.

The following comments refer to certain items on the Proof of Subscribing Witness form that may need further explanation:

Item 1: Attach a photocopy of the will to the Proof of Subscribing Witness form, showing the filing stamp of the court clerk and the probate case number. Label it "Attachment 1" at the bottom of the first page. If there are any codicils, attach a separate Proof of Subscribing Witness form for each one, and attach a copy of the codicil, labeled "Attachment 1," at the bottom of the first page of the codicil.

Item 1-a: If the decedent signed the will or codicil personally in the presence of the witnesses, check box 1-a and the first box under Item 1-a. In rare instances, wills are signed by someone else for the decedent because the decedent for some reason could not sign his own name (for instance, he was unable to write because of a stroke). If this is the case, check the second box under a.

Item 1-b: If the decedent didn't sign in the presence of the witnesses, but acknowledged to the witnesses that he personally signed the will or codicil, check box b and

the first box under Item 1-b. If the decedent acknowledged to the witnesses that another person signed for him at his direction and in his presence, then check the second box under Item 1-b.

Item 1-c: Check box 1-c and the additional box under Item 1-c that indicates whether the document is the decedent's will or codicil.

Item 2: If the Proof of Subscribing Witness is for the decedent's will, check the first box. If it is for a codicil, check the second box.

What happens if all the witnesses have died, or can't be found? Don't worry; the will is still good. However, you must prepare a declaration like the one just below, which describes your efforts and inability to locate any of the witnesses (or which states that they are dead) and a statement "proving" the handwriting of the decedent. The wording in our sample is usually sufficient to prove handwriting in the absence of evidence to the contrary. Anyone having personal knowledge of the decedent's handwriting can make a sworn statement proving it is the decedent's handwriting. Since you (the petitioner) are probably a relative or close friend, you are a suitable person to do this.

The sample we have provided is self-explanatory and may be modified to suit your particular situation. For instance, Paragraph 4 may be reworded to add additional information showing your efforts to locate the witnesses, and you may add (or omit) from Paragraph 5 any facts that explain why you are qualified to prove the decedent's handwriting. Be sure to attach a copy of the will as "Exhibit A."

Sample Cover Letter

July 5, 1989

CERTIFIED MAIL - RETURN RECEIPT REQUESTED

Clerk of the Superior Court
1735 Main Street
Santa Monica, California 90401

      Re: Estate of Anabelle Kidd, Deceased

Dear Sir:

Enclosed are the following documents:

1. Petition for Probate;

2. Notice of Petition to Administer Estate;

3. Original Will, plus four copies;

4. Certificate of Assignment;

5. Check in the amount of $117

Please file the original documents with the court and return the extra copies, conformed, in the enclosed stamped, self-addressed envelope, advising me of the time and date of the hearing.

                        Very truly yours,

                        Billy M. Kidd

Proof of Subscribing Witness

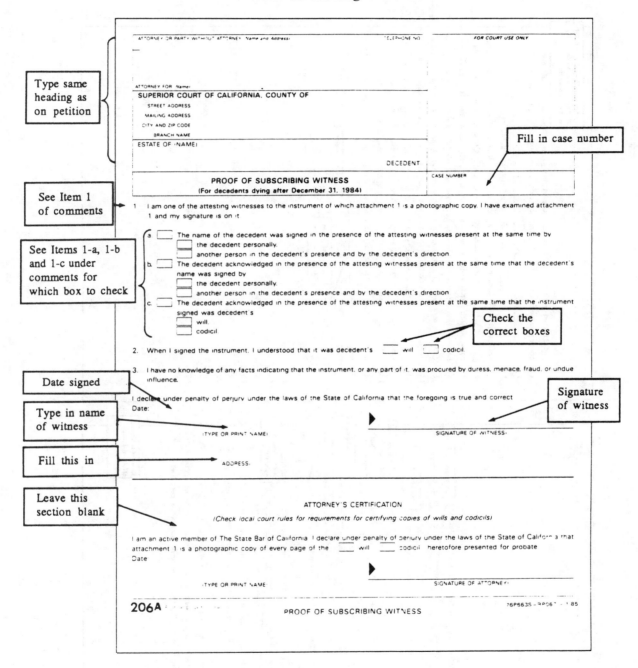

Declaration re Execution of Will

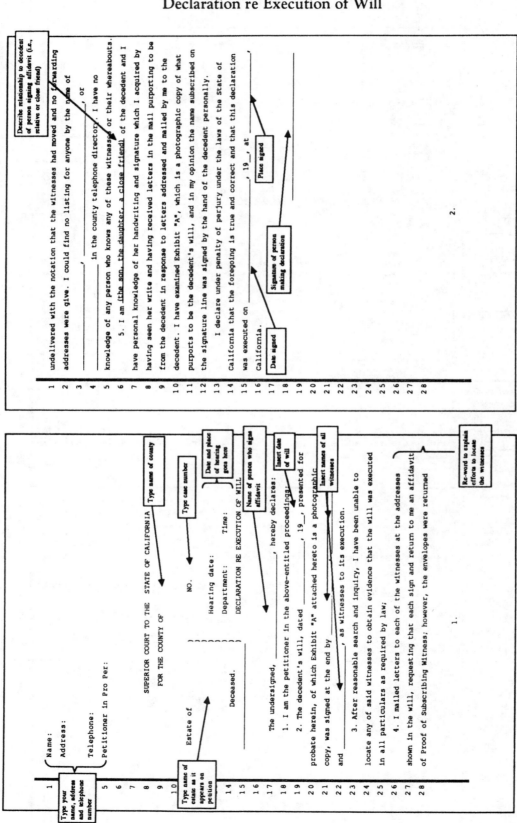

Step 7: Complete a Proof of Holographic Instrument

IF THE WILL IS A HOLOGRAPHIC will (in the decedent's handwriting), you will need someone who can prove the decedent's handwriting to sign a Proof of Holographic Instrument form. Anyone, including you (the petitioner), who has personal knowledge of the decedent's handwriting can sign this form, even if she is a person who will receive all or part of the estate by reason of the holographic will. Attach a clear photocopy of the handwritten will to the form, and label it "Attachment 1" at the bottom of the first page. We show you a sample of the form below, with instructions for filling it in.

Proof of Holographic Instrument

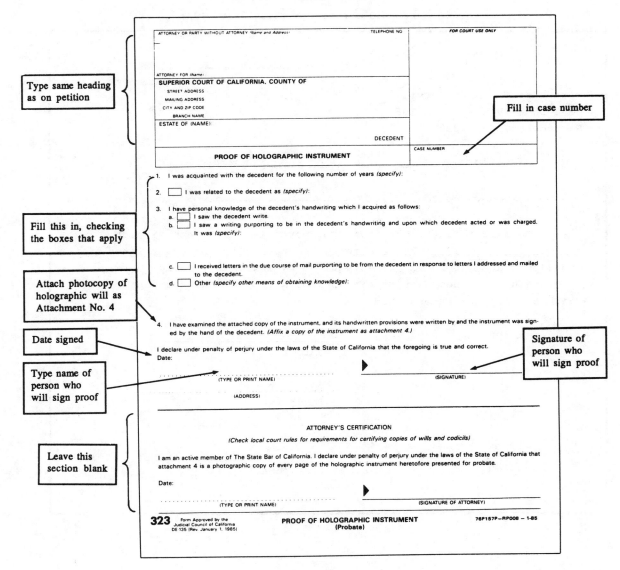

Step 8: Notify the Director of Health Services

IF THE DECEDENT was receiving health care under Medi-Cal, you must send a Notice within 90 days of the death to the Director of Health Services advising that office of the decedent's death. This is to give Medi-Cal a chance to file a claim for repayment of any benefits that should be returned. There is no special form for this, and the Notice may be given in a letter, as shown below. Enclose a copy of the decedent's death certificate.

Notice to the Director of Health Services

```
                                    _____, 19__


Director of Health Services
1250 Sutterville, Room 206
Sacramento, CA 95822


        Re:  Estate of _____, deceased

        Social Security No._____


    Notice is hereby given that the above-named decedent died on
_____, 19__. You are requested to notify the undersigned in
the manner and within the time required by law of any claim you may
have against the decedent or his estate. A copy of the decedent's
death certificate is enclosed.


                            _____
                            (Name)


                            _____
                            (Address)
                            _____


                            _____
                            (Telephone)
```

Step 9: Prepare Your Order for Probate

WHEN THE PETITION is approved, the petitioner must prepare an Order for Probate and submit it to the court for the signature of the judge. The purpose of the Order for Probate is to admit the will (if any) to probate and appoint an estate representative. Some counties require the order to be in the hands of the court three or more days prior to the hearing date so it may be examined before the judge signs it. In other counties, including Los Angeles, the order may be submitted on or after the date of the hearing. If you are unsure of the procedure followed by the court in your area, it is good practice to send it to the court several days ahead of the hearing date. You may mail your Letters and, for those counties that require it, the Application for Appointment of Probate Referee at the same time. (See Steps 11, 12 and 13.)

How to Fill Out the Order for Probate

Caption: Fill in your name, address, the court's name, and case number, as you have on your other court papers.

Order for Probate: Indicate whether an executor or administrator is being appointed. Also indicate that you petitioned for authority (full or limited) under the Independent Administration of Estates Act.

Item 1: Fill in the date, time, location and judge for the court hearing. Call the court for the name of the judge, or leave it blank.

Item 2: Fill in the date of death and check the correct box about residence. Indicate whether there was a will (testate) or not (intestate). If there is a will, fill in the date of the will and any codicils. For the date the will was admitted to probate, put the date of the court hearing.

Item 3: Fill in your name and check the appropriate box. Leave Item 3-d blank.

Item 4: Check box a if you petitioned for full authority to use the Independent Administration of Estates Act; check box b if you asked for limited authority.

Item 5: Check box a if bond is waived. If bond is required, check box b and fill in the amount. If cash is to be deposited in a blocked account, check box c and fill in the amount, and name and address of the depository. (You must file a receipt for the deposit with the court either before or shortly after Letters are issued. Some banks and trust companies request a certified copy of the Order for Probate naming them as depository.)

Item 6: Check this box and the court will complete it, unless you intend to request that the referee be waived. (See Step 15, Section C.)

Leave the rest of the form blank.

Step 10: Study and Respond to the Calendar Notes

AS DISCUSSED IN CHAPTER 13, Section D, "calendar notes" are shorthand terms used by the court's probate examiners to indicate whether a petition is approved or if there is a problem to be corrected. Some courts mail calendar notes to you, while others don't. In some counties, the probate clerk will call you if there are any problems. If you have not received a copy of the probate examiner's calendar notes two or three days before the hearing, call the probate department at the courthouse and ask if the petition has been approved. In some counties, on the day before the hearing, you can call a number and listen to a taped announcement of all the petitions granted without requiring a court appearance. If your case is on the tape, go to the next step. If it is not, call the court to find out what the problem is and how to correct it.

Order for Probate

ATTORNEY OR PARTY WITHOUT ATTORNEY *(Name and Address)*   TELEPHONE NO

BILLY M. KIDD   (715) 392-6408

1109 Sky Blue Mountain Trail

Billings, Montana 48906

FOR COURT USE ONLY

ATTORNEY FOR *(Name)*   Petitioner in Pro Per

SUPERIOR COURT OF CALIFORNIA, COUNTY OF LOS ANGELES

STREET ADDRESS: 1725 Main Street

MAILING ADDRESS:

CITY AND ZIP CODE: Santa Monica, California 90401

BRANCH NAME: West District

ESTATE OF (NAME): ANABELLE KIDD, aka

ANABELLE O. KIDD,   DECEDENT

ORDER FOR PROBATE

ORDER | [X] Executor
APPOINTING | [ ] Administrator with Will Annexed
[ ] Administrator   [ ] Special Administrator
[X] Order Authorizing Independent Administration of Estate
[X] with full authority   [ ] with limited authority

CASE NUMBER

WEP 14813

1. Date of hearing: 7-25-89   Time: 9:30 A.M.   Dept/Rm: A   Judge:

THE COURT FINDS

2. a. All notices required by law have been given.
   b. Decedent died on *(date)*: June 18, 1989
     (1) [X] a resident of the California county named above
     (2) [ ] a nonresident of California and left an estate in the county named above
   c. Decedent died
     (1) [ ] intestate
     (2) [X] testate and decedent's will dated: July 1, 1980
         and each codicil dated:
         was admitted to probate by Minute Order on *(date)*: July 25, 1989

THE COURT ORDERS

3. *(Name)*: BILLY M. KIDD
   is appointed personal representative:
   a. [X] Executor of the decedent's will   d. [ ] Special Administrator
   b. [ ] Administrator with will annexed   (1) [ ] with general powers
   c. [ ] Administrator   (2) [ ] with special powers as specified in Attachment 3d
                                    (3) [ ] without notice of hearing
   and letters shall issue on qualification.

4. a. [X] Full authority is granted to administer the estate under the Independent Administration of Estates Act.
   b. [ ] Limited authority is granted to administer the estate under the Independent Administration of Estates Act (there is no authority, without court supervision, to (1) sell or exchange real property or (2) grant an option to purchase real property or (3) borrow money with the loan secured by an encumbrance upon real property).

5. a. [X] Bond is not required.
   b. [ ] Bond is fixed at: $ to be furnished by an authorized surety company or as otherwise provided by law.
   c. [ ] Deposits of: $ are ordered to be placed in a blocked account at *(specify institution and location)*:
     and receipts shall be filed. No withdrawals shall be made without a court order.

6. [X] *(Name)*:   is appointed probate referee.

Date:

JUDGE OF THE SUPERIOR COURT

7. [ ] Number of pages attached: [ ] Signature follows last attachment

Form Approved by the
Judicial Council of California
DE-140 (Rev. July 1, 1988)
884 (8/88)

ORDER FOR PROBATE

Probate Code, § 329

Supplement to Petition for Probate of Will

```
 1    John J. Smith
 2    202 Park Street
 3    Los Angeles, California 90087
 4    Telephone: (213) 1198754
 5    Petitioner in Pro Per
 6
 7
 8              SUPERIOR COURT OF THE STATE OF CALIFORNIA
 9                   FOR THE COUNTY OF LOS ANGELES
10
11    Estate of                )         NO. P 394860
12        DOROTHY JANE SMITH    )    SUPPLEMENT TO PETITION FOR PROBATE
          aka DOROTHY SMITH     )    OF WILL AND FOR LETTERS TESTAMENTARY
13        aka DOROTHY J. SMITH  )
14              Deceased.       )    5/30/85, 9:15 A.M., Dept. 5
15    _____)
16            The undersigned is the petitioner in the above-entitled proceeding.
17    As a supplement to Paragraph 6 of the Petition for Probate of Will and For
18    Letters Testamentary on file herein, the undersigned alleges as follows:
19            Carol Brown, daughter of the decedent, is the same person named as
20    Carol Marie Smith in paragraph FIRST of the decedent's Will.
21            I declare under penalty of perjury under the laws of the State of
22    California that the foregoing is true and correct and that this declaration
23    is executed on May 27, 1985, at Los Angeles, California.
24
25
26            _____
                        JOHN J. SMITH
27
28
```

(This supplement corrects the following problem: The decedent's daughter, Carol Brown, was married after the will was made, and was listed as an heir in the petition under her married name. Since she was named in the will under her maiden name, the court wanted proof that Carol Marie Smith was the same person and not someone else who was inadvertently omitted as an heir.)

If you need to provide additional information, you must either appear at the hearing personally or file a "supplement" to the petition. The supplement must be typed and verified (under penalty of perjury) by the petitioner in the same way as the original petition. The hearing date must be inserted on the right hand side in the title of the document. It may be necessary to take the supplement to the court personally for it to be filed in time to have the petition approved on the hearing date. Be sure to tell the clerk at the court that the matter is set for hearing shortly, so the supplement will be placed in the case file in time for the hearing. Answering questions at the hearing is often an easier way to cure defects and, generally, is not intimidating.

If the calendar notes indicate bond is required, it must be filed with the court before Letters will be issued. See Chapter 13, Section D8, on how to arrange for bond. A sample of a bond that may be used for personal sureties is shown below. Remember, when personal sureties are used, the bond must be in twice the amount required. The court should be contacted in advance to determine what evidence, if any, of net worth the sureties will have to show.

Step 11: Prepare the Letters

WHEN THE ORDER FOR PROBATE is signed appointing you as the estate representative, the court clerk will issue the Letters you have prepared confirming that you have been appointed and have qualified. Letters testamentary or letters of administration are both prepared on the same form. Instructions and a sample form are shown below. You may sign the Letters prior to the hearing date and send them to the court at the same time you mail the Order for Probate, as discussed in Step 9.

You should order at least two certified copies of the Letters by enclosing a check payable to the "County Clerk" in an amount "Not to exceed $5.00." The certified copies are usually needed right away to transfer bank accounts from the decedent's name to that of the estate. You may order additional certified copies now, or later, if

you need them. Be sure that your signature on the Letters is not dated prior to the date you filed your petition.

How to Fill Out the Letters

Caption: Fill in your name, address, the court's name, and case number, as you have on your other court papers.

Letters: Check "testamentary" if there is a will. Check "of administration" if there is no will.

Item 1: If there is no will, go to Item 2. If there is a will, check the first box and type the name of the representative below it. Then check either box a or b, and go to Item 3.

Item 2: If there is no will, type in the name of the administrator and check box a.

Item 3: Check this box and indicate whether you petitioned for full or limited authority under the Independent Administration of Estates Act.

Leave the rest of this half blank.

Affirmation: Check box 2 and sign the form, and fill in the date and city.

Bond (Personal) on Qualifying
(front)

```
 1    Name:
 2    Address:
 3
 4    Telephone No.:
 5    Petitioner in Pro Per
 6
 7
 8                    SUPERIOR COURT OF CALIFORNIA
 9                       COUNTY OF _____
10
11    Estate of                   )      NO.
                                  )
12       (name of decedent),      )    BOND (PERSONAL) ON QUALIFYING
                                  )
13            deceased            )
                                  )
14    _____     )
15         I,  (name of representative) , as principal, and
16    (name of first surety)  , and  (name of second surety) , as
17    sureties, are bound to the State of California in the sum of
18    $_____.  We bind ourselves, our heirs, executors, and
19    administrators, jointly and severally, to pay in event of breach
20    of this bond.
21         This bond is being executed under an order of the
22    Superior Court of California for _____ County, made on
23    _____, 19___, by which  (name of representative)  was
24    appointed  (executor/administrator)  of the estate of the above-
25    named decedent, and letters  (testamentary/of administration)
26    were directed to be issued to ___(name of representative)_____
27    on executing a bond under the laws of California.
28         If  (name of representative) , as  (executor/adminis-
```

Bond (Personal) on Qualifying
(back)

```
1  |  tor)   , faithfully executes the duties of the trust according
2  |  to the law, this obligation shall become void; otherwise, it will
3  |  remain in effect.
4  |      DATED: _____
5  |
6  |                              _____
7  |      DATED: _____     (Name of Representative)
8  |                              _____
9  |      DATED: _____        (Name of First Surety)
10 |
11 |                              _____
12 |                                     (Name of Second Surety)
13 |                        DECLARATION OF SURETIES
14 |      _____ and _____, the
15 |  sureties named in the above bond state, each for himself, that
16 |  he/she is a householder or property owner and resident within
17 |  said state and is worth the sum of $_____ over and
18 |  above all his debts and liabilities, exclusive of property exempt
19 |  from execution.
20 |          Signed and dated at _____, California,
21 |  on _____, 19___.  I declare under penalty of perjury
22 |  under the laws of the State of California that the foregoing is
23 |  true and correct.
24 |                              _____
25 |                                        (First Surety)
26 |                              _____
27 |                                        (Second Surety)
28 |
```

Letters

ATTORNEY OR PARTY WITHOUT ATTORNEY *(Name and Address)*	TELEPHONE NO.	FOR COURT USE ONLY
BILLY M. KIDD 1109 Sky Blue Mountain Trail Billings, Montana 48906	(715) 392-6408	

ATTORNEY FOR *(Name)* In Pro Per

SUPERIOR COURT OF CALIFORNIA, COUNTY OF LOS ANGELES
STREET ADDRESS: 1725 Main Street
MAILING ADDRESS:
CITY AND ZIP CODE: Santa Monica, California 90401
BRANCH NAME West District

ESTATE OF (NAME):
    ANABELLE KIDD, aka
    ANABELLE O. KIDD,   DECEDENT

LETTERS

[X] TESTAMENTARY	[ ] OF ADMINISTRATION	CASE NUMBER
[ ] OF ADMINISTRATION WITH WILL ANNEXED	[ ] SPECIAL ADMINISTRATION	WEP 14813

LETTERS

1. [X] The last will of the decedent named above having been proved, the court appoints *(name)*:

    BILLY M. KIDD

    a. [X] Executor
    b. [ ] Administrator with will annexed

2. [ ] The court appoints *(name)*:

    a. [ ] Administrator of the decedent's estate
    b. [ ] Special administrator of decedent's estate
        (1) [ ] with the special powers specified in the Order for Probate
        (2) [ ] with the powers of a general administrator

3. [X] The personal representative is authorized to administer the estate under the Independent Administration of Estates Act [X] with full authority
[ ] with limited authority (no authority, without court supervision, to (1) sell or exchange real property or (2) grant an option to purchase real property or (3) borrow money with the loan secured by an encumbrance upon real property).

WITNESS, clerk of the court, with seal of the court affixed.

Date:

Clerk, by _____ , Deputy

(SEAL)

AFFIRMATION

1. [ ] PUBLIC ADMINISTRATOR: No affirmation required (Prob. Code, § 1140(b)).

2. [X] INDIVIDUAL: I solemnly affirm that I will perform the duties of personal representative according to law.

3. [ ] INSTITUTIONAL FIDUCIARY *(name)*:

    I solemnly affirm that the institution will perform the duties of personal representative according to law.
    I make this affirmation for myself as an individual and on behalf of the institution as an officer.
    (Name and title):

4. Executed on *(date)*: July 20, 1989
    at *(place)*: Santa Monica, , California.

▶ *(signature)* Billy M. Kidd
    (SIGNATURE) Billy M. Kidd

CERTIFICATION

I certify that this document is a correct copy of the original on file in my office and the letters issued the personal representative appointed above have not been revoked, annulled, or set aside, and are still in full force and effect.

(SEAL)	Date: Clerk, by _____ (DEPUTY)

Form Approved by the
Judicial Council of California
DE-150 (Rev. July 1, 1988)
373 (6/88)

LETTERS
(Probate)

Probate Code, §§ 463, 465, 501, 502, 540
Code of Civil Procedure, § 2015.6

Step 12: Prepare the Duties and Liabilities of Personal Representative Form

THIS FORM PROVIDES a summary of your duties as personal representative. You must read it, fill out and sign the acknowledgment of receipt, and file it along with the Letters before the clerk will formally issue the Letters. A sample is shown below, and a tear-out copy is in Appendix 2.

Step 13: Prepare the Application for Appointment of Probate Referee

ALL NON-CASH ASSETS must be appraised by a probate referee appointed by the court, unless the court waives the requirement. (See Step 15-C.) The sample form shown is used only in the Central District in Los Angeles County to appoint the referee. Some other counties also have their own forms. However, in most counties, and in the branch courts in Los Angeles, the referee is routinely appointed without special application, in which case the name of the probate referee is affixed on the Order for Probate or stamped on the petition when you file it.

As you will note from the sample form shown below, you are required to set forth the approximate value of the cash in the estate, as well as all real estate and non-cash personal property. These figures need only be estimates. If you submit a duplicate copy of this form to the court with a self-addressed, stamped envelope, the clerk will return a conformed copy with the name, address and telephone number of the referee. You can submit the application to the court with the Order for Probate. A sample cover letter is shown below.

Step 14: Prepare Notice of Proposed Action, If Necessary

AFTER LETTERS ARE ISSUED, you must wait four months before you may close the estate. This is to allow creditors time to file their claims against the estate. During this period, you will be taking care of such things as estate bank accounts, tax returns and the estate inventory.

Also during this time you may find it necessary to perform some of the acts allowed by the Independent Administration of Estates Act (discussed in Chapter 13, Section D), such as selling assets that may depreciate in value or cause expenses to the estate (such as automobiles or apartment furnishings). Some of these require a Notice of Proposed Action. It is usually required for the sale of estate property, with some exceptions as discussed in Chapter 13. Although the Probate Code doesn't require it, some courts want the original action notice, and any consent obtained, to be filed with the court (prior to or along with the Petition for Final Distribution) with proof that it was given to all interested persons. Instructions for filing out the Notice and sample Notice are shown below with a proof of sevice.

"Interested persons" are those whose interest in the estate would be affected by the proposed action. For example, if real property is to be sold, all persons entitled to inherit an interest in the property must be given the Notice. On the other hand, a beneficiary receiving only a cash gift, or other specific property, and who is not entitled to receive an interest in the property being sold, is not entitled to notice. Anyone who has filed a Request for Special Notice with the court, however, should be given the Notice, regardless of whether that person is entitled to any part of the property.

Note: When real property is sold under the Independent Administration of Estates Act, the title company will require the following documents:

- Copy of the Notice of Proposed Action, with a proof of mailing showing that the Notice was given within the time period required;

- Certified copy of Letters;

- A special deed, referred to as an "Executor's Deed." A sample is shown below. You can copy its format or buy a deed form in a legal stationery store.

Duties and Liabilities of Personal Representative

TO COURT CLERK: This form is CONFIDENTIAL if local rule requires the Acknowledgment of Receipt to have a Social Security or Driver's license number.

ATTORNEY OR PARTY WITHOUT ATTORNEY (Name and Address):   TELEPHONE NO.

BILLY M. KIDD   (715) 392-6408
1109 Sky Blue Mountain Trail
Billings, Montana 48906

FOR COURT USE ONLY

ATTORNEY FOR (Name): In Pro Per

SUPERIOR COURT OF CALIFORNIA, COUNTY OF   LOS ANGELES
STREET ADDRESS: 1725 Main Street
MAILING ADDRESS:
CITY AND ZIP CODE: Santa Monica, California 90401
BRANCH NAME: West District

ESTATE OF (NAME): ANABELLE KIDD, aka
ANABELLE O. KIDD,
          DECEDENT

DUTIES AND LIABILITIES OF PERSONAL REPRESENTATIVE
and Acknowledgment of Receipt

CASE NUMBER: WEP 14813

DUTIES AND LIABILITIES OF PERSONAL REPRESENTATIVE

When you have been appointed by the court as personal representative of an estate, you become an officer of the court and assume certain duties and obligations. An attorney is best qualified to advise you about these matters. You should clearly understand the following:

1. MANAGING THE ESTATE'S ASSETS

a. Prudent investments
You must manage the estate assets with the care of a prudent person dealing with someone else's property. This means you must be cautious and you may not make any speculative investments.

b. Keep estate assets separate
You must keep the money and property in this estate separate from anyone else's, including your own. When you open a bank account for the estate, the account name must indicate that it is an estate account and not your personal account. Securities in the estate must also be held in a name that shows they are estate property and not your personal property.
Never deposit estate funds in your personal account or otherwise commingle them with anyone else's property.

c. Interest-bearing accounts and other investments
Except for checking accounts intended for ordinary administration expenses, estate accounts must earn interest. You may deposit estate funds in insured accounts in financial institutions, but you should consult with an attorney before making other investments.

d. Other restrictions
There are many other restrictions on your authority to deal with estate property. You should not spend any of the estate's money unless you have received permission from the court or have been advised to do so by an attorney. You may reimburse yourself for official court costs paid by you to the county clerk and for the premium on your bond. Without prior order of the court, you may not pay fees to yourself or to your attorney, if you have one. If you do not obtain the court's permission when it is required, you may be removed as personal representative or you may be required to reimburse the estate from your own personal funds, or both. You should consult with an attorney concerning the legal requirements affecting sales, leases, mortgages, and investments of estate property.

2. INVENTORY OF ESTATE PROPERTY

a. Locate the estate's property
You must attempt to locate and take possession of all the decedent's property to be administered in the estate.

b. Determine the value of the property
You must arrange to have a court-appointed referee determine the value of the property unless the appointment is waived by the court. (You, rather than the referee, must determine the value of certain "cash items." An attorney can advise you about how to do this.)

c. File an inventory and appraisal
Within four months after your appointment as personal representative, you must file with the court an inventory and appraisal of all the assets in the estate.

(Continued on reverse)

Form Adopted by the
Judicial Council of California
DE-147 [Rev. July 1, 1989]

DUTIES AND LIABILITIES OF PERSONAL REPRESENTATIVE
(Probate)

Probate Code, § 8404

ESTATE OF (NAME): ANABELLE KIDD,   DECEDENT

CASE NUMBER: WEP 14813

d. File a change of ownership
At the time you file the inventory and appraisal, you must also file a change of ownership statement with the county recorder or assessor in each county where the decedent owned real property at the time of death, as provided in section 480 of the California Revenue and Taxation Code.

3. NOTICE TO CREDITORS

You must mail a notice of administration to each known creditor of the decedent within four months after your appointment as personal representative. If the decedent received Medi-Cal assistance you must notify the State Director of Health Services within 90 days after appointment.

4. INSURANCE

You should determine that there is appropriate and adequate insurance covering the assets and risks of the estate. Maintain the insurance in force during the entire period of the administration.

5. RECORD KEEPING

a. Keep accounts
You must keep complete and accurate records of each financial transaction affecting the estate. You will have to prepare an account of all money and property you have received, what you have spent, and the date of each transaction. You must describe in detail what you have left after the payment of expenses.

b. Court review
Your account will be reviewed by the court. Save your receipts because the court may ask to review them. If you do not file your accounts as required, the court will order you to do so. You may be removed as personal representative if you fail to comply.

6. CONSULTING AN ATTORNEY

If you have an attorney, you should cooperate with the attorney at all times. You and your attorney are responsible for completing the estate administration as promptly as possible. When in doubt, contact your attorney.

NOTICE: This statement of duties and liabilities is a summary and is not a complete statement of the law. Your conduct as a personal representative is governed by the law itself and not by this summary.

ACKNOWLEDGMENT OF RECEIPT

1. I have petitioned the court to be appointed as a personal representative of the estate of (specify): ANABELLE KIDD, aka ANABELLE O. KIDD, Deceased
2. I acknowledge that I have received a copy of this statement of the duties and liabilities of the office of personal representative.

Date: July 20, 1989

BILLY M. KIDD
(TYPE OR PRINT NAME)   _Beg M. Edd_ (SIGNATURE OF PETITIONER)

*Social Security No.: 567-20-8418   *Driver's License No.: B08339025

Date:

_____
(TYPE OR PRINT NAME)   (SIGNATURE OF PETITIONER)

*Social Security No.:   *Driver's License No.:

Date:

_____
(TYPE OR PRINT NAME)   (SIGNATURE OF PETITIONER)

*Social Security No.:   *Driver's License No.:

*Supply these numbers only if required to do so by local court rule. The law requires the court to keep this information CONFIDENTIAL (Probate Code, § 8404(a).)

DE-147 [Rev. July 1, 1989]   DUTIES AND LIABILITIES OF PERSONAL REPRESENTATIVE (Probate)   Page two

Letter to Court

July 12, 1989

Clerk of the Superior Court
1725 Main Street
Santa Monica, California 90401

Re: Estate of ANABELLE KIDD, Deceased

Case No. WEP 14813

Hearing Date: July 25, 1989

Dear Sir:

Enclosed are the original and one copy of the following documents:

1. Notice of Petition to Administer Estate (with proof of service by mail);

2. Order for Probate

3. Letters

4. Duties and Liabilities of Personal Representative

Please file the original documents with the court and return the extra copies, conformed, in the enclosed stamped self-addressed envelope.

Please return two certified copies of Letters. A check in the amount of "not to exceed $6.00" is enclosed to cover your certification fees.

Very truly yours,

Billy M. Kidd

Application for Appointment of Referee

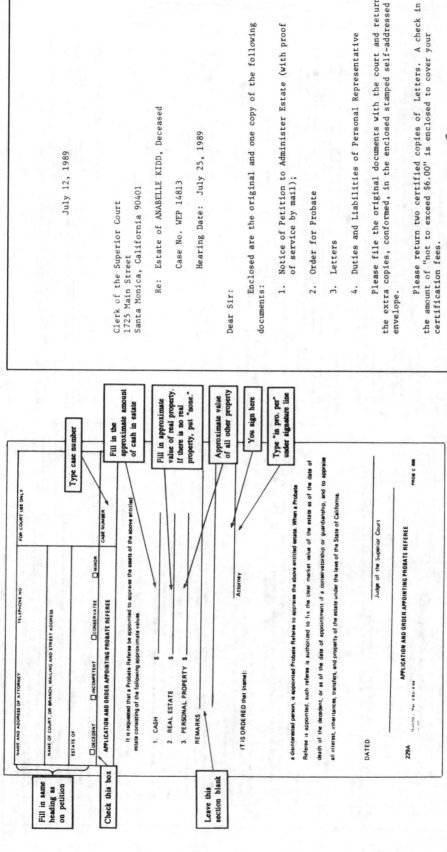

Deed to Real Property

I, ___BILLY M. KIDD___, as ___Executor___ of the

Estate of __Anabelle Kidd, aka Anabelle O. Kidd__, deceased, pursuant to authority
granted to me by Order of the Superior Court of California, for the County of

__Los Angeles__, on ___July 25___, 19_89_, in Case No. __WEP 14813__,

to administer the Estate of ___Anabelle Kidd___, deceased, under the
Independent Administration of Estates Act, and pursuant to Notice of Proposed Action
duly given under the provisions of Probate Code Sections l0580, et seq., do hereby

convey to __John A. Buyer, an unmarried man__, as __his separate property__,
without any representation, warranty, or covenant of any kind, express or implied, all
right, title, interest, and estate of the decedent at the time of death, and all right, title
and interest that the estate may have subsequently acquired in the real property

situated in the County of __Los Angeles__, State of California, described as follows:

    Lot 11 in Block 9 of Tract 5721, as per map recorded in Book 63,
    Page 31 of Maps in the office of the County Recorder of said county.

Commonly known as 9560 Euclid Street, Santa Monica, CA A.P.N. 3467-047-379

DATED: __August 30__, 19_89_   _Billy M. Kidd_
                            Billy M. Kidd

STATE OF CALIFORNIA   )
) SS.
COUNTY OF _LOS ANGELES_)

On ___August 30___, 19_89_, before me, the undersigned, a Notary
Public in and for said State, personally appeared ___Billy M. Kidd___, as
___Executor___ of the Estate of ___Anabelle Kidd___, deceased,
personally known to me (or proved to me on the basis of satisfactory evidence) to be
the person whose name is subscribed to the within instrument, and acknowledged to me
that _he_ executed the same as such _Executor_.

     WITNESS my hand and official seal.

                        Nancy Notary
(Notary's Seal)   Notary Public in and for said State

Notice of Proposed Action (front)

Notice of Proposed Action (back)

Front form

ATTORNEY OR PARTY WITHOUT ATTORNEY (Name and Address):
BILLY M. KIDD
1109 Sky Blue Mountain Trail
Billings, Montana 48906

TELEPHONE NO.: (715) 392-6408

FOR COURT USE ONLY

ATTORNEY FOR (Name): In Pro Per

SUPERIOR COURT OF CALIFORNIA, COUNTY OF LOS ANGELES
STREET ADDRESS: 1725 Main Street
MAILING ADDRESS:
CITY AND ZIP CODE: Santa Monica, California 90401
BRANCH NAME: West District

ESTATE OF (NAME): ANABELLE KIDD, aka
ANABELLE O. KIDD,   DECEDENT

CASE NUMBER: WEP 14813

NOTICE OF PROPOSED ACTION
Independent Administration of Estates Act
Objection—Consent

NOTICE: If you do not object in writing or obtain a court order preventing the action proposed below, you will be treated as if you consented to the proposed action and you may not object after the proposed action has been taken. If you object, the personal representative may take the proposed action only under court supervision. An objection form is on the reverse. If you wish to object, you may use the form or prepare your own written objection.

1. The personal representative (executor or administrator) of the estate of the deceased is (names):
   BILLY M. KIDD

2. The personal representative has authority to administer the estate without court supervision under the Independent Administration of Estates Act (Probate Code section 10400 et seq.)
   a. [X] with full authority under the act.
   b. [ ] with limited authority under the act (there is no authority, without court supervision, to (1) sell or exchange real property or (2) grant an option to purchase real property or (3) borrow money with the loan secured by an encumbrance upon real property).

3. On or after (date): August 20, 1989 , the personal representative will take the following action without court supervision (describe in specific terms here or in Attachment 3):
   [ ] The proposed action is described in an attachment labeled Attachment 3.
   The Executor will sell the real property located at 9560 Euclid Street, Santa Monica, California, for a total sales price of $129,900, all cash. Buyer to obtain own financing. Property to be sold as is, and seller will not make any repairs nor provide any warranty on house and other structures on lot. Sales price includes all built-in appliances. Seller to pay brokers a commission of 6% of sales price, allocated as follows: 3% to Exceptional Real Estate and 3% to J.F. Realty. Seller to furnish buyer, at seller's expense, a California Land Title Association policy issued by Commonwealth Land Title Insurance. County transfer tax and documentary transfer tax or transfer fee to be paid by seller.

4. [X] Real property transaction (Check this box and complete item 4b if the proposed action involves a sale or exchange or a grant of an option to purchase real property.)
   a. The material terms of the transaction are specified in item 3, including any sale price and the amount of or method of calculating any commission or compensation to an agent or broker.
   b. $ is the value of the subject property in the probate inventory. [X] No inventory yet.

NOTICE: A sale of real property without court supervision means that the sale will NOT be presented to the court for confirmation at a hearing at which higher bids for the property may be presented and the property sold to the highest bidder.

(Continued on reverse)

Form Approved by the Judicial Council of California DE-165 (Rev. July 1, 1988) | NOTICE OF PROPOSED ACTION Objection—Consent (Probate) | Probate Code § 10580 et seq.

Back form

ESTATE OF (NAME): ANABELLE KIDD,   DECEDENT
CASE NUMBER: WEP 14813

5. If you OBJECT to the proposed action
   a. Sign the objection form below and deliver or mail it to the personal representative at the following address (specify name and address):
      Billy M. Kidd
      1109 Sky Blue Mountain Trail, Billings, Montana 48906
      -OR-
   b. Send your own written objection to the address in item 5a. (Be sure to identify the proposed action and state that you object to it.)
      -OR-
   c. Apply to the court for an order preventing the personal representative from taking the proposed action without court supervision.
   d. NOTE: Your written objection or the court order must be received by the personal representative before the date in the box in item 3, or before the proposed action is taken, whichever is later. If you object, the personal representative may take the proposed action only under court supervision.

6. If you APPROVE the proposed action, you may sign the consent form below and return it to the address in item 5a. If you do not object in writing or obtain a court order, you will be treated as if you consented to the proposed action.

7. If you need more INFORMATION, call (name): Billy M. Kidd (telephone): (715) 392-6408

Date: August 3, 1989

BILLY M. KIDD
(TYPE OR PRINT NAME)   Billy M. Kidd
SIGNATURE OF PERSONAL REPRESENTATIVE OR ATTORNEY

OBJECTION TO PROPOSED ACTION

[ ] I OBJECT to the action proposed above in item 3.

NOTICE: Sign and return this form (both sides) to the address in item 5a. The form must be received before the date in the box in item 3, or before the proposed action is taken, whichever is later. (You may want to use certified mail, with return receipt requested. Make a copy of this form for your records.)

Date:
....
(TYPE OR PRINT NAME)
SIGNATURE OF OBJECTOR

CONSENT TO PROPOSED ACTION

[ ] I CONSENT to the action proposed above in item 3.

NOTICE: You may indicate your consent by signing and returning this form (both sides) to the address in item 5a. If you do not object in writing or obtain a court order, you will be treated as if you consented to the proposed action.

Date:
....
(TYPE OR PRINT NAME)
SIGNATURE OF CONSENTER

DE-165 (Rev. July 1, 1988) | NOTICE OF PROPOSED ACTION Objection—Consent (Probate) | Page two

Proof of Service

```
 1  BILLY M. KIDD
    1109 Sky Blue Mountain Trail
 2  Billings, Montana 48906

 3  Telephone:  (715) 392-6408

 4  In Pro Per

 5

 6

 7

 8              SUPERIOR COURT OF CALIFORNIA

 9                COUNTY OF LOS ANGELES

10

11  Estate of                    )    CASE NO. WEP 14813
                                 )
12    ANABELLE KIDD, aka         )    PROOF OF SERVICE BY MAIL OF
      ANABELLE O. KIDD,          )
13                               )    NOTICE OF PROPOSED ACTION
               Deceased          )
14  _____)

15  STATE OF MONTANA, COUNTY OF BILLINGS:

16       I am a resident of the county aforesaid; I am over the age of eighteen

17  years and not a party to the within entitled action; my business address is:

18  _____1809 - G Street, Billings, Montana_____.

19  On ____August 3_____, 1989, I served the attached NOTICE OF PROPOSED ACTION

20  on the interested parties by placing a true copy thereof enclosed in a sealed

21  envelope with postage thereon fully prepaid in the United States mail at

22  Billings, Montana_____, addressed as follows:

23       Mary Kidd Clark, 789 Main Street, Venice, California 90410

24       Carson Kidd, 711 Valley Road, Owens, California 98455

25

26       I declare under penalty of perjury under the laws of the State of

27  California that the foregoing is true and correct.

28  DATED: ___August 10_____, 1989   _Mary Smith_____
                                              Mary Smith
```

How to Fill Out a Notice of Proposed Action

Caption: Fill in your name, address, the court's name, and case number, as you have on your other court papers.

Item 1: Type in name of executor or administrator.

Item 2: Check the box that indicates whether you petitioned for full or limited authority under the Independent Administration of Estates Act.

Item 3: Fill in the date of the proposed action, which must be at least 15 days after the date of this notice, unless all interested persons sign the consent on the back of the notice. Describe the action if there is room, or check the box if you describe it in an attachment.

Item 4: Check this box if the proposed action is a real estate transaction, and fill in the requested information.

Item 5: Fill in your name and address.

Item 7: Type in your name and phone number.

Print or type your name, and sign and date the form.

Leave the rest of the form blank; it is for the recipient.

Step 15: Prepare the Inventory and Appraisement Form

A. General Instructions

The regulations governing the Inventory and Appraisement of the probate assets are in Probate Code §§ 8800-8980. The estate inventory should be prepared as soon as conveniently possible on the Inventory and Appraisement form shown below.[3] At this point, you should refer to your Schedule of Assets prepared in Chapter 5. The description of the probate assets on the Inventory and Appraisement form will follow the same general format as

---

[3]Probate Code § 8800 states that the inventory must be filed within four months after Letters are issued, but this rule is not strictly enforced.

on the Schedule of Assets, with these additional requirements:

1. If the decedent owned only a partial interest in an asset (for example, a one-half or one-third interest with others), you must be sure to indicate this in the beginning of your description on the Inventory and Appraisement form. For example, a "one-half interest in promissory note secured by deed of trust . . . " or a "one-third interest in real property located at . . . " It must be made clear in the description that the decedent owned only a part interest; otherwise the referee will appraise the asset at its full value, which would be incorrect.

2. Be sure you list only assets subject to probate that were owned at the date of death.

3. The full *legal description* of all real property must be given. It is also a good idea to include the assessor's parcel number, which you can find on the property tax bill, for all real property.

4. For a mortgage or deed of trust secured by real property, include the recording reference or, if not recorded, a legal description of the real property. (Note of caution: If an encumbrance on real property is unrecorded, you should immediately see an attorney to take steps to make an estate's lien claim a matter of record.)

5. Indicate whether the property is community, quasi-community or separate property of the decedent. If community property passes outright to the surviving spouse, it doesn't require probate (unless the surviving spouse wishes the property to be probated) and is not listed on the inventory. (See Chapter 15.) If the decedent willed his one-half interest in community property to someone else, however, it is listed.

As you can see, the form itself is fairly short. This is because the assets are listed on separate attachment sheets stapled to the face page, which is the first page of the inventory. These attachments (the inventory of the assets) should list everything owned by the decedent at the time of death, except joint tenancy property, property held in trust (including living trusts), bank trust accounts (also called pay-on-death accounts), death benefits and insurance proceeds payable to named beneficiaries. (You do, however, list insurance proceeds or death benefits payable to the estate.) Each asset must be numbered separately and fully described as shown in the samples below. Don't be afraid to call the referee and ask how to list a certain asset. If you have problems, obtain a pamphlet entitled "Probate Procedures Guide," put out by the California Probate Referees Association. You may be able to get a copy from the Los Angeles Daily Journal, 210 S. Spring, Los Angeles, CA 90054. But because the booklet is intended mostly for new attorneys, it isn't always available. You can probably get a copy from a local probate referee; ask the probate court for the name of a referee.

The first attachment (Attachment 1) is for assets for which the value is certain and which will be appraised by the personal representative. Under Probate Code § 8901, such assets include:

1. Money and checks, drafts, or money orders issued on or before the date of death that can be immediately converted to cash;

2. Checks issued after the date of death for wages, or for refunds of tax and utility bills, medical insurance, and Medicare payments;

3. Bank accounts and Certificates of Deposit;

4. Money market funds or accounts, including a brokerage cash account; and

5. Insurance proceeds or retirement fund benefits payable in lump sum to the estate.

Each item should be specifically described and numbered consecutively, as in our example below. Insert the value of each item in the column at the right, and show an overall total at the end.

All other property should be listed on "Attachment 2," with the values left blank so the referee may fill in her appraisals. Our sample of Attachment 2 shows how to describe most non-cash assets. The referee doesn't normally examine household items and personal effects, which means you should include an estimate of the value of these items in a cover letter when you forward the inventory to the referee. They are usually grouped together as one item and valued at what they would bring at a yard sale or if sold to someone who purchases household goods. In other words, they are not worth much. The referee will usually accept your suggested valuation, if it seems reasonable, and will insert it as the appraised value.

Instructions for the Inventory and Appraisement Form

Heading: In the large block titled "Inventory and Appraisement," check the first box which says "complete." The other boxes are checked when a partial, supplemental, or final inventory is filed; however, in a simple estate, the initial inventory is usually the complete inventory. In unusual circumstances, additional assets may be discovered after the filing of a complete inventory, in which case a supplemental inventory may be filed (checking the appropriate box) with separate attachments describing the additional assets. A supplemental inventory is sent to the referee and processed in the same way as the initial complete inventory.

Item 1 on the right-hand side is where you will fill in the total value of assets listed on Attachment 1 (as indicated on our sample form).

Item 2 on the front of the inventory is for the total value of the assets appraised by the referee on Attachment 2. The referee fills in this figure.

Item 3 only requires that you check the first box, as indicated on the sample form, unless you are filing a partial or supplemental inventory, in which case you should check the next box.

Item 4 on the front of the inventory is for special situations where a petition has been filed with the court requesting that no probate referee be appointed. (See Section C.) If the appointment of the referee has been waived, check box 4 and fill in the date of the court order.

Items 5, 6, 7, and 8 of "Statement Regarding Bond": Ordinarily, box 5 should be checked, assuming bond is waived either in the will or by all the heirs and beneficiaries. If bond was required, check box 7 and fill in the amount of the bond; when the appraised inventory is returned to you by the probate referee, you should check to make sure that the amount of the bond is sufficient. The two additional boxes in Item 7 which say "sufficient" or "insufficient" are for this purpose. To be sufficient, the amount of the bond should be equal to the value of all of the personal property plus the annual estimated income from real and personal property in the estate (or twice this amount if personal sureties are used), excluding cash or other personal property deposited in blocked accounts. If bond is insufficient, then an additional bond will be required by the court. We discuss bond requirements in more detail in Chapter 13, Section D. If blocked accounts were established, check box 8 and fill in the information. The box in Item 6 should be left blank.

When the inventory is completed, sign and date it on the front in the two places indicated and forward it to the probate referee. When you send the inventory to the referee, you should include additional information in your cover letter about unusual assets to help her with her appraisals. For instance, in the case of income property or business interests, the referee will probably need operating statements for at least the last three years (usually the handiest source is the decedent's income tax returns). If the inventory contains real property that is subject to depreciation for income tax purposes, the referee will appraise the land and improvements separately, if requested to do so, so the new owner can later justify a new basis for depreciation.

After the referee has completed her appraisals, she will insert the values of the assets she has appraised, sign it and return it to you for filing with the court. If the referee did not insert the total of Attachments 1 and 2, you should do this yourself.[4]

Note: If the inventory contains real property, you must file a Change in Ownership Statement with the County Assessor's office when the inventory is filed with the court. The statement is filed in the county where the real property is located. (See Chapter 8, Section C.) A copy of the form used in Los Angeles County is shown below. Each county has its own form, which may be obtained by calling the County Assessor's office. However, most accept forms furnished by other counties. The statement is required because passage of title by inheritance is generally considered a change in ownership, requiring a reassessment for property tax purposes, unless the real property goes to a surviving spouse or decedent's children. Even if the property does go to a spouse or decedent's children, you must still file the statement.

---

[4]Under Probate Code § 8803, you must mail a copy of the Inventory and Appraisement to anyone who has requested Special Notice within 15 days after the inventory is filed with the court. See Step 14 for a sample "proof of mailing" form that may be adapted for this purpose.

Inventory and Appraisement
(front)

ATTORNEY OR PARTY WITHOUT ATTORNEY (Name and Address)	TELEPHONE NO	FOR COURT USE ONLY
BILLY M. KIDD 1109 Sky Blue Mountain Trail Billings, Montana 48906 ATTORNEY FOR (Name) In Pro Per	(715) 392-6408	

SUPERIOR COURT OF CALIFORNIA, COUNTY OF LOS ANGELES
STREET ADDRESS 1725 Main Street
MAILING ADDRESS
CITY AND ZIP CODE Santa Monica, California 90401
BRANCH NAME West District

ESTATE OF (NAME): ANABELLE KIDD, aka ANABELLE O. KIDD,

[X] DECEDENT   [ ] CONSERVATEE   [ ] MINOR

INVENTORY AND APPRAISEMENT	CASE NUMBER
[X] Complete [ ] Final [ ] Partial No.: [ ] Supplemental [ ] Reappraisal for Sale	WEP 14813 Date of Death of Decedent or of Appointment of Guardian or Conservator 6-18-89

APPRAISALS

1. Total appraisal by representative (attachment 1) .... $ 38,590.38
2. Total appraisal by referee (attachment 2) .... $
                                                          TOTAL: $

DECLARATION OF REPRESENTATIVE

3. Attachments 1 and 2 together with all prior inventories filed contain a true statement of
   [X] all [ ] a portion of the estate that has come to my knowledge or possession, including particularly all money and all just claims the estate has against me. I have truly, honestly, and impartially appraised to the best of my ability each item set forth in attachment 1.
4. [ ] No probate referee is required [ ] by order of the court dated (specify):

I declare under penalty of perjury under the laws of the State of California that the foregoing is true and correct.

Date: August 28, 1989

BILLY M. KIDD
(TYPE OR PRINT NAME) (Include title if corporate officer)   ▶ *Billy M. Kidd*
                                                                (SIGNATURE OF PERSONAL REPRESENTATIVE)

STATEMENT REGARDING BOND
(Complete if required by local court rule)

5. [X] Bond is waived.
6. [ ] Sole personal representative is a corporate fiduciary.
7. [ ] Bond filed in the amount of: $ _____   [ ] Sufficient [ ] Insufficient
8. [ ] Receipts for: $ _____   have been filed with the court for deposits in a blocked account
      at (specify institution and location):

Date: August 28, 1989   ▶ *Billy M. Kidd*
                                                (SIGNATURE OF ATTORNEY OR PARTY WITHOUT ATTORNEY)

DECLARATION OF PROBATE REFEREE

9. I have truly, honestly, and impartially appraised to the best of my ability each item set forth in attachment 2.
10. A true account of my commission and expenses actually and necessarily incurred pursuant to my appointment is
    Statutory commission: $
    Expenses (specify): $
              TOTAL: $

I declare under penalty of perjury under the laws of the State of California that the foregoing is true and correct.
Date:

                                            ▶
(TYPE OR PRINT NAME)   (SIGNATURE OF REFEREE)

(Instructions on reverse)

| Form Approved by the
Judicial Council of California
DE-160, GC-040 [Rev. January 1, 1985] | INVENTORY AND APPRAISEMENT
(Probate) | Prob C 600-611,
2610-2616
(CEP JC-6)
(Rel 1-6/85 Pub.888) |

Inventory and Appraisement
Attachment 1

ESTATE OF ANABELLE KIDD, Deceased

CASE NUMBER WEP 14813

ATTACHMENT NO: 1

PAGE 1 OF 2 TOTAL PAGES

(IN DECEDENTS ESTATES ATTACHMENTS MUST CONFORM TO PROBATE CODE 601 REGARDING COMMUNITY AND SEPARATE PROPERTY) (ADD PAGES AS REQUIRED)

SEPARATE PROPERTY

Item No	Description	Appraised value
1	Cash in decedent's possession at time of death	$ 26.39
2.	Checking Account No. 345 778, Westside National Bank, Los Angeles; balance at date of death	1,366.49
3.	Certificate of Deposit No. 3459, Central Savings and Loan Association, Santa Monica Branch Principal balance on date of death: Accrued interest to date of death:	20,000.00 143.00
4.	Uncashed check dated 6-12-89 from Jon Harrad, payable to decedent	500.00
5.	Five $50 American Express travelers checks, Nos. 13765 to 13770	250.00
6.	Magazine refund from Fortune Magazine	10.50
7.	Merrill Lynch Ready Assets Trust, Account No. 063-215-29235	6,294.00
8.	Proceeds of Acme Insurance policy No. 54377, payable to decedent's estate	10,000.00
	Total Attachment 1 -	$ 38,590.38

Form Approved by the Judicial Council of California Effective January 1 1976

INVENTORY AND APPRAISEMENT (ATTACHMENT)

Prob C 481. 600-605, 784 1550 1901 ICSP JC-10 (Feb 1988)

Inventory and Appraisement
Attachment 2

ESTATE OF ANABELLE KIDD, Deceased

CASE NUMBER WEP 14813

ATTACHMENT NO: 2

PAGE 2 OF 2 TOTAL PAGES

(IN DECEDENTS ESTATES ATTACHMENTS MUST CONFORM TO PROBATE CODE 601 REGARDING COMMUNITY AND SEPARATE PROPERTY) (ADD PAGES AS REQUIRED)

Item No	Description	Appraised value
	SEPARATE PROPERTY	$
9.	Real property in the City of Santa Monica, County of Los Angeles, State of California, described as Lot 11 in Block 9 of Tract 5721, as per map recorded in Book 63, Page 31 of Maps in the office of the County Recorder of said county. Commonly known as 9560 Euclid Street, Santa Monica, improved with a single dwelling. A.P.N. 3467-047-379	
10.	One-third (1/3) interest as tenant in common with co-owners John and Mary Smith, in real property in the County of Contra Costa, described as Section 3, Township 20 North, Range 3 East (unimproved land) A.P.N. 4562-34-5770	
11.	250 shares, Federated Department Stores, Inc., common stock	
12.	75 shares, BestCo, Inc., $3 Cumulative, convertible preferred stock	
13.	Five $100 U.S. Series E bonds, issued June, 1960	
14.	$22,000 promissory note dated June 1, 1986, to decedent by R. E. Jones, interest at 9%, secured by deed of trust recorded June 15, 1976, in Book 4879, Page 98, in Official Records of Los Angeles County. Balance due at date of death: Accrued interest from June 1, 1989:	
15.	$10,000 promissory note of June 1, 1988, to decedent by David Hudson, unsecured, payable interest only at 7%	
16.	Decedent's interest as owner in Great Life Insurance Company Policy No. 36678, on life of decedent's daughter	
17.	Decedent's 50% interest in Valueless Mining Co., a limited partnership	
18.	Antique silver teapot, marked "Sheffield, 1893"	
19.	1987 Chevrolet Camaro automobile	
20.	Household furniture, furnishings, and personal effects located at decedent's residence	
	Total Attachment 2 -	

Form Approved by the Judicial Council of California Effective January 1 1976

INVENTORY AND APPRAISEMENT (ATTACHMENT)

Prob C 481. 600-605, 784 1550 1901 ICSP JC-10 (Feb 1988)

Letter to Probate Referee

September 15, 199_

Mr. Frank Adams
California Probate Referee
7856 Third Street
West Los Angeles, California

      Re: Estate of Anabelle Kidd, Deceased

          Los Angeles County Superior Court, Case No. WEP 14813

Dear Mr. Adams:

    I am advised that you have been appointed by the Court to appraise the assets in the above estate.

    Enclosed are the original and one copy of the Inventory and Appraisement. Please appraise the assets listed on Attachment 2 and return to me for filing with the Court.

    The approximate date of death value of the household furniture, furnishings and personal effects was $350.

    Should you require any addition information, please contact me at the address and phone number indicated below.

                 Very truly yours,

                 Billy M. Kidd
                 1109 Sky Blue Mountain Trail
                 Billings, Montana 48906

                 (715) 392-6408

Change in Ownership Statement
Death of Real Property Owner
(Los Angeles County form)

Instructions: *Complete a separate form for each property. Answer each question. Upon completion, mail this form and a copy of the death certificate to:*
Office of Assessor, 500 West Temple Street, Room 205, Los Angeles, California 90012.

1 NAME OF DECEDENT	2 DATE OF DEATH
ANABELLE KIDD, deceased	June 18, 1989

3 STREET ADDRESS OF REAL PROPERTY
9560 Euclid Street

Santa Monica, California

4. ASSESSOR'S IDENTIFICATION NUMBER

a Map Book			b Page			c Parcel		
3	4	6	7	0	4	7	3	7	9

5 DESCRIPTIVE INFORMATION *(Check a, b, or c, if applicable)*

a. ☐ Attached is copy of deed by which decedent acquired title.

b. ☒ Attached is copy of most recent tax bill.

c. ☐ Deed or tax bill are not available; attached is the legal description.

6 DISPOSITION OF REAL PROPERTY WILL BE BY *(Check one)*

a. ☐ Intestate succession.

b. ☐ PC 202 or PC 650 distribution of community property to surviving spouse.

c. ☐ Affidavit of death of joint tenant.

d. ☒ Decree of distribution pursuant to will.

e. ☐ Action of trustee pursuant to terms of a trust.

7 TRANSFEREE INFORMATION *(Check a, b, or c, if applicable)*

a. ☐ Transfer is to decedent's spouse. *(Check even if affidavit of death of joint tenant is to be recorded.)*

Name of spouse _____

b. ☐ Transfer is to a trust of which the spouse is the sole beneficiary or the income beneficiary.

Name of spouse _____

c. ☒ Transfer is to decedent's non-spousal beneficiaries. *(Where known, indicate names of beneficiaries and the percentage of ownership interest each is to receive.)*

Mary Kidd Clark, one-third (1/3) interest

Billy M. Kidd, one-third (1/3) interest

Carson Kidd, one-third (1/3) interest

8 SALE PRIOR TO DISTRIBUTION

☒ This property has been sold or will be sold prior to distribution. *(Where appropriate, attach the conveyance document and/or court order.)*

9 ADDITIONAL INFORMATION

☐ Additional sheets attached. *(Should you wish to explain any of the foregoing or provide additional information, please attach additional sheets.)*

_____

_____

_____

NAME *(Please print.)*	TITLE *(If corporate officer/partner)*	TELEPHONE NO *(8 a.m.-5 p.m.)*
Billy M. Kidd	Executor	(715) 392-6408

under the laws of the State of California
I declare under penalty of perjury that the foregoing is true and correct to the best of my knowledge and belief.

Signature of owner or corporate officer

Signed in Billings, Montana ~~California~~, this 10th day of September 1989

76C448 ASSR · 76 (rev 9/82)

B. Unique Assets

Appraisement of unique items, such as coin collections, art collections and the like, usually requires expertise beyond that of most probate referees. If the decedent owned a unique, artistic, unusual or special item of tangible personal property, you have the option of having it appraised by an independent expert instead of a probate referee. (Probate Code §§ 8904 and 8905.) List the asset on the main inventory with a notation that it will be appraised by the independent expert. Then prepare another separate inventory form, describing the unique asset in an attachment, and check the box on the face page indicating it is a "Partial" inventory. Have the expert complete the appraisal, sign the Declaration of Probate Referee at the bottom of the form and return it to you for filing with the court.

C. Waiver of Appraisal by Probate Referee

If good cause is shown, the court may waive the requirement that some or all non-cash assets be appraised by a probate referee. It is not clear what constitutes "good cause," but probably if the assets have readily ascertainable values, such as publicly traded securities or motor vehicles listed in Kelly's Blue Book, or the values are supported by independent appraisals by qualified persons, a waiver would be given if none of the beneficiaries objects. Application for the waiver may be filed either at the time the Petition for Probate is filed or later before the inventory is delivered to the referee, if one has been designated. (Probate Code § 8903.) Here is how you apply for the waiver:

1. List the assets on Attachment 1, since they will be appraised by you as personal representative instead of the referee, and insert the values opposite the assets in the right-hand column.

2. Prepare a Petition for Waiver of Appraisal by Probate Referee (a sample is shown below) setting forth the facts that constitute good cause for granting the waiver. Be specific as to how the valuations were obtained, as shown in our example. The Verification should be typed on a separate page and attached last, after the other attachments.

3. File the petition, with a copy of the proposed inventory attached, at which time the court will give you a hearing date. A $14 filing fee is required in most counties. Call the court clerk to find out if you must attach a blue document backer to the petition and/or punch holes at the top with a standard two-hole punch.

4. Prepare a Notice of Hearing in the manner described in Step 18 of this chapter inserting the name of this document in Item 1 of the Notice.

5. A copy of the Notice of Hearing and *a copy of the petition and proposed inventory* must be mailed (or personally delivered) by a disinterested person at least 15 days before the hearing to: (a) all beneficiaries of the will, if there is a will; (b) all heirs, if no will; (c) the state of California if any property may escheat to it; (d) the probate referee, if one has been designated by the court; and (e) any person who has requested special notice. You do not have to mail notice to yourself, however.

6. File the original Notice of Hearing with the court prior to the hearing date, with proof of the mailing. Be sure to indicate in the proof of mailing that a copy of the petition and the proposed inventory were mailed with the notice.

7. Check with the court a few days prior to the hearing to see if the petition has been approved. If so, prepare the Order and send it to the court for signature. A sample Order is shown below. Attach a "blue backer" and/or punch holes at the top, if required.

Petition for Waiver

1   (Name of Petitioner)
2   (Address)
3   (Telephone Number)
4   Petitioner in pro per

SUPERIOR COURT OF CALIFORNIA

COUNTY OF _____

Estate of

(Name of Decedent),

     Deceased.

CASE NO.

PETITION FOR WAIVER OF APPRAISAL
BY PROBATE REFEREE

(Probate Code Sec. 8903)

15   The undersigned, as personal representative of the estate of the
16   above-named decedent, states:
17   Attached is a copy of the proposed inventory and appraisement of the
18   estate assets. The date-of-death values of the non-cash assets listed in
19   Attachment 1 were obtained from the following reliable sources and an appraisal
20   by a probate referee is not required:
21   1. The value of the ABC Corporation stock (Item 1) was obtained from
22   newspaper financial pages by computing the mean between the highest and lowest
23   selling prices per share on the date of death.
24   2. The value of the 1985 Dodge Aries automobile (Item 2) was deter-
25   mined by taking the average between the wholesale and retail price listed in
26   Kelly's Blue Book for the month of death.
27   3. The value of the real property (Item 3) was provided by a
28   professional appraiser, and a copy of the appraisal is attached.

1.

---

1   WHEREFORE, petitioner prays that the court make an Order waiving the
2   requirement that a probate referee appraise the assets listed in Attachment 1
3   of the inventory and appraisement attached hereto.
4   DATED: _____, 19___

      _____
      (Type name of petitioner)

[Note: Also attach separate Verification page.
Use the form on page 14/76.]

2.

Order Waiving Appraisal

1	(Name of Petitioner)
2	(Address)
3	
4	(Telephone)
5	
6	Petitioner in Pro Per
7	
8	SUPERIOR COURT OF CALIFORNIA
9	COUNTY OF _____
10	

11 Estate of   )   CASE NO. _____
)
12   (Name of Decedent),   )   ORDER WAIVING APPRAISAL
)   BY PROBATE REFEREE
13   Deceased.   )
)
14 _____   )

15   The petition of _____, as personal representa-

16 tive of the estate of the above-named decedent, for a Waiver of Appraisal by

17 Probate Referee having come on regularly for hearing on _____, 19__,

18 the Honorable _____, Judge presiding, the Court finds that

19 due notice of the hearing has been given as prescribed by law; that all

20 allegations of the petition are true; and that an appraisal by a probate

21 referee of the non-cash assets listed in Attachment 1 of the Inventory and

22 Appraisement should be waived. Good cause appearing,

23   IT IS ORDERED that an appraisal by a probate referee of the assets

24 listed in Attachment 1 of the Inventory and Appraisement is hereby waived.

25   DATED: _____, 19__

26

27   _____
                                       JUDGE OF THE SUPERIOR COURT
28

Step 16: Notify Creditors and Deal with Creditor's Claims and Other Debts

AS ESTATE REPRESENTATIVE, you must handle the decedent's debts. If you have authority to administer the estate under the Independent Administration of Estates Act, you may allow, pay, reject, contest or compromise any claim against the estate without court supervision and without first giving a Notice of Proposed Action. (Probate Code § 10552(a) and (b).) Generally, the only proper claims are debts and obligations of the decedent that were due and unpaid as of the date of death, and funeral expenses. Expenses and obligations incurred *after* the date of death, such as court filing fees, certification fees, expenditures necessary to protect estate property, etc., don't require formal claims. Formal claims are also not required for tax bills, secured debts such as mortgages on real property or judgments secured by recorded liens.

Payment of debts and claims against a decedent's estate is subject to many technical rules which are set out in Probate Code Sections 9000 and following. If the estate you are settling involves large debts or claims other than the usual ordinary expenses, get the advice of an attorney.

A. Written Notice to Creditors

The law requires the personal representative to give actual written notice to all known creditors. (Probate Code § 9050.) The written notice is in addition to the published notice discussed in Step 4 (Section A). It is given on a printed form entitled "Notice of Administration to Creditors," which advises the creditor how and where to file a claim. A sample is shown below.

Here are the rules on when claims may be filed (Probate Code §§ 9051 and 9100):

- The notice must be given to all known creditors within four months after the date Letters are first issued to the personal representative. All creditors so notified must file their claims within the four-month period.

- If a creditor is discovered only during the last 30 days of the four-month period, notice must be given to that creditor within 30 days after discovery of the creditor. That creditor then has 30 days from the date notice is given to file a claim.

- If a creditor is discovered *after* the four-month period has expired, notice must be given to that creditor within 30 days. That creditor must then petition the court to file a late claim under Probate Code § 9103 if he wishes to pursue payment of his claim. A late claim cannot be allowed after one year from the date of death.

Generally, claims are barred from payment if they are not filed within the above time frames. In limited cases, a distributee of an estate may be liable for a claim if the creditor was known or reasonably ascertainable and the personal representative did not give the creditor written Notice of Administration. (Probate Code § 9392.) Actions against a distributee must be commenced within one year of date of the death for decedent's dying on or after January 1, 1991.

A personal representative is not liable to a creditor for failure to give written notice to that creditor unless the failure was in bad faith. The burden of proof of bad faith is on the person seeking to impose liablility. (Probate Code § 9053.)

Hint: At this point, you collect and examine all itemized bills and statements that have been sent to the decedent. If they are legitimate, you may be able to save time and paperwork by paying them under the provisions of Probate Code § 10552 or § 9154, without giving written notice or requiring a formal claim, as discussed in Section B, below.

There is no need to send the Notice to creditors who have filed formal claims, or creditors who have submitted bills and will be paid without a formal claim under Probate Code § 9154, discussed below. Other than creditors who have already submitted bills or filed claims, written notice should be given to all creditors, or potential creditors, who can be identified through reasonably diligent efforts. For your protection, make a thorough search of

Notice of Administration to Creditors

NOTICE OF ADMINISTRATION* OF THE ESTATE OF

ANABELLE KIDD, aka ANABELLE O. KIDD
(NAME)

DECEDENT

NOTICE TO CREDITORS

1. (Name): Billy M. Kidd
   (Address): 1109 Sky Blue Mountain Trail
   Billings, Montana 48906

is the personal representative of the ESTATE OF (name): ANABELLE KIDD, who is deceased.

2. The personal representative HAS BEGUN ADMINISTRATION of the decedent's estate in the

a. SUPERIOR COURT OF CALIFORNIA, COUNTY OF LOS ANGELES
   STREET ADDRESS: 1725 Main Street
   MAILING ADDRESS:
   CITY AND ZIP CODE: Santa Monica, California 90401
   BRANCH NAME: West District

b. Case Number (specify): WEP 14813

3. You must FILE YOUR CLAIM with the court clerk (address in item 2a) AND mail or deliver a copy to the personal representative before the later of the following dates as provided in section 9100 of the California Probate Code:
a. four months after (date): July 25, 1989, the date letters (authority to act for the estate) were first issued to the personal representative, OR
b. thirty days after (date): August 2, 1989, the date this notice was mailed or personally delivered to you.

or you must petition to file a late claim as provided in Section 9103 of the California Probate Code.

You may obtain a CREDITOR'S CLAIM FORM from any superior court clerk. (Judicial Council form No. DE-172. Creditor's Claim.) A letter is not sufficient.

If you use the mail to file your claim with the court, for your protection you should send your claim by certified mail, with return receipt requested. If you mail a copy of your claim to the personal representative, you should also use certified mail.

(Proof of Service on reverse)

* Use this form in estates begun on or after July 1, 1988
Form Approved by the Judicial Council of California
DE-157 (New July 1, 1988)
NOTICE OF ADMINISTRATION TO CREDITORS (Probate)
Probate Code, §§ 9050, 9052

(Optional)
PROOF OF SERVICE BY MAIL

1. I am over the age of 18 and not a party to this cause. I am a resident of or employed in the county where the mailing occurred.
2. My residence or business address is (specify):
   25 Sutter Street, Billings, Montana
3. I served the foregoing Notice of Administration to Creditors on each person named below by enclosing a copy in an envelope addressed as shown below AND
a. X depositing the sealed envelope with the United States Postal Service with the postage fully prepaid.
b. placing the envelope for collection and mailing on the date and at the place shown in item 4 following our ordinary business practices. I am readily familiar with this business' practice for collecting and processing correspondence for mailing. On the same day that correspondence is placed for collection and mailing, it is deposited in the ordinary course of business with the United States Postal Service in a sealed envelope with postage fully prepaid.

4. a. Date of deposit: August 2, 1989   b. Place of deposit (city and state): Billings, Montana

I declare under penalty of perjury under the laws of the State of California that the foregoing is true and correct.

Date: August 2, 1989

Samantha Long
(TYPE OR PRINT NAME)   (SIGNATURE OF DECLARANT)

NAME AND ADDRESS OF EACH PERSON TO WHOM NOTICE WAS MAILED

Bullocks Wilshire
P. O. Box 1990077
Los Angeles, CA 90002

Jon Barrad
1206 - 19th Street
Santa Monica, CA 90047

Sullivan's Catering
11560 Lincoln Boulevard
Marina del Rey, California 90488

DE-157 (New July 1, 1988)   NOTICE OF ADMINISTRATION TO CREDITORS (Probate)   Page two the decedent's files and records for evidence of any obligation or potential liability the decedent may have had at death. Look for such things as outstanding loans, mortgages, promissory notes, disputed bills, pending or anticipated lawsuits where the decedent is or could be a defendant, and outstanding judgments against the decedent.

For each possible creditor, make a list of the name of the individual, corporation or other entity, the mailing address, the account number and any other information relevant to the debt or obligation. Each creditor on this list should receive a written "Notice of Administration of Estate of _____, Decedent" and should be required to file a formal Creditor's Claim. This task can be simplified by preparing a master copy of the Notice, filling in all relevant information except the date in Item 3-b, and making several photocopies.

When you're ready to mail the Notice, fill in the date before sending it to the creditor. We recommend that you have a disinterested person mail the copies of the Notice and complete the proof of mailing on the back. Keep the original copy in your files as a record of who was given written notice in case of disputes.

How To Fill Out the Notice of Administration to Creditors

Caption: Fill in the decedent's name.

Item 1: Fill in the name and address of the executor or administrator, and the name of the decedent.

Item 2: Fill in the address and branch name of the court, and the case number.

Item 3: In the first box, put the date Letters were issued. In the second box, put the date you are mailing the Notice.

After Item 3.b, type in the following:

"or you must petition to file a late claim as provided in § 9103 of the California Probate Code."

This language was added to the creditor's claim statute, but the form has not yet been updated to reflect the change.

Proof of Service: Have a disinterested person mail copies of the Notice to creditors and fill out and sign the Proof of Service on the back of the original Notice. Keep the original Notice(s) until you are ready to close the estate and file them with the court when you file the Petition for Final Distribution.

B. Bills You May Pay Without a Claim or Giving Written Notice

Under Probate Code § 9154, a written demand for payment, such as an itemized bill or statement, may be treated as an established claim if it's received within four months after Letters are issued. You can pay these debts without giving written notice and without requiring a formal creditor's claim if they're bona fide debts and paid in good faith, and the estate is solvent.[5]

As a practical matter, in simple estates it's easier to pay ordinary expenses such as utility bills, charge account balances, doctor or other medical bills, funeral expenses, real estate and income taxes, and other clearly proper debts without giving written notice or requiring a formal claim as long as you're sure no one will object to the payment. Just remember these requirements: (1) you must have received a written demand for payment within four months after Letters were issued, (2) the debt must be justly due, (3) the amount you pay must take into account any previous payments or offsets, (4) payment must be made within 30 days after the four-month period that begins with issuance of your Letters, and (5) the estate must be solvent.

---

[5]If the estate is insolvent, there is an order of priority for payment set by law in Probate Code § 11420. As you might guess, attorneys get paid first, before other creditors, except for priority debts due the U.S. Government.

Creditor's Claim

Page one

ATTORNEY OR CREDITOR WITHOUT ATTORNEY:
Michael Sullivan
11560 Lincoln Boulevard,
Marina del Rey, California 90488
TELEPHONE NO.: (213) 393-6632
ATTORNEY FOR: In Pro Per

SUPERIOR COURT OF CALIFORNIA, COUNTY OF LOS ANGELES
STREET ADDRESS: 1725 Main Street
MAILING ADDRESS:
CITY AND ZIP CODE: Santa Monica, California 90401
BRANCH NAME: West District

ESTATE OF (NAME): ANABELLE KIDD, aka
ANABELLE O. KIDD, DECEDENT

CASE NUMBER: WEP 14F13

CREDITOR'S CLAIM*
(for estate administration proceedings filed after June 30, 1988)

You must file this claim with the court clerk at the court address above before the LATER of (a) four months after the date letters (authority to act for the estate) were first issued to the personal representative, or (b) thirty days after the date Notice of Administration was given to the creditor, if notice was given as provided in Probate Code section 9051. Mail or deliver a copy of this claim to the personal representative. A proof of service is on the reverse.

1. Total amount of the claim: $ 347.00
2. Claimant (name): Michael Sullivan
   a. ☐ an individual.
   b. ☒ an individual or entity doing business under the fictitious name of (specify): Sullivan's Catering
   c. ☐ a partnership. The person signing has authority to sign on behalf of the partnership.
   d. ☐ a corporation. The person signing has authority to sign on behalf of the corporation.
   e. ☐ other (specify):
3. Address of claimant (specify): 11560 Lincoln Boulevard, Marina del Rey, California 90488

4. Claimant is ☒ the creditor ☐ a person acting on behalf of creditor (state reason):
5. Claimant is ☐ the personal representative ☐ the attorney for the personal representative.
   (Claims against the estate by the personal representative and the attorney for the personal representative must be filed within the claim period allowed in Probate Code section 9100 See the notice box above.)
6. I am authorized to make this claim which is just and due or may become due. All payments on or offsets to the claim have been credited. Facts supporting this claim are ☒ on reverse ☐ attached.

I declare under penalty of perjury under the laws of the State of California that this creditor's claim is true and correct.
Date: August 15, 1989

Michael Sullivan
(TYPE OR PRINT NAME AND TITLE)
► [signature] (SIGNATURE OF CLAIMANT)

INSTRUCTIONS TO CLAIMANT

A. On the reverse, itemize the claim and show the date the service was rendered or the debt incurred. Describe the item or service in detail, and indicate the amount claimed for each item. Do not include debts incurred after the date of death, except funeral claims.
B. If the claim is not due or contingent, or the amount is not yet ascertainable, state the facts supporting the claim.
C. If the claim is secured by a note or other written instrument, the original or a copy must be attached (state why original is unavailable). If secured by mortgage, deed of trust, or other lien on property that is of record, it is sufficient to describe the security and refer to the date or volume and page, and county where recorded. (See Probate Code section 9152.)
D. Mail or take this original claim to the court clerk's office for filing. If mailed, use certified mail, with return receipt requested.
E. Mail or deliver a copy to the personal representative. Complete the Proof of Mailing or Personal Delivery on the reverse.
F. The personal representative will notify you when your claim is allowed or rejected.
(Continued on reverse)

* See instructions before completing. Use Creditor's Claim form No. DE-170 for access filed before July 1, 1988.
Form Approved by the Judicial Council of California
DE-172 (Rev. July 1, 1988)
370 to (880)

CREDITOR'S CLAIM
(Probate)

Probate Code §§ 9000 et seq. 9153

Page two

ESTATE OF (NAME): ANABELLE KIDD, DECEDENT
CASE NUMBER: WEP 14813

FACTS SUPPORTING THE CREDITOR'S CLAIM
☐ See attachment (if space is insufficient)

Date of Item	Item and Supporting Facts	Amount Claimed
June 10, 1989	Food and services provided decedent per the attached statement	$ 347.00
	TOTAL	$ 347.00

PROOF OF ☒ MAILING ☐ PERSONAL DELIVERY TO PERSONAL REPRESENTATIVE
(Be sure to mail or take the original to the court clerk's office for filing)

1. I am the creditor or a person acting on behalf of the creditor. At the time of mailing or delivery I was at least 18 years of age.
2. My residence or business address is (specify): 11560 Lincoln Boulevard, Marina del Rey, Calif.
3. I mailed or delivered a copy of this Creditor's Claim to the personal representative as follows (check either a or b below):
   a. ☒ First-class mail. I deposited a copy of the claim with the United States Postal Service, in a sealed envelope with postage fully prepaid. I used first-class mail. I am a resident of or employed in the county where the mailing occurred.
   The envelope was addressed and mailed as follows:
   (1) Name of personal representative served: Billy M. Kidd
   (2) Address on envelope: 1109 Sky Blue Mountain Trail
   Billings, Montana 48906
   (3) Date of mailing: August 15, 1989
   (4) Place of mailing (city and state): Marina del Rey, California
   b. ☐ Personal delivery. I personally delivered a copy of the claim to the personal representative as follows:
   (1) Name of personal representative served:
   (2) Address where delivered:
   (3) Date delivered:
   (4) Time delivered:

I declare under penalty of perjury under the laws of the State of California that the foregoing is true and correct.
Date: August 15, 1989

Michael Sullivan
(TYPE OR PRINT NAME OF CLAIMANT)
► [signature] (SIGNATURE OF CLAIMANT)

DE-172 (New July 1, 1988)

CREDITOR'S CLAIM
(Probate)

Page two

C. Formal Creditor's Claims

The published "Notice of Petition to Administer Estate" advises creditors how and when to file claims. Subject to the few exceptions discussed in Section A above, a creditor must file a formal Creditor's Claim directly with the court and mail or personally deliver a copy to the personal representative within four months after Letters are issued. Failure to deliver a copy to the personal representative, however, doesn't invalidate a claim that has been properly filed with the court. Generally, you're not legally required to pay any claims not filed within this four-month period, so make note of this important cut-off date.

Few formal claims, if any, are filed in uncomplicated estates. Usually, you just receive bills addressed to the decedent at his last address, because most creditors don't know of the death.

D. Claim By Personal Representative

If you, as personal representative, have paid any of the decedent's debts from your personal funds (funeral expenses or utility bills, for example), or have any other claim against the estate, you must file a formal Creditor's Claim with the court. Copies of cancelled checks or other evidence of payment must be attached. A claims examiner will review the claim, and the court's approval or rejection will be endorsed on the "Allowance or Rejection of Creditor's Claim" form (discussed below), which you should submit with the claim when it is filed. After the court has approved the claim, you only pay yourself the amount allowed out of estate funds. As stated previously, payment of administrative expenses such as court filing fees don't require formal claims and you may be reimbursed immediately from the estate bank account for these expenses after your appointment.

E. Allowance or Rejection of Creditor's Claims

If formal claims are filed, you must allow, reject or partially allow each one. You prepare an "Allowance or Rejection of Creditor's Claim" form to let the creditor and the court know what action you've taken on the claim. You file the original form with the court (with a copy of the claim attached) and send a copy to the creditor. The mailing or personal delivery to the creditor must be done by a disinterested adult, who afterwards must complete the proof of mailing or personal delivery on the back of the original form before it's filed. If you have independent powers, no further court action is required; however, if you don't have independent powers, the court must review your action and endorse its allowance or rejection on the original form.

You should examine each Creditor's Claim carefully to make sure (1) it's signed and dated, (2) the debt was incurred or the service was rendered before the date of death, and (3) the claim was filed within the four-month claim period or within 30 days after written notice was given. Otherwise, it may be defective and not an allowable claim.

If you receive a Creditor's Claim for a debt you question for some reason (for example, the amount is too high, or the service rendered wasn't satisfactory), you may reject the claim in whole or in part. A creditor who refuses to accept the amount you allow has three months from the date of the rejection within which to file suit against the estate. If he doesn't file suit within such time, the claim is barred forever. If he files suit, you'll need an attorney. Whenever a claim is rejected you must wait three months from the date of rejection before filing a petition to close the estate.

F. Payment of Claims

Claims for funeral expenses, last illness expenses, and wage claims that have been allowed and approved should be paid promptly as soon as there are sufficient funds in the estate, after retaining enough to pay administration expenses and debts owed to the United States or California. (Probate Code § 11421.)

Allowance or Rejection of Creditor's Claim
(front)

ATTORNEY OR PARTY WITHOUT ATTORNEY (Name and Address):	TELEPHONE NO.	FOR COURT USE ONLY
BILLY M. KIDD 1109 Sky Blue Mountain Trail Billings, Montana 48906	(715) 392-6408	Personal representative's allowance or rejection filed

ATTORNEY FOR (Name): In Pro Per

SUPERIOR COURT OF CALIFORNIA, COUNTY OF LOS ANGELES

STREET ADDRESS: 1725 Main Street

MAILING ADDRESS:

CITY AND ZIP CODE: Santa Monica, California 90401

BRANCH NAME: West District

(date) (Deputy)

☐ No court approval required.

Presented to court for approval or rejection:

(date) (Deputy)

ESTATE OF (NAME):
ANABELLE KIDD, aka
ANABELLE O. KIDD,   DECEDENT

ALLOWANCE OR REJECTION OF CREDITOR'S CLAIM (for estate administration proceedings filed after June 30, 1988)	CASE NUMBER: WEP 14813

NOTE: Attach a copy of the creditor's claim.

PERSONAL REPRESENTATIVE'S ALLOWANCE OR REJECTION

1. Name of creditor (specify): Michael Sullivan
2. The claim was filed on (date):
3. Date of first issuance of letters: July 25, 1989
4. Date of Notice of Administration: August 2, 1989
5. Date of decedent's death: June 18, 1989
6. Estimated value of estate: $ 250,000
7. Total amount of the claim: $ 347.00
8. [X] Claim is allowed for: $ 347.00   (The court must approve certain claims before they are paid.)
9. [ ] Claim is rejected for: $ (A creditor has three months to act on a rejected claim. See box below.)
10. Notice of allowance or rejection given on (date): August 20, 1989
11. [X] The personal representative is authorized to administer the estate under the Independent Administration of Estates Act.

Date: August 20, 1989

............Billy M. Kidd.............   ▶ _Billy M. Kidd_ (signature)
(TYPE OR PRINT NAME)   (SIGNATURE OF PERSONAL REPRESENTATIVE)

REJECTED CLAIMS: From the date notice of rejection is given, the creditor must act on the rejected claim (e.g., file a lawsuit) as follows:
a. **Claim due:** within three months after the notice of rejection.
b. **Claim not due:** within three months after the claim becomes due.

COURT'S APPROVAL OR REJECTION

12. [ ] Approved for: $

13. [ ] Rejected for: $

Date:

                                              ▶
                                                 SIGNATURE OF [ ] JUDGE [ ] COMMISSIONER
14. [ ] Number of pages attached: [ ] Signature follows last attachment.

(Proof of Service on reverse)

Form Approved by the Judicial Council of California DE-174 (New July 1, 1988) 370 05 (6/88)	ALLOWANCE OR REJECTION OF CREDITOR'S CLAIM (Probate)	Probate Code, § 9000 et seq., 9250

Allowance or Rejection of Creditor's Claim
(back)

ESTATE OF (NAME): ANABELLE KIDD, DECEDENT	CASE NUMBER: WEP 14813

PROOF OF [X] MAILING [ ] PERSONAL DELIVERY   TO CREDITOR

1. At the time of mailing or personal delivery I was at least 18 years of age and not a party to this proceeding.

2. My residence or business address is *(specify)*:   25 Sutter Street, Billings, Montana

3. I mailed or personally delivered a copy of the **Allowance or Rejection of Creditor's Claim** as follows *(complete either a or b)*:

    a. [X] **Mail.** I am a resident of or employed in the county where the mailing occurred.
        (1) I enclosed a copy in an envelope AND
           (i) [X] deposited the sealed envelope with the United States Postal Service with the postage fully prepaid.
           (ii) [ ] placed the envelope for collection and mailing on the date and at the place shown in items below following our ordinary business practices. I am readily familiar with this business' practice for collecting and processing correspondence for mailing. On the same day that correspondence is placed for collection and mailing, it is deposited in the ordinary course of business with the United States Postal Service in a sealed envelope with postage fully prepaid.
        (2) The envelope was addressed and mailed first-class as follows:
           (i) Name of creditor served: Michael Sullivan
           (ii) Address on envelope: 11560 Lincoln Boulevard
                                          Marina del Rey, California 90488

           (iii) Date of mailing: August 20, 1989
           (iv) Place of mailing *(city and state)*:   Billings, Montana

    b. [ ] **Personal delivery.** I personally delivered a copy to the creditor as follows:
        (1) Name of creditor served:
        (2) Address where delivered:

        (3) Date delivered:
        (4) Time delivered:

I declare under penalty of perjury under the laws of the State of California that the foregoing is true and correct.

Date: August 20, 1989

Samantha Long
....
(TYPE OR PRINT NAME OF DECLARANT)

▶ *Samantha Long*
                     (SIGNATURE OF DECLARANT)

DE 174 (New July 1, 1988)   **ALLOWANCE OR REJECTION OF CREDITOR'S CLAIM**   Page two
                                                    (Probate)

Strictly speaking, you're not required to pay any other claims without a court order. However, this rule isn't strictly observed and you may safely pay other allowed and approved claims as long as (1) the time for filing or presenting claims has expired, (2) the estate is solvent and there is cash available for payment, and (3) no one having an interest in the estate is going to challenge the payment. If the claim is based on a written contract, interest accrues at the rate and in accordance with the contract. (Probate Code § 11423.)

How to Fill Out the Allowance or Rejection of Creditor's Claim

Caption: Fill in your name, address, the court's name, and case number, as you have on your other court papers.

Items 1—7: Fill in the requested information (most of it is on the Creditor's Claim). Leave Item 2 blank if you don't know when the claim was filed with the court.

Items 8 and 9: Fill in the amount you are approving and/or rejecting.

Item 10: Enter the date you mail this form to the creditor.

Item 11: Check the box if you are authorized to administer the estate under the Independent Administration of Estates Act.

Print your name, and date and sign the form. Leave the rest of the front page blank.

Proof of Service: Whoever mails or gives the form to the creditor should fill out and sign the Proof of Service on the original of the form, after a copy has been sent to the creditor. Then, you should file the original with the court.

Step 17: Prepare the Petition for Final Distribution

AFTER THE CREDITOR'S CLAIM period has expired (four months from the issuance of Letters), you may file a petition with the court requesting an Order Distributing the Assets to the Beneficiaries—if the estate is in a condition to be closed. Following is a checklist of the requirements to help you determine whether or not the estate is ready to be closed:

1. The Creditor's Claim period must have expired;

2. All Creditor's Claims must either have been allowed and approved, or if any were rejected, the time to file suit on the rejected claims must have expired. (See Step 16, above.);

3. All expenses of administration, including charges for legal advertising, have been paid;

4. A California Income Tax Clearance certificate must be obtained, if the estate requires one. This is required only for estates that have a gross value exceeding $400,000, and where assets of $100,000 or more will be distributed to one or more beneficiaries who are not residents of California. (See Chapter 13, Section E.)

Application for the certificate is made using Form FTB-3571, called "Request for Estate Income Tax Certificate" (as required under Section 19262), which may be obtained by calling the nearest Franchise Tax Board office. The form is self-explanatory and should be filled in and mailed to the Franchise Tax Board, Sacramento, California 95867 at least 30 days prior to the hearing date on the Petition for Final Distribution. (The hearing date is usually three to four weeks from the time you file the petition with the court.) Therefore, to coordinate this, you should wait to file the petition to close the estate until about a week or ten days after you mail the Form FTB-3571 to the Franchise Tax Board to allow time for the certificate to be processed before the hearing date. When the certificate is received, it should be filed with the court prior to the hearing date on the petition.

Petition for Final Distribution
(front)

1   BILLY M. KIDD
     1109 Sky Blue Mountain Trail
2   Billings, Montana 48906
     (715) 392-6408
3

4   Petitioner in pro per

5

6

7

8   SUPERIOR COURT OF CALIFORNIA

9   COUNTY OF LOS ANGELES

10

11   Estate of   )   CASE NO. WEP 14813
)
12   ANABELLE KIDD, aka   )   PETITION FOR FINAL DISTRIBUTION ON
)   WAIVER OF ACCOUNT (AND FOR ALLOWANCE
13   ANABELLE O. KIDD,   )   OF STATUTORY COMMISSIONS)
)
14   Deceased.   )   (Probate Code Sec. 10400-10406,
     _____)   10954, 11600-11642)
15

16   Petitioner, BILLY M. KIDD, as personal representative of the estate

17   of the above-named decedent, states:

18   1. ANABELLE KIDD, aka ANABELLE O. KIDD, died on June 18, 1989, a

19   resident of the county named above.

20   2. Notice of Petition to Administer Estate was duly published as re-

21   quired by law. In addition, petitioner made a diligent search for all reasonably

22   ascertainable creditors.   No such creditors were found beyond those who sub-

23   mitted bills in the ordinary course within the four-month period, all of which

24   have been paid. (Or, if applicable: All such creditors were given written

25   Notice of Administration as required by Probate Code Sec. 9052, and the Notices

26   are on file herein.)   The time for filing claims has expired.

27   3. The decedent did not receive Medi-Cal benefits, and notice to

28   the Director of Health Services is not required.

                                    1.

Petition for Final Distribution
(back)

1	(or)
2	3. Notice to the Director of Health Services has been given.
3	4. No claims were filed against the estate.
4	(or)
5	4. The following claims were filed against the estate and were allowed
6	and paid. There were no rejected claims:

7	Name of Claimant	Nature of Claim	Amount
8	Sullivan's Catering	Food and services provided decedent	$ 347.00

9.   5. All administration expenses, including charges for legal

10. advertising and bond premiums, if any, have been paid and the estate is ready

11. for distribution and in a condition to be closed.

12.   6. An inventory and appraisement of the estate assets was filed, showing

13. the value of the estate to be $211,480.38.

14.   7. The estate was administered under the Independent Administration of

15. Estates Act. Petitioner performed the following actions without court super-

16. vision, after having given Notice of Proposed Action when required:

17.   a. Sold the decedent's residence at 9560 Euclid Street, Santa

18. Monica, for the sales price of $129,900, after giving Notice of Proposed Action

19. to all persons whose interest was affected by such action;

20.   b. Sold the decedent's 1987 Chevrolet automobile, without notice,

21. for cash in the sum of $8,000. Said automobile would have depreciated in

22. value and caused undue expense to the estate by being kept.

23.   8. No personal property taxes are due or payable by the estate.

24.   9. All income taxes due by the decedent or the estate as of the date of

25. this petition have been paid. (Add, if applicable: The value of the estate

26. assets at the date of decedent's death exceeded $400,000, and assets of at

27. least $100,000 are distributable to nonresident beneficiaries. The certificate

28. of the California Franchise Tax Board required by Revenue and Taxation Code

2.

Petition for Final Distribution

1   Section 19262 is on file herein.)

2   10.   No California or federal estate tax return is required.

3   (or)

4   10.   The California and federal estate tax returns have been filed

5 for the estate, and the taxes shown to be due have been paid.

6   11.   The assets on hand, including their community or separate

7 character, are set forth in Exhibit "A", attached hereto.

8   12.   The names, present addresses, ages and relationship to decedent

9 of all persons entitled to receive property of the estate and the plan of

10 distribution are set forth in Exhibit "B", attached.

11   13.   Petitioner waives the filing of a final account. (Add, if

12 appropriate: Waivers of Account by the remaining beneficiaries are attached

13 as Exhibits "C" and "D".

14   14.   Petitioner waives any right to statutory commissions.

15   (or)

16   14.   Petitioner's statutory commissions are computed as follows:

17   Amount of Inventory and Appraisement $ 211,480.38

18   4% on $ 15,000.00   =   600.00

19   3% on next $ 85,000.00   =   2,550.00

20   2% on next $ 111,480.38   =   2,229.61

21   Total Commissions - $ 5,379.61

22   WHEREFORE, petitioner prays that the administration of the

23 estate be brought to a close without the requirement of an accounting; that

24 all acts and proceedings of petitioner as herein set forth be approved;

25 (Insert, if applicable: that petitioner be allowed $ 5,379.61 as statutory

26 commissions;) that distribution of the estate of the decedent in petitioner's

27 hands, and any other property of decedent or the estate not now known or

28 discovered, be made to the persons entitled to it as set forth in the petition:

3.

---

1   and that the Court make such other and further Orders as may be proper.

2   DATED: December 10, 1989

3

4   *[signature]*   BILLY M. KIDD

5

6

7

8

9

10

11

12

13   [Note: Also attach separate Verification page.

14   Use the form on page 14/76.]

15

16

17

18

19

20

21

22

23

24

25

26

27

28

4.

There is no printed form for the Petition for Final Distribution, but you should have no trouble typing it if you carefully follow the sample shown below. As you will note, alternative paragraphs are listed next to some numbers, such as 3, 4 and 7, which take care of different situations. Use only the provision that fits your situation, which you can determine after reading the notes below that are keyed to each numbered provision.

Note: Our sample forms should be acceptable for most counties. However, some courts have requirements of their own for the preparation of petitions and orders, so be sure to carefully read their printed Probate Rules. You might even examine some probate files at the courthouse for specific examples of these forms.

To prepare the Petition for Final Distribution, you will need the numbered court paper which we discussed in Chapter 13, Section C, on the preparation of court documents. You should review the instructions in that section before you begin. Here are a few reminders:

- The title of the court must start on or below line 8.

- The title of the estate usually starts on line 11 on the left side of the paper, as shown.

- On the right side, type in the case number as shown in our sample above (this was assigned to you when you filed your first petition).

- Under the case number, type in the title of the petition as shown. Add the words in parentheses if you will request commissions.(If distribution will be made to a trust, add "AND DISTRIBUTION TO TESTAMENTARY TRUST.") Some courts (for example, Riverside County) require that the applicable Probate Code section be shown under the title.

- The body of the petition starts on the next numbered line after your heading—in our sample, this happens to be line 16.

- Be sure to double-space the body of the petition so each typewritten line is opposite one of the numbers on the left side of the paper. Also, be sure to keep within the margins.

Here are some guidelines for preparing the petition:

Paragraph 2: If written Notice of Administration was given to any creditor (see Step 16), use the alternate sentence in parentheses. (Remember, if the notice was given during the last 30 days of the four-month period, the claims period doesn't expire until 30 days after that notice was given.)

Paragraph 3: Use whichever paragraph applies.

Paragraph 4: If no formal claims were filed, use the first Paragraph 4. If formal claims were filed with the court, list them as shown in the second Paragraph 4. (If the accounting is waived, you do not have to list debts paid without formal claims under Probate Code § 9154.)

Note: If there were rejected claims, leave out the last sentence in the second Paragraph 4 and add another paragraph stating: "The following claims were rejected: (list and describe and give the date the Notice of Rejection was given). Petitioner has no knowledge of suit having been filed on said claims and no service of process has been served upon petitioner. The time to file suit has now expired." (See Step 16.)

Paragraph 6: Fill in the total appraised value of the estate inventory. You can get this figure from the Inventory and Appraisement form. (See Step 15.)

Paragraph 7: If you performed any actions without court supervision under the Independent Administration of Estates Act (see Chapter 13, Section C), especially those that require a Notice of Proposed Action, you should list and describe them here. Ordinary steps taken in administering the estate and in caring for and preserving the estate assets, such as making ordinary repairs, paying taxes and other expenses, terminating a lease or storing personal property, need not be listed. However, describe major transactions which substantially affect or alter the property contained in the estate and the assets that remain on hand for distribution. For instance, if property was sold or additional assets were acquired, such actions should be described. Some examples might be:

- "Sold the real property commonly known as 123 Elm Street, Anywhere, California, listed as Item 1 on the Inventory and Appraisement, for its appraised value of $150,000";

- "Sold decedent's 1965 Ford Mustang automobile for cash in the sum of $500, to avoid the expense of storing and maintaining the automobile during the period of administration of the estate";

- "Sold 100 shares of General Oil Corp., common stock, for cash on an established stock exchange";

- "Invested funds of the estate in a $10,000 U.S. Treasury Bond, series 1991, due August 15, 1991";

- "Continued the operation of the decedent's business known as 'John's Auto Repair Shop,' to preserve the interest of the estate and those persons interested in such business";

- "Executed a $5,000 promissory note, dated January 7, 1986, interest at 10%, all due and payable January 7, 1989, secured by deed of trust on real property of the estate located at 1801 Cove Street, Seaside, California."

Note: If a Notice of Proposed Action was given, some counties require that the original be filed with the court (before or at the same time as the petition for final distribution) with a proof of mailing attached, or the consent of the parties shown on the form. A "proof of mailing" may be typed separately, as shown in Step 14.

Paragraphs 8, 9 and 10: These allegations are not required but are recommended to show the condition of the estate.

Paragraph 9: Add the last two sentences of Paragraph 9, shown in parentheses, if this applies to your situation. (See Chapter 13, Section D.)

Paragraph 11: The petition must have a schedule attached to it describing in detail all property in the probate estate that is to be distributed. If there is real property, the legal description must be given. With the exception of the cash remaining on hand, the value of the assets will be the same as the appraised value shown on the Inventory and Appraisement form (Step 15, above). This is called the "carry value." If any of the assets have been sold, they will not be listed on this schedule because they are not "on hand" for distribution. Instead, the cash received from the sale will be in the estate's bank account. The amount of cash on hand will be whatever is left in the estate account (both checking and savings) at the time you prepare the petition. Any assets that have been acquired since the estate was opened will also be included in the schedule. A sample of the schedule, which will be attached to the petition as "Exhibit A," is shown below. Cash or other personal property held in blocked accounts should be so indicated, with the name of the depository given. The court order will then direct the depository to distribute the property to the beneficiaries on the closing of the estate.

Paragraph 12: Another schedule ("Exhibit B") must be prepared naming all persons who are entitled to receive property from the estate, showing their addresses, ages, relationship to the decedent, and the amount of property each will receive. The schedule will differ somewhat, depending on whether or not there is a will.

- **When there is no will:** In this instance, the schedule must list all the heirs who are entitled to the estate according to the laws of intestate succession (as explained in Chapter 3), and the share (fraction) each will receive. Usually, you don't have to itemize the property going to each heir, because each will merely receive his or her proportionate share of each and every asset listed in Exhibit A of the petition. However, some counties (for example, San Diego) require a separate distribution schedule specifically describing the assets going to each distributee. If any heir is deceased, be sure to indicate this and show the date of death, and then list the issue of the deceased heir. A sample of a schedule for an intestate estate is shown below.

- **When there is a will:** The decedent's will determines how the property is to be distributed. Therefore, you must set out the will provisions and list all of the beneficiaries and the property they receive. The easiest way to do this is to simply quote the paragraphs in the will that say how the property is to go. After that, list the beneficiaries' names, addresses, ages ("over 18" or "under 18") and relationship to the decedent, and what they are to get. Persons who are not related to the decedent are listed as "strangers."

As we discussed in Chapter 3, occasionally a will may be written in such a way that makes it difficult to determine how the property is to be distributed and you may have some doubt as to how to proceed. This might be the case if the will gives away a lot more than the decedent had, or if a beneficiary under a will predeceased the decedent (or didn't survive him by the number of days required by the will) and there is no alternate beneficiary. In this situation, your best bet is to arrange for a consultation with a lawyer. Once your questions are answered, you can complete the probate of the estate on your own. See Chapter 16 for material on how to hire and compensate lawyers.

If the will directs that all of the property is to go to one person, or to several persons in equal shares, this schedule will be much like the one in an intestate estate where each beneficiary receives a percentage, or fraction. Many wills direct that specific gifts be given to certain persons, such as "I give $1,000 to John, and I give my antique blue china dishes to Mary, and the remainder of my estate to my daughter, Jane." Unless the will provides otherwise, the specific gifts must normally be paid or distributed first, and whatever property is left is called the "remainder" or "residue" of the estate. If it should so happen that no residue is left after the specific gifts are distributed or paid, then the person or persons entitled to

the residue are simply out of luck, *unless there is a provision in the will to prevent this from happening.* The samples below show how this schedule might be prepared for a testate estate (one having a will).

A specific gift (for example, "I give my 200 shares of IBM stock to Jane") carries with it income on the property from the date of death, less taxes and other expenses attributable to the property during administration. (Probate Code § 12002.) Also, unless a will provides otherwise, gifts for a specific amount of money receive interest one year after the date of death if not paid within that time. (Probate Code § 12003.) To compute the interest, see Probate Code § 12001. Most estates are closed within a year and don't have to deal with this problem.

Our fourth example of Exhibit B shows how you would prepare the distribution schedule if you encounter a will that makes only specific gifts of property and does not contain a provision disposing of the residue of the estate. The property not disposed of by the will passes to the decedent's heirs under intestate succession laws (discussed in Chapter 3, Section F). Therefore, it passes one-third to each of the two brothers, and the children of the deceased sister share the one-third their mother would have inherited, or one-sixth each. Poor Albert, the decedent's nephew, doesn't receive anything because the decedent disposed of the Pontiac automobile prior to his death.

Petition for Final Distribution

Exhibit A

Estate of Anabelle Kidd, Deceased

Exhibit "A"

Assets on Hand

	SEPARATE PROPERTY	Carry Value
1.	One-third (1/3) interest as tenant in common with co-owners John and Mary Smith, in real property in the County of Contra Costa, described as Section 3, Township 20 North, Range 3 East; unimproved land. Assessor's Parcel No. 4562-34-5770	$ 5,000.00
2.	250 shares, Federated Stores, Inc. common stock	6,000.00
3.	75 shares, Bestco, Inc., $3 Cumulative, convertible preferred stock	1,500.00
4.	Five $100 U.S. Series E bonds, issued June, 1960	500.00
5.	$22,000 promissory note dated June 1, 1986, to decedent by R. E. Jones, interest at 9%, secured by deed of trust recorded June 15, 1976, in Book 4879, Page 98, in Official Records of Los Angeles County	
	Balance at date of death:	20,000.00
	Accrued interest:	150.00
6.	$10,000 promissory note of June 1, 1988, to decedent by David Hudson, unsecured, interest at 7%, payable interest only	10,000.00
7.	Decedent's interest as owner in Great Life Insurance Company Policy No. 36678	1,300.00
8.	Decedent's 50% interest in Valueless Mining Co., a Limited Partnership	
9.	Antique silver teapot, marked "Sheffield, 1893"	250.00
10.	Household furniture, furnishings, and personal effects located at decedent's residence	90.00
11.	Cash on deposit in checking Account No. 345 778, Westside National Bank, Los Angeles	350.00
12.	Certificate of Deposit No. 3459, Central Savings and Loan Association, Santa Monica Branch	40,000.00
		100,000.00
		$ 185,140.00

Petition for Final Distribution

Exhibit B

(Example 1)

Estate of Anabelle Kidd, Deceased

Exhibit "B"

Beneficiaries Under Decedent's Will
and Proposed Distribution

1. The decedent's Will disposes of her estate as follows:

   "I give to my friend, ALBERTINE TERREUX, that certain silver teapot marked 'Sheffield, 1893.'

   "I give, devise and bequeath all the rest, residue and remainder of my property, of whatsoever kind and character and wheresoever situated, to my husband, CALVIN KIDD. If my husband should predecease me, then in that event I give the residue of my estate to my three children, MARY KIDD CLARK, BILLY M. KIDD, and JON KIDD, in equal shares. If any of my children should predecease me, then that child's share shall go to his or her then living lawful issue, by right of representation."

2. The decedent's husband, CALVIN KIDD, predeceased the decedent. The decedent's son, JON KIDD, also predeceased the decedent, and under the terms of the decedent's Will his share of the estate passes to his son, CARSON KIDD.

3. Petitioner proposes to distribute the estate on hand as follows:

Name and Address	Age	Relationship	Share
Albertine Terreux 17 Rue Madeleine Paris, France	Adult	Stranger	Silver teapot marked "Sheffield, 1893"
Mary Kidd Clark 789 Main Street Venice, California 90410	Adult	Daughter	1/3 Residue
Billy M. Kidd 1109 Sky Blue Mountain Trail Billings, Montana 48906	Adult	Son	1/3 Residue
Carson Kidd 711 Valley Road Owens, California 98455	Adult	Grandson	1/3 Residue

Petition for Final Distribution

Exhibit B

(Example 3)

EXHIBIT "B"

Beneficiaries Under Decedent's Will

And

Proposed Distribution

1. The decedent's Will disposes of his estate as follows:

"I hereby give, devise and bequeath all of my estate, of every kind and character, to my wife, JANE DOE.

Should my wife, JANE DOE, predecease me or fail to survive a period of six months following my death, then and in that event I give, devise and bequeath the sum of $1,000 to my daughter, MARY CLARK, I hereby give, devise and bequeath all the rest, residue and remainder of my estate, both real and personal of whatsoever kind and character and wheresoever situated to my son, ROBERT DOE.

In the event that either of my said two children shall predecease me, or fail to survive a period of six months following my death, then I direct that the share which would otherwise have been paid to him or her be distributed to my surviving child."

2. The decedent's wife, JANE DOE, predeceased the decedent. The decedent's daughter, MARY CLARK, and the decedent's son, ROBERT DOE, survived the decedent for six months and are now living.

Name and Address	Age	Relationship	Share
Mary Clark 789 Main Street Venic, CA 90000	Over 18	Daughter	$1,000
Robert Doe 21 Kelley Court Santa Ana, CA 90000	Over 18	Son	100% Residue

5.

Petition for Final Distribution

Exhibit B

(Example 2)

EXHIBIT "B"

Heirs of Decedent and Proposed Distribution

Decedent's heirs at law and the respective shares to which they are entitled are:

Name and Address	Age	Relationship	Share
Robert Doe 100 Ocean Avenue Santa Monica, CA 90000	Over 18	Son	1/2
Mary Smith (Deceased January 10, 1976)		Daughter	
Margaret Smith 1022 - 10th Street Culver City, CA 90000	Over 18	Granddaughter (daughter of Mary Smith)	1/4
William Smith 123 Main Street Los Angeles, CA 90000	Over 18	Grandson (son of Mary Smith)	1/4

5.

Petition for Final Distribution
Exhibit B
(Example 4)

EXHIBIT "B"

Beneficiaries Under Decedent's Will

And

Proposed Distribution

1. The decedent's will disposes of his estate as follows:

"FIRST: I give my collection of tennis trophies to my niece, Eileen.

SECOND: I give my 1974 Pontiac automobile to my nephew, Albert.

THIRD: I give my household furniture, furnishings and personal effects and artwork to my brother, Mark.

FOURTH: I give my condominium located at 2009 Sagebrush Circle in Palm Springs, to my brother Ron.

FIFTH: I give the sum of $10,000 to my sister, Mary."

2. Petitioner, as personal representative of the estate, did not come into possession of the 1974 Pontiac automobile referred to in Article Second of the decedent's Will, and said property was not among the assets of the decedent's estate.

3. The decedent's sister, Mary Smith, predeceased the decedent on January 3, 1986. Accordingly, the gift of $10,000 given to Mary Smith in Article Fifth of the Will should be distributed to Mary Smith's surviving issue, her daughter Betty Smith and her son James Smith, in equal shares.

4. Included among the assets of the decedent's estate were 200 shares of Miracle Corporation stock and a 1984 Buick automobile. The decedent's Will does not dispose of these assets, and under the laws of intestate succession such property should be distributed to the decedent's heirs at law whose names, ages, and relationships are set forth below.

5. Proposed Distribution:

Name and Address	Age	Relationship	Share
Mark Jones 1835 Navajo Circle Palm Springs, CA	Over 18	Brother	Household furniture, furnishings, personal effects, and artwork, plus 1/3 interest as an heir at law in 200 shares of Miracle Corporation stock and 1984 Buick automobile
Ron Jones 89 Thermal Dr. Apt. 8 Needles, CA	Over 18	Brother	Condominium at 2009 Sagebrush Circle, Palm Springs, plus 1/3 interest as an heir at law in 200 shares of Miracle Corporation stock and 1984 Buick
Mary Smith (deceased 1-3-86)	-	Sister	-
Eileen Jones 1835 Navajo Circle Palm Springs, CA	Under 18	Niece	Tennis trophies
Betty Smith 190 Main Street Redlands, CA	Over 18	Niece (Daughter of Mary Smith)	$5,000, plus 1/6 interest as an heir at law in 200 shares of Miracle Corporation stock and 1984 Buick automobile
James Smith 190 Main Street Redlands CA	Over 18	Nephew (Son of Mary Smith)	$5,000, plus 1/6 interest as an heir at law in 200 shares of Miracle Corporation stock and 1984 Buick automobile

- **When the Will Contains a Trust:** If the will distributes property in trust for one or more of the beneficiaries, the proposed distribution schedule (Exhibit B) will list the trustee as a beneficiary, showing the amount distributed to the trust. You do not have to list the trust beneficiaries, nor the property they each receive from the trust. The distribution schedule must also quote the language in the will providing for the trust and the trust provisions. Wills containing trusts are usually many pages long, which in turn makes Exhibit B longer. In Example 5 of Exhibit B we show you an abridged sample of a distribution schedule for a will that contains a simple trust. A Consent to Act and Waiver of Accounting signed by the trustee must be attached to the petition or filed separately before the hearing date.

If the trustee (as well as the successor trustee, if the will named one) cannot serve or declines to act, you will have to see an attorney to have a trustee appointed by the court before distribution will be ordered. You will also have to file a Declination to Act as Trustee in addition to the successor trustee's Consent to Act. Samples of these forms are shown below.

A. Distribution to Minors (Under 18)

Usually, you cannot safely distribute property to a minor unless a guardian has been appointed for the minor's estate. However, there are exceptions if the amount to be distributed is small, or the decedent's will names a custodian to receive the minor's property, or the minor has a court-appointed guardian. Here are some guidelines.

1. Minor Has a Court-Appointed Guardian

If there is a guardian appointed for the minor's estate, you may distribute the minor's property to the guardian.[6] In this case, add a paragraph to Paragraph 12 of the petition in the following basic form:

" (Name of minor) , one of the beneficiaries, is a minor, and petitioner proposes to distribute the property belonging to said minor to (name of guardian) as guardian of the minor's estate. A copy of Letters of Guardianship issued to said guardian is attached to petition as Exhibit __."

2. Decedent's Will Names a Custodian to Receive Minor's Property

If there is no guardian for the minor's estate, but the decedent has nominated a custodian in her will (or in some other document) to receive the minor's property, then the personal representative may transfer the property to that person to be held for the benefit of the minor under the California Uniform Gifts to Minors Act or under the California Uniform Transfers to Minors Act. Specific language must be used when transferring title to the property to the custodian, for example, "John Doe, as Custodian for Mary Doe, under the California Uniform Transfers to Minors Act." Any type of property may be transferred under the California Uniform Transfers to Minors Act. However, the custodian has certain duties with respect to the custodial property, such as keeping records of all transactions regarding the property, including information necessary for the minor's tax return, and making them available for inspection. The custodian also has certain powers with respect to the management of the custodial property. The regulations governing transfers under the Uniform Transfers to Minors Act are set out in Probate Code §§ 3900-3925.

---

[6]People who need to have a court appoint a guardian for a minor should refer to *The Guardianship Book*, by Goldoftas and Brown (Nolo Press).

Petition for Final Distribution
Exhibit B
(Example 5)

EXHIBIT "B"

Beneficiaries Under Decedent's Will

and Proposed Distribution

1. The decedent's Will disposes of his estate as follows:

"THIRD: I hereby give to:

A. My nephew ARTHUR JONES, the sum of $5,000. If he should predecease me, this gift shall lapse and become part of the residue of my estate.

B. My niece, FRIEDA JONES, the sum of $5,000. If she should precedease me, this gift shall lapse and become part of the residue of my estate.

C. I give, devise, bequeath all the rest, residue and remainder of my estate, both real and personal and wherever situated, to my children, SHARON SMITH, SALLY SMITH and LINDA SMITH, in equal shares. All of my children are over the age of twenty-one (21) as of the date of this will, with the exception of LINDA. It is my wish that the portion of my estate bequeathed and devised to LINDA be held in trust by ALEXANDER BROWN, as Trustee, to be held, administered, and distributed in accordance with the following provisions:

1. I direct that my Trustee provide for the health, education, welfare and support and other needs of LINDA, so long as she is living and is under age thirty-five (35). The Trustee shall pay to or apply for her benefit, as much of the net income and principal of the trust as in the Trustee's discretion he deems necessary, after taking into consideration to the extent the Trustee deems advisable any other income or resources she may possess. Any unexpended income shall be added to the principal.

2. When LINDA for whom a share has been so allocated in trust attains the age of twenty-five (25), the Trustee shall distribute to the said child one-half (1/2) of the principal of said child's trust as then constituted; when said child attains age thirty-five (35) the Trustee shall distribute to said child the undistributed balance of her trust.

3. To carry out the purpose of the trust created for LINDA and subject to any limitations stated elsewhere in this will, the Trustee is vested with the following powers with respect to the trust estate and any part of it, in addition to those powers now or hereafter conferred by law:

EXHIBIT "B" - Page 2

a. To continue to hold any property including shares of the Trustee's own stock, and to operate at the risk of the trust estate any business that the Trustee receives or acquires under the trust as long as the Trustee deems advisable;

b. To manage, control, grant options on, sell (for cash or on deferred payments), convey, exchange, partition, divide, improve and repair trust property;

c. To borrow money, and to encumber or hypothecate trust property by mortgage, deed of trust, pledge, or otherwise;

4. If LINDA dies before becoming entitled to receive distribution of her share of the estate, the undistributed balance of her portion shall be distributed to her issue, if any, by right of representation, and if none then to my surviving children in equal shares."

2. Proposed Distribution:

Name and Address	Age	Relationship	Share
Arthur Jones 35 Berkeley Square, No. 6 Newhall, California	Adult	Nephew	$10,000
Frieda Jones 3885 Overlook Drive Ojai, California	Adult	Niece	$10,000
Sharon Smith 2332 - 20th Street, Apt. C Santa Monica, California	Adult	Daughter	1/3 residue
Sally Smith 1139 Oak Avenue Ocean Park, California	Adult	Daughter	1/3 residue
Alexander Brown 477 Palisades Park Drive Brentwood Park, California	Adult	Trustee	1/3 residue

3. Alexander Brown has consented to act as Trustee, and a Consent to Act as Trustee and Waiver of Accounting by Alexander Brown is attached to this petition.

Consent to Act as Trustee and Waiver of Accounting

```
 1   Name:
 2   Address:
 3
 4   In Pro Per
 5
 6
 7
 8            SUPERIOR COURT OF CALIFORNIA
 9                 COUNTY OF
10
11   Estate of            NO.
12                        CONSENT TO ACT AS TRUSTEE
13   MARY BROWN,          AND WAIVER OF ACCOUNTING
14        Deceased
15
        The undersigned, named in the Will of the above-named
16   decedent to act as Trustee of the testamentary trust provided
17   for therein, hereby consents to act as Trustee and waives the
18   filing and settlement of a final account by the estate representa-
19   tive.
20        DATED:            , 19
21
22
23
24
25
26
27
28
```

Declination to Act as Trustee

```
 1   Name:
 2   Address:
 3   Telephone No.:
 4
 5   Petitioner in pro per
 6
 7
 8            SUPERIOR COURT OF CALIFORNIA
 9                 COUNTY OF
10
11   Estate of            NO.
12            , aka         DECLINATION TO ACT AS TRUSTEE
13            ,
14        Deceased.
15
16        The undersigned, being nominated by name to act as
17   Trustee of the trust created under the decedent's will, does
18   hereby decline to act as Trustee.
19        DATED:            , 19
20
21
22
23
24
25
26
27
28
```

When making a distribution to a custodian nominated by the decedent to receive a minor's property, add the following paragraph to Paragraph 12 of the petition:

"Petitioner proposes to distribute the property belonging to ___(name of minor)___, a minor, to ___(name of custodian)___ as custodian for the minor under the California Uniform Transfers to Minors Act, as authorized by the decedent's will. A consent to act as custodian, signed by ___(name of custodian)___, is attached hereto as Exhibit __ ."

Note: The consent may be a simple statement, signed and dated by the custodian, such as: "I hereby consent to act as custodian for ___(name of minor)___, under the California Uniform Transfers to Minors Act."

3. Minor's Estate Does Not Exceed $5,000

If there is no appointed guardian and the decedent did not nominate a custodian to receive the minor's property but the total estate of the minor (that is, what she already owns plus what she gets under the will or by intestate succession) does not exceed $5,000, then money or other personal property belonging to the minor may be delivered to a parent of the minor to be held in trust for her until she reaches age 18. To accomplish this, a declaration signed by the parent under oath (under penalty of perjury) should be attached to the petition attesting to the fact that the total estate of the minor, including the money or other property delivered to the parent, does not exceed $5,000 in value. A sample of such a declaration is shown below. In this situation, add the following paragraph to Paragraph 12 of the petition:

"___(Name of minor)___, one of the beneficiaries entitled to receive property of the estate, is a minor. The total estate of the minor does not exceed $5,000, and petitioner proposes to distribute the property belonging to the minor to the minor's mother, ___(name of parent)___, to be held in trust for the benefit of the minor until she reaches age 18, pursuant to Probate Code § 3400 and 3401. A declaration signed by

___(name of parent)___ attesting to the fact that the total estate of the minor, including the money or other property to be paid or delivered to the parent, does not exceed $5,000 in value, is attached hereto as Exhibit ___."

4. Property to Be Distributed Does Not Exceed $10,000

If the minor has no guardian of the estate and a custodian has not been nominated by the decedent, but the property to be transferred does not exceed $10,000 in value, the personal representative may, under certain conditions, designate another adult as custodian under the California Uniform Transfers to Minors Act. This is true even if the will contains no express authorization for such a distribution or if the decedent died intestate (without a will). This is allowed by Probate Code § 3906. The conditions are:

- The personal representative must consider the transfer to be in the best interests of the minor; and

- The will must not prohibit the transfer or contain provisions inconsistent with such a transfer.

If the estate you are settling fits this situation and you wish to make this type of transfer, we suggest adding a paragraph in substantially the following form to Paragraph 12 of the petition:

"___(Name of minor)___, one of the beneficiaries entitled to receive property of the estate, is a minor. Said minor does not have a guardian appointed for his estate, nor did the decedent designate a guardian or custodian to receive property belonging to the minor. The property to be distributed to ___(name of minor)___ does not exceed a value of $10,000, and petitioner, in his capacity as personal representative of the decedent's estate, believes it will be in the best interest of the minor to transfer the property belonging to said minor to ___(name of custodian)___, the minor's ___(state relationship, for example, parent, adult sister) , as custodian for (name of minor) under the California Uniform Transfers to Minors Act to hold without bond until said minor attains the age of 18 years, pursuant to the provision of Probate Code § 3906. [*Add, if the decedent left a will:* The custodianship is not prohibited by or inconsistent with the terms of the decedent's will or any other governing instrument.] (Name of custodian) has consented to act as custodian and her written consent is attached hereto as Exhibit ___."

Note: Prepare a consent as described in Item b, above.

5. Property to Be Distributed Consists of Money

If the minor has no guardian of the estate and money is to be distributed to the minor, the court may order that the money be deposited in a bank in California, or in a trust company authorized to transact a trust business in this state, or invested in an account in an insured savings and loan association, subject to withdrawal only upon authorization of the court. (Probate Code § 3413.) In this situation, you may add the following paragraph to Paragraph 12 of the petition:

"The cash distribution to (name of minor) , should be deposited in an account at (name of institution) , subject to withdrawal only on order of the court."

Note: You should contact the bank or trust company in advance to make arrangements for the deposit. A form of receipt and agreement to be signed by the depository is shown under Item 2-d of the instructions for preparing the Petition for Probate.

6. Other Types of Property Distributed to a Minor

In the absence of a guardian or designated custodian for the minor's estate, transfer of other types of property to a minor must normally be authorized by the court. However, transfer to a custodian under the California Uniform Transfers to Minors Act may still be made if the court approves the transfer. If you are faced with this situation, we suggest you see an attorney to handle the transfer for you.

Paragraph 13: This is the paragraph that waives the requirement of an accounting. (See Chapter 13, Section E.) When the accounting is waived, the representative does not have to prepare a detailed list of receipts and disbursements during probate administration, which makes the closing of the estate much easier. All beneficiaries or heirs receiving property from the estate must sign waivers before the court will allow the accounting to be waived. The form, called "Waiver of Account," is shown as Exhibit C to the sample petition. If you are the sole beneficiary, you may waive the accounting by a statement in the petition as shown in Paragraph 13. If there are other beneficiaries, a separate waiver may be attached for each one, or all of the beneficiaries may sign one waiver.

Declaration re Distribution to a Minor

```
 1   Name:
 2   Address:
 3
 4   Telephone Number:
 5   Petitioner in pro per
 6
 7
 8                    SUPERIOR COURT OF CALIFORNIA
 9                    FOR THE COUNTY OF _____
10
11   Estate of                    )     NO. _____
12                                 )
                                   )     DECLARATION UNDER SECTION 3401 OF
13                                 )     THE CALIFORNIA PROBATE CODE
14              Deceased.          )
15   _____  )
16        The undersigned declares:
17        I am one of the parents of ____(name of minor)____, a minor, who is a
18   distributee of the estate of the above-named decedent, and as such I am
19   entitled to said minor's custody; no guardian has been appointed for said
20   minor's estate, nor has said minor an estate in excess of $5,000; the said
21   minor has due from the above estate money or personal property not exceeding
22   $5,000; I agree to account to said minor for all of the said property that I
23   may receive from the above estate on behalf of said minor, upon said minor
24   reaching the age of majority; I further agree to receipt for the said
25   property due the minor, and to fully release and hold harmless the personal
26   representative of the above estate upon payment or delivery of the said money
27   or personal property.
28        I declare under penalty of perjury under the laws of the State of
     California that the foregoing is true and correct. Executed this _____
     day of _____, 19_____.

                                        _____
```

Petition for Final Distribution
Exhibit C

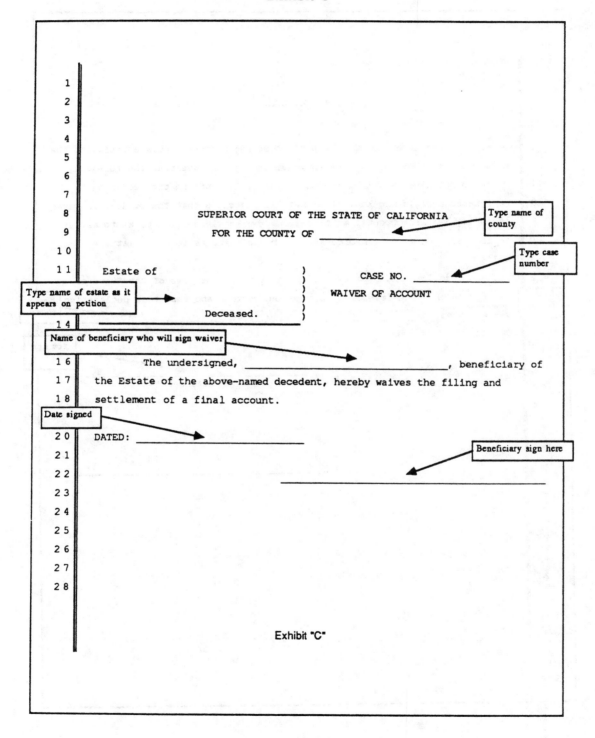

Verification

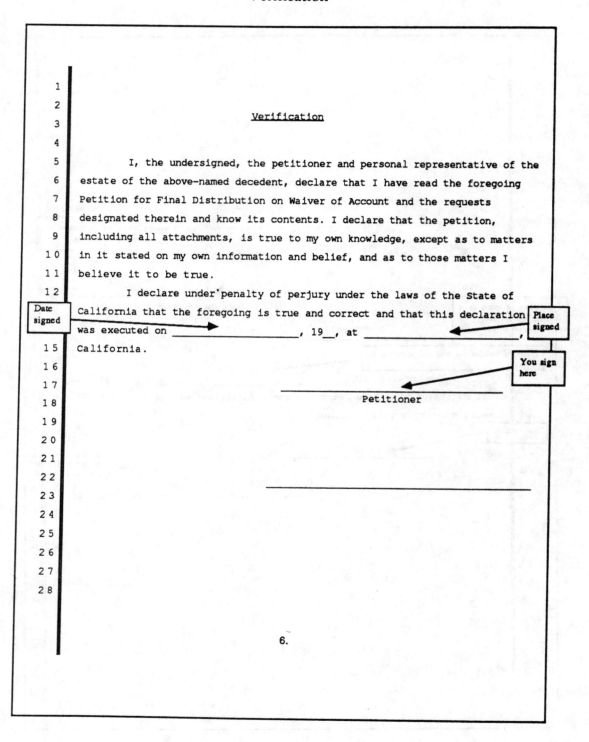

Verification

    I, the undersigned, the petitioner and personal representative of the estate of the above-named decedent, declare that I have read the foregoing Petition for Final Distribution on Waiver of Account and the requests designated therein and know its contents. I declare that the petition, including all attachments, is true to my own knowledge, except as to matters in it stated on my own information and belief, and as to those matters I believe it to be true.

    I declare under penalty of perjury under the laws of the State of California that the foregoing is true and correct and that this declaration was executed on _____, 19__, at _____, California.

_____
Petitioner

6.

Note: Persons who receive property as surviving joint tenants, as named beneficiaries under the decedent's life insurance policies or from living trusts, do not have to sign waivers.

If an accounting is required because all beneficiaries or heirs will not sign the waiver, contact a lawyer to find out how the courts in your county want the accounting prepared.

Paragraph 14: This paragraph refers to the commissions to which you are entitled as estate representative. (See Chapter 13, Section F.) If you waive your commissions, type the first Paragraph 14. If you claim them, type the second Paragraph 14 and fill in the computation.

The last page of the petition after the exhibits is always the "verification" page.

B. Filing the Petition for Final Distribution

When you have completed the Petition for Final Distribution, this is how you get it ready to file:

a. Staple it together at the top in at least two places. Some courts (including Los Angeles) require a blue document backer to be attached to all documents (except printed Judicial Council forms) with the name of the document typed at the bottom. Other courts require that all documents be two-hole punched at the top, so check with the court before you file.

b. Sign and date it at the end and don't forget to sign the verification page. (This is very important.)

c. Staple a self-addressed, stamped envelope to the petition so a conformed (file stamped) copy can be returned to you. In some counties the probate examiner may mail you a copy of the calendar notes if you attach another self-addressed, stamped envelope marked "calendar notes."

d. Make two copies of the petition, one for your file and one to send to the court with the original to be conformed and returned to you for your file.

e. Enclose a transmittal letter (a sample is shown below). In some court districts (San Bernardino, for example) you are required to send in the Order for Final Distribution at the same time you file the petition. In some other courts, you will also have to enclose a Notice of Hearing (Probate), which is discussed in Step 18, below.

f. A fee is required by some courts when the petition is filed, so check with the court regarding its policy. If you are filing in Los Angeles County, you must enclose a $50 fee to the Los Angeles County Clerk to cover the cost of a clerk order prepared by that court. This may not apply if the Order must list real property with a long legal description, or if property is distributed to a trust, in which case no fee will be collected and you will be asked to prepare the Order and submit it to the court. Los Angeles courts also require an extra copy of the petition.

Transmittal Letter

County Clerk

(Address)

      Re: Estate of _____

           Case No. _____

Dear Sir or Madam:

    Enclosed are the following documents:

    1. Original and two copies of the Petition for Final Distribution in the above estate. Please file the original petition and return the extra copies to me, conformed, in the enclosed stamped self-addressed envelope. (If filing in Los Angeles County, add: A check in the amount of $50 is enclosed to cover the cost of a Clerk Order on the petition.)

    2. Original and ____ copies of Notice of Hearing. Please fill in the date, time and place of the hearing and return all copies to me for processing.

                Very truly yours,

Step 18: Prepare Notice of Hearing (Probate)

NOTICE OF THE HEARING on the Petition for Final Distribution must be mailed at least 15 days before the date of hearing to the following persons:

1. If there is a will, to all the beneficiaries affected;

2. If no will, to all heirs who succeed to the estate;

3. If any portion of the estate escheats to the State of California, to the Attorney General at Sacramento;

4. To anyone who has requested Special Notice;

5. If a distributee is a trustee of a trust, to the trustee;

6. If the trustee is also the personal representative, Notice must also be given to certain trust beneficiaries. (Probate Code §1208.)

The Notice is given on the printed form shown below. In many counties the Notice must be prepared ahead of time and sent to the court at the time you file the petition so the court clerk may insert the date of the hearing on the Notice and return it to you. In some counties (Los Angeles, for example), you don't have to send in the Notice form when you file the petition. Instead, the date of the hearing is stamped or written on the petition form by the court clerk. You then must fill in this date on the Notice of Hearing form. Inquire locally as to the required procedure. Make a copy of the Notice for each beneficiary, plus an extra one to be stamped and returned to you for your file.

Caption: Fill in your name, address, the court's name, and case number, as you have on your other court papers.

Item 1: Fill in your name and title (executor, administrator), and that you have filed "A Petition for Final Distribution on Waiver of Accounting." If the petition requests statutory commissions, be sure to add this to the title.

Item 3: Fill in the requested information about the hearing. If the street address of the court is not shown in the caption, check the second box and type in the street address.

Type and sign your name. Check the box next to "attorney or party." Fill in the date when you sign the notice below.

Item 4: Fill in the date the Notice was mailed and the place (city).

On the back of the form, fill in the name of the estate at the top, and the case number. Leave the top section (Clerk's Certificate of Posting/Mailing) blank. Complete the Proof of Service by Mail the same way as on the back of the Notice of Administration of Estate (explained in Step 4, paragraph 2). In the space at the bottom, type in the name and address of everyone who is entitled to Notice. (See Step 18.) The person who mails the Notice should fill in and sign the Proof of Service on the original Notice, after all copies of the Notice are sent. You must file the original Notice with the court before the hearing.

Step 19: Prepare Order of Final Distribution

IN THE CENTRAL DISTRICT and branch courts in Los Angeles County, the Order of Final Distribution is prepared by the court clerk, and you don't have to worry about typing it. However, in most other counties you will have to type the Order of Final Distribution form and mail it to the court for the judge's signature. A sample transmittal letter is shown below. Some courts require the Order three or four days before the hearing date. Again, it's always wise to ask about local rules.

Notice of Hearing

ATTORNEY OR PARTY WITHOUT ATTORNEY *(Name and Address):*	TELEPHONE NO.:	FOR COURT USE ONLY
BILLY M. KIDD 1109 Sky Blue Mountain Trail Billings, Montana 48906	(715) 392-6408	

ATTORNEY FOR *(Name):* Petitioner in Pro Per

SUPERIOR COURT OF CALIFORNIA, COUNTY OF LOS ANGELES
- STREET ADDRESS: 1725 Main Street
- MAILING ADDRESS:
- CITY AND ZIP CODE: Santa Monica, California 90401
- BRANCH NAME: West District

ESTATE OF (NAME):
ANABELLE KIDD, aka
ANABELLE O. KIDD,
                                             DECEDENT

NOTICE OF HEARING (Probate)	CASE NUMBER: WEP 14813

> This notice is required by law. This notice does not require you to appear in court, but you may attend the hearing if you wish.

1. NOTICE is given that *(name):*   BILLY M. KIDD

   (representative capacity, if any):   Executor

   has filed *(specify):** a Petition for Final Distribution on Waiver of Account

2. You may refer to the filed documents for further particulars. *(All of the case documents filed with the court are available for examination in the case file kept by the court clerk.)*

3. A HEARING on the matter will be held as follows:

   Date: December 30, 1989   **Time:** 9:30 A.M.   **Dept.:** A   **Room:**
   Address of court [ ] shown above [ ] is:

....   [X] Attorney or party _____
BILLY M. KIDD   *(SIGNATURE)*
(TYPE OR PRINT NAME)

Date: December 14, 1989   [ ] Clerk, by _____, Deputy

4. This notice was mailed on *(date):* December 14, 1989   at *(place):* Billings, Montana

(Continued on reverse)

* Do not use this form to give notice of hearing of the petition for administration *(see Probate Code, § 8100).*

Form Approved by the
Judicial Council of California   **NOTICE OF HEARING**   Probate Code, §§ 1211, 1215, 1216, 1230
DE-120 [Rev. July 1, 1989]   (Probate)

ESTATE OF (NAME):	CASE NUMBER:
ANABELLE KIDD, DECEDENT	WEP 14813

CLERK'S CERTIFICATE OF ☐ POSTING ☐ MAILING

I certify that I am not a party to this cause and that a copy of the foregoing Notice of Hearing (Probate)

1. ☐ was posted at *(address)*:

   on *(date)*:

2. ☐ was served on each person named below. Each notice was enclosed in an envelope with postage fully prepaid. Each envelope was addressed to a person whose name and address is given below, sealed, and deposited with the United States Postal Service at *(place)*:   California,

   on *(date)*:

Date: Clerk, by _____, Deputy

PROOF OF SERVICE BY MAIL

1. I am over the age of 18 and not a party to this cause. I am a resident of or employed in the county where the mailing occurred.

2. My residence or business address is *(specify)*:

   1809 - "G" Street, Billings, Montana

3. I served the foregoing **Notice of Hearing (Probate)** on each person named below by enclosing a copy in an envelope addressed as shown below AND

   a. ☒ depositing the sealed envelope with the United States Postal Service with the postage fully prepaid.

   b. ☐ placing the envelope for collection and mailing on the date and at the place shown in item 4 following our ordinary business practices. I am readily familiar with this business' practice for collecting and processing correspondence for mailing. On the same day that correspondence is placed for collection and mailing, it is deposited in the ordinary course of business with the United States Postal Service in a sealed envelope with postage fully prepaid.

4. a. Date mailed: December 14, 1989   b. Place mailed *(city, state)*:   Billings, Montana

5. ☐ I served with the *Notice of Hearing (Probate)* a copy of the petition or other document referred to in the notice.

I declare under penalty of perjury under the laws of the State of California that the foregoing is true and correct.

Date: December 14, 1989

Mary Smith   ▶ *[signature]*
....   _____
(TYPE OR PRINT NAME)   (SIGNATURE OF DECLARANT)

NAME AND ADDRESS OF EACH PERSON TO WHOM NOTICE WAS MAILED

Mary Kidd Clark
789 Main Street
Venice, California 90410

Carson Kidd
711 Valley Road
Owens, California 98455

Albertine Terreux
17 Rue Madeleine
Paris, France

Consulate of France
8350 Wilshire Blvd.
Los Angeles, California 90035

DE-120 (Rev. July 1, 1989)	**NOTICE OF HEARING** (Probate)	Page two
		Probate Code. §§ 1261, 1264

The sample Order shown below should fulfill the requirements of most courts, and may be modified to conform to your particular situation. The Order must always list in detail the property to be distributed to each person and its appraisal value. In the case of real property, the legal description must be given. Be sure to proofread the legal description with the deed to the property to make sure it is accurate, since the Order will be recorded with the County Recorder's office as evidence of the transfer of ownership. We suggest one person read aloud from the deed while another reads the description in the Order carefully. Or, if you have a legible copy of the legal description on a deed, title insurance report or homestead declaration, you can photocopy the document, cut out the legal description, tape it on to the Order and photocopy the whole document.

The persons receiving specific gifts of property are always listed first, and those receiving the assets making up the balance of the estate (residue) are described after that. Make sure you don't include any of the specific gifts in the residue. No riders or exhibits may be attached to any court order, and nothing should appear after the signature of the judge.

If property will be distributed to a trust, you must set out the terms of the trust in full, again, in the Order of Final Distribution, changing the wording to the present tense and the third person. For example, "my daughter" should be changed to "decedent's daughter," or "I direct that my Trustee provide. . ." should be changed to "The Trustee shall provide. . ." Based on Example No. 5 of Exhibit B in the instructions for Paragraph 12 of the Petition for Final Distribution, this is what the Order would recite:

"IT IS FURTHER ORDERED, ADJUDGED AND DECREED that the following property shall be and the same is hereby distributed as follows:

To ARTHUR JONES, the sum of $5,000;

To FRIEDA JONES, the sum of $5,000;

All the rest, residue and remainder of said estate, hereinafter more particularly described, together with any and all other property not now known or discovered which may belong to said decedent or

her estate, or in which said decedent or her estate may have an interest, be and the same is hereby distributed as follows:

To SHARON SMITH, one-third (1/3) thereof;

To SALLY SMITH, one-third (1/3) thereof;

To ALEXANDER BROWN, as Trustee, one-third (1/3) thereof in trust for decedent's daughter, LINDA SMITH, to be held, administered and distributed in accordance with the following provisions:

The Trustee shall provide for the health, education, welfare and support and other needs of LINDA, so long as she is living and is under age thirty-five (35). The Trustee shall pay to or apply for her benefit, as much of the net income and principal of the trust as in the Trustee's discretion. . . (etc.)"

If property will be distributed to a minor, here are some examples of the wording that may be used:

"To _____, the parent of _____, a minor, the sum of $5,000 to hold in trust for the minor until the minor's majority."

"To _____, as Custodian for _____, a minor, under the California Uniform Transfers to Minors Act, the following property: (describe property)."

You will also need to record a Preliminary Change in Ownership Report if real property has been transferred. (See Chapter 8, Section C.)

Step 20: Transfer the Assets and Obtain Court Receipts

ALTHOUGH THE ORDER for Final Distribution is proof in itself of a beneficiary's right to property from an estate, the estate representative must still see that title is transferred in the case of certain types of assets.

A formal receipt, typed on numbered court paper, should be prepared and signed by each person who receives property in the Order for Final Distribution. The receipt should list the property received by the distributee, as shown below. If real property is being distributed, the personal representative must file a statement that identifies the date and place or location of the recording of the Order for Distribution. (Probate Code §11753.) This can usually be typed on the affidavit for Final Discharge, shown below.

Note on Missing Beneficiaries: If you can't locate a beneficiary who is entitled to receive a cash gift, you may deposit the money, in the name of the beneficiary, with the county treasurer. (Probate Code § 1060.) If the beneficiary turns up, she can claim the money by petitioning the probate court. If the gift is other personal property and remains unclaimed for a year, the court will order that it be sold and the proceeds paid to the county. (Probate Code §1062.)

A. Real Property

Real property is transferred by recording a certified copy of the Order for Final Distribution, containing a legal description of the property, in each county in which any part of the property lies. (See Chapter 8 on how to record documents with the Recorder's office.) The new owner(s) should tell the county tax collector where to mail tax bills. Fire insurance policies should also be changed to show the new ownership.

B. Promissory Notes

Promissory notes should be endorsed over and delivered to the distributee by the personal representative together with any deed of trust, pledge or other security, and a copy of the Order for Final Distribution. The endorsement may be typed on the note in substantially the following form:

"___(Name of city)___, California, ___(date)___, 19___. For value received, I hereby transfer and assign to ___(name of beneficiary)___ all right, title and interest of ___(name of decedent)___ at the time of his/her death in the within note. [*Add, if applicable*: and the deed of trust securing the same, so far as the same pertains to said note, without recourse.]"

_____

Executor/Administrator of the Estate of _____, deceased.

C. Trust Deed Notes

If there are trust deed notes to be transferred, this is also handled by recording a certified copy of the Order for Final Distribution in the county in which the property described in the deed of trust is located. This will establish a record of the transfer from the name of the decedent to the name of the new owner. If the note itself is being held by a bank, the new owner should send a copy of the Order to the bank with directions on where to send future statements and payment requests.

Order of Final Distribution

page 1

1 BILLY M. KIDD
   1109 Sky Blue Mountain Trail
2 Billings, Montana 48906

3 Telephone: (715) 392-6408

4 Petitioner in Pro Per

5

6

7

8   SUPERIOR COURT OF CALIFORNIA

9   COUNTY OF LOS ANGELES

10

11 Estate of   )   CASE NO. WEP 14813
)
12   ANABELLE KIDD, aka   )   ORDER OF FINAL DISTRIBUTION
)   ON WAIVER OF ACCOUNT
13   ANABELLE O. KIDD,   )
)
14   Deceased.   )
)
15

16   BILLY M. KIDD, as personal representative of the estate of the above-

17 named decedent, having filed a Petition for Final Distribution without render-

18 ing account, and the report and petition coming on this day, December 30, 1989,

19 regularly for hearing in Department A of the above-entitled Court, the

20 Honorable Herbert Wise, Judge presiding, the Court, after examining the petition

21 and hearing the evidence, finds that due notice of the hearing of the petition

22 has been regularly given as prescribed by law; that all of the allegations of

23 the petition are true; that the assets described in this decree of distribution

24 comprise the entire estate on hand for distribution; that no federal estate

25 taxes were due from the estate; that all personal property taxes due and payable

26 by said estate have been paid; and that said report and petition should be

27 approved and distribution ordered as prayed for.

28   IT IS THEREFORE ORDERED by the Court that notice to creditors has

1.

Order of Final Distribution
page 2

1	been duly given as required by law, and that BILLY M. KIDD has in his possess-
2	ion belonging to said estate, after deducting credits to which he is entitled,
3	the assets described later herein; that said report is approved; (Add, if
4	applicable: that said BILLY M. KIDD is hereby authorized to pay to himself
5	the sum of $5,379.61, hereby allowed as statutory commissions.)
6	IT IS FURTHER ORDERED that the decedent's will disposes of his
7	estate as follows: (Quote dispositive provisions of the will verbatim. If
8	there is no will, leave this paragraph out.)
9	IT IS FURTHER ORDERED that the following property shall be and the
10	same is hereby distributed as follows:
11	To ALBERTINE TERREUX, the decedent's antique silver teapot, marked
12	"Sheffield, 1893;"
13	All the rest, residue and remainder of said estate, hereinafter more
14	particularly described, together with any and all other property not now known
15	or discovered which may belong to said decedent or her estate, or in which
16	said decedent or her estate may have an interest, be and the same is hereby
17	distributed to MARY KIDD CLARK, BILLY M. KIDD, AND CARSON KIDD, in equal shares.
18	The residue of the estate, insofar as is now known, consists of the
19	following property:

Carry Value

20	1. One-third (1/3) interest as tenant in common	
21	with co-owners John and Mary Smith, in real property	
22	in the County of Contra Costa, described as Section 3	
23	Township 20 North, Range 3 East. Unimproved land.	
24	Assessor's Parcel No. 4562-34-5770	$ 5,000.00
25	2. 250 shares, Federated Stores, Inc. common stock	6,000.00
26	3. 75 shares, Bestco, Inc., $3 Cumulative, convertible	
27	preferred stock	1,500.00
28	4. Five $100 U. S. Series E bonds, issued June, 1960	500.00

2.

Order of Final Distribution
page 3

1	5. $22,000 promissory note dated June 1, 1986, to	
2	decedent by R. E. Jones, interest at 9%, secured	
3	by deed of trust recorded June 15, 1976, in	
4	Book 4879, Page 98, in Official Records of Los	
5	Angeles County	
6	Balance at date of death:	$ 20,000.00
7	Accrued interest:	150.00
8	6. $10,000 promissory note of June 1, 1988, to	
9	decedent by David Hudson, unsecured, interest	
10	at 7%, payable interest only	10,000.00
11	7. Decedent's interest as owner in Great Life	
12	Insurance Company Policy No. 36678	1,300.00
13		
14	8. Decedent's 50% interest in Valueless Mining Co.,	
15	a Limited Partnership	250.00
16	9. Household furniture, furnishings, and personal	
17	effects located at decedent's residence	350.00
18		
19	10. Cash on deposit in checking Account No. 345 778,	
20	Westside National Bank, Los Angeles	40,000.00
21	11. Certificate of Deposit No. 3459, Central Savings	
22	and Loan Association, Santa Monica Branch	100,000.00
23		
24	DATED: _____, 19___	
25		
26		
27	_____	
	JUDGE OF THE SUPERIOR COURT	
28		

3.

D. Stocks and Bonds

Stocks and bonds should be transferred as discussed in Chapter 9. When stock shares must be divided among two or more persons and the shares do not come out even, an extra share may be taken by one person and the others given cash to make up the difference, if the distributees agree. For instance, if twenty-five shares of stock were to be divided among three beneficiaries, each would take eight shares (twenty-four total). Then the extra share could be given to one beneficiary, who would give cash to the other beneficiaries equal to the value of their interest in the extra share so everyone would receive assets of the same value.

E. Mutual Funds and Money Market Funds

Transferring record ownership of mutual funds and money market funds is usually handled by the fund custodian. Therefore, the easiest way to deal with these assets is to contact the fund management directly (the monthly statement should tell you the address) and ask what is required to transfer or redeem the shares.

F. Tangible Personal Property

Items of tangible personal property, such as household furnishings, and other personal effects, usually have no record of title and require only physical delivery.

G. Automobiles, Motor Vehicles and Small Boats

The Department of Motor Vehicles will help in the transfer of title to these assets. Usually, they require the representative to endorse the pink slip as "owner" and present a certified copy of Letters and pay a transfer fee.

The insurance company should be notified of the change in ownership as well.

H. Cash in Blocked Accounts

Cash or other assets that were placed in blocked accounts to reduce bond will be released if you present the bank, or institution holding the assets, with a certified copy of the Order of Final Distribution. The assets can then get distributed to the beneficiaries.

Court Receipt

```
 1    Name:
 2    Address:
 3
 4    Telephone Number:
 5    Petitioner In pro per
 6
 7
 8                    SUPERIOR COURT OF THE STATE OF CALIFORNIA
 9                        FOR THE COUNTY OF LOS ANGELES
10
11    Estate of                    )        NO. _____
12    _____    )        RECEIPT OF DISTRIBUTEE
13    _____    )
14              Deceased.          )
15    _____    )
16
17        The undersigned hereby acknowledges receipt from _____
18    _____, as personal representative of the estate of the
19    above-named decedent, of the following listed property:
20            Cash in the sum of $_____;
21            1/3 interest in 200 shares of Miracle Corporation stock;
22            1984 Buick automobile;
23            Household furniture, furnishings, personal effects, and artwork.
24        The undersigned acknowledges that the above property constitutes all
25    of the property to which the undersigned is entitled pursuant to the Order of
26    Final Distribution made in the above estate on _____, 19__.
27        Dated: _____, 19__.
28

                                    _____
                                              (signature)
```

Step 21: Request Discharge From Your Duties

AFTER YOU'VE DELIVERED all property to the persons who are entitled to it, you may request that the court discharge you from your duties as the estate representative. The printed form for Los Angeles County is shown below (and a copy is in the Appendix), with instructions on how to fill it in. If your county doesn't have a printed form, you may type one on numbered court paper based on this example. Some courts require all receipts to be filed at the same time you file the Request for Final Discharge. Some courts also require a copy of the court order. This is to make it easier for the probate examiners to make sure there is a receipt from everybody.

If everything is in order, the judge will sign the Order on the bottom of the form, discharging you as the representative, and this concludes the court proceeding. If you had to post a bond while serving as representative, be sure to send a copy of the Order of Final Discharge to the bonding company to terminate the bond.

If the Order of Final Distribution listed real property, add a sentence just above the date, as follows: "The Order of Final Distribution was recorded on _____, 19___, as Instrument No. _____, in the office of the County Recorder of __(name of county where property is located)__ showing distribution of the real property." Some attorneys like to file a copy of the recorded order with the court as evidence of the transfer of real property.

Affidavit for Final Discharge

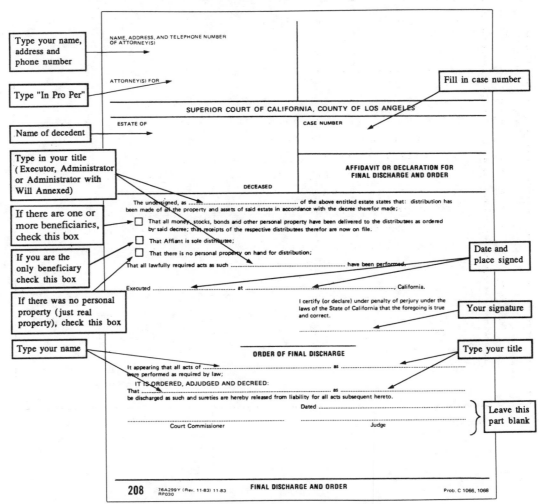

CHAPTER 15

Handling Property that Passes Outright to the Surviving Spouse

A. Introduction

ALL PROPERTY that a surviving spouse is entitled to receive outright from a deceased spouse, regardless of the size of the estate, may be "set aside" to the survivor without formal probate. This includes community property, separate property and quasi-community property.[1]

Technically, under Probate Code § 13500, the surviving spouse has the right to possession and control of such property without any administration procedures whatsoever. A surviving spouse will normally have no problem acquiring assets that don't have official title documents, such as household furniture and personal effects. However, title companies, stock transfer agents and others that have control over other kinds of property often require some kind of official document establishing that the property really belongs to the surviving spouse. This makes sense; without documentation, no one dealing with the surviving spouse has any real assurance that the surviving spouse's position is valid.

Two kinds of documents are used, depending on the type of property involved. For community real property, a simple form affidavit can usually be used. For other property, the surviving spouse can obtain a Spousal Property Order from the superior court. This chapter shows you how to use both methods to transfer property to a surviving spouse.

---

[1]Quasi-community property, or property acquired by married couples outside California that would have been community property if acquired in California, is treated just like community property. We discuss this in Chapter 4, Section I.

B. When to Use These Simplified Procedures

THE SIMPLIFIED PROCEDURES outlined in this chapter should not be used in complex property situations. They apply only to simple estates with assets such as houses, cars, household goods, bank accounts, stocks, bonds, mutual funds, promissory notes, personal belongings and antiques. If there are complex investments, large or complex claims by creditors, strained family relations, or if the decedent owned an interest in a good-sized business, the surviving spouse should consult an attorney. We discuss how to hire and compensate a lawyer in Chapter 16.

The "abbreviated" procedures discussed in this chapter apply only to property that goes *outright* to a surviving spouse, either under the deceased spouse's will or by intestate succession. To qualify as a "surviving spouse," the survivor must have been legally married to the decedent at the time of her death. If any of the decedent's property passes to the surviving spouse under a "qualified" form of ownership, formal probate is usually required. "Qualified ownership" means there is some sort of limitation on the spouse's ownership—for example, if property is willed to the surviving spouse and someone else as joint tenants or tenants in common, or under a trust in which the "time of enjoyment" is deferred or limited, such as giving the surviving spouse the right to use the property only during her lifetime (called a "life estate"), or the surviving spouse's use of the property is restricted in some way.

If the will says, "I give my entire estate to my wife providing she survives me for 30 days," this is not considered a "qualified" interest and, if the surviving spouse survives for the required period, the property may be transferred or confirmed to the surviving spouse without probate by the procedures described in this chapter. Property that is inherited under intestate succession in the absence of a will has, by definition, no limitation as to ownership.

These "short-cut" procedures to transfer property to a surviving spouse will also not work if the decedent willed all or part of her interest in the community property or separate property to someone else. Here are a couple of examples of will provisions that necessitate probate:

- "I give my husband a life estate in my interest in our home in Montebello. Upon my husband's death, I give my interest in said property to my two granddaughters, Holly and Celeste."

  The husband is given a life estate (a qualified ownership) in the home; because it doesn't pass outright to him as surviving spouse, it will require probate.

- "I give my residence located at 18865 Navajo Circle, Indio, to my son, Raymond. I give the sum of $50,000 to my daughter, Elsa. I give the residue of my estate to my husband, Anthony."

Since the decedent's interest in the residence in Indio and the $50,000 do not pass to the decedent's surviving spouse, these assets will require probate; however, the assets contained in the residue of the estate, which pass outright to the decedent's husband, Anthony, can be transferred without formal probate administration using the "abbreviated" procedures described here.

Small Estate Note: Remember, if the total gross value of the decedent's real and/or personal property that is willed to someone else (or passes to someone else under intestate succession) is less than $60,000, it may be possible to use the transfer procedures outlined in Chapter 11.

Note re Creditors' Claims: The surviving spouse is responsible for any debts chargeable against community or separate property she receives using these procedures, no matter when claims are made to her. When formal probate proceedings are used, however, creditor's claims are cut off four months after probate is begun. In most estates, because no (or a very few) creditors even present claims in the first place, using the spousal set-aside procedures outlined in this chapter will cause no problems. If, however, after examining the decedent's affairs you realize that she owed a number of debts and you anticipate the possibility of substantial creditor's claims against the estate, consider putting the property through formal probate. It will give you peace of mind knowing that no additional claims can be brought after the four-month period ends.

C. Before You Begin

IF A WILL GIVES a decedent's entire estate to a spouse, it is not crucial to know the character of the property. However, in most instances, before going ahead with these unsupervised transfer procedures in the estate you are settling, you must know whether the decedent's property is community property or separate property, and of course, you must be sure the surviving spouse is entitled to inherit it. In the absence of a will, it is essential that you know whether the property is community or separate, to determine who will inherit it. How to classify property as community or separate is discussed in detail in Chapter 4. If you are not absolutely sure as to the community and separate property ownership of the property you are dealing with, read this chapter before continuing. How to identify who will inherit property, whether or not there is a will, is covered in Chapter 3.

D. Collecting Compensation Owed the Decedent

A SURVIVING SPOUSE may collect salary or other compensation owed by an employer for personal services of the deceased spouse, including compensation for unused vacation, by presenting the employer with a declaration in the form shown below. The procedure may be used immediately by the surviving spouse, regardless of the size of the estate; however, the amount collected cannot exceed $5,000, and the surviving spouse must be entitled to the compensation under the decedent's will or by intestate succession.

Declaration for Collection of Compensation
Owed to Deceased Spouse

DECLARATION FOR COLLECTION OF COMPENSATION

OWED TO DECEASED SPOUSE

(California Probate Code Section 13600)

STATE OF CALIFORNIA   )
)   ss.
COUNTY OF _____   )

        I, _____, being duly sworn, state:

        1. _____ died on _____, at
_____, and at the time of death was a resident of
California;

        2. ___ I am the surviving spouse of the decedent;

        ___ I am the guardian or conservator of the estate of the
decedent;

        3. The surviving spouse of the decedent is entitled to the
earnings of the decedent under the decedent's will or by intestate
succession and no one else has a superior right to the earnings;

        4. No proceeding is now being or has been conducted in California
for administration of the decedent's estate;

        5. Sections 13600 to 13605 of the California Probate Code require
that the earnings of the decedent, including compensation for unused
vacation, not in excess of five thousand dollars ($5,000) net, be paid
promptly to me;

        6. Neither the surviving spouse, nor anyone acting on behalf of
the surviving spouse, has a pending request to collect compensation owed
by another employer for personal services of the decedent under Sections
13600 to 13605 of the California Probate Code;

        7. Neither the surviving spouse, nor anyone acting on behalf of
the surviving spouse, has collected any compensation owed by an employer
for personal services of the decedent under Sections 13600 to 13605 of
the California Probate Code except the sum of _____ dollars
($_____);

        8. I request that I be paid the salary or other compensation owed
by you for personal services of the decedent, including compensation for
unused vacation, not to exceed five thousand dollars ($5,000) net, less
the _____ dollars ($_____) which was previously collected;

        I declare under penalty of perjury under the laws of the State of
California that the foregoing is true and correct.

DATED: _____

                                        _____

E. Affidavit for Transferring Community Real Property

CALIFORNIA LAW PROVIDES that the surviving spouse may take over all community property without probate administration, unless the deceased spouse willed his one-half interest or a portion of it to someone else. The only restriction is a 40-day waiting period before the surviving spouse may sell or otherwise dispose of any community real property—a provision that allows others (creditors, or anyone else who claims an interest in the property) to file their claims against it. If someone does claim an interest in the real property, you should see a lawyer.

For community real property, most title insurance companies will accept a simple form affidavit to clear title in the name of the surviving spouse. To use the affidavit, the deed to the property must clearly show that title is held as community property; that is, the deed must show ownership in the names of the spouses "as community property," or as "husband and wife." The affidavit cannot be used for community property held in joint tenancy, or in the deceased spouse's name alone; instead, the Death of Joint Tenant affidavit (see Chapter 10) or Spousal Property Petition (see Section F, below) is required. To complete the community property affidavit, insert the legal description of the property and other recording information which can be taken from the original deed. The surviving spouse signs the affidavit in the presence of a notary public and then records it in the county where the real property is located, along with a certified copy of the decedent's death certificate. (See Chapter 8 on how to record documents.) A sample is shown below with instructions on how to fill it in. It is a good idea to check with the title company before using the affidavit, since it may have specific requirements.

F. The Spousal Property Petition

IN OTHER SITUATIONS, a slightly more involved procedure is required for real property and certain other assets. This involves the surviving spouse (or the personal representative of the surviving spouse if the surviving spouse is deceased, or conservator of the surviving spouse if the surviving spouse is incapacitated) filing a Spousal Property Petition with the superior court in the county of the decedent's residence (or in the county where the property is located, if the decedent was not a California resident). This petition is appropriate for the following types of property:

- Real property held in the names of the spouses in joint tenancy or where the deed does not indicate the manner in which title is held, or real property held in the name of the decedent alone, or in the name of the decedent with a third party. Absent a court order in a formal probate proceeding, the title company will want a Spousal Property Order specifying that the property belongs to the surviving spouse before it will insure title, unless the deed says title is held by the spouses as community property, in which case the affidavit discussed in Section D, above, may be used instead.

- Securities, stocks and bonds that are in the names of the spouses "as community property" or as "tenants in common," or are held in the name of the decedent alone. The stock transfer agent will require a Spousal Property Order before transferring title to the securities.

Affidavit of Surviving Spouse Succeeding to Title
to Community Property
(California Probate Code § 13500)

WHEN RECORDED MAIL TO:

(Type name and address of
    surviving spouse)

AFFIDAVIT OF SURVIVING SPOUSE
SUCCEEDING TO TITLE TO COMMUNITY PROPERTY

I, the undersigned, declare that:

1. The real property described below is the community property of the under-signed and ___(name of decedent)___.

2. ___(name of decedent)___ died on _(date of death)_, 19___, as evidenced by the attached certified copy of the decedent's death certificate.

3. I am the surviving spouse of ___(name of decedent)___, and title to the real property described below devolved to me under the provisions of Section 13500 of the California Probate Code.

4. I have not filed in any court of competent jurisdiction an election under Section 13502 of the California Probate Code to subject the real property described below to administration.

5. ___(name of decedent)___ is the person named in that certain deed, dated___(date of deed)___, 19___, executed by _(names of grantors)_ _____ to _(name of decedent and spouse and how title was taken)_ recorded as instrument No. _____, on _____, 19___, in Book No. _____, Page No. _____, of Official Records of _(name of county)_ County, California, covering the property described below, which is situated in the City of _(name of city)_, County of ___(name of county)___, State of California:

(Insert legal description. If not enough room, put
See Exhibit "A", and attach a full page showing
legal description)

I certify (or declare) under penalty of perjury under the laws of the State of California that the foregoing is true and correct.

DATED: __(date signed)__, 19___   ___(signature of surviving spouse)___
                                         (Type name of surviving spouse here)

STATE OF CALIFORNIA   )
COUNTY OF _(insert county)_) SS.

On __(date signed)__, 19___, before me, a notary public for the State of California, personally appeared __(name of surviving spouse)_,personally known to me (or proved to me on the basis of satisfactory evidence) to be the person whose name is subscribed to this instrument, and acknowledged that _she_ executed the same. WITNESS my hand and official seal.

                              ___(signature of Notary Public)___
                                   NOTARY PUBLIC

(Notary's Seal)

Recording Affidavit by Mail
(Form Letter)

```
                                July 30, 19__

County Recorder
227 North Broadway
Los Angeles, California

          Re: John Doe, Deceased

To Whom It May Concern:

     Enclosed is an Affidavit by Surviving Spouse
Succeeding to Title to Community Property. Please record
the Affidavit, and after it is recorded return it to me
at the address indicated in the upper left-hand corner of
the Affidavit. A certified copy of the decedent's death
certificate is attached to the Affidavit.

     Also enclosed is a Preliminary Change in Ownership
Report.

     A check in the amount of $7.00 is enclosed to cover
your recording fee.

                         Very truly yours,



                         Mary Doe
```

- Trust deed notes or promissory notes payable to the decedent alone, or to the decedent and the surviving spouse. The person or entity making payment on the notes will normally require evidence in the form of a court order before making payments to the new owner. In the case of a trust deed note, a certified copy of the Spousal Property Order should be recorded in the county where the real property securing the note is located as evidence of the transfer of ownership.

- Motor vehicles held in the name of the decedent alone, or in the names of the decedent and the surviving spouse if their names are not joined by "or." The DMV has many simple transfer documents for motor vehicles and it is worthwhile to check with them before applying for a court order authorizing the transfer. However, if you have to file a Spousal Property Petition for other assets anyway, it is no more trouble to add the motor vehicle to the petition.

- Bank accounts in the name of the decedent alone, or in the name of the decedent and spouse as community property or as tenants in common. Since banks sometimes follow different procedures, you should check with the bank first to see if the transfer can be made without a court order.

If so, you may be able to avoid having to obtain the Spousal Property Order to transfer a bank account.

Caution: If it is claimed that property held in joint tenancy is community property, the petition must explain the way in which the property was converted to community property and give the date. If the decedent and the surviving spouse changed joint tenancy property to community property after December 31, 1984, it must be based on a document (Civil Code Sec. 5110.730), and the court will require that a photocopy of the document, showing signatures, be attached to the petition. If the joint tenancy property was converted to community property before January 1, 1985, it may be proved either by a writing or other supporting facts (for example, that there was an oral agreement between the spouses) which must be set forth in the petition.

The Spousal Property Petition is a printed court form with schedules attached that describe the property and give facts to support the surviving spouse's claim. One schedule describes the surviving spouse's one-half interest in community property (the half already owned by the surviving spouse), which the court is requested to "confirm" as belonging to the surviving spouse. Another schedule describes the decedent's one-half interest in community property and his 100% interest in any separate property that the court is requested to transfer to the surviving spouse.

Once filed, the court will set the petition for hearing.[2] A notice of the hearing must then be mailed to a number of people established by law (close relatives, others interested in the estate, etc., as explained in Step 3, below) at least 15 days prior to the hearing. An appearance in court is not usually required, unless someone objects to the petition.

---

[2]If probate court proceedings are required to transfer other assets (meaning if a Petition for Probate has been or will be filed), the Spousal Property Petition must be filed in the probate proceeding using the same case number.

If everything is in order, and there are no objections, the court will routinely approve the petition and grant an order declaring that the property "passes to" and "belongs to" the surviving spouse. If the decedent's will requires the surviving spouse to survive for a specified period of time (for example, 30 days, 90 days or 180 days), you must wait to file the petition because the court will not order property transferred to the surviving spouse until the expiration of the required survivorship period. Once obtained, the court order is used as the "official document" to transfer or clear title to the property, and no further proceedings are required. The entire procedure takes about a month.

G. The Spousal Property Petition Checklist

ASSUMING YOU HAVE concluded that you may use the Spousal Property Petition to transfer property to a surviving spouse, here is a step-by-step checklist showing you how to obtain a court order declaring property to be community or separate property "passing to" and "belonging to" a surviving spouse. Each item in the checklist is discussed in the notes that immediately follow the list. All forms needed for this procedure are included in Appendix 2 at the back of this book. If you need extra copies you may obtain them from the court where you file your papers, or make photocopies. We recommend that you review Chapter 13 on court procedures before you begin.

Prepare and file with the court:

- Spousal Property Petition;

- Notice of Hearing, if required;

- Certificate of Assignment, if required (see Chapter 14, Step 3);

- Filing Fee.

Before the hearing date on the petition:

- Mail Notice of Hearing;

- File original Notice of Hearing which shows date of mailing;

- Prepare Spousal Property Order;

- File Spousal Property Order, if required;

- Check Calendar Notes (see Chapter 13, Section D).

After hearing date:

- File Spousal Property Order;

- Record Spousal Property Order in counties where real property (or real property securing trust deed notes) is located;

- Transfer assets to surviving spouse.

Step 1: Prepare the Spousal Property Petition

Caption boxes: In the first box, type petitioner's name, address and telephone number. After "Attorney for," type "Petitioner In Pro Per." In the second box, fill in the court's address (including county) and branch name, if any. In the "Estate of" box, type the decedent's name, including all variations used. Leave the case number and hearing date boxes blank; the court clerk will give you a case number when you file the petition.

Item 1: Usually the surviving spouse is the petitioner. However, the personal representative of the surviving spouse's estate (executor or administrator in a formal probate proceeding), may be the petitioner if the surviving spouse is deceased, or a conservator acting on behalf of the surviving spouse may be the petitioner if the surviving spouse is incapacitated. In this case, you would type:

"_____ , as Executor of the Estate of _____ , deceased," or "_____ , as Conservator of the Estate of _____ ."

Item 1-a, 1-b and 1-c: Box 1-a, which should always be checked, refers to the decedent's one-half interest in community property or quasi-community property, or a 100% interest in separate property owned by the decedent, that the surviving spouse contends should be transferred to her without probate administration. Check box 1-b, which refers only to the one-half interest in community property that is already owned by the surviving spouse, if the decedent owned community property (as is normally the case) and the surviving spouse will request that the other one-half interest in the community property be "confirmed" as belonging to her. If the decedent didn't own any community property, don't check box 1-b. Box 1-c, pertaining to attorney's fees, should be left blank.

Item 1-c: Check this item if it is necessary to commence probate court proceedings for other assets owned by the decedent (such as for separate or community property over $60,000 in value willed to someone other than the surviving spouse). In this case, the Spousal Property Petition must be filed in the same proceeding as the Petition for Probate, using the same case number. The petitions are then considered "joined," and only one filing fee is required. Both petitions may be filed at the same time, or filed separately, with the Petition for Probate filed first. If no probate proceeding is necessary, the Spousal Property Petition is filed alone and there will be a filing fee. Inquire at the court clerk's office for the amount.

Item 1-d: Although it is usually not required for these proceedings, this item gives you the option of requesting that the court appoint a probate referee to appraise the non-cash assets listed in the petition. The referee charges a fee of one-tenth of one percent of the value of all non-cash assets. Some counties *require* the filing of an Inventory and Appraisement before hearing a Spousal Property Petition, so check local practice. Unless the court requires it, however, it shouldn't be necessary to have a referee appointed unless you are dealing with property that has appreciated in value, such as stocks or real property. You should have an official record of the date-of-death value of appreciated property, because all of the decedent's separate property and both halves of the community property receive a new "stepped-up" federal income tax basis equal to the date-of-death value of the asset. This substantially reduces the amount of capital gains tax paid by the surviving spouse, if and when the property is sold. (See Chapter 7.) The value of stocks and bonds can usually be established by contacting a stockbroker or by referring to newspaper financial pages which provide an official date-of-death record. However, in the case of real property, you should obtain an appraisal documenting the date-of-death value of the property. The appraisal should be obtained as soon as possible after the death because it may be more difficult to establish value later if much time has elapsed. Some people rely on a letter from a real estate broker, supported by a list of recent comparable sales in the area, to establish fair market value. Private appraisers (most are in the Yellow Pages) may charge from $200 to $300 to appraise a piece of real property, while many probate referees will appraise assets outside of a court proceeding for the same fee charged in a probate matter (for example, one-tenth of one percent of the value of the asset). Call the probate department of the courthouse for the names of referees in the county where the real property is located.

If you request the appointment of a probate referee in the court proceeding, the referee's name, address and telephone number are stamped on the conformed copy of the petition when it is filed. You must then prepare an Inventory and Appraisement with the attachments describing the property, following the procedures outlined in Chapter 14 for formal probate court proceedings, and forward it to the referee, who will appraise the assets and

return it to you for filing with the court prior to the hearing. Ordinarily, if you have a probate referee appraise the assets, you will not get the appraised inventory back in time to file it with the court prior to the hearing date (usually four or five weeks from the day you file your petition), which means you will have to request that the court continue the hearing to a later date. A simple phone call to the court can accomplish this. The appraised value of each asset will be shown in the Spousal Property Order, thereby providing an official record for future use.

Item 2: Check box 2-a if the surviving spouse is the petitioner, which is usually the case. However, if the petitioner is the personal representative of the surviving spouse's estate, check box 2-b. Box 2-c is to be checked if the petition is filed by a conservator or guardian of the surviving spouse.

Note: If the surviving spouse signed a Durable Power of Attorney to cover his other financial affairs, the person acting as "attorney-in-fact" under such a power *cannot* file a Spousal Property Petition on behalf of the surviving spouse.

Items 3-a and 3-b: Fill in the date and place of death.

Item 3-c: If the decedent died without a will, check the first box. If the decedent left a will, check the second box and be sure to attach a copy of the will (and any codicils) to the petition as "Attachment 3-c." If the will (or codicil) is handwritten, also attach an exact typewritten version.

Item 4: If the decedent is survived by a child or children, check the first box under (1) and then check one or more of the additional boxes on the same line indicating whether the child is natural or adopted, or a stepchild or foster child.

If there are no surviving children of decedent, check the box under (1) indicating this.

If the decedent had a child or children who died before the decedent (predeceased child) leaving a child or children or grandchildren (issue) living, check the first box under (2).

Spousal Property Petition
(front)

ATTORNEY OR PARTY WITHOUT ATTORNEY *(Name and Address)*:   TELEPHONE NO: FOR COURT USE ONLY

MARY DOE   (213) 365-4084
1022 Ninth Street
Santa Monica, California 90403

ATTORNEY FOR *(Name)*:   Petitioner In Pro Per

SUPERIOR COURT OF CALIFORNIA, COUNTY OF   LOS ANGELES
STREET ADDRESS: 1725 Main Street
MAILING ADDRESS:
CITY AND ZIP CODE: Santa Monica, California 90401
BRANCH NAME: West District

ESTATE OF (NAME):
          JOHN DOE, aka
          JOHN C. DOE,   DECEDENT

SPOUSAL PROPERTY PETITION

CASE NUMBER

HEARING DATE:

DEPT: TIME:

1. Petitioner *(name)*:   Mary Doe
   requests
   a. [X] determination of property passing to the surviving spouse without administration (Probate Code, § 13500).
   b. [X] confirmation of property belonging to the surviving spouse (Probate Code, §§ 100 and 101).
   c. [ ] this petition be joined with the petition for probate or administration of the decedent's estate.
   d. [X] immediate appointment of a probate referee.

2. Petitioner is
   a. [X] surviving spouse of the decedent.
   b. [ ] personal representative of *(name)*:   surviving spouse.
   c. [ ] guardian of the estate or conservator of the estate of *(name)*:   surviving spouse.

3. Decedent died on *(date)*:   July 14, 1989
   a. [X] a resident of the California county named above.
   b. [ ] a nonresident of California and left an estate in the county named above.
   c. [ ] intestate [X] testate and a copy of the will and any codicil is affixed as attachment 3c or 6d. *(Attach will.)*

4. a. *(Complete in all cases)* The decedent is survived by
      (1) [X] child as follows: [X] natural or adopted [ ] natural adopted by a third party [ ] step [ ] foster
          [ ] no child
      (2) [ ] issue of a predeceased child [X] no issue of a predeceased child
   b. Petitioner [X] has no [ ] has actual knowledge of facts reasonably giving rise to a parent-child relationship under Probate Code section 6408(b).
   c. [X] All surviving children and issue of predeceased children have been listed in item 7.

5. *(Complete only if no issue survived the decedent. Check only the first box that applies.)*
   a. [ ] The decedent is survived by a parent or parents who are listed in item 7.
   b. [ ] The decedent is survived by a brother, sister, or issue of a deceased brother or sister, all of whom are listed in item 7.

6. a. Administration of all or part of the estate is not necessary for the reason that all or a part of the estate is property passing to the surviving spouse.
   b. [X] The legal description of the deceased spouse's property that petitioner requests to be determined as passing to the surviving spouse is set forth in attachment 6b,¹ and includes the trade or business name of any unincorporated business or an interest in any unincorporated business the deceased spouse was operating or managing at the time of death.
   c. [X] The legal description of the community or quasi-community property petitioner requests the court to confirm to the surviving spouse as belonging to the surviving spouse under Probate Code sections 100 and 101 is set forth in attachment 6c.
   d. The facts upon which the petitioner bases the allegation that the property described in attachments 6b and 6c is property that should pass or be confirmed to the surviving spouse are stated in attachment 6d.²

(Continued on reverse)

Form Approved by the
Judicial Council of California
DE-221 (Rev. July 1, 1987)

SPOUSAL PROPERTY PETITION
(Probate)

See reverse for footnotes
Probate Code, § 13650

Spousal Property Petition
(back)

ESTATE OF (NAME): JOHN DOE, DECEDENT	CASE NUMBER:

7. The names, relationships, ages, and residence or mailing addresses of all persons checked in items 4 or 5 and all other heirs and
   devisees of the decedent, so far as known to petitioner, including stepchild and foster child heirs and devisees to whom notice
   is to be given [X] are listed below [ ] are listed in attachment 7.

NAME AND RELATIONSHIP	AGE	RESIDENCE OR MAILING ADDRESS
Jane Doe , daughter	Adult	1022 Ninth Street Santa Monica, California 90403

8. The names and address of all persons named as executors in the decedent's will or appointed as personal representatives
   [ ] are listed below [X] are listed in attachment 8 [ ] none.

9. [ ] The personal representative is the trustee of a trust that is a devisee under decedent's will. The names and addresses of
   all persons interested in the trust who are entitled to notice under Probate Code section 13655(b)(2) are listed in attachment 9.

10. A petition for probate or for administration of the decedent's estate
    a. [ ] is being filed with this petition and published notice will be given.
    b. [ ] was filed on (date):
    c. [X] has not been filed and is not being filed with this petition.

11. [X] Number of pages attached: 3

I declare under penalty of perjury under the laws of the State of California that the foregoing is true and correct.
Date: July 28, 1989

MARY DOE
(TYPE OR PRINT NAME)   (SIGNATURE OF PETITIONER)

¹ See Probate Code, § 13658 for required filing of a list of known creditors of a business and other information in certain instances. If required, include in attachment 6b.
² See Probate Code, § 13651(b) for the requirement that a copy of the will be attached in certain instances. If required, include in attachment 3c or 6d.

DE-221 (Rev. 1-1987)

SPOUSAL PROPERTY PETITION
(Probate)

Page two

If there are no living issue of a predeceased child of the decedent, check the second box under (2).

Check the first box in Item 4-b unless the decedent (1) did not leave a will, and (2) had a foster child he would have adopted but for a legal barrier.

Be sure to list all surviving children, plus any surviving issue of predeceased children in Item 7 (discussed below). If you do this, check box 4-c.

Item 5: Complete this section only if the deceased spouse left no children, grandchildren or great-grand-children (issue) surviving. Only one of the two boxes should be checked. If there are surviving parents, check box 5-a, and list them in Item 7, below. If there are no parents, but a surviving brother, or sister, or children of a predeceased brother or sister, check box 5-b and list their names, addresses and ages under Item 7, below.

Items 6-b and 6-c: Prepare two separate attachments on plain white bond paper the same size as the petition. Attachment 6-b should list and describe the decedent's interest in community or separate property that passes outright to the surviving spouse. The decedent's interest in community property should be shown as one-half, and in separate property 100%. (See sample below.) Attachment 6-c should list only the surviving spouse's one-half interest in community property. Be sure to describe the property fully, as shown in the sample below, indicating whether it is community property or separate property. Pay particular attention to the legal description for real estate; identify the property exactly as it is shown on the real property deed. Community property held in joint tenancy may be included in the attachments if you wish to have a court order finding the joint tenancy property to be community property. As we mentioned earlier, the court order may help establish a new "stepped-up" income tax basis for both the surviving spouse's and the decedent's interest in the community property that joint tenancy property would not otherwise receive. (See Chapter 7, Section D.)

If the decedent owned an interest in a going trade or business, additional information, including a list of creditors, is required, and the surviving spouse should have the help of an attorney.

Item 6-d: Here the court requires an attachment giving information to support the surviving spouse's contention that the property listed in Attachments 6-b and 6-c is community property or separate property and why it should pass to or be confirmed as belonging to the surviving spouse. Some samples of Attachment 6-d that may be adapted to your particular situation are shown below. Normally, to establish that property is community property, most courts require the following information:

- Date and place of marriage;

- Description and approximate value of any real or personal property owned by decedent on the date of marriage. (This tells the court whether the decedent owned a substantial amount of separate property when he married the surviving spouse. Property acquired after the date of marriage through the combined efforts of the spouses will be presumed to be community property, absent evidence to the contrary.);

- Decedent's occupation at time of marriage;

- Decedent's net worth at time of marriage;

- Description, approximate value and date of receipt of any property received by decedent after date of marriage by gift, bequest, devise, descent, proceeds of life insurance or joint tenancy survivorship. These assets are the decedent's separate property (unless they have been converted to community property by an agreement between the spouses);

- Identification of any property received by decedent under any of the devices listed directly above that is still a part of this estate;

- If claim is based on any document, a photocopy showing signatures; (normally, these would be the decedent's will, a deed to real property, or a written agreement between the spouses);

- Date decedent first came to California; and

- Any additional facts upon which claim of community property is based. (Here you may add anything of significance that would support a claim by the surviving spouse to community property, such as a commingling of community and separate property, or actions by the spouses showing an intention to treat property either as community property or separate property.)

For separate property, you should provide the following information:

• If the separate property passes outright to the surviving spouse under the decedent's will, the paragraph number in the will. (See example of Attachment 6-d);

• If there is no will, how the surviving spouse's share of the separate property is computed under intestate succession law. (See Chapter 3.) For example, if the decedent is survived by two children as well as the surviving spouse, put:

"The decedent died without a will, and is survived by a son and daughter in addition to the surviving spouse. Under the laws of intestate succession, the surviving spouse is entitled to receive one-third of the decedent's separate property."

Item 7: This section is for listing all persons potentially interested in the estate so they may be given notice of the filing of the petition. If the decedent left a will, you must list here the name, relationship, age and residence or mailing address of everyone mentioned in the decedent's will or codicil as a beneficiary, whether living or deceased. In addition, the name, relationship, age and residence of all persons checked in Items 4 and 5 of the petition should be listed (these are the decedent's heirs under intestate succession laws). Even if the surviving spouse claims the entire estate, the heirs must be given notice so they may present any adverse claims. Often, the heirs are the same as the beneficiaries named in the will; if so, you need list each person only once. Persons not related to the decedent by blood are described as "strangers." Ages may be shown as either "under eighteen" or "over eighteen." For a detailed explanation of the persons who should be included in this listing, see Item 8 of the instructions for preparing the Petition for Probate in Chapter 14, Step 1. If you don't have enough room for all

the names, prepare an attachment in the same format and attach it to the petition as "Attachment 7."

Item 8: List here the names and addresses of all persons named as executors in the decedent's will (or appointed as executors or administrators, if a probate proceeding is pending). If there is enough space on the petition to list them, check the first box. Otherwise, check the second box and prepare a separate schedule and attach it to the petition as "Attachment 8." If the surviving spouse is the executor or administrator, you should also enter her name here.

Item 9: Check this box if the decedent left a will and the executor or administrator, CTA is the trustee of a trust that is entitled to receive property under the will, and prepare a list of the names and addresses of all persons in being who are potential beneficiaries of the trust (now or in the future) so far as known to any petitioner and attach it as "Attachment 9."

Item 10: If a Petition for Probate or administration of the decedent's estate is required, check the appropriate box and fill in the filing date, if any.

Item 11: Check box 11 and enter the number of attachments.

Signatures: Sign the petition in the two places indicated.

Attachment 6-b

Estate of John Doe, Deceased

Spousal Property Petition

Attachment 6-b

Legal description of the deceased spouse's property passing
to the surviving spouse:

Community Property:

Undivided one-half (1/2) interest in the following community
property assets:

1. Real property, improved with a single dwelling and
    separate garage, commonly known as 1022 Ninth Street,
    Santa Monica, California, standing in the name of John
    Doe and Mary Doe, husband and wife as joint tenants, legally
    described as Lot 23, Block 789, in Tract ZYZ, per map re-
    corded in Book 73, Pages 91-94 of Maps, Records of Los
    Angeles County. Assessors I.D. No. 435-22-477

2. $25,000 trust deed note of Robert Smith, dated October 1,
    1967, payable to John Doe and Mary Doe, interest at 6%,
    payable $400 per month, principal and interest, secured by
    deed of trust dated October 1, 1967, recorded October 25,
    1967, as Instrument No. 3645 in Book T5553, Page 578,
    covering real property in the City of Santa Monica, County
    of Los Angeles, State of California, described as:

        Lot 231 of Tract No. 1234, in the City of Santa
        Monica, County of Los Angeles, State of California,
        as per map recorded in Book 29, Pages 33 to 37 in-
        clusive of Maps, in the office of the County Recorder
        of said County. Assessors I.D. No. 345-35-588

3. 454 shares of W. R. Grace Company, common stock (held in
    the name of the decedent, acquired as community property)

Separate Property:

A 100% interest in the following separate property assets:

4. 200 shares of XYX Corporation, common stock

5. 50% interest in Desert Sands West, a limited partnership

Attachment 6-c

Estate of John Doe, Deceased

Spousal Property Petition

Attachment 6-c

Legal description of the community or quasi-community property
to be confirmed to the surviving spouse -

Community Property:

Undivided one-half (1/2) interest in the following community
property assets:

1. Real property, improved with a single dwelling and
    separate garage, commonly known as 1022 Ninth Street,
    Santa Monica, California, standing in the name of John
    Doe and Mary Doe, husband and wife as joint tenants, legally
    described as Lot 23, Block 789, in Tract ZYZ, per map re-
    corded in Book 73, Pages 91-94 of Maps, Records of Los
    Angeles County. Assessors I.D. No. 435-22-477

2. $25,000 trust deed note of Robert Smith, dated October 1,
    1967, payable to John Doe and Mary Doe, interest at 6%,
    payable $400 per month, principal and interest, secured by
    deed of trust dated October 1, 1967, recorded October 25,
    1967, as Instrument No. 3645 in Book T5553, Page 578,
    covering real property in the City of Santa Monica, County
    of Los Angeles, State of California, described as:

        Lot 231 of Tract No. 1234, in the City of Santa
        Monica, County of Los Angeles, State of California,
        as per map recorded in Book 29, Pages 33 to 37 in-
        clusive of Maps, in the office of the County Recorder
        of said County. Assessors I.D. No. 345-35-588

3. 454 shares of W. R. Grace Company, common stock (held in
    the name of the decedent, acquired as community property)

Attachment 6-d

(Example 1)

Estate of John Doe, Deceased

Spousàl Property Petition

Attachment 6-d

The facts upon which petitioner bases the allegation that the property listed in Items 1, 2, and 3, of Attachments 6-b and 6-c is community property passing to and belonging to the surviving spouse are:

1. Petitioner and the decedent were married on July 10, 1945 in New York City. They remained married and continuously lived together as husband and wife from 1945 to the date of decedent's death;

2. At the time of marriage, the decedent owned no real property and the extent of the personal property then owned by the decedent consisted of clothing, personal effects and a checking account, the total value of which did not then exceed more than Five Hundred Dollars ($500);

3. Decedent was not indebted at that time to any significant extent, and his net worth was approximately Five Hundred Dollars ($500);

4. Decedent's occupation at the time of marriage was that of a bookkeeper;

5. Decedent and his surviving spouse first came to California in 1952;

6. Decedent's net worth upon arrival in California was no more than a few thousand dollars. All community property assets were acquired as community property of the spouses, and not as separate property, subsequent to their arrival in California.

7. During the marriage, the decedent inherited 200 shares of XYX Corporation common stock and a 50% interest in Desert Sands West, a Limited Partnership, from his mother, Jane Doe, who died in Los Angeles County in 1963. Said stock and partnership interest are the decedent's separate property. During the marriage of petitioner and decedent, decedent did not receive any other property by inheritance, nor did he receive any property of significant value by way of gift.

The facts upon which the petitioner bases the allegation that the separate propety listed as Items 4 and 5 of Attachment 6-b should pass to the surviving spouse are:

1. The decedent's entire estate passes to the surviving spouse under Article Fourth of the decedent's will, as shown in the copy of the will attached to the petition as Attachment 3-c.

Step 2: File the Petition

Make one photocopy for your files, and another photocopy if local court rules require the petition to be filed in duplicate. Read the petition over carefully to make sure all the required boxes are checked. If there is a will, don't forget to attach a copy to the petition.

The petition, along with the other required documents and filing fee, should be filed with the court clerk's office in the superior court of the county in which the decedent resided (or in the county where the property is located, if the decedent was not a resident of California), in person or by mail.

Prepare a certificate of assignment, if necessary. This form is normally required only if you file your papers in a branch court in your county. (See Chapter 13 on general court procedures for instructions on how to fill it in.)

The fee for filing the petition varies from county to county, and you should call the court for the amount of the fee. The check should be made payable to the county clerk of the county in which you file your papers. Most courts accept personal checks.

The sample form letter shown below may be adapted to your particular situation when mailing the petition and other documents to the court for filing. Not all items listed in the form letter will apply in all situations, so be sure to include only those that apply to your particular estate. Be sure to include a self-addressed, stamped envelope so the court clerk will return conformed (file stamped) copies of your documents to you.

Letter to Court

```
                              August 16, 19__
County Clerk
1500 Main Street
Santa Monica, CA 90402

RE: Estate of John Doe, Deceased

  Enclosed are the following documents:

1.  Original and two copies of Spousal Property Petition
2.  Original and four copies of Notice of Hearing
3.  Original and one copy of Certificate of Assignment
4.  Filing fee of $_____.

  Please file the original documents with the Court and
return the extra copies to me, conformed with your filing
stamp, indicating the case number and time and date of the
hearing on the Petition. A stamped, self-addressed envelope
is enclosed for your convenience.

                              Very truly yours,




                              Mary Doe
```

Probate Note: When the Spousal Property Petition is joined with a Petition for Probate, notice of the hearing on the Spousal Property Petition is combined with the "Notice of Death" given in the probate proceedings. In this case, wording is added to the Notice of Death to indicate that the hearing is on the Spousal Property Petition as well as the Petition for Probate, and that a copy of the Spousal Property Petition (if required) was mailed with the Notice of Death. (We show you how to do this in Chapter 14.)

Step 3: Mail and File a Notice of Hearing

When you file the petition, the court clerk will establish a hearing date, and all persons listed in Items 7 and 8 of the petition (except the petitioner) must be given notice of the time, date and place of the hearing. You provide this notice on a printed form called Notice of Hearing. The person filing the petition is responsible for preparing the Notice and seeing that it is properly given. A copy of the Notice is shown below, with instructions on how to fill it in. You will find a blank Notice of Hearing form in Appendix 2.

In some counties, the Notice of Hearing must be presented or mailed to the court when you file the petition, and the court clerk fills in the time and date of the hearing on the original copy and returns your conformed copy of the petition in the stamped, self-addressed envelope you provided. In other counties, the petitioner must choose a hearing date according to when such matters are heard on the court calendar. Check with the court where you file your papers for the procedures it follows. If you pick a date, be sure to allow enough time to give the 15 days' notice to the people it must be served on.

When the Notice of Hearing is completed, with the time, date and place of the hearing, mail a copy (not the original) 15 days prior to the hearing date to all the persons, other than the petitioner, named in Item 7 and Item 8 of the petition. The mailing must be done by someone over 18 years of age who is not a person interested in the estate. Thus, the Notice cannot be mailed by the surviving spouse, any of the heirs or beneficiaries, or others named in Item 7 or 8 of the petition. After the Notice is mailed, the person giving the Notice must complete the affidavit on the reverse side of the original copy of the Notice, giving proof of the mailing.

File the original Notice, with the Proof of Mailing, with the court prior to the hearing date.

Front

Heading: Fill in the same information as on the Spousal Property Petition, and insert case number.

Item 1: Type your name on the first line. On the second line, type representative capacity (for example, "Surviving spouse of Decedent"). On the third line type "a Spousal Property Petition."

Item 3: Fill in the date and place of the hearing and address of the court. Type your name on the dotted line and sign your name on the signature line. Fill in the date below.

Item 4: Fill in the date and place (city) of mailing.

Back

Heading: Fill in name of estate and case number. Leave the next section (Clerk's Certificate of Posting/Mailing) blank.

Proof of Service by Mail: Complete this section the same as on the back of the Notice of Administration (explained in Step 4, paragraph 2). In the space at the bottom, list the name and address of each person to whom a copy of the Notice was mailed. (This must be everyone listed in Attachment 7 and 8 of the petition.)

Notice of Hearing

(front)

ATTORNEY OR PARTY WITHOUT ATTORNEY (Name and Address)   TELEPHONE NO.   FOR COURT USE ONLY
MARY DOE   (213) 365-4084
1022 Ninth Street
Santa Monica, California 90403

ATTORNEY FOR (Name): Petitioner in Pro Per

SUPERIOR COURT OF CALIFORNIA, COUNTY OF LOS ANGELES
STREET ADDRESS   1725 Main Street
MAILING ADDRESS
CITY AND ZIP CODE   Santa Monica, California 90401
BRANCH NAME   West District

ESTATE OF (NAME):
                    JOHN DOE, aka
                    JOHN C. DOE,   DECEDENT

NOTICE OF HEARING   CASE NUMBER:
(Probate)   WEP 4084

This notice is required by law. This notice does not require you to appear in court, but you may attend the hearing if you wish.

1. NOTICE is given that (name):   MARY DOE

   (representative capacity, if any): Surviving Spouse of decedent

   has filed (specify):*   a Spousal Property Petition

2. You may refer to the filed documents for further particulars. (All of the case documents filed with the court are available for examination in the case file kept by the court clerk.)

3. A HEARING on the matter will be held as follows:

   Date: August 24, 1989   Time: 9:30 A.M.   Dept.: A   Room:
   Address of court [X] shown above [ ] is:

        Mary Doe
   . . . .   [X] Attorney or party   *Mary Doe*
              (TYPE OR PRINT NAME)   (SIGNATURE)

Date: August 7, 1989   [ ] Clerk, by _____, Deputy

4. This notice was mailed on (date): August 7, 1989   at (place): Santa Monica, California

(Continued on reverse)

---

* Do not use this form to give notice of hearing of the petition for administration (see Probate Code, § 8100).

Form Approved by the
Judicial Council of California   **NOTICE OF HEARING**   Probate Code, §§ 1211, 1215, 1216, 1230
DE-120 [Rev. July 1, 1989]   (Probate)

Notice of Hearing

(back)

ESTATE OF (NAME).	CASE NUMBER
JOHN DOE, DECEDENT	WEP 4084

CLERK'S CERTIFICATE OF ☐ POSTING ☐ MAILING

I certify that I am not a party to this cause and that a copy of the foregoing Notice of Hearing (Probate)

1. ☐ was posted at (address):

   on (date):

2. ☐ was served on each person named below. Each notice was enclosed in an envelope with postage fully prepaid. Each envelope was addressed to a person whose name and address is given below, sealed, and deposited with the United States Postal Service at (place): , California, on (date):

Date: Clerk, by _____ , Deputy

PROOF OF SERVICE BY MAIL

1. I am over the age of 18 and not a party to this cause. I am a resident of or employed in the county where the mailing occurred.
2. My residence or business address is (specify):

   2332 - 20th Street, Santa Monica, California

3. I served the foregoing Notice of Hearing (Probate) on each person named below by enclosing a copy in an envelope addressed as shown below AND
   a. [X] depositing the sealed envelope with the United States Postal Service with the postage fully prepaid.
   b. ☐ placing the envelope for collection and mailing on the date and at the place shown in item 4 following our ordinary business practices. I am readily familiar with this business' practice for collecting and processing correspondence for mailing. On the same day that correspondence is placed for collection and mailing, it is deposited in the ordinary course of business with the United States Postal Service in a sealed envelope with postage fully prepaid.

4. a. Date mailed August 7, 1989   b. Place mailed (city, state): Santa Monica, California

5. ☐ I served with the Notice of Hearing (Probate) a copy of the petition or other document referred to in the notice.

I declare under penalty of perjury under the laws of the State of California that the foregoing is true and correct.

Date: August 7, 1989

Laura Jones
(TYPE OR PRINT NAME)   *Laura Jones* (SIGNATURE OF DECLARANT)

NAME AND ADDRESS OF EACH PERSON TO WHOM NOTICE WAS MAILED

Jane Doe
1022 Ninth Street
Santa Monica, California 90403

DE-120 (Rev. July 1, 1989)   **NOTICE OF HEARING** (Probate)   Page two   Probate Code, §§ 1261, 1264

Step 4: Prepare Your Spousal Property Order

The point of filing a Spousal Property Petition is to obtain an Order from the court stating that the property described in the petition belongs to the surviving spouse. To accomplish this, it is the responsibility of the petitioner to prepare the Order for the judge's signature by following the instructions outlined below.

A sample Spousal Property Order is shown below.

Instructions for Filling Out the Spousal Property Order

Caption boxes: Fill in as you did on the Spousal Property Petition, except that now you can add the case number.

Item 1: Fill in date, time and department (courtroom) of hearing as it appears on your Notice of Hearing.

Item 3: Fill in date of death.

Item 3-a or 3-b: Check correct box.

Item 3-c: Indicate whether decedent died intestate (without a will) or testate (with a will).

Items 4-a and 6-a: Type in name of surviving spouse and prepare an Attachment 4-a describing the decedent's one-half interest in the community property and any separate property that passes outright to the surviving spouse. To do this, you can resubmit Attachment 6-b of your petition; just change the title to Attachment 4-a. For Item 6-a, also type in name of surviving spouse and prepare Attachment 6-a which will describe only the surviving spouse's one-half interest in the community property. You can resubmit Attachment 6-c of your petition. Just be sure to change the title to Attachment 6-a. The attachments should be typed on plain white bond paper, the same size as the petition, and the property described the same way as in the petition.

Items 4-b and 6-b: These items refer to attachments "for further order respecting transfer of the property to the surviving spouse." Such orders would be required only in unusual circumstances. In most estates you can leave this blank.

Item 5: This section applies only to a trade or business owned by a decedent.

Item 7: If during the proceedings it has been ascertained that some part of the property described in the petition does not pass to or belong to the surviving spouse, check this box. (This has the effect of ordering the property to be subjected to probate administration, unless the entire estate is worth less than $60,000. See Chapter 11.)

Item 8: Check box and add up pages of attachment, and fill in.

Some counties, such as Los Angeles, do not permit attachments to a court order after the judge's signature. Because you will have at least one or two attachments, this means you should check the box at the bottom of the Spousal Property Order and then type lines at the bottom of the last page attached to the Order for the judge's signature and the date, as shown in the example.

In most counties, if the petition is unopposed, the Spousal Property Order will be signed without an appearance in court by anyone. Because of this, some counties require the Spousal Property Order to be submitted to the court for review a certain number of days prior to the hearing date. In other counties, the Spousal Property Order may be sent in after the hearing date for the judge's signature, so local practice should be checked. In either case, once the Spousal Property Order is signed, you will need one certified copy for each issue of security to be transferred, and one certified copy to record in each county in which any item of real property is located. A sample form letter for mailing the Order and requesting certified copies is shown below.

Spousal Property Order

ATTORNEY OR PARTY WITHOUT ATTORNEY *(Name and Address)*:		TELEPHONE NO.	FOR COURT USE ONLY

ATTORNEY OR PARTY WITHOUT ATTORNEY *(Name and Address)*:
MARY DOE   (213) 365-4084
1022 Ninth Street
Santa Monica, California 90403

ATTORNEY FOR *(Name)*:   Petitioner in Pro Per

SUPERIOR COURT OF CALIFORNIA. COUNTY OF LOS ANGELES
STREET ADDRESS: 1725 Main Street
MAILING ADDRESS:
CITY AND ZIP CODE: Santa Monica, California 90401
BRANCH NAME: West District

ESTATE OF (NAME):
        JOHN DOE, aka
        JOHN C. DOE,   DECEDENT

SPOUSAL PROPERTY ORDER	CASE NUMBER:
	WEP 4084

1. Date of hearing: August 24, 1989   Time: 9:30 A.M.   Dept.: A   Room:

THE COURT FINDS

2. All notices required by law have been given.

3. Decedent died on *(date)*: July 14, 1989
   a. [X] a resident of the California county named above.
   b. [ ] a nonresident of California and left an estate in the county named above.
   c. [ ] intestate [X] testate.

THE COURT FURTHER FINDS AND ORDERS

4. a. [X] The property described in attachment 4a is property passing to the surviving spouse,
      (name):   MARY DOE   , and no administration of it is necessary.
   b. [ ] See attachment 4b for further order respecting transfer of the property to the surviving spouse.

5. [ ] To protect the interests of the creditors of *(business name)*:

   an unincorporated trade or business, a list of all its known creditors and the amount owed each is on file.
   a. [ ] Within *(specify)*:   days from this date, the surviving spouse shall file an undertaking in the amount of
         $, upon condition that the surviving spouse pay the known creditors of the business.
   b. [ ] See attachment 5b for further order protecting the interests of creditors of the business.

6. a. [X] The property described in attachment 6a is property that belongs to the surviving spouse,
      (name):   MARY DOE   , under Probate Code sections 100 and 101, and the surviving
      spouse's ownership is hereby confirmed.
   b. [ ] See attachment 6b for further order respecting transfer of the property to the surviving spouse.

7. [ ] All property described in the Spousal Property Petition that is not determined to be property passing to the surviving spouse
      under Probate Code section 13500, or confirmed as belonging to the surviving spouse under Probate Code sections 100
      and 101, shall be subject to administration in the estate [ ] described in attachment 7.
8. [ ] Other *(specify)*:

Date:

9. [X] Number of pages attached: 2

JUDGE OF THE SUPERIOR COURT

[X] Signature follows last attachment

Form Approved by the
Judicial Council of California
CF 226 (Rev July 1, 1987)

SPOUSAL PROPERTY ORDER
(Probate)

Probate Code. § 13656

H. How to Transfer the Assets to the Surviving Spouse

ASSUMING YOU HAVE now obtained a copy of the Spousal Property Order (as well as a number of certified copies), you are ready to actually transfer the property. Here is how you do it.

1. Real Property

Title to real property is transferred by recording a certified copy of the Spousal Property Order in the office of the County Recorder for each county where the real property is located. If there are several items of real property in one county, you need record only one certified copy of the Order in that county. See Chapter 8 on how to record documents with the County Recorder.

2. Securities

Send the transfer agent the following items by registered mail, insured, for each issue:

1. Certified copy of Spousal Property Order;

2. Stock power signed by the surviving spouse, with signature guaranteed;

3. Original stock or bond certificates;

4. Affidavit of Domicile;

5. Stock transfer tax (if transfer agent is located in New York); and

6. Transmittal letter, giving instructions.

   See Chapter 9 on how to transfer securities, where to get the forms and how to fill them in.

3. Promissory Notes and Trust Deed Notes

Usually, if the surviving spouse notifies the person making payments on the note that the note is now the sole property of the surviving spouse (or owned by the surviving spouse with another), and furnishes the payor with a certified copy of the Spousal Property Order, the payor will adjust his records and make future checks payable to the new owner. The surviving spouse should keep a certified copy of the Spousal Property Order with his or her other important papers as evidence of ownership of any promissory notes. If the note is secured by a deed of trust on real property, recording a certified copy of the Spousal Property Order in the county in which the property described in the deed of trust is located will establish a record of transfer to the new owner.

4. Automobiles

The surviving spouse should go in person to the Department of Motor Vehicles to transfer title to any community property automobiles or other motor vehicles. Upon being presented with the Certificate of Ownership (pink slip) and a copy of the Spousal Property Order, the DMV will provide the surviving spouse with the required forms to complete the transfer of title.

5. Bank Accounts

Bank accounts usually can be transferred into the name of the surviving spouse without loss of interest by simply submitting the passbook or time certificate of deposit together with a certified copy of the Spousal Property Order to the bank or savings and loan association with a request that the account or accounts be transferred.

6. Money Market Funds and Mutual Funds

Transferring record ownership in these types of assets is handled by the fund management, which will transfer title to the surviving spouse when presented with a certified copy of the Spousal Property Order.

7. Miscellaneous Assets

Any tangible personal property held by third parties, as well as other property interests such as partnership and joint venture interests, usually can be transferred by presenting a certified copy of the court Order to the persons having possession or control over the property.

CHAPTER 16

If You Need Expert Help

EVEN SIMPLE ESTATES sometimes have quirks that can't be resolved by a layperson. An estate that appears to be straightforward and uncomplicated at the outset may suddenly turn out to be neither if someone challenges the will or otherwise intervenes in the probate court proceedings.

When To Get Help

- Separate and community property of a married couple are commingled, and you don't know how to distribute the decedent's property.
- A creditor files a large disputed claim against the estate.
- The will gives away property that is no longer owned by the decedent.
- An heir or beneficiary can't be located.
- Someone challenges your right to settle the estate.
- The will is ambiguous.
- A would-be beneficiary contests the will or otherwise interferes with settlement of the estate.

The most sensible approach to settling an estate without professional help is to be pragmatic. Do as much of the routine estate work by yourself as you are able to, and be prepared to seek help if you need it.

A. What Kind of Expert Do You Need?

DON'T ASSUME THAT EVERY TIME you have a probate question, you need to hire a probate lawyer. You may be able to get the help you need more quickly and cheaply from another kind of expert. For example, a tax accountant will be able to assist you with estate tax or income tax problems. And a non-lawyer who specializes in probate paperwork can help you fill out and file your probate forms.

B. Using a Probate Paralegal

IF YOU JUST WANT some help preparing and filing your probate paperwork, you may want to hire a probate paralegal, who will charge much less than a lawyer. Many paralegals now operate independent offices, so customers can go to them directly instead of hiring a lawyer (who, often as not, gives the actual paperwork to a paralegal the law firm employs).

These independent paralegals (sometimes called "legal technicians") don't offer legal advice. You are responsible for making decisions about how to proceed and for providing the information to fill out the papers. The typing service can prepare your papers and file them with the court for you.

Most typing services specialize in one or two areas; for example, some handle only divorce paperwork, and others just do bankruptcy or eviction papers. Be sure to use a typing service that is experienced in probate paperwork.

The author of this book, Julia Nissley, now operates a probate typing service. You can write to her at P.O. Box 1832, Cathedral City, CA 92235 or call (619) 321-1993. The National Association for Independent Paralegals also maintains a list of reputable typing services. Write to NAIP at 585 Fifth St. West, Suite 111, Sonoma, CA 95476, or call (800) 542-0034. You can also look in the Yellow Pages under "Typing Services" or "Attorney Services."

C. Using a Lawyer

IF YOU DO NEED A LAWYER, find one who does not object to your doing most of your own legal work and who will charge a reasonable hourly rate for occasional help and advice. While this isn't impossible, it may be difficult, because some lawyers may not want to accept piecemeal work in a field where much higher fees are available for handling an entire probate.

As a general rule, you will be better off using a lawyer who specializes to some extent in probate matters. Many attorneys devote a large part of their practice to probate and will do a competent job while charging fairly for their services. However, because this area is so specialized, you simply can't expect much creative help from someone who doesn't work regularly with these matters. In Northern California, Consumer's Group Legal Services in Berkeley provides good services at a very reasonable cost and is open to its members helping themselves. The membership cost for CGLS is very reasonable, as are hourly consultation fees.

If your employer or union offers a pre-paid legal services plan, which offers you some free or low-cost consultation with a lawyer, take advantage of it. But remember that you need to talk to someone who is familiar with probate law and practice. And if the lawyer starts telling you that you need to turn everything over to him, you may want to get a second opinion.

Finding a lawyer who charges reasonable rates and who you feel you can trust is not always easy. Picking a name out of the telephone book may get you the right attorney the first time, but you might also end up with an unsympathetic attorney or one who charges too much or someone who isn't really knowledgeable about probate matters. This sorry result is not necessarily inevitable. Just as you can competently handle much of your own probate work, if you take the time to inform yourself on how to do it, you can also find the right attorney to help you if you need it.

The best way to find a suitable attorney is through a friend or some trusted person who has had a satisfactory experience with one. Ask small business people and others you know who deal with their own investment or business decisions who they use and what it usually costs.

Generally, we advise you to comparison shop before dealing with one of the advertised legal clinics. You can often get better service from a specialist who doesn't buy television time at thousands of dollars per minute. If you do deal with a legal clinic, make sure the price you are quoted includes all the services you need. It is not unusual for legal clinics to advertise a very low basic price and then add to it considerably, based on the assertion that your particular problem costs more.

Referral panels set up by local bar associations are also not high on our list of favorite ways to find a lawyer. Although some lawyers are given minimal screening as to their expertise in certain areas of the law before they qualify to be listed, the emphasis more often than not is on the word "minimal." You might get a good referral from these panels, but sometimes they just serve as a haven for the inexperienced practitioner who does not have enough clients.

Once you get a few referrals that sound good, call the law offices that have been recommended and state your problem. Ask how much an initial interview will cost, and if you want advice on a particular problem, explain the situation to the lawyer to see if she is willing to see you on this basis.

As your own intuition should tell you, the world provides little or nothing of value for free. This is doubly true when it comes to buying legal services.

When you do locate a lawyer who seems good, be sure to ask how much her rates are. Hourly rates can run anywhere from $80 to $300 per hour, with $100 per hour being fairly common. When you find an attorney you like, make an appointment to discuss your situation personally. Be ready to pay for this consultation. It is unwise to accept an offer of a free initial consultation, as you put the attorney in a position of profiting only if she sells you some service, whether you need it or not. Be sure to bring all the relevant documents and information with you when you go, so your time and money will be well spent.

If you want an attorney to review all of your work, and you are dealing with a good-sized estate, this is not a job that can be handled in a consultation of an hour or two and, consequently, will be fairly costly. When compared to how much it would cost to have a lawyer probate the entire estate, however, it should be a bargain.

EVEN SIMPLE ESTATES sometimes have quirks that can't be resolved by a layperson. An estate that appears to be straightforward and uncomplicated at the outset may suddenly turn out to be neither if someone challenges the will or otherwise intervenes in the probate court proceedings.

When To Get Help

- Separate and community property of a married couple are commingled, and you don't know how to distribute the decedent's property.
- A creditor files a large disputed claim against the estate.
- The will gives away property that is no longer owned by the decedent.
- An heir or beneficiary can't be located.
- Someone challenges your right to settle the estate.
- The will is ambiguous.
- A would-be beneficiary contests the will or otherwise interferes with settlement of the estate.

The most sensible approach to settling an estate without professional help is to be pragmatic. Do as much of the routine estate work by yourself as you are able to, and be prepared to seek help if you need it.

A. What Kind of Expert Do You Need?

DON'T ASSUME THAT EVERY TIME you have a probate question, you need to hire a probate lawyer. You may be able to get the help you need more quickly and cheaply from another kind of expert. For example, a tax accountant will be able to assist you with estate tax or income tax problems. And a non-lawyer who specializes in probate paperwork can help you fill out and file your probate forms.

B. Using a Probate Paralegal

IF YOU JUST WANT some help preparing and filing your probate paperwork, you may want to hire a probate paralegal, who will charge much less than a lawyer. Many paralegals now operate independent offices, so customers can go to them directly instead of hiring a lawyer (who, often as not, gives the actual paperwork to a paralegal the law firm employs).

These independent paralegals (sometimes called "legal technicians") don't offer legal advice. You are responsible for making decisions about how to proceed and for providing the information to fill out the papers. The typing service can prepare your papers and file them with the court for you.

Most typing services specialize in one or two areas; for example, some handle only divorce paperwork, and others just do bankruptcy or eviction papers. Be sure to use a typing service that is experienced in probate paperwork.

The author of this book, Julia Nissley, now operates a probate typing service. You can write to her at P.O. Box 1832, Cathedral City, CA 92235 or call (619) 321-1993. The National Association for Independent Paralegals also maintains a list of reputable typing services. Write to NAIP at 585 Fifth St. West, Suite 111, Sonoma, CA 95476, or call (800) 542-0034. You can also look in the Yellow Pages under "Typing Services" or "Attorney Services."

C. Using a Lawyer

IF YOU DO NEED A LAWYER, find one who does not object to your doing most of your own legal work and who will charge a reasonable hourly rate for occasional help and advice. While this isn't impossible, it may be difficult, because some lawyers may not want to accept piecemeal work in a field where much higher fees are available for handling an entire probate.

Glossary

Abatement: Cutting back certain gifts under a will when necessary to create a fund to meet expenses, pay taxes, satisfy debts or to have enough to take care of other bequests which are given priority under law or under the will.

Ademption: The failure of a specific bequest of property because the property is no longer owned by the testator at the time of his death.

Administrator: The title given to the person who is appointed by the probate court, when there is no will, to collect assets of the estate, pay its debts and distribute the rest to the appropriate beneficiaries.

Administrator With Will Annexed: Sometimes termed "Administrator CTA," this title is given to the administrator when there is a will but the will either fails to nominate an executor or the named executor is unable to serve.

Adopted Child: Any person, whether an adult or a minor, who is legally adopted as the child of another in a court proceeding.

Affidavit: A voluntary written or printed statement of facts that is signed under oath before a notary public (or other officer having authority to administer oaths) by any person having personal knowledge of the facts. Affidavits are used in lieu of live testimony to support the facts contained in a petition or other document submitted in the course of the probate process.

Anti-Lapse Statute: A statute that prevents dispositions in a will from failing in the event the beneficiary predeceases the testator. See *Lapse*.

Appraiser: A person possessing expertise in determining the market or fair value of real or personal property. The probate court appoints an appraiser to place a value on the estate for tax purposes.

Attestation: The act of witnessing the signing of a document by another, and the signing of the document as a witness. Thus, a will requires both the signature by the person making the will and attestation by at least two witnesses.

Beneficiary: A person (or organization) receiving benefits under a legal instrument such as a will, trust or life insurance policy. Except when very small estates are involved, beneficiaries of wills only receive their benefits after the will is examined and approved by the probate court. Beneficiaries of trusts receive their benefits directly as provided in the trust instrument.

Bequeath: The first-person legal term used to leave someone personal property in the will; for example, "I bequeath my antique car collection to my brother Jody."

Bequest: The legal term used to describe personal property left in a will.

Bond: A document guaranteeing that a certain amount of money will be paid to the victim if a person occupying a position of trust does not carry out his legal and ethical responsibilities. Thus, if an executor, trustee or guardian who is bonded (covered by a bond) wrongfully deprives a beneficiary of her property (say by taking it on a one-way trip to Las Vegas), the bonding company will replace it, up to the limits of the bond. Bonding companies, which are normally divisions of insurance companies, issue a bond in exchange for a premium (usually about 10% of the face amount of the bond). Because the cost of any required bond is paid out of the estate, most wills provide that no bond shall be required.

Children: Children are (1) the biological offspring of the person making the will (the testator) unless they have been legally adopted by another, (2) persons who were legally adopted by the testator, (3) children born out of wedlock if the testator is the mother, (4) children born out of wedlock if the testator is the father and has acknowledged the child as being his under California law (this can be done in writing or by the conduct of the father—for more information see *The Living Together Kit*, Warner and Ihara, Nolo Press)), and (5) stepchildren and foster children if the relationship began during the person's minority, continued throughout the parties' joint lifetimes, and it is established by clear and convincing evidence that the decedent would have adopted the person but for a legal barrier.

Class: A group of beneficiaries or heirs that is designated only by status—for example, "children" or "issue." A class member is simply anyone who fits in the category.

Codicil: A supplement or addition to a will. It may explain, modify, add to, subtract from, qualify, alter, restrain or revoke provisions in the will. Because a codicil changes a will, it must be executed with the same formalities as a will. When admitted to probate, it forms a part of the will.

Collateral: Property pledged as security for a debt.

Community Property: Very generally, all property acquired by a couple after marriage and before permanent separation, except for gifts to and inheritances by one spouse only, or unless the nature of property has been changed by agreement between the spouses. In most marriages, the main property accumulated is a family home, a retirement pension belonging to one or both spouses, motor vehicles, a joint bank account, a savings account and, perhaps, some stocks or bonds. So long as these were purchased during the marriage with the income earned by either spouse during the marriage, they are usually considered to be community property, unless the spouses have entered into an agreement to the contrary. If the property was purchased with the separate property of a spouse, it is separate property, unless it has been given to the community by gift or agreement. If separate property and community property are mixed together (commingled) in a bank account and expenditures are made from this bank account, then the goods purchased will usually be treated as community property unless they can be specifically linked with the separate property. (This is called "tracing.")

Conformed Copy: A copy of a document filed with the court that has been stamped with the filing date by the court clerk.

Consanguinity: An old-fashioned term referring to the relationship enjoyed by people who have a common ancestor. Thus, consanguinity exists between brothers and sisters but not between husbands and wives.

Contingent Beneficiary: Any person entitled to property under a will in the event one or more prior conditions are satisfied. Thus, if Fred is entitled to take property under a will on the condition that Harry does not survive the testator, Fred is a contingent beneficiary. Similarly, if Ellen is named to receive a house only in the event her mother, who has been named to receive the house, moves out of it, then Ellen is a contingent beneficiary.

Creditor: For probate purposes, a creditor is any person or entity to whom the decedent was liable for money at the time of her death, and any person or entity to whom the estate owes money (say a taxing authority, funeral home, etc.).

Conditional Bequest: A bequest which only passes under certain specified conditions or upon the occurrence of a specific event. For example, if you leave property to Aunt Millie provided she is living in Cincinnati when you die, and otherwise to Uncle Fred, you have made a "conditional bequest."

CTA: An abbreviation for the Latin phrase "Cum Testamento Annexo," meaning "with the will annexed." Thus, an administrator who is appointed to serve in a context where a will exists but no executor was either named or able to serve is termed an "administrator CTA" or "administrator with will annexed."

Decedent: For probate purposes, the person who died, either testate or intestate, and left the estate under consideration.

Decree: A court order.

Deductions: Items that cause the value of the estate to be reduced. They include the decedent's debts, any expenses associated with a last illness, funeral expenses, taxes and costs of administration (for example, court filing fees, certification fees, bond premiums, fees for public notices, etc.).

Deed: A document that describes a transfer of ownership in respect to a particular parcel of real property, a description of which is also set out in the document. There are many types of deeds, including quitclaim deeds (a naked transfer of the property ownership without any guarantees), grant deeds (a transfer of ownership accompanied by a number of standard guarantees or warranties, including the fact that the person making the transfer has the power to do so), as well as joint tenancy deeds, gift deeds, etc.

Deed of Trust: A special type of deed (similar to a mortgage) that places legal title to real property in the hands of one or more trustees as security for repayment of a loan. Thus, if Ida borrows $100,000 to buy a house, she will be required as a condition of the loan to sign a deed of trust in favor of the designated trustees, who will retain the deed of trust until the loan has been paid off. It is not uncommon for homes to carry two deeds of trust—one executed as security for a loan to buy the house and another (termed the "second deed of trust") executed at a later time as security for another loan (for example, for home improvement, purchase of another parcel, cash to buy stocks, etc.).

Devise: A legal term that now means any real or personal property that is transferred under the terms of a will. Previously, the term only referred to real property.

Devisee: A person or entity who receives real or personal property under the terms of a will.

Discharge: The term used to describe the court order releasing the administrator or executor from any further duties regarding the estate being subjected to probate proceedings. This typically occurs when the duties have been completed but can also happen in the middle of the probate proceedings when the executor or administrator wishes to withdraw.

Donee: One who receives a gift. Thus, the beneficiary of a trust is generally referred to as the "donee."

Donor: One who, while alive, gives property to another, usually in the form of a trust.

Encumbrances: Debts (for example, taxes, mechanic's liens, judgment liens) and loans (for example, mortgages, deeds of trust, security interests) which use property as collateral for payment of the debt or loan are considered to encumber the property because they must be paid off before title to the property can pass from one owner to the next. Generally, the value of a person's ownership in such property (called the "equity") is measured by the market value of the property less the sum of all encumbrances.

Escheat: A legal doctrine under which property belonging to a deceased person with no heirs passes to the state.

Estate: Generally, the property you own when you die. There are different ways to measure your estate, depending on whether you are concerned with tax reduction (taxable estate), probate avoidance (probate estate), net worth (net estate) or attorney fees for probate (gross estate).

Estate Planning: The art of dying with the smallest taxable estate and probate estate possible while continuing to prosper when you're alive and yet passing your property to your loved ones with a minimum of fuss and expense.

Estate Taxes: See Federal Estate Taxes.

Equity: The difference between the fair market value of your real and personal property and the amount you still owe on it, if any.

Executor/Executrix: The person specified in a will to manage the estate, deal with the probate court, collect the assets and distribute them as the will has specified. If there is no will, or no executor nominated under the will, the probate court will appoint such a person, who is then called the "administrator" of the estate.

Expenses of Administration: The expenses incurred by an executor or administrator in carrying out the terms of a will or in administering an estate in accordance with the law applicable to persons dying intestate. These include probate court fees, fees charged by the executor or administrator, attorneys' fees, accountant fees and appraisers' fees.

Fair Market Value: That price for which an item of property would be purchased by a willing buyer, and sold by a willing seller, both knowing all the facts and neither being under any compulsion to buy or sell. All estates are appraised for their fair market value, and taxes are computed on the basis of the estate's net fair market value.

Federal Estate Taxes: Taxes imposed by the federal government on property as it passes from the dead to the living. The first $600,000 of property is exempt from tax. Also, all property left to a surviving spouse is exempt. Taxes are only imposed on property actually owned by the decedent at the time of her death. Thus, estate planning techniques designed to reduce taxes usually concentrate on the legal transfer of ownership of property while the decedent is still living, to minimize the amount of property owned at death. For example, a person can give away up to $10,000 per year per person free of gift and estate taxation.

Gift: Property passed to others for no return or substantially less than its actual market value is considered a gift when the giver ("donor") is still alive, and a bequest, legacy or devise when left by a will. Any gift of more than $10,000 per year to an individual is subject to the Federal Estate and Gift Tax. A donor is required to take the Estate and Gift Tax credit for gifts over $10,000 and the amount of the credit thus used up will not be available when the donor dies. In other words, if enough property is given away in gifts over $10,000 during a donor's life, the full amount of the donor's estate may be subject to federal estate taxation. On the other hand, if gifts are kept within the $10,000 annual limit, the tax exemption available to the estate will not be adversely affected.

Gross Estate: For federal estate tax filing purposes, the total of all property a decedent owned at the time of death, without regard to any debts or liens against such property or the expenses of administration of the estate. However, taxes are due only on the value of the property the decedent actually owned. The gross estate is also used when computing attorneys' fees for probating estates. These are established by statute as a percentage of the gross estate, the percentage varying with the size of the estate.

Heir: Any person who is entitled by law to inherit in the event an estate is not completely disposed of under a will, and any person or institution named in a will.

Heir at Law: A person entitled to inherit under intestate succession laws.

Holographic Will: A will in which the signature and material provisions are in the handwriting of the person making it. Any statement of testamentary intent contained in a holographic will may be either in the testator's own handwriting or as part of a commercially printed form will. Holographic wills are valid in California but they are not recommended as a means to dispose of property because the lack of witnesses raises the possibility of difficulties in proving the decedent's handwriting and/or mental competency.

Inheritance Tax: A tax imposed prior to June 1982 by the state of California on property owned by a deceased person. At present, there is no longer a state inheritance tax as such, but the federal estate tax return includes a table for figuring an amount that is paid to the state and allowed as a credit on the amount of federal tax owed. See Chapter 7, Section F.

Intangible Personal Property: Personal property that does not assume a physical form but which derives its value from the rights and powers that it gives to its owner. Thus, stock in a corporation, the right to receive a pension, and a patent or copyright, are all examples of intangible personal property. Intangible personal property is as a matter of law deemed to be located where the decedent resides at the time of her death, even if in fact a title slip (e.g., a stock or bond certificate) is physically located elsewhere.

Inter Vivos Trusts: See *Living Trusts*.

Intestate Succession: The method by which property is distributed when a person fails to leave a will. In such cases, California law and the law of all other states provide that the property be distributed in certain shares to the closest surviving relatives. The intestate succession laws of the various states are similar, but not identical. In most states, the surviving spouse, children, parents, siblings, nieces and nephews, and next of kin, inherit in that order. In California, intestate succession rules can be different depending on whether separate or community property is involved (see Chapter 3). The intestate succession laws are also used in the event certain close relatives are found to be pretermitted (that is, overlooked in the will) or if the beneficiary named to inherit the residuary estate predeceases the testator and there is no alternate.

Intestate: When a person dies without having made a will he is said to die "intestate." In that event, the estate is distributed according to the laws governing intestate succession.

Inventory: A complete listing of all property owned by the decedent at death that is filed with the probate court in the event a probate petition is filed.

Issue: A term generally meaning all natural children and their children down through the generations. Thus, a person's issue includes her children, grandchildren, great-grandchildren, and so on. Adopted children are considered the issue of their adopting parents and the children of the adopted children (and so on) are also considered issue. A term often used in place of issue is "lineal descendants."

Joint Tenancy: A way to hold title to jointly owned real or personal property. When two or more people own property as joint tenants, and one of the owners dies, the others automatically become owners of the deceased owner's share. Thus, if a parent and child own a house as joint tenants, and the parent dies, the child automatically becomes full owner. Because of this "right of survivorship," a joint tenancy interest in property does not go through probate, or, put another way, is not part of the probate estate. Instead, it goes directly to the surviving joint tenant(s) once some tax and transfer forms are completed. Placing property in joint tenancy is therefore a common tool used in estate planning to avoid probate. However, when property is placed in joint tenancy, a gift is made to any persons who become owners as a result. Thus, if Tom owns a house and places it in joint tenancy with Karen, Tom will have made a gift to Karen equal to one-half the house's value. This will normally have gift tax consequences if the gift is worth more than $10,000.

Kindred: All persons described as relatives of the decedent under the California Probate Code.

Lapse: The failure of a gift of property left in a will because when the testator dies, the beneficiary is deceased and no alternate has been named. California has a statute (termed an "anti-lapse" statute) which prevents gifts to relatives from lapsing unless the relative has no heirs of his or her own.

Lawful Issue: This phrase used to distinguish between legitimate and illegitimate children (and their issue). Now, the phrase means the same as "issue" and "lineal descendant."

Legacy: An old legal word meaning a transfer of personal property by will. The more common term for this type of transfer is bequest or devise.

Letters of Administration: A document issued by the court that designates an administrator of an estate and authorizes her to carry out her proper duties.

Letters Testamentary: The formal instrument of authority given to an executor by the probate court, empowering her to carry out her duties as executor. If an administrator has been appointed, letters of administration are granted.

Life Estate: The type of ownership a person possesses in real estate when he has only the right of possession for his life, and the ownership passes to someone else after his death.

Lineal Descendants: Persons who are in the direct line of descent from an ancestor, such as children, grandchildren and great grandchildren. The term does not include non-descendant relatives such as siblings, nieces and nephews, and cousins.

Living Trust: A trust set up while a person is alive and which remains under the control of that person during the remainder of her life. Also referred to as "inter vivos trusts," living trusts are an excellent way to minimize the value of property passing through probate. This is because they enable people (called "trustors") to specify that money or other property (called the "trust corpus") will pass directly to their beneficiaries at the time of their death, free of probate, and yet allow the trustors to continue to control the property during their lifetime and even end the trust or change the beneficiaries if they wish.

Marriage: A specific status conferred on a couple by the state. In California it is necessary to file papers with a county clerk and have a marriage ceremony conducted by authorized individuals in order to be married, unless there is a valid marriage in another state.

Marital Exemption: A deduction allowed by the federal estate tax laws for all property passed to a surviving spouse. This deduction (which really acts like an exemption) allows anyone, even a billionaire, to pass his entire estate to a surviving spouse without any tax at all.

Minor: In California, any person under 18 years of age.

Net Estate: The value of all property owned at death less liabilities.

Next of Kin: A term used to describe those living relatives of a decedent who are considered closest to the decedent under the California law governing intestate succession.

Personal Effects: Belongings of a personal nature, such as clothes and jewelry.

Personal Property: All items, both tangible and intangible, that are considered susceptible to ownership and that are not real property (for example, house, land, crops, cabin, etc.) are termed personal property. Property in an estate may be treated differently depending on whether it is considered "personal" or "real."

Personal Representative: The generic title applied to the person who is authorized to act on behalf of the decedent's estate. Almost always, this person is either the administrator or executor.

Per Stirpes: A Latin term meaning that a beneficiary inherits through a deceased ancestor by right of representation. In real life, the term is normally used in wills to control the way property should be divided when one or more joint beneficiaries of a gift has died before the testator, leaving living children of his own. For example, suppose Fred leaves his house jointly to his son Alan and his daughter Julie, and when Fred dies, Julie is alive but Alan has already died, leaving two living children. If Fred's will indicated that heirs of a deceased beneficiary were to receive the property "per stirpes," Julie would receive one-half of the property, and Alan's two children would take the other half per stirpes (that is, through Alan by right of representation). If, on the other hand, Fred's will indicated that the property was to be divided "per capita," Julie and the two grandchildren would each take a third.

Under California law, multiple heirs of an intestate estate also take their property per stirpes (termed "right of representation" in the law).

Petition: Any document filed with a court requesting a court order. In the probate context, the term is normally used to describe the initial document filed with the probate court requesting that the estate be probated, subsequent requests by the executor for court permission to take certain actions in respect to the estate, and a final request to discharge the executor or administrator from her duties.

Predeceased Spouse: The term applies to a spouse who has died before the decedent while married to him or her.

Pretermitted Heir: A child or spouse who, under certain circumstances, is not mentioned in the will and who the court believes was accidentally overlooked by the testator when making her will. This typically occurs when a child has been born or adopted after the will was made. Because state law presumes that persons want their children to inherit, the failure to provide for them in a will is considered unintentional unless there is evidence of an intent to disinherit. Mentioning them in the will and then not providing for them is considered sufficient evidence of intent to disinherit in California. If the court determines that an heir was pretermitted, that heir is entitled to receive the same share of the estate as she would have had the testator died intestate.

Probate: Generally, the process by which (1) the authenticity of your will (if any) is established, (2) your executor or administrator is appointed, (3) your debts and taxes are paid, (4) your heirs are identified and (5) property in your probate estate is distributed according to your will or intestate succession laws. Many people feel that formal court-supervised probate is a costly, time-consuming process which is best avoided if possible. Accordingly, instead of leaving their property in a will, they use probate avoidance devices, such as joint tenancy, trusts (including savings bank, "living," insurance and testamentary trusts) or life insurance.

Probate Estate: All the assets owned at death that require some form of legal proceeding before title may be transferred to the proper heirs. Accordingly property that passes automatically at death (property in a trust, life insurance proceeds or property held in joint tenancy) is not in the probate estate.

Public Administrator: A publicly-appointed person who handles the administration of an estate when no other person has been appointed as executor or administrator. This usually occurs when there are no known heirs.

Quasi-Community Property: Property acquired by a husband and wife during their marriage while residing outside California which would have been community property had it been acquired in California. California law treats it the same as community property. In essence, this means that in assessing whether or not a decedent's property is community property, the residence of the decedent when the property was acquired is irrelevant. An important exception: real property located outside California is not considered quasi-community property.

Real Property: Land, things affixed to the land such as trees and crops, buildings, stationary mobile homes, cabins and camps are all termed real property. All property that is not real property is termed personal property. See *Personal Property*.

Residence: The physical location that a person considers and treats as her home, both presently and for the indefinite future. For example, although congressmen typically spend most of their time in Washington D.C., they generally consider the states they come from as their residences. With rare exceptions, a person may have only one residence. The concept of residence is important to the subject of probate since a decedent's estate, with the exception of certain property located in other states, is subject to the laws of the state where the decedent was residing.

Residuary Estate: All the property contained in the probate estate except for property that has been specifically and effectively left to designated beneficiaries.

Right of Representation: When the descendants of a deceased beneficiary take the same share collectively that the deceased beneficiary would have taken if living at the time of a decedent's death. See *Per Stirpes*.

Self-Proving Will: A will that is executed in a way that allows the court to accept it as the true will of the decedent without further proof. In California, a will is self-proving when two witnesses to the will sign under penalty of perjury that they observed the testator sign it and that the testator told them it was his will.

Separate Property: In the probate context, all property owned by a married California decedent that is not considered community or quasi-community property. Separate property generally includes all property acquired by the decedent before the marriage and after a legal separation, property acquired by separate gift or inheritance at any time, property acquired from separate property funds, and property that has been designated separate property by agreement of the spouses.

Specific Bequest: A specific item, distinguished from all others of the same kind belonging to the testator, that is designated in the will as going to a specific beneficiary. If the specific item is no longer in the estate when the decedent dies, the bequest fails and resort cannot be made to other property of the decedent. Thus, if John leaves his 1954 Mercedes to Patti, and when John dies the 1954 Mercedes is long gone, Patti doesn't receive John's current car or the cash equivalent of the Mercedes.

Succession: The act of acquiring title to property when it has not been disposed of by will. Thus, when Abbie receives her mother's coin collection through "succession," she gets it under the intestate laws rather than as a beneficiary under a will.

Tangible Personal Property: Personal property that takes a tangible form, such as automobiles, furniture and heirlooms. Although such items as stock ownership and copyrights may be represented in the form of paper certificates, the actual property is not in physical form and is therefore considered intangible personal property. See *Intangible Personal Property*.

Taxable Estate: The fair market value of all assets owned by a decedent at date of death (gross estate) less certain allowable deductions, such as debts of the decedent, last illness and funeral expenses, and expenses of administering the decedent's estate (attorneys' fees, court costs and newspaper publication fees).

Tenancy in Common: The ownership of property by two or more persons in such a manner that each has an undivided interest in the whole and each can pass his or her interest upon death to his or her own heirs/beneficiaries instead of to the other owners (as is the case with joint tenancy). Also, unlike joint tenancies, the ownership shares need not be equal.

Testamentary Disposition: A disposition of property in a will.

Testate: One who has made a will; one who dies leaving a will. Thus, if Elmer dies having made a will, he is said to have died "testate."

Testator: A person who makes a will.

Transfer Agent: A representative of a corporation who is authorized to transfer ownership of a corporation's stock from one person to another. An executor or administrator must use a transfer agent when passing title to a decedent's stock to an heir or beneficiary.

Trust: A legal arrangement under which one person or institution (called a "trustee") controls property given by another person (termed a "trustor") for the benefit of a third person (called a "beneficiary"). The property itself is termed the "corpus" of the trust.

Uniform Transfers to Minors Act: A set of statutes adopted by the California legislature which provides a way for someone to give or leave property to a minor by appointing a "custodian" to manage the property for the minor. It is common for wills to use the Act to appoint a custodian for property left to minors in the will.

Will: A written document, signed and witnessed as required by law in which a person expresses what he wants to happen in respect to his property, children, pets, etc. after his death.

Appendix 1

1. California Probate Code Sections 13100-13106

2. Declaration Re Property Passing to Decedent's Surviving Spouse under Probate Code Section 13500

3. Who Inherits Under a Will?

4. Schedule of Assets

5. Affidavit—Death of Joint Tenant

6. Affidavit of Surviving Spouse Succeeding to Title to Community Property (California Probate Code 13500)

7. Affidavit Under California Probate Code Section 13100

California Probate Code Sections 13100-13106
Affidavit Procedure for Collection or Transfer of Personal Property

§13100. Successor of Decedent May Collect Personal Property Without Letters of Administration If Less Than $60,000

Excluding the property described in Section 13050, if the gross value of the decedent's real and personal property in this state does not exceed sixty thousand dollars ($60,000) and if 40 days have elapsed since the death of the decedent, the successor of the decedent may, without procuring letters of administration or awaiting probate of the will, do any of the following with respect to one or more particular items of property:

(a) Collect any particular item of property that is money due the decedent.

(b) Receive any particular item of property that is tangible personal property of the decedent.

(c) Have any particular item of property that is evidence of a debt, obligation, interest, right, security, or chose in action belonging to the decedent transferred, whether or not secured by a lien or real property.

(1986 ch. 783 oper. July 1, 1987)

§13101. Affidavit Shall Be Furnished to Holder of Decedent's Property

(a) To collect money, receive tangible personal property, or have evidences transferred under this chapter, an affidavit or a declaration under penalty of perjury under the laws of this state shall be furnished to the holder of the decedent's property stating all of the following:

(1) The decedent's name.

(2) The date and place of the decedent's death.

(3) "At least 40 days have elapsed since the death of the decedent, as shown in a certified copy of the decedent's death certificate attached to this affidavit or declaration."

(4) "No proceeding is now being or has been conducted in California for administration of the decedent's estate."

(5) "The gross value of the decedent's real and personal property in California, excluding the property described in Section 13050 of the California Probate Code, does not exceed sixty thousand dollars ($60,000)."

(6) A description of the property of the decedent that is to be paid, transferred, or delivered to the affiant or declarant.

(7) The name of the successor of the decedent (as defined in Section 13006 of the California Probate Code) to the described property.

(8) Either of the following, as appropriate:

(A) "The affiant or declarant is the successor of the decedent (as defined in Section 13006 of the California Probate Code) to the decedent's interest in the described property."

(B) "The affiant or declarant is authorized under Section 13051 of the California Probate Code to act on behalf of the successor of the decedent (as defined in Section 13006 of the California Probate Code) with respect to the decedent's interest in the described property."

(9) "No other person has a right to the interest of the decedent in the described property."

(10) "The affiant or declarant requests that the described property be paid, delivered, or transferred to the affiant or declarant."

(11) "The affiant or declarant affirms or declares under penalty of perjury under the laws of the State of California that the foregoing is true and correct."

(b) Where more than one person executes the affidavit or declaration under this section, the statements required by subdivision (a) shall be modified as appropriate to reflect that fact.

(c) A certified copy of the decedent's death certificate shall be attached to the affidavit or declaration.

(1986 ch. 783 oper. July 1, 1987)

§13102. Evidence of Ownership of Property Shall Be Presented with Affidavit to the Holder of Decedent's Property

(a) If the decedent had evidence of ownership of the property described in the affidavit or declaration and the holder of the property would have had the right to require presentation of the evidence of ownership before the duty of the holder to pay, deliver, or transfer the property to the decedent would have arisen, the evidence of ownership, if available, shall be presented with the affidavit or declaration to the holder of the decedent's property.

(b) If the evidence of ownership is not presented to the holder pursuant to subdivision (a), the holder may require, as a condition for the payment, delivery, or transfer of the property, that the person presenting the affidavit or declaration provide the holder with a bond or undertaking in a reasonable amount determined by the holder to be sufficient to indemnify the holder against all liability, claims, demands, loss, damages, costs, and expenses that the holder may incur or suffer by reason of the payment, delivery, or transfer of the property. Nothing in this subdivision precludes the holder and the person presenting the affidavit or declaration from dispensing with the requirement that a bond or undertaking be provided and instead entering into an agreement satisfactory to the holder concerning the duty of the person presenting the affidavit or declaration to indemnify the holder.

(1986 ch. 783 oper. July 1, 1987)

§13103. Inventory and Appraisement of Decedent's Real Property Shall Be Included with Affidavit

If the estate of the decedent includes any real property, the affidavit or declaration shall be accompanied by an inventory and appraisement of the real property. The form, content, and manner of making the inventory and appraisement of the real property shall be as set forth in Chapter 9 (commencing with Section 600) of Division 3. The inventory and appraisement shall be made by a probate referee selected by the affiant or declarant from those probate referees appointed by the Controller under Section 1305 to appraise property in the county where the real property is located.

(1986 ch. 783 oper. July 1, 1987)

§13104. Reasonable Proof of Identity of Persons Executing Affidavit Shall Be Provided to Holder of Decedent's Property

(a) Reasonable proof of the identity of each person executing the affidavit or declaration shall be provided to the holder of the decedent's property.

(b) Reasonable proof of identity is provided for the purposes of this section if both of the following requirements are satisfied:

(1) The person executing the affidavit or declaration is personally known to the holder.

(2) The person executes the affidavit or declaration in the presence of the holder.

(c) If the affidavit or declaration is executed in the presence of the holder, a written statement under penalty of perjury by a person personally known to the holder affirming the identity of the person executing the affidavit or declaration is reasonable proof of identity for the purposes of this section.

(d) If the affidavit or declaration is executed in the presence of the holder, the holder may reasonably rely on any of the following as reasonable proof of identity for the purposes of this section:

(1) An identification card or driver's license issued by the Department of Motor Vehicles of this state that is current or was issued during the preceding five years.

(2) A passport issued by the Department of State of the United States that is current or was issued during the preceding five years.

(3) Any of the following documents if the document is current or was issued during the preceding five years and contains a photograph and description of the person named on it, is signed by the person, and bears a serial or other identifying number:

(A) A passport issued by a foreign government that has been stamped by the United States Immigration and Naturalization Service.

(B) A driver's license issued by a state other than California.

(C) An identification card issued by a state other than California.

(D) An identification card issued by any branch of the armed forces of the United States.

(e) For the purposes of this section, a notary public's certificate of acknowledgment identifying the person executing the affidavit of declaration is reasonable proof of identity of the person executing the affidavit or declaration.

(f) Unless the affidavit or declaration contains a notary public's certificate of acknowledgment of the identity of the person, the holder shall note on the affidavit or declaration either that the person executing the affidavit or declaration is personally known or a description of the identification provided by the person executing the affidavit or declaration.

(1986 ch. 783 oper. July 1, 1987)

§13105. Entitlement of Successor of Decedent to Have Property of Decedent Transferred When Requirements Are Met

(a) If the requirements of Sections 13100 to 13104, inclusive, are satisfied:

(1) The person or persons executing the affidavit or declaration as successor of the decedent are entitled to have the property described in the affidavit or declaration paid, delivered, or transferred to them.

(2) A transfer agent of a security described in the affidavit or declaration shall change the registered ownership on the books of the corporation from the decedent to the person or persons executing the affidavit or declaration as successor of the decedent.

(b) If the holder of the decedent's property refuses to pay, deliver, or transfer any personal property or evidence thereof to the successor of the decedent within a reasonable time, the successor may recover the property or compel its payment, delivery, or transfer in an action brought for that purpose against the holder of the property. If an action is brought against the holder under this section, the court shall award attorney's fees to the person or persons bringing the action if the court finds that the holder of the decedent's property acted unreasonably in refusing to pay, deliver, or transfer the property to them as required by subdivision (a)

(1986 ch. 783 oper. July 1, 1987)

§13106. Reception of Affidavit by Holder—Sufficient Acquittance

(a) If the requirements of Sections 13100 to 13104, inclusive, are satisfied, receipt by the holder of the decedent's property of the affidavit or declaration constitutes sufficient acquittance for the payment of money, delivery of property, or changing registered ownership of property pursuant to this chapter and discharges the holder from any further liability with respect to the money or property. The holder may rely in good faith on the statements in the affidavit or declaration and has no duty to inquire into the truth of any statement in the affidavit or declaration.

(b) If the requirements of Sections 13100 to 13104, inclusive, are satisfied, the holder of the decedent's property is not liable for any taxes due to this state by reason of paying money, delivering property, or changing registered ownership of property pursuant to this chapter.

(1986 ch. 783 oper. July 1, 1987)

Declaration Regarding Property Passing to Decedent's Surviving Spouse Under Probate Code § 13500

The undersigned declares:

1. _____
died on _____, 19___, and on the date of
death was a resident of California.

2. On the date of death, decedent was married to
_____, who survives the decedent.

3. Among the decedent's assets was
_____ (insert
description of bank account, savings and loan account or
safe-deposit box, by account or box number, name and
location of bank and balance of account).

4. The decedent's interest in the described
property passed to decedent's surviving spouse upon
decedent's death by the terms of decedent's will and any
codicils to it.

or

4. The decedent died intestate and the above
described property is the community property of the
decedent and the decedent's surviving spouse, having been
acquired during the parties' marriage while domiciled in
California, and not having been acquired by gift or
inheritance, and passes to the decedent's surviving
spouse by the laws of inheritance governing passage of
title from decedent in the absence of a will.

5. Decedent's surviving spouse therefore is
entitled to have the described property delivered to that
spouse without probate administration, pursuant to
California Probate Code § 13500.

The undersigned declares under penalty of perjury
that the foregoing is true and correct and that this
declaration was executed on _____, 19___, at
_____, California.

_____

Who Inherits Under a Will?

Beneficiaries Named in the Will	Property Inherited

Estate of_____**, Deceased**

Schedule of Assets

Description of Asset	A Total Value of Asset on Date/Death	B How is Asset Owned?	C Portion Owned by Decedent	D Value of Decedent's Interest	E Probate or Non- Probate
1. **Cash Items:**					
Cash in decedent's possession:					
Uncashed checks payable to decedent:	_____	_____	_____	_____	_____
_____	_____	_____	_____	_____	_____
_____	_____	_____	_____	_____	_____
_____	_____	_____	_____	_____	_____
2. **Bank and Savings and Loan Accounts:** (Name and location of bank, type of account, account number, account balance)					
_____	_____	_____	_____	_____	_____
_____	_____	_____	_____	_____	_____
_____	_____	_____	_____	_____	_____
_____	_____	_____	_____	_____	_____
_____	_____	_____	_____	_____	_____
3. **Real Property:** (common address, brief description)					
_____	_____	_____	_____	_____	_____
_____	_____	_____	_____	_____	_____
_____	_____	_____	_____	_____	_____
_____	_____	_____	_____	_____	_____
_____	_____	_____	_____	_____	_____
4. **Securities:** <u>Stock:</u> (Name of company, type and number of shares)					
_____	_____	_____	_____	_____	_____
_____	_____	_____	_____	_____	_____
_____	_____	_____	_____	_____	_____
_____	_____	_____	_____	_____	_____

Bonds:
(Type of bond, face amount)

_____ ___ ___ ___ ___ ___
_____ ___ ___ ___ ___ ___
_____ ___ ___ ___ ___ ___
_____ ___ ___ ___ ___ ___

U.S. Savings Bonds/Treasury Bills:
(Series, amount, date of issue)

_____ ___ ___ ___ ___ ___
_____ ___ ___ ___ ___ ___
_____ ___ ___ ___ ___ ___
_____ ___ ___ ___ ___ ___

    Mutual funds:
(Name of fund, number of shares)

_____ ___ ___ ___ ___ ___
_____ ___ ___ ___ ___ ___
_____ ___ ___ ___ ___ ___
_____ ___ ___ ___ ___ ___

5. Insurance:
(Name of company, policy number, name
of beneficiary, name of owner)
Policies on decedent's life:

_____ ___ ___ ___ ___ ___
_____ ___ ___ ___ ___ ___
_____ ___ ___ ___ ___ ___
_____ ___ ___ ___ ___ ___

Policies owned by decedent on another:

_____ ___ ___ ___ ___ ___
_____ ___ ___ ___ ___ ___
_____ ___ ___ ___ ___ ___
_____ ___ ___ ___ ___ ___

6. **Retirement and Death Benefits:**
(Description, beneficiary, amount)
Employee Benefits:

_____ ___ ___ ___ ___ ___
_____ ___ ___ ___ ___ ___
_____ ___ ___ ___ ___ ___

Pension, profit-sharing, savings plans:

_____ ___ ___ ___ ___ ___
_____ ___ ___ ___ ___ ___
_____ ___ ___ ___ ___ ___

Social Security/Railroad Retirement:

_____   _____ _____ _____ _____ _____

7. **Amounts Due the Decedent:**
   (Name of payor, amount)

_____   _____ _____ _____ _____ _____
_____   _____ _____ _____ _____ _____
_____   _____ _____ _____ _____ _____

8. **Promissory Notes:**
   (Name of payor, date amount, balance)

_____   _____ _____ _____ _____ _____
_____   _____ _____ _____ _____ _____
_____   _____ _____ _____ _____ _____
_____   _____ _____ _____ _____ _____

9. **Tangible Personal Property:**
   (Household furniture, furnishings,
   personal effects, books, jewelry, artwork,
   valuable collections, antiques, etc.)

_____   _____ _____ _____ _____ _____
_____   _____ _____ _____ _____ _____
_____   _____ _____ _____ _____ _____
_____   _____ _____ _____ _____ _____
_____   _____ _____ _____ _____ _____
_____   _____ _____ _____ _____ _____
_____   _____ _____ _____ _____ _____

10. **Automobiles:**
    (Year, make, model)

_____   _____ _____ _____ _____ _____
_____   _____ _____ _____ _____ _____
_____   _____ _____ _____ _____ _____

11. **Business Interests:**
    (Partnerships, sole proprietorships,
    family corporations, brief description)

_____   _____ _____ _____ _____ _____
_____   _____ _____ _____ _____ _____
_____   _____ _____ _____ _____ _____

12. **Other Assets:**
    (Copyrights, royalty interests, patents,
    any other property not listed above)

_____   _____ _____ _____ _____ _____
_____   _____ _____ _____ _____ _____
_____   _____ _____ _____ _____ _____
_____   _____ _____ _____ _____ _____
_____   _____ _____ _____ _____ _____

Total Value of Decedent's Gross Estate . . . . $_____

Deductions (for Federal Estate Tax Purposes):

a. Debts owned by decedent at date of death: Amount

_____ $_____

b. Expenses of estate administration:

_____   _____

c. Last illness expenses:

_____   _____

_____   _____

d. Funeral expenses:

_____   _____

e. Sales contracts (automobiles, furniture, television):

_____   _____

f. Mortgages/promissory notes due:

_____   _____

                                    Total: $_____

RECORDING REQUESTED BY

AND WHEN RECORDED MAIL TO

Name _____

Street Address _____

City & State _____

_____ SPACE ABOVE THIS LINE FOR RECORDER'S USE _____

Affidavit — Death of Joint Tenant

A.P.N. _____

STATE OF CALIFORNIA, }
COUNTY OF_____ } ss.

_____ , of legal age, being first duly sworn, deposes and says:

That_____ , the decedent mentioned in the attached certified copy of Certificate of Death, is the same person as_____ named as one of the parties in that certain _____ dated_____ ,

executed by_____

to_____ ,

as joint tenants, recorded as Instrument No._____ , on_____ , in Book/Reel_____ , Page/Image_____ , of Official Records of_____ County, California, covering the following described property situated in the_____ _____ . County of_____ , State of California:

That the value of all real and personal property owned by said decedent at date of death, including the full value of the property above described, did not then exceed the sum of $_____ .

Dated_____   _____

SUBSCRIBED AND SWORN TO before me   _____

this_____ day of_____

Signature_____

(This area for official notarial seal)

Title Order No._____   Escrow or Loan No._____

WHEN RECORDED MAIL TO:

AFFIDAVIT OF SURVIVING SPOUSE
SUCCEEDING TO TITLE TO COMMUNITY PROPERTY

I, the undersigned, declare that:

1. The real property described below is the community property of the under-signed and _____.

2. _____ died on _____, 19___, as evidenced by the attached certified copy of the decedent's death certificate.

3. I am the surviving spouse of _____, and title to the real property described below devolved to me under the provisions of Section 13500 of the California Probate Code.

4. I have not filed in any court of competent jurisdiction an election under Section 13502 of the California Probate Code to subject the real property described below to administration.

5. _____ is the person named in that certain deed, dated_____, 19___, executed by_____

_____ to _____

recorded as instrument No. _____, on _____, 19___, in

Book No. _____, Page No. _____, of Official Records of _____

County, California, covering the property described below, which is situated in the City

of _____, County of _____, State of

California:

I certify (or declare) under penalty of perjury under the laws of the State of California that the foregoing is true and correct.

DATED: _____, 19___   _____

STATE OF CALIFORNIA   )
COUNTY OF _____) SS.

On _____, 19___, before me, a notary public for the State of California, personally appeared _____, personally known to me (or proved to me on the basis of satisfactory evidence) to be the person whose name is subscribed to this instrument, and acknowledged that _____executed the same.
WITNESS my hand and official seal.

_____
NOTARY PUBLIC

I certify (or declare) under penalty of perjury
under the laws of the State of California that the foregoing
is true and correct.

Dated: _____, 19___

_____

STATE OF CALIFORNIA   )
) ss.
COUNTY OF _____   )

   On _____, 19___, before me, a notary
public for the State of California, personally appeared
_____, personally known to me (or
proved to me on the basis of satisfactory evidence) to be the
person whose name is subscribed to this instrument, and
acknowledged that _(he/she)_ executed the same.

   WITNESS my hand and official seal.

_____
                    Notary Public

AFFIDAVIT
FOR COLLECTION OF PERSONAL PROPERTY
UNDER CALIFORNIA PROBATE CODE §13100

The undersigned state(s) as follows:

1. _____ died on _____, 19___, in the County of _____, State of California.

2. At least 40 days have elapsed since the death of the decedent, as shown by the attached certified copy of the decedent's death certificate.

3. No proceeding is now being or has been conducted in California for administration of the decedent's estate.

4. The gross value of the decedent's real and personal property in California, excluding the property described in Section 13050 of the California Probate Code, does not exceed $60,000.

5. ☐ An inventory and appraisement of the real property included in the decedent's estate is attached; ☐ There is no real property in the decedent's estate.

6. The following property is to be paid, transferred, or delivered to the undersigned under the provisions of California Probate Code Section 13100:

7. The successor(s) of the decedent, as defined in Probate Code Section 13006, is/are: _____.

8. The undersigned ☐ is/are successor(s) of the decedent to the decedent's interest in the described property, or ☐ is/are authorized under California Probate Code Section 13051 to act on behalf of the successor(s) of the decedent with respect to the decedent's interest in the described property.

9. No other person has a right to the interest of the decedent in the described property.

10. The undersigned request(s) that the described property be paid, delivered or transferred to the undersigned.

I/we declare under penalty of perjury under the laws of the State of California that the foregoing is true and correct.

DATED: _____, 19___

_____   _____

_____   _____

_____   _____

(See reverse side for Notarial Acknowledgments)

STATE OF CALIFORNIA, COUNTY OF *(specify)*:

(Name): , whose name is subscribed to the foregoing affidavit,

on *(date)*: personally appeared before me and acknowledged that he or she executed the affidavit, and

a. ☐ is known to me to be that person, or

b. ☐ was proved to be that person by satisfactory evidence.

[NOTARY SEAL]

_____
(SIGNATURE OF NOTARY PUBLIC)

STATE OF CALIFORNIA, COUNTY OF *(specify)*:

(Name): , whose name is subscribed to the foregoing affidavit,

on *(date)*: personally appeared before me and acknowledged that he or she executed the affidavit, and

a. ☐ is known to me to be that person, or

b. ☐ was proved to be that person by satisfactory evidence.

[NOTARY SEAL]

_____
(SIGNATURE OF NOTARY PUBLIC)

STATE OF CALIFORNIA, COUNTY OF *(specify)*:

(Name): , whose name is subscribed to the foregoing affidavit,

on *(date)*: personally appeared before me and acknowledged that he or she executed the affidavit, and

a. ☐ is known to me to be that person, or

b. ☐ was proved to be that person by satisfactory evidence.

[NOTARY SEAL]

_____
(SIGNATURE OF NOTARY PUBLIC)

STATE OF CALIFORNIA, COUNTY OF *(specify)*:

(Name): , whose name is subscribed to the foregoing affidavit,

on *(date)*: personally appeared before me and acknowledged that he or she executed the affidavit, and

a. ☐ is known to me to be that person, or

b. ☐ was proved to be that person by satisfactory evidence.

[NOTARY SEAL]

_____
(SIGNATURE OF NOTARY PUBLIC)

STATE OF CALIFORNIA, COUNTY OF *(specify)*:

(Name): , whose name is subscribed to the foregoing affidavit,

on *(date)*: personally appeared before me and acknowledged that he or she executed the affidavit, and

a. ☐ is known to me to be that person, or

b. ☐ was proved to be that person by satisfactory evidence.

[NOTARY SEAL]

_____
(SIGNATURE OF NOTARY PUBLIC)

STATE OF CALIFORNIA, COUNTY OF *(specify)*:

(Name): , whose name is subscribed to the foregoing affidavit,

on *(date)*: personally appeared before me and acknowledged that he or she executed the affidavit, and

a. ☐ is known to me to be that person, or

b. ☐ was proved to be that person by satisfactory evidence.

[NOTARY SEAL]

_____
(SIGNATURE OF NOTARY PUBLIC)

Appendix 2

1. Affidavit Re Real Property of Small Value ($10,000 or Less)
2. Petition to Determine Succession to Real Property (Estates of $60,000 or Less)
3. Order Determining Succession to Real Property
4. Petition for Probate
5. Notice of Petition to Administer Estate
6. Proof of Subscribing Witness
7. Proof of Holographic Instrument
8. Order for Probate
9. Letters
10. Duties and Liabilities of Personal Representative
11. Application and Order Appointing Probate Referee
12. Notice of Proposed Action
13. Inventory and Appraisement
14. Inventory and Appraisement Attachment
15. Notice of Administration to Creditors
16. Allowance or Rejection of Creditor's Claim
17. Final Discharge and Order
18. Spousal Property Petition
19. Notice of Hearing
20. Spousal Property Order

ATTORNEY OR PARTY WITHOUT ATTORNEY *(Name and Address)* *(After recording return to)* :

TELEPHONE NO.:

FOR COURT USE ONLY

ATTORNEY FOR *(Name)*:

SUPERIOR COURT OF CALIFORNIA, COUNTY OF

STREET ADDRESS:

MAILING ADDRESS:

CITY AND ZIP CODE:

BRANCH NAME:

MATTER OF (NAME):

DECEDENT

CASE NUMBER:

AFFIDAVIT RE REAL PROPERTY OF SMALL VALUE
($10,000 or Less)

FOR RECORDER'S USE ONLY

1. Decedent *(name)* :   died on *(date)* :

2. Decedent died at *(city, state)* :

3. At least **six months** have elapsed since the date of death of decedent as shown in the certified copy of decedent's death certificate attached to this affidavit. *(Attach a certified copy of decedent's death certificate.)*

4. a. ☐ Decedent was domiciled in this county at the time of death.

   b. ☐ Decedent was **not** domiciled in California at the time of death. Decedent died owning real property in this county.

5. a. The following is a **legal description** of decedent's real property claimed by the declarants *(copy description from deed or other legal instrument)* :

     ☐ described in an attachment labeled "Attachment 5a."

   b. Decedent's interest in this real property is as follows *(specify)* :

6. Each declarant is a successor of decedent (as defined in Probate Code section 13006) and a successor to decedent's interest in the real property described in item 5a, and no other person has a superior right, because each declarant is

   a. ☐ **(will)** a beneficiary who succeeded to the property under decedent's will. *(Attach a copy of the will.)*

   b. ☐ **(no will)** a person who succeeded to the property under Probate Code sections 6401 and 6402.

7. Names and addresses of each guardian or conservator of decedent's estate at date of death

   ☐ none   ☐ are as follows* *(specify)* :

8. The **gross value** of all real property in decedent's estate located in California as shown by the inventory and appraisal, excluding the real property described in section 13050 of the Probate Code (joint tenancy, property passing to decedent's spouse, etc.), does not exceed $10,000.

9. An **inventory and appraisal** of decedent's **real property** in California is attached. The inventory and appraisal was made by a probate referee appointed for the county in which the property is located. *(You may use Judicial Council form DE-160.)*

10. No proceeding is now being or has been conducted in California for administration of decedent's estate.

(Continued on reverse)

*You must personally serve or mail a copy of this affidavit with attachments to each person named in item 7.

Form Adopted by the
Judicial Council of California
DE-305 [Rev. January 1, 1989]

AFFIDAVIT RE REAL PROPERTY OF SMALL VALUE
(Probate)

Probate Code, § 13200

11. Funeral expenses, expenses of last illness, and all known unsecured debts of the decedent have been paid. *[NOTE: You may be personally liable for decedent's unsecured debts up to the fair market value of the real property and any income you receive from it.]*

I declare under penalty of perjury under the laws of the state of California that the foregoing is true and correct.

Date:

. . . .
Date: (TYPE OR PRINT NAME)   ▶   (SIGNATURE OF DECLARANT)

. . . .
Date: (TYPE OR PRINT NAME)   ▶   (SIGNATURE OF DECLARANT)

. . . .
       (TYPE OR PRINT NAME)   ▶   (SIGNATURE OF DECLARANT)

NOTARY ACKNOWLEDGMENTS   *(NOTE: No notary acknowledgment may be affixed as a rider (small strip) to this page. If additional notary acknowledgments are required, they must be attached as 8½- by 11-inch pages.)*

STATE OF CALIFORNIA, COUNTY OF *(specify)*:

(Name):   , whose name is subscribed to the foregoing affidavit,
on *(date)*:   personally appeared before me and acknowledged that he or she executed the affidavit, and

a. ☐   is known to me to be that person, or

b. ☐   was proved to be that person by satisfactory evidence.

[NOTARY SEAL]

_____
(SIGNATURE OF NOTARY PUBLIC)

STATE OF CALIFORNIA, COUNTY OF *(specify)*:

(Name):   , whose name is subscribed to the foregoing affidavit,
on *(date)*:   personally appeared before me and acknowledged that he or she executed the affidavit, and

a. ☐   is known to me to be that person, or

b. ☐   was proved to be that person by satisfactory evidence.

[NOTARY SEAL]

_____
(SIGNATURE OF NOTARY PUBLIC)

STATE OF CALIFORNIA, COUNTY OF *(specify)*:

(Name):   , whose name is subscribed to the foregoing affidavit,
on *(date)*:   personally appeared before me and acknowledged that he or she executed the affidavit, and

a. ☐   is known to me to be that person, or

b. ☐   was proved to be that person by satisfactory evidence.

[NOTARY SEAL]

_____
(SIGNATURE OF NOTARY PUBLIC)

[SEAL]

CLERK'S CERTIFICATE

I certify that the foregoing, including any attached notary acknowledgements and any attached legal description of the property (but **excluding** other attachments), is a true and correct copy of the original affidavit on file in my office. *(Certified copies of this affidavit do not include the (1) death certificate, (2) will, or (3) inventory and appraisal. See Probate Code section 13202.)*

Date: _____   Clerk, by _____ , Deputy

ATTORNEY FOR *(Name)*:

SUPERIOR COURT OF CALIFORNIA, COUNTY OF

STREET ADDRESS:

MAILING ADDRESS:

CITY AND ZIP CODE:

BRANCH NAME:

MATTER OF (NAME):

DECEDENT

PETITION TO DETERMINE SUCCESSION TO REAL PROPERTY (Estates $60,000 or Less)	CASE NUMBER:
	HEARING DATE:
	DEPT.: TIME:

1. **Petitioner** *(name of each)*:

   requests a determination that the real property described in this petition is property passing to petitioner and that no administration of decedent's estate is necessary.

2. Decedent *(name)*:
   a. Date of death:
   b. Place of death *(city, state)*:

3. At least **40 days** have elapsed since the date of decedent's death.

4. a. ☐ Decedent was a resident of this county at the time of death.
   b. ☐ Decedent was **not** a resident of California at the time of death. Decedent died owning property in this county.

5. Decedent died ☐ intestate ☐ testate and a copy of the will and any codicil is affixed as attachment 5 or 12a.

6. a. No proceeding for the administration of decedent's estate is being conducted or has been conducted in California.
   b. No administration of decedent's estate is necessary in California.

7. Proceedings for the administration of decedent's estate in another jurisdiction
   a. ☐ have **not** been commenced.
   b. ☐ have been commenced ☐ and completed.
      (Specify state, county, court, and case number):

8. The **gross value** of all real and personal property in decedent's estate located in California as shown by the inventory and appraisal attached to this petition, excluding the property described in Probate Code section 13050 (joint tenancy, property passing to decedent's spouse, etc.), does not exceed $60,000. *(Attach an inventory and appraisal as attachment 8.)*

9. a. The decedent is survived by
   (1) ☐ spouse ☐ no spouse as follows: ☐ divorced or never married ☐ spouse deceased
   (2) ☐ child as follows: ☐ natural or adopted ☐ natural adopted by a third party ☐ step ☐ foster
       ☐ no child
   (3) ☐ issue of a predeceased child ☐ no issue of a predeceased child
   b. Petitioner ☐ has no actual knowledge of facts ☐ has actual knowledge of facts reasonably giving rise to a parent-child relationship under Probate Code section 6408(b).
   c. ☐ All surviving children and issue of predeceased children have been listed in item 14.

10. *(Complete if decedent was survived by (1) a spouse but no issue (only a or b apply); or (2) no spouse or issue. Check the **first** box that applies)*:
    a. ☐ The decedent is survived by a parent or parents who are listed in item 14.
    b. ☐ The decedent is survived by a brother, sister, or issue of a deceased brother or sister, all of whom are listed in item 14.
    c. ☐ The decedent is survived by other heirs under Probate Code section 6400 et seq., all of whom are listed in item 14.

11. The **legal description** of decedent's real property in California passing to petitioner and decedent's interest in the property are stated in attachment 11. *(Attach the legal description of the real property and state decedent's interest.)*

(Continued on reverse)

Form Approved by the
Judicial Council of California
DE-310 [Rev. January 1, 1989]

PETITION TO DETERMINE SUCCESSION TO REAL PROPERTY
(Probate)

Probate Code, § 13151

12. Each petitioner is a successor of decedent (as defined in Probate Code section 13006) and a successor to decedent's interest in the real property described in item 11 because each petitioner is

a. ☐ **(will)** a beneficiary who succeeded to the property under decedent's will.[1]

b. ☐ **(no will)** a person who succeeded to the property under Probate Code sections 6401 and 6402.

13. The specific property interest claimed by each petitioner in the real property described in item 11 ☐ is stated in attachment 13 ☐ is as follows (specify):

14. The names, relationships, ages, and residence or mailing addresses of (a) all persons checked in items 9 or 10, (b) all other heirs of decedent, and (c) all devisees of decedent (persons designated in the will to receive any property), so far as known to petitioner, **including** stepchild and foster child heirs and devisees to whom notice is to be given

☐ are listed below ☐ are listed in attachment 14.

NAME AND RELATIONSHIP	AGE	RESIDENCE OR MAILING ADDRESS

15. The names and addresses of all persons named as executors in decedent's will

☐ are listed below ☐ are listed in attachment 15 ☐ none named ☐ no will.

16. ☐ The petitioner is the trustee of a trust that is a devisee under decedent's will. The names and addresses of all persons interested in the trust, as determined in cases of future interests pursuant to paragraphs (1), (2), or (3) of subdivision (a) of Probate Code section 15804 ☐ are listed in attachment 16.

17. ☐ Decedent's estate was under a ☐ guardianship ☐ conservatorship at decedent's death. The names and addresses of all persons serving as guardian or conservator ☐ are listed in attachment 17.

18. ☐ Number of pages attached:

I declare under penalty of perjury under the laws of the State of California that the foregoing is true and correct.

Date:

....
(TYPE OR PRINT NAME)

▶ _____
(SIGNATURE OF PETITIONER)

....
(TYPE OR PRINT NAME)

▶ _____
(SIGNATURE OF PETITIONER)

[1] See Probate Code section 13151(c) for the requirement that a copy of the will be attached in certain instances. If required, include as attachment 5 or 12a.

ATTORNEY OR PARTY WITHOUT ATTORNEY *(Name and Address)*   TELEPHONE NO.:   **FOR RECORDER'S USE ONLY**

☐ Recording requested by and return to:

ATTORNEY FOR *(Name)*:

SUPERIOR COURT OF CALIFORNIA, COUNTY OF

STREET ADDRESS:

MAILING ADDRESS:

CITY AND ZIP CODE:

BRANCH NAME:

MATTER OF (NAME):

DECEDENT

ORDER DETERMINING SUCCESSION TO REAL PROPERTY (Estates $60,000 or Less)	CASE NUMBER:

1. Date of hearing: Time: Dept.:   Rm.: | **FOR COURT USE ONLY** |

THE COURT FINDS

2. All notices required by law have been given.
3. Decedent died on *(date)*:
   a. ☐ a resident of the California county named above.
   b. ☐ a nonresident of California and left an estate in the county named above.
   c. ☐ intestate ☐ testate.
4. At least 40 days have elapsed since the date of decedent's death.
5. No proceeding for the administration of decedent's estate is being conducted or has been conducted in California.
6. The gross value of decedent's real and personal property in California, excluding property described in Probate Code section 13050, does not exceed $60,000.
7. Each petitioner is a successor of decedent (as defined in Probate Code section 13006) and a successor to decedent's interest in the real property described in item 9a because each petitioner is
   a. ☐ **(will)** a beneficiary who succeeded to the property under decedent's will.
   b. ☐ **(no will)** a person who succeeded to the property under Probate Code sections 6401 and 6402.

THE COURT FURTHER FINDS AND ORDERS

8. No administration of decedent's estate is necessary in California.
9. a. The following described real property is property of decedent passing to each petitioner *(give legal description)*:
      ☐ described in attachment 9a.

   b. Each petitioner's **name** and specific property interest ☐ is stated in attachment 9b ☐ is as follows *(specify)*:

10. ☐ Other *(specify)*:

Date: _____   _____
                                          JUDGE OF THE SUPERIOR COURT

11. ☐ Number of pages attached: ☐ Signature follows last attachment

Form Approved by the
Judicial Council of California
DE-315 [Rev. January 1, 1989]

ORDER DETERMINING SUCCESSION TO REAL PROPERTY
(Probate)

Probate Code, § 13154

ATTORNEY OR PARTY WITHOUT ATTORNEY *(Name and Address)*:	TELEPHONE NO.:	FOR COURT USE ONLY

ATTORNEY FOR *(Name)*:

SUPERIOR COURT OF CALIFORNIA, COUNTY OF

STREET ADDRESS:

MAILING ADDRESS:

CITY AND ZIP CODE:

BRANCH NAME:

ESTATE OF (NAME):

DECENT

PETITION FOR	☐ Probate of Will and for Letters Testamentary	CASE NUMBER:
	☐ Probate of Will and for Letters of Administration with Will Annexed	
	☐ Letters of Administration	HEARING DATE:
(For deaths after December 31, 1984)	☐ Letters of Special Administration	
	☐ Authorization to Administer Under the Independent Administration of Estates Act ☐ with limited authority	DEPT.: TIME:

1. Publication will be in *(specify name of newspaper)*:

    a. ☐ Publication requested.

    b. ☐ Publication to be arranged.

    ▶ _____

    (Signature of attorney or party without attorney)

2. **Petitioner** *(name of each)*:

    requests

    a. ☐ decedent's will and codicils, if any, be admitted to probate.

    b. ☐ *(name)*:

    be appointed (1) ☐ executor   (3) ☐ administrator

    (2) ☐ administrator with will annexed   (4) ☐ special administrator

    and Letters issue upon qualification.

    c. ☐ that ☐ full ☐ limited   authority be granted to administer under the Independent Administration of Estates Act.

    d. ☐ bond not be required for the reasons stated in item 3d.

    ☐ $ bond be fixed. It will be furnished by an admitted surety insurer or as otherwise provided by law. *(Specify reasons in Attachment 2d if the amount is different from the maximum required by Probate Code, § 8482.)*

    ☐ $ in deposits in a blocked account be allowed. Receipts will be filed. *(Specify institution and location)*:

3. a. Decedent died on *(date)*:   at *(place)*:

    ☐ a resident of the county named above.

    ☐ a nonresident of California and left an estate in the county named above located at *(specify location permitting publication in the newspaper named in item 1)*:

    b. Street address, city, and county of decedent's residence at time of death:

    c. Character and estimated value of the property of the estate

    (1) Personal property . . . . $

    (2) Annual gross income from

    (i) ☐ real property . . . . $

    (ii) ☐ personal property . . . . . . $

    Total . . . . . . $

    (3) Real property: $ *(If full authority under the Independent Administration of Estates Act is requested, state the fair market value of the real property less encumbrances.)*

    d. ☐ Will waives bond. ☐ Special administrator is the named executor and the will waives bond.

    ☐ All beneficiaries are adults and have waived bond, and the will does not require a bond. *(Affix waiver as Attachment 3d.)*

    ☐ All heirs at law are adults and have waived bond. *(Affix waiver as Attachment 3d.)*

    ☐ Sole personal representative is a corporate fiduciary.

    (Continued on reverse)

3. e. ☐ Decedent died intestate.

☐ Copy of decedent's will dated: ☐ codicils dated: are affixed as Attachment 3e.

☐ The will and all codicils are self-proving (Probate Code, § 8220).

f. **Appointment of personal representative** (check all applicable boxes)

> Attach a typed copy of a holographic will and a translation of a foreign language will.

(1) Appointment of executor or administrator with will annexed

☐ Proposed executor is named as executor in the will and consents to act.

☐ No executor is named in the will.

☐ Proposed personal representative is a nominee of a person entitled to Letters. (Affix nomination as Attachment 3f(1).)

☐ Other named executors will not act because of ☐ death ☐ declination ☐ other reasons (specify in Attachment 3f(1)).

(2) Appointment of administrator

☐ Petitioner is a person entitled to Letters. (If necessary, explain priority in Attachment 3f(2).)

☐ Petitioner is a nominee of a person entitled to Letters. (Affix nomination as Attachment 3f(2).)

☐ Petitioner is related to the decedent as (specify):

(3) ☐ Appointment of special administrator requested. (Specify grounds and requested powers in Attachment 3f(3).)

g. Proposed personal representative is a ☐ resident of California ☐ nonresident of California (affix statement of permanent address as Attachment 3g) ☐ resident of the United States ☐ nonresident of the United States.

4. ☐ Decedent's will does not preclude administration of this estate under the Independent Administration of Estates Act.

5. a. The decedent is survived by

(1) ☐ spouse ☐ no spouse as follows: ☐ divorced or never married ☐ spouse deceased

(2) ☐ child as follows: ☐ natural or adopted ☐ natural adopted by a third party ☐ step ☐ foster

☐ no child

(3) ☐ issue of a predeceased child ☐ no issue of a predeceased child

b. Petitioner ☐ has no actual knowledge of facts ☐ has actual knowledge of facts reasonably giving rise to a parent-child relationship under Probate Code section 6408(b).

c. ☐ All surviving children and issue of predeceased children have been listed in item 8.

6. (Complete if decedent was survived by (1) a spouse but no issue (only a or b apply); or (2) no spouse or issue. Check the **first** box that applies):

a. ☐ The decedent is survived by a parent or parents who are listed in item 8.

b. ☐ The decedent is survived by issue of deceased parents, all of whom are listed in item 8.

c. ☐ The decedent is survived by a grandparent or grandparents who are listed in item 8.

d. ☐ The decedent is survived by issue of grandparents, all of whom are listed in item 8.

e. ☐ The decedent is survived by issue of a predeceased spouse, all of whom are listed in item 8.

f. ☐ The decedent is survived by next of kin, all of whom are listed in item 8.

g. ☐ The decedent is survived by parents of a predeceased spouse or issue of those parents, if both are predeceased, all of whom are listed in item 8.

7. (Complete only if no spouse or issue survived the decedent) Decedent ☐ had no predeceased spouse ☐ had a predeceased spouse who (1) ☐ died not more than 15 years before decedent owning an interest in **real property** that passed to decedent, (2) ☐ died not more than five years before decedent owning **personal property** valued at $10,000 or more that passed to decedent, (3) ☐ neither (1) nor (2) apply. (If you checked (1) or (2), check only the **first** box that applies):

a. ☐ The decedent is survived by issue of a predeceased spouse, all of whom are listed in item 8.

b. ☐ The decedent is survived by a parent or parents of the predeceased spouse who are listed in item 8.

c. ☐ The decedent is survived by issue of a parent of the predeceased spouse, all of whom are listed in item 8.

d. ☐ The decedent is survived by next of kin of the decedent, all of whom are listed in item 8.

e. ☐ The decedent is survived by next of kin of the predeceased spouse, all of whom are listed in item 8.

8. **Listed in Attachment 8** are the names, relationships, ages, and addresses of all persons named in decedent's will and codicils, whether living or deceased, and all persons checked in items 5, 6, and 7, so far as known to or reasonably ascertainable by petitioner, **including** stepchild and foster child heirs and devisees to whom notice is to be given under Probate Code section 1207.

9. ☐ Number of pages attached:

Date:

▶ _____
(SIGNATURE OF PETITIONER*)

▶ _____
(SIGNATURE OF PETITIONER*)

I declare under penalty of perjury under the laws of the State of California that the foregoing is true and correct.

Date:

. . . . ▶ _____
(TYPE OR PRINT NAME)   (SIGNATURE OF PETITIONER*)

* All petitioners must sign the petition. Only one need sign the declaration.

ATTORNEY OR PARTY WITHOUT ATTORNEY *(Name and Address)*:	TELEPHONE NO.:	*FOR COURT USE ONLY*

ATTORNEY FOR *(Name)*:

SUPERIOR COURT OF CALIFORNIA, COUNTY OF
  STREET ADDRESS:
  MAILING ADDRESS:
  CITY AND ZIP CODE:
  BRANCH NAME:

ESTATE OF (NAME):

DECEDENT

CASE NUMBER:

NOTICE OF PETITION TO ADMINISTER ESTATE

OF *(name)*:

1. To all heirs, beneficiaries, creditors, contingent creditors, and persons who may otherwise be interested in the will or estate, or both, of *(specify all names by which decedent was known)*:

2. A PETITION has been filed by *(name of petitioner)*:
   in the Superior Court of California, County of *(specify)*:

3. THE PETITION requests that *(name)*:
   be appointed as personal representative to administer the estate of the decedent.

4. ☐ THE PETITION requests the decedent's WILL and codicils, if any, be admitted to probate. The will and any codicils are available for examination in the file kept by the court.

5. ☐ THE PETITION requests authority to administer the estate under the Independent Administration of Estates Act. (This authority will allow the personal representative to take many actions without obtaining court approval. Before taking certain very important actions, however, the personal representative will be required to give notice to interested persons unless they have waived notice or consented to the proposed action.) The independent administration authority will be granted unless an interested person files an objection to the petition and shows good cause why the court should not grant the authority.

6. ☐ A PETITION for determination of or confirmation of property passing to or belonging to a surviving spouse under California Probate Code section 13650 IS JOINED with the petition to administer the estate.

7. A HEARING on the petition will be held

   on *(date)*:   at *(time)*:   in Dept.:   Room:

   located at *(address of court)*:

8. IF YOU OBJECT to the granting of the petition, you should appear at the hearing and state your objections or file written objections with the court before the hearing. Your appearance may be in person or by your attorney.

9. IF YOU ARE A CREDITOR or a contingent creditor of the deceased, you must file your claim with the court and mail a copy to the personal representative appointed by the court within four months from the date of first issuance of letters as provided in section 9100 of the California Probate Code. The time for filing claims will not expire before four months from the hearing date noticed above.

10. YOU MAY EXAMINE the file kept by the court. If you are a person interested in the estate, you may file with the court a formal Request for Special Notice of the filing of an inventory and appraisal of estate assets or of any petition or account as provided in section 1250 of the California Probate Code. A Request for Special Notice form is available from the court clerk.

11. ☐ Petitioner   ☐ Attorney for petitioner *(name)*:

    (address):

    ▶

    (SIGNATURE OF ☐ PETITIONER ☐ ATTORNEY FOR PETITIONER)

12. This notice was mailed on *(date)*:   at *(place)*:   , California.
    (Continued on reverse)

NOTE: If this notice is published, print the caption, beginning with the words NOTICE OF PETITION, and do not print the information from the form above the caption. The caption and decedent's name must be printed in at least 8-point type and the text in at least 7-point type. Print the case number as part of the caption. Print items preceded by a box only if the box is checked. Do not print the *italicized* instructions in parentheses, the paragraph numbers, the mailing information, or the material on the reverse.

Form Approved by the
Judicial Council of California
DE-121 [Rev. July 1, 1989]

NOTICE OF PETITION TO ADMINISTER ESTATE

Probate Code, § 8100

ESTATE OF (NAME):	
DECEDENT	
CASE NUMBER:	

PROOF OF SERVICE BY MAIL

1. I am over the age of 18 and not a party to this cause. I am a resident of or employed in the county where the mailing occurred.

2. My residence or business address is (specify):

3. I served the foregoing **Notice of Petition to Administer Estate** on each person named below by enclosing a copy in an envelope addressed as shown below AND

   a. ☐ **depositing** the sealed envelope with the United States Postal Service with the postage fully prepaid.

   b. ☐ **placing** the envelope for collection and mailing on the date and at the place shown in item 4 following our ordinary business practices. I am readily familiar with this business' practice for collecting and processing correspondence for mailing. On the same day that correspondence is placed for collection and mailing, it is deposited in the ordinary course of business with the United States Postal Service in a sealed envelope with postage fully prepaid.

4. a. Date of deposit: b. Place of deposit (city and state):

5. ☐ I served with the Notice of Petition to Administer Estate a copy of the petition and other documents referred to in the notice.

I declare under penalty of perjury under the laws of the State of California that the foregoing is true and correct.

Date:

....   ►

(TYPE OR PRINT NAME)   (SIGNATURE OF DECLARANT)

NAME AND ADDRESS OF EACH PERSON TO WHOM NOTICE WAS MAILED

ATTORNEY FOR *(Name)*

SUPERIOR COURT OF CALIFORNIA, COUNTY OF

STREET ADDRESS:

MAILING ADDRESS:

CITY AND ZIP CODE:

BRANCH NAME:

ESTATE OF (NAME):

DECEDENT

PROOF OF SUBSCRIBING WITNESS (For decedents dying after December 31, 1984)	CASE NUMBER:

1.　I am one of the attesting witnesses to the instrument of which attachment 1 is a photographic copy. I have examined attachment 1 and my signature is on it.

　　a. ☐　The name of the decedent was signed in the presence of the attesting witnesses present at the same time by
　　　　☐　the decedent personally.
　　　　☐　another person in the decedent's presence and by the decedent's direction.

　　b. ☐　The decedent acknowledged in the presence of the attesting witnesses present at the same time that the decedent's name was signed by
　　　　☐　the decedent personally.
　　　　☐　another person in the decedent's presence and by the decedent's direction.

　　c. ☐　The decedent acknowledged in the presence of the attesting witnesses present at the same time that the instrument signed was decedent's
　　　　☐　will.
　　　　☐　codicil.

2.　When I signed the instrument, I understood that it was decedent's ☐ will ☐ codicil.

3.　I have no knowledge of any facts indicating that the instrument, or any part of it, was procured by duress, menace, fraud, or undue influence.

I declare under penalty of perjury under the laws of the State of California that the foregoing is true and correct.

Date:

▶

....
(TYPE OR PRINT NAME)

_____
(SIGNATURE OF WITNESS)

....
(ADDRESS)

ATTORNEY'S CERTIFICATION

(Check local court rules for requirements for certifying copies of wills and codicils)

I am an active member of The State Bar of California. I declare under penalty of perjury under the laws of the State of California that attachment 1 is a photographic copy of every page of the ☐ will ☐ codicil heretofore presented for probate.

Date:

▶

....
(TYPE OR PRINT NAME)

_____
(SIGNATURE OF ATTORNEY)

206A Form Approved by the
Judicial Council of California
DE-131 [New January 1, 1985]

PROOF OF SUBSCRIBING WITNESS
(Probate)

76P663S—RP067 — 1-85

ATTORNEY FOR *(Name)*

SUPERIOR COURT OF CALIFORNIA, COUNTY OF

STREET ADDRESS

MAILING ADDRESS

CITY AND ZIP CODE

BRANCH NAME

ESTATE OF (NAME):

DECEDENT

PROOF OF HOLOGRAPHIC INSTRUMENT

CASE NUMBER

1. I was acquainted with the decedent for the following number of years *(specify)*:

2. ☐ I was related to the decedent as *(specify)*:

3. I have personal knowledge of the decedent's handwriting which I acquired as follows:
   a. ☐ I saw the decedent write.
   b. ☐ I saw a writing purporting to be in the decedent's handwriting and upon which decedent acted or was charged. It was *(specify)*:

   c. ☐ I received letters in the due course of mail purporting to be from the decedent in response to letters I addressed and mailed to the decedent.
   d. ☐ Other *(specify other means of obtaining knowledge)*:

4. I have examined the attached copy of the instrument, and its handwritten provisions were written by and the instrument was signed by the hand of the decedent. *(Affix a copy of the instrument as attachment 4.)*

I declare under penalty of perjury under the laws of the State of California that the foregoing is true and correct.
Date:

▶

. . . .
(TYPE OR PRINT NAME)   (SIGNATURE)

. . . .
(ADDRESS)

ATTORNEY'S CERTIFICATION

(Check local court rules for requirements for certifying copies of wills and codicils)

I am an active member of The State Bar of California. I declare under penalty of perjury under the laws of the State of California that attachment 4 is a photographic copy of every page of the holographic instrument heretofore presented for probate.

Date:

▶

. . . .
(TYPE OR PRINT NAME)   (SIGNATURE OF ATTORNEY)

Form Approved by the
Judicial Council of California
DE-135 [Rev. January 1, 1985]

PROOF OF HOLOGRAPHIC INSTRUMENT
(Probate)

76P157P—RP008 — 1-85

ATTORNEY OR PARTY WITHOUT ATTORNEY *(Name and Address)*:

TELEPHONE NO.:

FOR COURT USE ONLY

ATTORNEY FOR *(Name)*:

SUPERIOR COURT OF CALIFORNIA, COUNTY OF

STREET ADDRESS:

MAILING ADDRESS:

CITY AND ZIP CODE:

BRANCH NAME:

ESTATE OF (NAME):

DECEDENT

ORDER FOR PROBATE

ORDER ☐ Executor
APPOINTING ☐ Administrator with Will Annexed
☐ Administrator ☐ Special Administrator
☐ Order Authorizing Independent Administration of Estate
☐ with full authority ☐ with limited authority

CASE NUMBER:

1. Date of hearing: Time: Dept/Rm: Judge:

THE COURT FINDS

2. a. All notices required by law have been given.
   b. Decedent died on *(date)*:
      (1) ☐ a resident of the California county named above
      (2) ☐ a nonresident of California and left an estate in the county named above
   c. Decedent died
      (1) ☐ intestate
      (2) ☐ testate   and decedent's will dated:
          and each codicil dated:
          was admitted to probate by Minute Order on *(date)*:

THE COURT ORDERS

3. *(Name)*:

   is appointed **personal representative**:
   a. ☐ Executor of the decedent's will   d. ☐ Special Administrator
   b. ☐ Administrator with will annexed   (1) ☐ with general powers
   c. ☐ Administrator   (2) ☐ with special powers as specified in Attachment 3d
                                                     (3) ☐ without notice of hearing

   and letters shall issue on qualification.

4. a. ☐ **Full authority** is granted to administer the estate under the Independent Administration of Estates Act.
   b. ☐ **Limited authority** is granted to administer the estate under the Independent Administration of Estates Act (there is no authority, without court supervision, to (1) sell or exchange real property or (2) grant an option to purchase real property or (3) borrow money with the loan secured by an encumbrance upon real property).

5. a. ☐ Bond is not required.
   b. ☐ Bond is fixed at: $ to be furnished by an authorized surety company or as otherwise provided by law.
   c. ☐ Deposits of: $ are ordered to be placed in a blocked account at *(specify institution and location)*:
      and receipts shall be filed. No withdrawals shall be made without a court order.

6. ☐ *(Name)*:   is appointed probate referee.

Date: _____

_____
JUDGE OF THE SUPERIOR COURT

7. ☐ Number of pages attached: ☐ Signature follows last attachment.

Form Approved by the
Judicial Council of California
DE-140 [Rev. July 1, 1988]

ORDER FOR PROBATE

Probate Code, § 329

SUPERIOR COURT OF CALIFORNIA, COUNTY OF

STREET ADDRESS:

MAILING ADDRESS:

CITY AND ZIP CODE:

BRANCH NAME:

ESTATE OF (NAME):

DECEDENT

LETTERS

☐ **TESTAMENTARY**

☐ **OF ADMINISTRATION WITH WILL ANNEXED**

☐ **OF ADMINISTRATION**

☐ **SPECIAL ADMINISTRATION**

CASE NUMBER:

LETTERS

1. ☐ The last will of the decedent named above having been proved, the court appoints (name):

   a. ☐ Executor

   b. ☐ Administrator with will annexed

2. ☐ The court appoints (name):

   a. ☐ Administrator of the decedent's estate

   b. ☐ Special administrator of decedent's estate

     (1) ☐ with the special powers specified in the Order for Probate

     (2) ☐ with the powers of a general administrator

3. ☐ The personal representative is authorized to administer the estate under the Independent Administration of Estates Act ☐ **with full authority** ☐ **with limited authority** (no authority, without court supervision, to (1) sell or exchange real property or (2) grant an option to purchase real property or (3) borrow money with the loan secured by an encumbrance upon real property).

WITNESS, clerk of the court, with seal of the court affixed.

Date:

Clerk, by _____ , Deputy

(SEAL)

AFFIRMATION

1. ☐ PUBLIC ADMINISTRATOR: No affirmation required (Prob. Code, § 1140(b)).

2. ☐ INDIVIDUAL: **I solemnly affirm** that I will perform the duties of personal representative according to law.

3. ☐ INSTITUTIONAL FIDUCIARY (name):

   I solemnly affirm that the institution will perform the duties of personal representative according to law.

   I make this affirmation for myself as an individual and on behalf of the institution as an officer.
(Name and title):

4. Executed on (date):
at (place): , California.

▶

_____
(SIGNATURE)

CERTIFICATION

I certify that this document is a correct copy of the original on file in my office and the letters issued the personal representative appointed above have not been revoked, annulled, or set aside, and are still in full force and effect.

(SEAL)

Date:

Clerk, by

_____
(DEPUTY)

ATTORNEY OR PARTY WITHOUT ATTORNEY *(Name and Address):*	TELEPHONE NO.:	FOR COURT USE ONLY

ATTORNEY FOR *(Name)*:

SUPERIOR COURT OF CALIFORNIA, COUNTY OF

STREET ADDRESS:

MAILING ADDRESS:

CITY AND ZIP CODE:

BRANCH NAME:

ESTATE OF (NAME):

DECEDENT

DUTIES AND LIABILITIES OF PERSONAL REPRESENTATIVE and Acknowledgment of Receipt	CASE NUMBER:

DUTIES AND LIABILITIES OF PERSONAL REPRESENTATIVE

When you have been appointed by the court as personal representative of an estate, you become an officer of the court and assume certain duties and obligations. An attorney is best qualified to advise you about these matters. You should clearly understand the following:

1. MANAGING THE ESTATE'S ASSETS

a. Prudent investments

You must manage the estate assets with the care of a prudent person dealing with someone else's property. This means you must be cautious and you may not make any speculative investments.

b. Keep estate assets separate

You must keep the money and property in this estate separate from anyone else's, including your own. When you open a bank account for the estate, the account name must indicate that it is an estate account and not your personal account. Never deposit estate funds in your personal account or otherwise commingle them with anyone else's property. Securities in the estate must also be held in a name that shows they are estate property and not your personal property.

c. Interest-bearing accounts and other investments

Except for checking accounts intended for ordinary administration expenses, estate accounts must earn interest. You may deposit estate funds in insured accounts in financial institutions, but you should consult with an attorney before making other investments.

d. Other restrictions

There are many other restrictions on your authority to deal with estate property. You should not spend any of the estate's money unless you have received permission from the court or have been advised to do so by an attorney. You may reimburse yourself for official court costs paid by you to the county clerk and for the premium on your bond. Without prior order of the court, you may not pay fees to yourself or to your attorney, if you have one. If you do not obtain the court's permission when it is required, you may be removed as personal representative or you may be required to reimburse the estate from your own personal funds, or both. You should consult with an attorney concerning the legal requirements affecting sales, leases, mortgages, and investments of estate property.

2. INVENTORY OF ESTATE PROPERTY

a. Locate the estate's property

You must attempt to locate and take possession of all the decedent's property to be administered in the estate.

b. Determine the value of the property

You must arrange to have a court-appointed referee determine the value of the property unless the appointment is waived by the court. (You, rather than the referee, must determine the value of certain "cash items." An attorney can advise you about how to do this.)

c. File an inventory and appraisal

Within four months after your appointment as personal representative, you must file with the court an inventory and appraisal of all the assets in the estate.

(Continued on reverse)

Form Adopted by the
Judicial Council of California
DE-147 [New July 1, 1989]

DUTIES AND LIABILITIES OF PERSONAL REPRESENTATIVE
(Probate)

Probate Code, § 8404

ESTATE OF (NAME):		
DECEDENT		
	CASE NUMBER:	

d.   File a change of ownership

At the time you file the inventory and appraisal, you must also file a change of ownership statement with the county recorder or assessor in each county where the decedent owned real property at the time of death, as provided in section 480 of the California Revenue and Taxation Code.

3.   NOTICE TO CREDITORS

You must mail a notice of administration to each known creditor of the decedent within four months after your appointment as personal representative. If the decedent received Medi-Cal assistance you must notify the State Director of Health Services within 90 days after appointment.

4.   INSURANCE

You should determine that there is appropriate and adequate insurance covering the assets and risks of the estate. Maintain the insurance in force during the entire period of the administration.

5.   RECORD KEEPING

a.   Keep accounts

You must keep complete and accurate records of each financial transaction affecting the estate. You will have to prepare an account of all money and property you have received, what you have spent, and the date of each transaction. You must describe in detail what you have left after the payment of expenses.

b.   Court review

Your account will be reviewed by the court. Save your receipts because the court may ask to review them. If you do not file your accounts as required, the court will order you to do so. You may be removed as personal representative if you fail to comply.

6.   CONSULTING AN ATTORNEY

If you have an attorney, you should cooperate with the attorney at all times. You and your attorney are responsible for completing the estate administration as promptly as possible. When in doubt, contact your attorney.

> **NOTICE: This statement of duties and liabilities is a summary and is not a complete statement of the law. Your conduct as a personal representative is governed by the law itself and not by this summary.**

ACKNOWLEDGMENT OF RECEIPT

1.   I have petitioned the court to be appointed as a personal representative of the estate of
(specify):

2.   I acknowledge that I have received a copy of this statement of the duties and liabilities of the office of personal representative.

Date:

▶

....
(TYPE OR PRINT NAME)

_____
(SIGNATURE OF PETITIONER)

*Social Security No.: _____   *Driver's License No.: _____

Date:

▶

....
(TYPE OR PRINT NAME)

_____
(SIGNATURE OF PETITIONER)

*Social Security No.: _____   *Driver's License No.: _____

Date:

▶

....
(TYPE OR PRINT NAME)

_____
(SIGNATURE OF PETITIONER)

*Social Security No.: _____   *Driver's License No.: _____

*Supply these numbers only if required to do so by local court rule. The law requires the court to keep this information CONFIDENTIAL. (Probate Code, § 8404(a).)

NAME AND ADDRESS OF ATTORNEY	TELEPHONE NO:	FOR COURT USE ONLY

NAME OF COURT, OR BRANCH, MAILING AND STREET ADDRESS

ESTATE OF

☐ DECEDENT ☐ INCOMPETENT ☐ CONSERVATEE ☐ MINOR

APPLICATION AND ORDER APPOINTING PROBATE REFEREE

CASE NUMBER

It is requested that a Probate Referee be appointed to appraise the assets of the above entitled estate consisting of the following approximate values:

1. CASH $ _____

2. REAL ESTATE $ _____

3. PERSONAL PROPERTY $ _____

REMARKS _____

_____

_____
Attorney

IT IS ORDERED that (name):

a disinterested person, is appointed Probate Referee to appraise the above entitled estate. When a Probate Referee is appointed, such referee is authorized to fix the clear market value of the estate as of the date of death of the decedent, or as of the date of appointment if a conservatorship or guardianship, and to appraise all interest, inheritances, transfers, and property of the estate under the laws of the State of California.

DATED:

_____
Judge of the Superior Court

APPLICATION AND ORDER APPOINTING PROBATE REFEREE

229A

76A650Q (Rev. 9-83) 4-84
RP005

PROB C 605

ATTORNEY OR PARTY WITHOUT ATTORNEY (Name and Address):	TELEPHONE NO.:	FOR COURT USE ONLY

ATTORNEY FOR (Name):

SUPERIOR COURT OF CALIFORNIA, COUNTY OF

STREET ADDRESS:

MAILING ADDRESS:

CITY AND ZIP CODE:

BRANCH NAME:

ESTATE OF (NAME):

DECEDENT

NOTICE OF PROPOSED ACTION Independent Administration of Estates Act Objection—Consent	CASE NUMBER:

> **NOTICE:** If you do not object in writing or obtain a court order preventing the action proposed below, you will be treated as if you consented to the proposed action and you may not object after the proposed action has been taken. If you object, the personal representative may take the proposed action only under court supervision. An objection form is on the reverse. If you wish to object, you may use the form or prepare your own written objection.

1. The personal representative (executor or administrator) of the estate of the deceased is (names):

2. The personal representative has authority to administer the estate without court supervision under the Independent Administration of Estates Act (Probate Code section 10400 et seq.)
   a. ☐ with **full authority** under the act.
   b. ☐ with **limited authority** under the act (there is no authority, without court supervision, to (1) sell or exchange real property or (2) grant an option to purchase real property or (3) borrow money with the loan secured by an encumbrance upon real property).

3. **On or after** (date): _____ , the personal representative will take the following action without court supervision (describe in specific terms here or in Attachment 3):
   ☐ The proposed action is described in an attachment labeled Attachment 3.

4. ☐ **Real property transaction** (Check this box and complete item 4b if the proposed action involves a sale or exchange or a grant of an option to purchase real property.)
   a. The material terms of the transaction are specified in item 3, including any sale price and the amount of or method of calculating any commission or compensation to an agent or broker.
   b. $_____ is the value of the subject property in the probate inventory. ☐ No inventory yet.

> **NOTICE:** A sale of real property without court supervision means that the sale will NOT be presented to the court for confirmation at a hearing at which higher bids for the property may be presented and the property sold to the highest bidder.

(Continued on reverse)

Form Approved by the
Judicial Council of California
DE-165 [Rev. July 1, 1988]

NOTICE OF PROPOSED ACTION
Objection—Consent
(Probate)

Probate Code, § 10580 et seq.

ESTATE OF (NAME):		
	DECEDENT	CASE NUMBER:

5. If you OBJECT to the proposed action

a. **Sign** the objection form below and deliver or mail it to the personal representative at the following address (*specify name and address*):

b. **Send** your own written objection to the address in item 5a. *(Be sure to identify the proposed action and state that you object to it.)*

-OR-

c. **Apply** to the court for an order preventing the personal representative from taking the proposed action without court supervision.

-OR-

d. **NOTE:** Your written objection or the court order must be received by the personal representative before the date in the box in item 3, or before the proposed action is taken, whichever is later. If you object, the personal representative may take the proposed action only under court supervision.

6. **If you APPROVE the proposed action,** you may sign the consent form below and return it to the address in item 5a. If you do not object in writing or obtain a court order, you will be treated as if you consented to the proposed action.

7. **If you need more INFORMATION, call** (*name*):
(*telephone*): ( )

Date: _____

(TYPE OR PRINT NAME)
....

▶ _____
(SIGNATURE OF PERSONAL REPRESENTATIVE OR ATTORNEY)

OBJECTION TO PROPOSED ACTION

☐ **I OBJECT** to the action proposed above in item 3.

NOTICE: Sign and return this form (both sides) to the address in item 5a. The form must be received before the date in the box in item 3, or before the proposed action is taken, whichever is later. (You may want to use certified mail, with return receipt requested. Make a copy of this form for your records.)

Date: _____

(TYPE OR PRINT NAME)
....

▶ _____
(SIGNATURE OF OBJECTOR)

CONSENT TO PROPOSED ACTION

☐ **I CONSENT** to the action proposed above in item 3.

NOTICE: You may indicate your **consent** by signing and returning this form (both sides) to the address in item 5a. If you do not object in writing or obtain a court order, you will be treated as if you consented to the proposed action.

Date: _____

(TYPE OR PRINT NAME)
....

▶ _____
(SIGNATURE OF CONSENTER)

ATTORNEY OR PARTY WITHOUT ATTORNEY *(Name and Address)*	TELEPHONE NO.	*FOR COURT USE ONLY*

ATTORNEY FOR *(Name)*

SUPERIOR COURT OF CALIFORNIA, COUNTY OF

STREET ADDRESS:

MAILING ADDRESS:

CITY AND ZIP CODE:

BRANCH NAME:

ESTATE OF (NAME):

☐ DECEDENT ☐ CONSERVATEE ☐ MINOR

INVENTORY AND APPRAISEMENT

☐ Complete   ☐ Final

☐ Partial No.:   ☐ Supplemental

☐ Reappraisal for Sale

CASE NUMBER:

Date of Death of Decedent or of Appointment of Guardian or Conservator:

APPRAISALS

1. Total appraisal by representative (attachment 1) $
2. Total appraisal by referee (attachment 2) $

TOTAL: $

DECLARATION OF REPRESENTATIVE

3. Attachments 1 and 2 together with all prior inventories filed contain a true statement of ☐ all ☐ a portion of the estate that has come to my knowledge or possession, including particularly all money and all just claims the estate has against me. I have truly, honestly, and impartially appraised to the best of my ability each item set forth in attachment 1.

4. ☐ No probate referee is required ☐ by order of the court dated *(specify)*:

I declare under penalty of perjury under the laws of the State of California that the foregoing is true and correct.

Date:

▶

. . . .

(TYPE OR PRINT NAME) (Include title if corporate officer)   (SIGNATURE OF PERSONAL REPRESENTATIVE)

STATEMENT REGARDING BOND

(Complete if required by local court rule)

5 ☐ Bond is waived.

6. ☐ Sole personal representative is a corporate fiduciary.

7. ☐ Bond filed in the amount of: $ ☐ Sufficient ☐ Insufficient

8. ☐ Receipts for: $ have been filed with the court for deposits in a blocked account at *(specify institution and location)*:

Date:

▶

(SIGNATURE OF ATTORNEY OR PARTY WITHOUT ATTORNEY)

DECLARATION OF PROBATE REFEREE

9. I have truly, honestly, and impartially appraised to the best of my ability each item set forth in attachment 2.

10. A true account of my commission and expenses actually and necessarily incurred pursuant to my appointment is

Statutory commission: $

Expenses *(specify)*: $

TOTAL: $

I declare under penalty of perjury under the laws of the State of California that the foregoing is true and correct.

Date:

▶

. . . .

(TYPE OR PRINT NAME)   (SIGNATURE OF REFEREE)

(Instructions on reverse)

Form Approved by the
Judicial Council of California
DE-160, GC-040 (Rev. January 1, 1985)

INVENTORY AND APPRAISEMENT
(Probate)

761552H
RP007 — 1-85

Prob C 600-611,
2610-2616

INSTRUCTIONS

See Probate Code, §§ 604, 608, 609, 611, 2610-2616 for additional instructions.

If required in a decedent's estate proceeding by local court rule, furnish an extra copy for the clerk to transmit to the assessor (Probate Code, § 600).

See Probate Code, §§ 600-602 for items to be included.

If the minor or conservatee is or has been during the guardianship or conservatorship confined in a state hospital under the jurisdiction of the State Department of Mental Health or the State Department of Developmental Services, mail a copy to the director of the appropriate department in Sacramento (Probate Code, § 2611).

The representative shall list on attachment 1 and appraise as of the date of death of the decedent or date of appointment of the guardian or conservator at fair market value moneys, currency, cash items, bank accounts and amounts on deposit with any financial institution (as defined in Probate Code, § 605), and the proceeds of life and accident insurance policies and retirement plans payable upon death in lump sum amounts to the estate, except items whose fair market value is, in the opinion of the representative, an amount different from the ostensible value or specified amount.

The representative shall list on attachment 2 all other assets of the estate which shall be appraised by the referee.

If joint tenancy and other assets are listed for appraisal purposes only and not as part of the probate estate, they must be separately listed on additional attachments and their value excluded from the total valuation of attachments 1 and 2.

Each attachment should conform to the format approved by the Judicial Council (see form Inventory and Appraisement (Attachment) (DE-161, GC-041) and Cal. Rules of Court, rule 201).

ESTATE OF:

ATTACHMENT NO:

(IN DECEDENTS' ESTATES. ATTACHMENTS MUST CONFORM TO PROBATE CODE 601
REGARDING COMMUNITY AND SEPARATE PROPERTY)

PAGE   OF   TOTAL PAGES
(ADD PAGES AS REQUIRED)

Item No.   Description   Appraised value
1. $

200A

Form Approved by the
Judicial Council of California
Effective January 1, 1976

INVENTORY AND APPRAISEMENT (ATTACHMENT)

Prob C 481,
600–605, 784.
1550 1901
761350C-RP-34 — PS 4-79

NOTICE OF ADMINISTRATION*
OF THE ESTATE OF

_____

(NAME)
DECEDENT

NOTICE TO CREDITORS

1.   *(Name)* :
     (Address) :

     is the **personal representative** of the **ESTATE OF** *(name)* :   , who is deceased.

2.   The personal representative HAS BEGUN ADMINISTRATION of the decedent's estate in the

     a. **SUPERIOR COURT OF CALIFORNIA, COUNTY OF**

     STREET ADDRESS:

     MAILING ADDRESS:

     CITY AND ZIP CODE:

     BRANCH NAME:

     b. Case Number *(specify)* :

3.   You must FILE YOUR CLAIM with the court clerk (address in item 2a) AND mail or deliver a copy to the personal representative before the **later** of the following dates as provided in section 9100 of the California Probate Code:

     a. **four months** after *(date)* : [   ] , the date letters (authority to act for the estate) were first issued to the personal representative, OR

     b. **thirty days** after *(date)* : [   ] , the date this notice was mailed or personally delivered to you.

   You may obtain a CREDITOR'S CLAIM FORM from any superior court clerk. *(Judicial Council form No. DE-172, Creditor's Claim.)* **A letter is not sufficient.**

   If you use the mail to file your claim with the court, for your protection you should send your claim by certified mail, with return receipt requested. If you mail a copy of your claim to the personal representative, you should also use certified mail.

(Proof of Service on reverse)

Use this form in estates begun on or after July 1, 1988.

Form Approved by the
Judicial Council of California

NOTICE OF ADMINISTRATION TO CREDITORS
(Probate)

Probate Code, §§ 9050, 9052

PROOF OF SERVICE BY MAIL

1. I am over the age of 18 and not a party to this cause. I am a resident of or employed in the county where the mailing occurred.
2. My residence or business address is *(specify)*:

3. I served the foregoing **Notice of Administration to Creditors** on each person named below by enclosing a copy in an envelope addressed as shown below AND

   a. ☐ **depositing** the sealed envelope with the United States Postal Service with the postage fully prepaid.

   b. ☐ **placing** the envelope for collection and mailing on the date and at the place shown in item 4 following our ordinary business practices. I am readily familiar with this business' practice for collecting and processing correspondence for mailing. On the same day that correspondence is placed for collection and mailing, it is deposited in the ordinary course of business with the United States Postal Service in a sealed envelope with postage fully prepaid.

4. a. Date of deposit: b. Place of deposit *(city and state)*:

   I declare under penalty of perjury under the laws of the State of California that the foregoing is true and correct.

Date:

. . . .   ▶ _____
(TYPE OR PRINT NAME)   (SIGNATURE OF DECLARANT)

NAME AND ADDRESS OF EACH PERSON TO WHOM NOTICE WAS MAILED

NOTICE OF ADMINISTRATION TO CREDITORS
(Probate)

ATTORNEY OR PARTY WITHOUT ATTORNEY *(Name and Address)*:	TELEPHONE NO.:	*FOR COURT USE ONLY*

ATTORNEY FOR *(Name)*:

SUPERIOR COURT OF CALIFORNIA, COUNTY OF

STREET ADDRESS:

MAILING ADDRESS:

CITY AND ZIP CODE:

BRANCH NAME:

ESTATE OF (NAME):

DECEDENT

FOR COURT USE ONLY

Personal representative's allowance or rejection filed:

. . . .
(date)　　　　　(Deputy)

☐　No court approval required.

Presented to court for approval or rejection:

. . . .
(date)　　　　　(Deputy)

CASE NUMBER:

ALLOWANCE OR REJECTION OF CREDITOR'S CLAIM
(for estate administration proceedings filed after June 30, 1988)

NOTE: Attach a copy of the creditor's claim.

PERSONAL REPRESENTATIVE'S ALLOWANCE OR REJECTION

1. Name of creditor *(specify)*:
2. The claim was filed on *(date)*:
3. Date of first issuance of letters:
4. Date of Notice of Administration:
5. Date of decedent's death:
6. Estimated value of estate:
7. Total amount of the claim: $
8. ☐ Claim is allowed for: $
9. ☐ Claim is rejected for: $
10. Notice of allowance or rejection given on *(date)*:
11. ☐ The personal representative is authorized to administer the estate under the Independent Administration of Estates Act.

(The court must approve certain claims before they are paid.)
(A creditor has three months to act on a rejected claim. See box below.)

Date:

. . . .
(TYPE OR PRINT NAME)

▶

(SIGNATURE OF PERSONAL REPRESENTATIVE)

REJECTED CLAIMS: From the date notice of rejection is given, the creditor must act on the rejected claim (e.g., file a lawsuit) as follows:
a. **Claim due:** within three months after the notice of rejection.
b. **Claim not due:** within three months after the claim becomes due.

COURT'S APPROVAL OR REJECTION

12. ☐ Approved for: $

13. ☐ Rejected for: $

Date:

14. ☐ Number of pages attached:

▶

SIGNATURE OF ☐ JUDGE ☐ COMMISSIONER

☐ Signature follows last attachment.

(Proof of Service on reverse)

Probate Code, § 9000 et seq., 9250

Form Approved by the
Judicial Council of California
DE-174 [New July 1, 1988]

ALLOWANCE OR REJECTION OF CREDITOR'S CLAIM
(Probate)

ESTATE OF (NAME):	
	DECEDENT
	CASE NUMBER:

PROOF OF ☐ **MAILING** ☐ **PERSONAL DELIVERY**   **TO CREDITOR**

1. At the time of mailing or personal delivery I was at least 18 years of age and not a **party** to this proceeding.

2. **My residence or business address is (specify):**

3. I **mailed or personally delivered** a copy of the **Allowance or Rejection of Creditor's Claim** as follows (complete either a or b):

   a. ☐   **Mail.** I am a resident of or employed in the county where the mailing occurred.

     (1) I enclosed a copy in an envelope AND

       (i) ☐   **deposited** the sealed envelope with the United States Postal Service with the postage fully prepaid.

       (ii) ☐   **placed** the envelope for collection and mailing on the date and at the place shown in items below following our ordinary business practices. I am readily familiar with this business' practice for collecting and processing correspondence for mailing. On the same day that correspondence is placed for collection and mailing, it is deposited in the ordinary course of business with the United States Postal Service in a sealed envelope with postage fully prepaid.

     (2) The envelope was addressed and mailed first-class as follows:

       (i) Name of creditor served:

       (ii) Address on envelope:

       (iii) Date of mailing:

       (iv) Place of mailing (city and state):

   b. ☐   **Personal delivery.** I personally delivered a copy to the creditor as follows:

     (1) Name of creditor served:

     (2) Address where delivered:

     (3) Date delivered:

     (4) Time delivered:

I declare under penalty of perjury under the laws of the State of California that the foregoing is true and correct.

Date:

. . . .   ▶   . . . .

(TYPE OR PRINT NAME OF DECLARANT)   (SIGNATURE OF DECLARANT)

NAME, ADDRESS, AND TELEPHONE NUMBER
OF ATTORNEY(S)

ATTORNEY(S) FOR

SUPERIOR COURT OF CALIFORNIA, COUNTY OF LOS ANGELES

ESTATE OF

CASE NUMBER

**AFFIDAVIT OR DECLARATION FOR
FINAL DISCHARGE AND ORDER**

DECEASED

The undersigned, as .... of the above entitled estate states that: distribution has been made of all the property and assets of said estate in accordance with the decree therefor made;

☐ That all money, stocks, bonds and other personal property have been delivered to the distributees as ordered by said decree; that receipts of the respective distributees therefor are now on file.

☐ That Affiant is sole distributee;

☐ That there is no personal property on hand for distribution;

That all lawfully required acts as such .... have been performed.

Executed .... at ...., California.

I certify (or declare) under penalty of perjury under the laws of the State of California that the foregoing is true and correct.

....

ORDER OF FINAL DISCHARGE

It appearing that all acts of .... as .... were performed as required by law;

  IT IS ORDERED, ADJUDGED AND DECREED:
That .... as .... be discharged as such and sureties are hereby released from liability for all acts subsequent hereto.

Dated ....

....
Court Commissioner

....
Judge

ATTORNEY OR PARTY WITHOUT ATTORNEY *(Name and Address)*:	TELEPHONE NO.:	FOR COURT USE ONLY

ATTORNEY FOR *(Name)*:

SUPERIOR COURT OF CALIFORNIA, COUNTY OF

STREET ADDRESS:

MAILING ADDRESS:

CITY AND ZIP CODE:

BRANCH NAME:

ESTATE OF (NAME):

DECEDENT

SPOUSAL PROPERTY PETITION	CASE NUMBER:
	HEARING DATE:
	DEPT.: TIME:

1. **Petitioner** *(name)*:

   requests

   a. ☐ determination of property passing to the surviving spouse without administration (Probate Code, § 13500).

   b. ☐ confirmation of property belonging to the surviving spouse (Probate Code, §§ 100 and 101).

   c. ☐ this petition be joined with the petition for probate or administration of the decedent's estate.

   d. ☐ immediate appointment of a probate referee.

2. Petitioner is

   a. ☐ surviving spouse of the decedent.

   b. ☐ personal representative of *(name)*: , surviving spouse.

   c. ☐ guardian of the estate or conservator of the estate of *(name)*: , surviving spouse.

3. Decedent died on *(date)*:

   a. ☐ a resident of the California county named above.

   b. ☐ a nonresident of California and left an estate in the county named above.

   c. ☐ intestate ☐ testate and a copy of the will and any codicil is affixed as attachment 3c or 6d. *(Attach will.)*

4. a. *(Complete in all cases)* The decedent is survived by

   (1) ☐ child as follows: ☐ natural or adopted ☐ natural adopted by a third party ☐ step ☐ foster

   ☐ no child

   (2) ☐ issue of a predeceased child ☐ no issue of a predeceased child

   b. Petitioner ☐ has no ☐ has actual knowledge of facts reasonably giving rise to a parent-child relationship under Probate Code section 6408(b).

   c. ☐ All surviving children and issue of predeceased children have been listed in item 7.

5. *(Complete only if no issue survived the decedent. Check only the first box that applies.)*

   a. ☐ The decedent is survived by a parent or parents who are listed in item 7.

   b. ☐ The decedent is survived by a brother, sister, or issue of a deceased brother or sister, all of whom are listed in item 7.

6. a. Administration of all or part of the estate is not necessary for the reason that all or a part of the estate is property passing to the surviving spouse.

   b. ☐ The legal description of the deceased spouse's property that petitioner requests to be determined as passing to the surviving spouse is set forth in attachment 6b,[1] and includes the trade or business name of any unincorporated business or an interest in any unincorporated business the deceased spouse was operating or managing at the time of death.

   c. ☐ The legal description of the community or quasi-community property petitioner requests the court to confirm to the surviving spouse as belonging to the surviving spouse under Probate Code sections 100 and 101 is set forth in attachment 6c.

   d. The facts upon which the petitioner bases the allegation that the property described in attachments 6b and 6c is property that should pass or be confirmed to the surviving spouse are stated in attachment 6d.[2]

(Continued on reverse)

Form Approved by the
Judicial Council of California
DE-221 [Rev. July 1, 1987]

SPOUSAL PROPERTY PETITION
(Probate)

See reverse for footnotes.
Probate Code, § 13650

Post-Record Catalog #DE-221

7. The names, relationships, ages, and residence or mailing addresses of all persons checked in items 4 or 5 and all other heirs and devisees of the decedent, so far as known to petitioner, **including** stepchild and foster child heirs and devisees to whom notice is to be given ☐ are listed below ☐ are listed in attachment 7.

NAME AND RELATIONSHIP	AGE	RESIDENCE OR MAILING ADDRESS

8. The names and address of all persons named as executors in the decedent's will or appointed as personal representatives ☐ are listed below ☐ are listed in attachment 8 ☐ none.

9. ☐ The personal representative is the trustee of a trust that is a devisee under decedent's will. The names and addresses of all persons interested in the trust who are entitled to notice under Probate Code section 13655(b)(2) are listed in attachment 9.

10. A petition for probate or for administration of the decedent's estate
   a. ☐ is being filed with this petition and published notice will be given.
   b. ☐ was filed on (date):
   c. ☐ has not been filed and is not being filed with this petition.

11. ☐ Number of pages attached:

I declare under penalty of perjury under the laws of the State of California that the foregoing is true and correct.

Date:

▶

....
(TYPE OR PRINT NAME)

_____
(SIGNATURE OF PETITIONER)

[1] See Probate Code, § 13658 for required filing of a list of known creditors of a business and other information in certain instances. If required, include in attachment 6b.
[2] See Probate Code, § 13651(b) for the requirement that a copy of the will be attached in certain instances. If required, include in attachment 3c or 6d.

SPOUSAL PROPERTY PETITION
(Probate)

DE-221 [Rev. July 1, 1987]

Page two

ATTORNEY OR PARTY WITHOUT ATTORNEY *(Name and Address)*:	TELEPHONE NO.:	*FOR COURT USE ONLY*
ATTORNEY FOR *(Name)*:		

SUPERIOR COURT OF CALIFORNIA, COUNTY OF

STREET ADDRESS:

MAILING ADDRESS:

CITY AND ZIP CODE:

BRANCH NAME:

ESTATE OF (NAME):

DECEDENT

NOTICE OF HEARING (Probate)	CASE NUMBER:

> **This notice is required by law. This notice does not require you to appear in court, but you may attend the hearing if you wish.**

1. NOTICE is given that *(name)*:

   (representative capacity, if any):

   has filed *(specify)*:*

2. You may refer to the filed documents for further particulars. *(All of the case documents filed with the court are available for examination in the case file kept by the court clerk.)*

3. A HEARING on the matter will be held as follows:

   Date: Time: Dept.:   Room:

   Address of court ☐ shown above ☐ is:

. . . .   ☐ Attorney or party _____
(TYPE OR PRINT NAME)   (SIGNATURE)

Date: ☐ Clerk, by _____ , Deputy

4. This notice was mailed on *(date)*:   at *(place)*:

(Continued on reverse)

---

* Do not use this form to give notice of hearing of the petition for administration *(see Probate Code,* § 8100).

Form Approved by the
Judicial Council of California
DE-120 [Rev. July 1, 1989]

NOTICE OF HEARING
(Probate)

Probate Code, §§ 1211, 1215, 1216, 1230

ESTATE OF (NAME):	CASE NUMBER:
DECEDENT	

CLERK'S CERTIFICATE OF ☐ POSTING ☐ MAILING

I certify that I am not a party to this cause and that a copy of the foregoing **Notice of Hearing (Probate)**

1. ☐ **was posted** at *(address)*:

   on *(date)*:

2. ☐ **was served** on each person named below. Each notice was enclosed in an envelope with postage fully prepaid. Each envelope was addressed to a person whose name and address is given below, sealed, and deposited with the United States Postal Service at *(place)*: , California,

   on *(date)*:

Date: Clerk, by _____ , Deputy

PROOF OF SERVICE BY MAIL

1. I am over the age of 18 and not a party to this cause. I am a resident of or employed in the county where the mailing occurred.
2. My residence or business address is *(specify)*:

3. I served the foregoing **Notice of Hearing (Probate)** on each person named below by enclosing a copy in an envelope addressed as shown below AND
   a. ☐ **depositing** the sealed envelope with the United States Postal Service with the postage fully prepaid.
   b. ☐ **placing** the envelope for collection and mailing on the date and at the place shown in item 4 following our ordinary business practices. I am readily familiar with this business' practice for collecting and processing correspondence for mailing. On the same day that correspondence is placed for collection and mailing, it is deposited in the ordinary course of business with the United States Postal Service in a sealed envelope with postage fully prepaid.

4. a. Date mailed: b. Place mailed *(city, state)*:

5. ☐ I served with the *Notice of Hearing (Probate)* a copy of the petition or other document referred to in the notice.

I declare under penalty of perjury under the laws of the State of California that the foregoing is true and correct.

Date:

. . . .   ▶ _____

(TYPE OR PRINT NAME)   (SIGNATURE OF DECLARANT)

NAME AND ADDRESS OF EACH PERSON TO WHOM NOTICE WAS MAILED

TELEPHONE NO.:

FOR COURT USE ONLY

ATTORNEY FOR *(Name)*:

SUPERIOR COURT OF CALIFORNIA, COUNTY OF

STREET ADDRESS:

MAILING ADDRESS:

CITY AND ZIP CODE:

BRANCH NAME:

ESTATE OF (NAME):

DECEDENT

SPOUSAL PROPERTY ORDER

CASE NUMBER:

1. Date of hearing: Time: Dept.:   Room:

THE COURT FINDS

2. All notices required by law have been given.

3. Decedent died on *(date)*:
  a. ☐ a resident of the California county named above.
  b. ☐ a nonresident of California and left an estate in the county named above.
  c. ☐ intestate ☐ testate.

THE COURT FURTHER FINDS AND ORDERS

4. a. ☐ The property described in attachment 4a is property passing to the surviving spouse,
    (name):   , and no administration of it is necessary.
  b. ☐ See attachment 4b for further order respecting transfer of the property to the surviving spouse.

5. ☐ To protect the interests of the creditors of *(business name)*:

  an unincorporated trade or business, a list of all its known creditors and the amount owed each is on file.
  a. ☐ Within *(specify)*:   days from this date, the surviving spouse shall file an undertaking in the amount of
    $, upon condition that the surviving spouse pay the known creditors of the business.
  b. ☐ See attachment 5b for further order protecting the interests of creditors of the business.

6. a. ☐ The property described in attachment 6a is property that belongs to the surviving spouse,
    (name):   , under Probate Code sections 100 and 101, and the surviving
    spouse's ownership is hereby confirmed.
  b. ☐ See attachment 6b for further order respecting transfer of the property to the surviving spouse.

7. ☐ All property described in the Spousal Property Petition that is not determined to be property passing to the surviving spouse
  under Probate Code section 13500, or confirmed as belonging to the surviving spouse under Probate Code sections 100
  and 101, shall be subject to administration in the estate ☐ described in attachment 7.

8. ☐ Other *(specify)*:

Date:

_____
JUDGE OF THE SUPERIOR COURT

9. ☐ Number of pages attached: ☐ Signature follows last attachment

Form Approved by the
Judicial Council of California
DE-226 [Rev. July 1, 1987]

SPOUSAL PROPERTY ORDER
(Probate)

Probate Code, § 13656

Index

ESTATE PLANNING & PROBATE

Plan Your Estate With a Living Trust
Attorney Denis Clifford
National 1st Edition
This book covers every significant aspect of estate planning and gives detailed specific, instructions for preparing a living trust, a document that lets your family avoid expensive and lengthy probate court proceedings after your death. Includes all the tear-out forms and step-by-step instructions you need
$19.95/NEST

Nolo's Simple Will Book
Attorney Denis Clifford
National 2nd Edition
It's easy to write a legally valid will using this book. The instructions and forms enable people to draft a will for all needs and updating a will when necessary. Good in all states except Louisiana.
$17.95/SWIL

The Conservatorship Book
Lisa Goldoftas &
Attorney Carolyn Farren
California 1st Edition
When a family member or close relative becomes incapacitated due to illness or age, it may be necessary to name a conservator for taking charge of their medical and financial affairs. This book will help you determine when and what kind of conservatorship is necessary. Includes complete instructions and all the forms to file a conservatorship.
$24.95/CON

How to Probate an Estate
Julia Nissley
California 6th Edition
If you find yourself responsible for winding up the legal and financial affairs of a deceased family member or friend, you can often save costly attorneys' fees by handling the probate process yourself. This book shows you the simple procedures you can use to transfer assets that don't require probate, including property held in joint tenancy or living trusts or as community property.
$34.95/PAE

The Power of Attorney Book
Attorney Denis Clifford
National 4th Edition
Who will take care of your affairs, and make your financial and medical decisions if you can't? With this book you can appoint someone you trust to carry out your wishes and stipulate exactly what kind of care you want or don't want. Includes Durable Power of Attorney and Living Will Forms.
$19.95/POA

GOING TO COURT

Everybody's Guide to Small Claims Court
Attorney Ralph Warner
National 5th Edition
California 9th Edition
These books will help you decide if you should sue in small claims court, show you how to file and serve papers, tell you what to bring to court and how to collect a judgment.
National $15.95/NSCC
California $14.95/ CSCC

Fight Your Ticket
Attorney David Brown
California 4th Edition
This book shows you how to fight an unfair traffic ticket—when you're stopped, at arraignment, at trial and on appeal.
$17.95/FYT

The Criminal Records Book
Attorney Warren Siegel
California 3rd Edition
This book shows you step-by-step how to seal criminal records, dismiss convictions, destroy marijuana records and reduce felony convictions.
$19.95/CRIM

Collect Your Court Judgment
Gini Graham Scott, Attorney Stephen Elias &
Lisa Goldoftas
California 2nd Edition
This book contains step-by-step instructions and all the forms you need to collect a court judgment from the debtor's bank accounts, wages, business receipts, real estate or other assets.
$24.95/JUDG

Dog Law
Attorney Mary Randolph
National 1st Edition
Dog Law is a practical guide to the laws that affect dog owners and their neighbors. You'll find answers to common questions on such topics as biting, barking, veterinarians and more.
$12.95/DOG

How to Change Your Name
Attorneys David Loeb &
David Brown
California 5th Edition
This book explains how to change your name legally and provides all the necessary court forms with detailed instructions on how to fill them out.
$19.95/NAME

BUSINESS

Marketing Without Advertising
Michael Phillips & Salli Rasberry
National 1st Edition
This book outlines practical steps for building and expanding a small business without spending a lot of money on advertising.
$14.00/MWA

How to Write a Business Plan
Mike McKeever
National 3rd Edition
If you're thinking of starting a business or raising money to expand an existing one, this book will show you how to write the business plan and loan package necessary to finance your business and make it work.
$17.95/SBS

The Partnership Book
Attorneys Denis Clifford &
Ralph Warner
National 4th Edition
This book shows you step-by-step how to write a solid partnership agreement that meets your needs. It covers initial contributions to the business, wages, profit-sharing, buy-outs, death or retirement of a partner and disputes.
$24.95/PART

How to Form Your Own Nonprofit Corporation
Attorney Anthony Mancuso
National 1st Edition
This book explains the legal formalities involved and provides detailed information on the differences in the law among 50 states. It also contains forms for the Articles, Bylaws and Minutes you need, along with complete instructions for obtaining federal 501 (c) (3) tax exemptions and qualifying for public charity status.
$24.95/NNP

How to Form Your Own Corporation
Attorney Anthony Mancuso
California 7th Edition
New York 2nd Edition
Florida 3rd Edition
These books contain the forms, instructions and tax information you need to incorporate a small business yourself and save hundreds of dollars in lawyers' fees.
California $29.95/CCOR
New York $24.95/NYCO
Florida $24.95/FLCO

The California Nonprofit Corporation Handbook
Attorney Anthony Mancuso
California 6th Edition
This book shows you step-by-step how to form and operate a nonprofit corporation in California. It includes the latest corporate and tax law changes, and the forms for the Articles, Bylaws and Minutes.
$29.95/NON

The California Professional Corporation Handbook
Attorney Anthony Mancuso
California 4th Edition
Health care professionals, lawyers, accountants and members of certain other professions must fulfill special requirements when forming a corporation in California. This book contains up-to-date tax information plus all the forms and instructions necessary to form a California professional corporation.
$34.95/PROF

The Independent Paralegal's Handbook
Attorney Ralph Warner
National 2nd Edition
The Independent Paralegal's Handbook provides legal and business guidelines for those who want to take routine legal work out of the law office and offer it for a reasonable fee in an independent business.
$19.95/PARA

Getting Started as an Independent Paralegal
(Two Audio Tapes)
Attorney Ralph Warner
National 1st Edition
Approximately three hours in all, these tapes are a carefully edited version of a seminar given by Nolo Press founder Ralph Warner. They are designed to be used with *The Independent Paralegal's Handbook.*
$44.95/GSIP

FAMILY MATTERS

The Living Together Kit
Attorneys Toni Ihara &
Ralph Warner
National 6th Edition
The Living Together Kit is a detailed guide designed to help the increasing number of unmarried couples living together understand the laws that affect them. Sample agreements and instructions are included.
$17.95/LTK

California Marriage & Divorce Law
Attorneys Ralph Warner,
Toni Ihara & Stephen Elias
California 11th Edition
This book explains community property, pre-nuptial contracts, foreign marriages, buying a house, getting a divorce, dividing property, and more.
$19.95/MARR

A Legal Guide for Lesbian and Gay Couples
Attorneys Hayden Curry & Denis Clifford
National 6th Edition
Laws designed to regulate and protect unmarried couples don't apply to lesbian and gay couples. This book shows you step-by-step how to write a living-together contract, plan for medical emergencies, and plan your estates. Includes forms, sample agreements and lists of both national lesbian and gay legal organizations, and AIDS organizations.
$17.95/LG

The Guardianship Book
Lisa Goldoftas &
Attorney David Brown
California 1st Edition
The Guardianship Book provides step-by-step instructions and the forms needed to obtain a legal guardianship without a lawyer.
$19.95/GB

How to Adopt Your Stepchild in California
Frank Zagone &
Attorney Mary Randolph
California 3rd Edition
There are many emotional, financial and legal reasons to adopt a stepchild, but among the most pressing legal reasons is the need to avoid confusion over inheritance or guardianship. This book provides sample forms and step-by-step instructions for completing a simple uncontested adoption by a stepparent
$19.95/ADOP

How to Do Your Own Divorce
Attorney Charles Sherman
(Texas Ed. by Sherman & Simons)
California 17th Edition &
Texas 2nd Edition
These books contain all the forms and instructions you need to do your divorce without a lawyer.
California $18.95/CDIV
Texas $14.95/TDIV

Practical Divorce Solutions
Attorney Charles Sherman
California 2nd Edition
This book is a valuable guide to the emotional aspects of divorce as well as an overview of the legal and financial decisions that must be made.
$12.95/PDS

HOMEOWNERS, LANDLORDS & TENANTS

How to Buy a House in California
Attorney Ralph Warner, Ira Serkes &
George Devine
California 1st Edition
This book shows you how to find a house, work with a real estate agent, make an offer and negotiate intelligently. Includes information on all types of mortgages as well as private financing options.
$18.95/BHC

For Sale By Owner
George Devine
California 1st Edition
For Sale By Owner provides essential information about pricing your house, marketing it, writing a contract and going through escrow.
$24.95/FSBO

The Deeds Book
Attorney Mary Randolph
California 1st Edition
If you own real estate, you'll need to sign a new deed when you transfer the property or put it in trust as part of your estate planning. This book shows you how
$15.95/DEED

Homestead Your House
Attorneys Ralph Warner,
Charles Sherman & Toni Ihara
California 7th Edition
This book shows you how to file a Declaration of Homestead and includes complete instructions and tear-out forms.
$9.95/HOME

Neighbor Law: Fences, Trees, Boundaries & Noise
Attorney Cora Jordan
National 1st Edition
Neighbor Law answers common questions about the subjects that most often trigger disputes between neighbors. It explains how to find the law and resolve disputes without a nasty lawsuit.
$14.95 NEI

The Landlord's Law Book: Vol.1, Rights & Responsibilities
Attorneys David Brown &
Ralph Warner
California 3rd Edition
This book contains information on deposits, leases and rental agreements, inspections (tenant's privacy rights), habitability (rent withholding), ending a tenancy, liability and rent control.
$29.95/LBRT

The Landlord's Law Book: Vol. 2, Evictions
Attorney David Brown
California 3rd Edition
Updated for 1991, this book will show you step-by-step how to go to court and get an eviction for a tenant who won't pay rent—and won't leave. Contains all the tear-out forms and necessary instructions.
$29.95/LBEV

Tenant's Rights
Attorneys Myron Moskovitz & Ralph Warner
California 11th Edition
This book explains the best way to handle your relationship both your landlord and your legal rights when you find yourself in disagreement. A special section on rent control cities is included.
$15.95/CTEN

MONEY MATTERS

Simple Contracts for Personal Use
Attorney Stephen Elias &
Marcia Stewart
National 2nd Edition
This book contains clearly written legal form contracts to buy and sell property, borrow and lend money, store and lend personal property, release others from personal liability, or pay a contractor to do home repairs.
$16.95/CONT

How to File for Bankruptcy
Attorneys Stephen Elias,
Albin Renauer & Robin Leonard
National 3rd Edition
Trying to decide whether or not filing for bankruptcy makes sense? How to File for Bankruptcy contains an overview of the process and all the forms plus step-by-step instructions on the procedures to follow.
$24.95/HFB

Barbara Kaufman's Consumer Action Guide
Barbara Kaufman
California 1st Edition
This practical handbook is filled with information on hundreds of consumer topics. Barbara Kaufman, the Bay Area's award-winning host and producer of KCBS Radio's *Call for Action,* gives consumers access to their legal rights, providing addresses and phone numbers of where to complain where things to wrong, and providing resources if more help is necessary.
$14.95/CAG

Money Troubles: Legal Strategies to Cope With Your Debts
Attorney Robin Leonard
National 1st Edition
Are you behind on your credit card bills or loan payments? If you are, then *Money Troubles* is exactly what you need. Covering everything from knowing what your rights are—and asserting them to helping you evaluate your individual situation, this practical, straightforward book is for anyone who needs help understanding and dealing with the complex and often scary topic of debts.
$16.95/MT

LEGAL REFORM

Legal Breakdown: 40 Ways to Fix Our Legal System
Nolo Press Editors and Staff
National 1st Edition
Legal Breakdown presents 40 common sense proposals to make our legal system fairer, faster, cheaper and more accessible. It explains such things as why we should abolish probate, take divorce out of court, treat jurors better and give them more power, and make a host of other fundamental changes.
$8.95/LEG

RESEARCH & REFERENCE

Legal Research: How to Find and Understand the Law
Attorney Stephen Elias
National 2nd Edition
A valuable tool on its own or as a companion to just about every other Nolo book. This book gives easy-to-use, step-by-step instructions on how to find legal information.
$14.95/LRES

Legal Research Made Easy: A Roadmap Through the Law Library Maze
2-1/2 hr. videotape and 40-page manual
Nolo Press/Legal Star Communications
If you're a law student, paralegal or librarian—or just want to look up the law for yourself—this video is for you. University of California law professor Bob Berring explains how to use all the basic legal research tools in your local law library.
$89.95/LRME

Family Law Dictionary
Attorneys Robin Leonard & Stephen Elias
National 2nd Edition
Finally, a legal dictionary that's written in plain English, not "legalese"! *The Family Law Dictionary* is designed to help the nonlawyer who has a question or problem involving family law—marriage, divorce, adoption or living together.
$13.95/FLD

Patent, Copyright & Trademark: The Intellectual Property Law Dictionary
Attorney Stephen Elias
National 2nd Edition
This book explains the terms associated with trade secrets, copyrights, trademarks, patents and contracts.
$15.95/IPLD

OLDER AMERICANS

Elder Care: Choosing & Financing Long-Term Care
Attorney Joseph Matthews
National 1st Edition
This book will guide you in choosing and paying for long-term care, alerting you to practical concerns and explaining laws that may affect your decisions.
$16.95/ELD

Social Security, Medicare & Pensions
Attorney Joseph Matthews with
Dorothy Matthews Berman
National 5th Edition
This book contains invaluable guidance through the current maze of rights and benefits for those 55 and over, including Medicare, Medicaid and Social Security retirement and disability benefits and age discrimination protections.
$15.95/SOA

PATENT, COPYRIGHT & TRADEMARK

The Inventor's Notebook
Fred Grissom &
Attorney David Pressman
National 1st Edition
This book helps you document the process of successful independent inventing by providing forms, instructions, references to relevant areas of patent law, a bibliography of legal and non-legal aids and more.
$19.95/INOT

Patent It Yourself
Attorney David Pressman
National 3rd Edition
From the patent search to the actual application, this book covers everything from use and licensing, successful marketing and how to deal with infringement.
$34.95/PAT

How to Copyright Software
Attorney M.J. Salone
National 3rd Edition
This book tells you how to register your copyright for maximum protection and discusses who owns a copyright on software developed by more than one person.
$39.95/copy

JUST FOR FUN

29 Reasons Not to Go to Law School
Attorneys Ralph Warner &
Toni Ihara
National 3rd Edition
Filled with humor and piercing observations, this book can save you three years, $70,000 and your sanity.
$9.95/29R

Devil's Advocates: The Unnatural History of Lawyers
by Andrew & Jonathan Roth
National 1st Edition
This book is a painless and hilarious education, tracing the legal profession. Careful attention is given to the world's worst lawyers, most preposterous cases and most ludicrous courtroom strategies.
$12.95/DA

Poetic Justice: The Funniest, Meanest Things Ever Said About Lawyers
Edited by Jonathan & Andrew Roth
National 1st Edition
A great gift for anyone in the legal profession who has managed to maintain a sense of humor.
$8.95/PJ

SOFTWARE

WillMaker
Nolo Press/Legisoft
National 4th Edition
This easy-to-use software program lets you prepare and update a legal will—safely, privately and without the expense of a lawyer. Leading you step-by-step in a question-and-answer format, *WillMaker* builds a will around your answers, taking into account your state of residence. *WillMaker* comes with a 200-page legal manual which provides the legal background necessary to make sound choices. Good in all states except Louisiana.
IBM PC
(3-1/2 & 5-1/4 disks included) $69.95/WI4
MACINTOSH $69.95/WM4

For the Record
Carol Pladsen &
Attorney Ralph Warner
National 2nd Edition
For the Record program provides a single place to keep a complete inventory of all your important legal, financial, personal and family records. It can compute your net worth and also create inventories of all insured property to protect your assets in the event of fire or theft. Includes a 200-page manual filled with practical and legal advice.
IBM PC
(3-1/2 & 5-1/4 disks included) $59.95/FRI2
MACINTOSH $59.95/FRM2

California Incorporator
Attorney Anthony Mancuso/Legisoft
California 1st Edition
Answer the questions on the screen and this software program will print out the 35-40 pages of documents you need to make your California corporation legal. Comes with a 200-page manual which explains the incorporation process.
IBM PC
(3-1/2 & 5-1/4 disks included) $129.00/INCI

The California Nonprofit Corporation Handbook
(computer edition)
Attorney Anthony Mancuso
California 1st Edition
This book/software package shows you step-by-step how to form and operate a nonprofit corporation in California. Included on disk are the forms for the Articles, Bylaws and Minutes.
IBM PC 5-1/4 $69.95/ NPI
IBM PC 3-1/2 $69.95/ NP3I
MACINTOSH $69.95/ NPM

How to Form Your Own New York Corporation
How to Form Your Own Texas Corporation
Computer Editions
Attorney Anthony Mancuso
These book/software packages contain the instructions and tax information and forms you need to incorporate a small business and save hundreds of dollars in lawyers' fees. All organizational forms are on disk. Both come with a 250-page manual.

New York 1st Edition
IBM PC 5-1/4 $69.95/ NYCI
IBM PC 3-1/2 $69.95/ NYC3I
MACINTOSH $69.95/ NYCM

Texas 1st Edition
IBM PC 5-1/4 $69.95/ TCI
IBM PC 3-1/2 $69.95/ TC3I
MACINTOSH $69.95/ TCM

VISIT OUR STORE

If you live in the Bay Area, be sure to visit the Nolo Press Bookstore on the corner of 9th & Parker Streets in West Berkeley. You'll find our complete line of books and software—new and "damaged"—all at a discount. We also have t-shirts, posters and a selection of business and legal self-help books from other publishers.

Hours

Monday to Friday	10 a.m. to 5 p.m.
Thursdays	Until 6 p.m
Saturdays	10 a.m. to 4:30 p.m.
Sundays	10 a.m. to 3 p.m.

**950 Parker Street,
Berkeley, California 94710**

ORDER FORM

Name

Address (UPS to street address, Priority Mail to P.O. boxes)

Catalog Code	Quantity	Item	Unit price	Total

Subtotal		
Sales tax (California residents only)		
Shipping & handling		
2nd day UPS		
TOTAL		

OR FASTER SERVICE, USE YOUR CREDIT CARD AND OUR TOLL-FREE NUMBERS:

Monday-Friday, 7 a.m. to 5 p.m. Pacific Time

US	1 (800) 992-6656
CA (outside 415 area code)	1 (800) 640-6656
(inside 415 area code)	549-1976
General Information	1 (510) 549-1976
Fax us your order	1 (510) 548-5902

METHOD OF PAYMENT

▯ Check enclosed

▯ VISA ▯ Mastercard ▯ Discover Card ▯ American Express

Account #   Expiration Date

Authorizing Signature

Phone

SALES TAX

California residents add your local tax

SHIPPING & HANDLING

$4.00	1 item
$5.00	2-3 items
+$.50	each additional item

Allow 2-3 weeks for delivery

IN A HURRY?

UPS 2nd day delivery is available: Add $5.00 (contiguous states) or $8.00 (Alaska & Hawaii) to your regular shipping and handling charges

Prices Subject to Change

FREE NOLO NEWS SUBSCRIPTION

When you register, we'll send you our quarterly newspaper, the *Nolo News*, free for two years. (U.S. addresses only.) Here's what you'll get in every issue:

INFORMATIVE ARTICLES

Written by Nolo editors, articles provide practical legal information on issues you encounter in everyday life: family law, wills, debts, consumer rights, and much more.

UPDATE SERVICE

The *Nolo News* keeps you informed of legal changes that affect any Nolo book and software program.

BOOK AND SOFTWARE REVIEWS

We're always looking for good legal and consumer books and software from other publishers. When we find them, we review them and offer them in our mail order catalog.

ANSWERS TO YOUR LEGAL QUESTIONS

Our readers are always challenging us with good questions on a variety of legal issues. So in each issue, "Auntie Nolo" gives sage advice and sound information.

COMPLETE NOLO PRESS CATALOG

The *Nolo News* contains an up-to-the-minute catalog of all Nolo books and software, which you can order using our toll-free "800" order line. And you can see at a glance if you're using an out-of-date version of a Nolo product.

LAWYER JOKES

Nolo's famous lawyer joke column continually gets the goat of the legal establishment. If we print a joke you send in, you'll get a $20 Nolo gift certificate.

We promise *never* to give your name and address to any other organization.

Your Registration Card

Complete and Mail Today

HOW TO PROBATE AN ESTATE   Registration Card

We'd like to know what you think! Please take a moment to fill out and return this postage paid card for a free two-year subscription to the *Nolo News*. If you already receive the *Nolo News*, we'll extend your subscription.

Name _____ Ph.(   ) _____

Address _____

City _____ State _____ Zip _____

Where did you hear about this book? _____

For what purpose did you use this book? _____

Did you consult a lawyer?	Yes	No		Not Applicable		
Was it easy for you to use this book?	(very easy)	5	4	3	2	1	(very difficult)
Did you find this book helpful?	(very)	5	4	3	2	1	(not at all)

Comments _____

_____

_____

_____

_____

_____

[Nolo books are]..."written in plain language, free of legal mumbo jumbo, and spiced with witty personal observations."

—ASSOCIATED PRESS

"Well-produced and slickly written, the [Nolo] books are designed to take the mystery out of seemingly involved procedures, carefully avoiding legalese and leading the reader step-by-step through such everyday legal problems as filling out forms, making up contracts, and even how to behave in court."

—SAN FRANCISCO EXAMINER

"...Nolo publications...guide people simply through the how, when, where and why of law."

—WASHINGTON POST

"Increasingly, people who are not lawyers are performing tasks usually regarded as legal work... And consumers, using books like Nolo's, do routine legal work themselves."

—NEW YORK TIMES

"...All of [Nolo's] books are easy-to-understand, are updated regularly, provide pull-out forms...and are often quite moving in their sense of compassion for the struggles of the lay reader."

—SAN FRANCISCO CHRONICLE

NO POSTAGE
NECESSARY
IF MAILED
IN THE
UNITED STATES

BUSINESS REPLY MAIL
FIRST-CLASS MAIL PERMIT NO 3283 BERKELEY CA

POSTAGE WILL BE PAID BY ADDRESSEE

NOLO PRESS
950 Parker Street
Berkeley CA 94710-9867